Innovative Korea

Innovative Korea

Leveraging Innovation and Technology for Development

Edited by
HOON SAHIB SOH, YOUNGSUN KOH, AND ANWAR ARIDI

 WORLD BANK GROUP

Contents

Foreword		*xv*
Acknowledgments		*xvii*
About the Editors		*xix*
Overview		*xxi*
Abbreviations		*lxv*
Chapter 1	**The Foundation of Korea's Long-Run Growth**	**1**
	Introduction	1
	Korea's Rapid Development	1
	Conclusions and Implications for Developing Countries	19
	Notes	19
	References	20
Chapter 2	**Korea's Transition to a High-Income Economy**	**25**
	Introduction	25
	Macroeconomic Performance and Key Sources of Growth	26
	Structural Transformation of the Economy	35
	Firm Dynamics	48
	Inclusive Growth	56
	Green, Sustainable Growth	61
	Conclusions and Implications for Developing Countries	65
	Notes	66
	References	66
Chapter 3	**Transformation of Korea's Growth Paradigm**	**69**
	Introduction	69
	Development of the Private Sector	70
	Transformation of the State-Market Paradigm	76
	The Asian Financial Crisis	80

	Comprehensive Financial Sector Reforms	82
	Promoting Private Markets: From State-Led to Market-Led Development	94
	Korea's Growing Focus on SME and Entrepreneurship Development	101
	Conclusions and Implications for Developing Countries	109
	Notes	112
	References	113
Chapter 4	**Leveraging Global Integration and International Trade**	**121**
	Introduction	121
	Trade Liberalization in the GVC Era	122
	Financial Integration and Economic Consequences	147
	Trade and Financial Integration and Macroeconomic Stability	151
	Conclusion and Policy Implications for Developing Countries	158
	Notes	159
	References	160
Chapter 5	**Promoting Innovation and Technology**	**165**
	Introduction	165
	Korea's Innovation Leadership	166
	National Innovation System and R&D in Korea	170
	Evolution of Korea's STI Policy	174
	Innovation and Growth: Remaining Challenges	191
	Conclusion and Policy Implications for Developing Countries	196
	Notes	198
	References	200
Chapter 6	**Investing in Human Capital and Strengthening the Labor Market**	**205**
	Introduction	205
	Human Capital Development in Korea	206
	The Labor Market in Korea	220
	Conclusions and Lessons for Developing Countries	239
	Notes	242
	References	243

Boxes

1.1	The Middle-Income Trap	3
1.2	Industrialization and the Industrial Policy Debate	8
1.3	Korea's Five Largest Chaebols	10
2.1	How Have Global Productivity Trends Evolved?	34
2.2	Is Korea Capturing the Promise of Services-Led Growth?	46
3.1	The Republic of Korea's Digital Government Reforms	93
3.2	Public Procurement and SME Growth and Innovation in the Republic of Korea	103
4.1	Republic of Korea-US Free Trade Agreement	143
4.2	Reserve Accumulation and Global Imbalances	152
4.3	Empirical Analysis of the Impact of Global Trade Shocks on Macroeconomic Fluctuations	154

5.1	Korea's Semiconductor Industry	176
5.2	Pangyo Techno Valley	185
5.3	Case Study of the Information Technology Gaming Industry in the Republic of Korea	187
6.1	Brain Korea 21	212

Figures

O.1	Gross Domestic Product per Capita in the Republic of Korea, the OECD, and EMDEs, 1960–2020	xxii
O.2	Relative Income Dynamics, OECD Countries, 1960–2019	xxiii
O.3	Capital Formation and Its Contribution to Gross Domestic Product Growth	xxiii
O.4	Gross Capital Formation, 1960–2020	xxiv
O.5	Total Factor Productivity, 1960–2019	xxv
O.6	Changes in Industrial Economic and Employment Structure, 1970–2018	xxvi
O.7	Within- and Between-Sector Labor Productivity Growth, 1980–2017	xxvii
O.8	Sectoral Labor Productivity, Republic of Korea, 1970–2018	xxvii
O.9	TFP Growth Decomposition Based on Enterprise Data, 1991–2018	xxviii
O.10	Trade Openness, 1970–2018	xxix
O.11	Foreign Direct Investments of Republic of Korea, China, and Other Countries, 1982–2018	xxx
O.12	Structural Changes in Korean Merchandise Exports, 1980–2010	xxx
O.13	Value-Added Share, by Level of Technology, Republic of Korea, 1980–2018	xxxii
O.14	Digital Adoption Index, OECD Countries, 2021	xxxiii
O.15	Value Added of the ICT Sector, 2020	xxxiii
O.16	Gini Coefficients, 1990–2016	xxxiv
O.17	Greenhouse Gas Emissions, GDP, and Carbon Intensity, 1990–2019	xxxvi
O.18	Impartial Administration and Predictable Enforcement of Laws, Republic of Korea, 1900–2015	xxxvii
O.19	Relative Strength of Elite Actors, Republic of Korea, 1904–2015	xxxviii
O.20	Legal Enforcement by the KFTC, 1981–2019	xli
O.21	Effectively Applied Weighted Tariff Rates, Republic of Korea, 1989–2019	xliii
O.22	R&D versus GDP per Capita, across Countries, 1965–2020	xliv
O.23	Sources of R&D Expenditure, Republic of Korea, 1995–2018	xlv
O.24	Targeting of Beneficiaries by Ministry as Share of Total Resources Allocated, 2018	xlvii
O.25	Estimated Technology Sophistication in Manufacturing, Selected Countries	xlix
O.26	Changing Trend in Gross Enrollment Rates, by Level of Education, Republic of Korea, 1965–2019	li
O.27	Labor Market Development since the AFC, Republic of Korea, 1997–2016	liv
1.1	Relative Income Dynamics, 1960–2019	2
1.2	Income Level and Long-Run Economic Growth in Subsequent Years	3
1.3	Central Government Financial Balance, 1970–2019	5

1.4	Outstanding Stock of External Assets and Liabilities, 1965–2019	6
1.5	Imports and Exports, 1955–2019	7
1.6	Trend in Import Liberalization, 1955–99	8
1.7	Relationship between Government Effectiveness and per Capita Income	12
1.8	Gross Capital Formation, 1960–2020	14
1.9	Gross Enrollment Rate, by Level of Education, 1965–2019	16
1.10	Wage Premium Compared to High School, by Level of Education, 1980–2016	16
1.11	Share of Students Attending Private Institutions, 1965–2019	17
1.12	Infant Mortality Rate, 1970–2018	18
1.13	Life Expectancy at Birth, 1965–2020	18
2.1	GDP and GDP per Capita, 1960–2020	27
2.2	Capital Formation and Its Contribution to GDP Growth	28
2.3	Human Capital	29
2.4	Total Factor Productivity, 1960–2019	30
2.5	Capital Contribution to Growth and Capital Returns	31
2.6	Public and Private Capital Stock per Capita, 2017	32
2.7	Total Factor Productivity Growth, 1974–2019	33
2.8	Changes in Industrial Economic and Employment Structure, 1970–2018	35
2.9	International Comparison of Industrial Structural Transformation	36
2.10	Labor Productivity, Republic of Korea, by Sector	37
2.11	Sectoral Labor Productivity Compared to Global Frontiers, 1970–2018	38
2.12	Productivity Growth and Structural Transformation, 1980–2017	39
2.13	Key Capital-Intensive Industries, Republic of Korea	40
2.14	Shares of Technology (Research and Development)–Intensive Manufacturing Industries, 1980–2018	41
2.15	Electrical Manufacturing, Republic of Korea	42
2.16	Labor Productivity of Manufacturing Subsectors, 1970–2018	43
2.17	Key Industries versus Non-Key Industries, Republic of Korea, 2002–17	44
2.18	Labor Productivity of the Service Sector, 1998–2018	45
2.19	Employment Share of Traditional Services in Total Services	46
B2.2.1	Compound Annual Growth Rate of Value Added per Worker in the Service and Industry Sectors, 1991–2019	47
2.20	Performance of Manufacturing Firms, by Size, 1980–2019	49
2.21	Employment Shares, by Firm Size: Manufacturing and Selected Services across Countries	51
2.22	TFP Growth Decomposition, 1991–2018	52
2.23	Total Factor Productivity and Employment Growth, by Plant Age	53
2.24	Productivity Decomposition of Within Effects, by Plant Age, 1991–2018	54
2.25	Productivity Decomposition into Different Tech Sectors, 1995–2013	55

2.26	Average TFP Growth of Young Plants and Productivity Decomposition by Age, 1991–2018	55
2.27	Productivity and Export Growth in Manufacturing, 2000–17	56
2.28	Gini Coefficients, 1990–2016	57
2.29	Wage, by Establishment Size, 1980–2019	58
2.30	Labor Productivity of Small and Medium-Size Manufacturing Firms Relative to Large Firms, OECD Countries, 2017 or Most Recent Year	58
2.31	Use of Maternity and Childcare Leaves, by Firm Size, 2018	59
2.32	Employment-to-Population Ratio, by Sex and Age, Republic of Korea, 2020	59
2.33	Employment-to-Population Ratio for Prime Working-Age (25–54) Women, OECD Countries, 2019	60
2.34	Total Fertility Rate and GDP per Capita across Countries, 2017	60
2.35	Share of the Elderly (65 years and older) in the Population, 1950–2060	60
2.36	Relative Poverty in the OECD Area, 2018 or Most Recent Year	61
2.37	Greenhouse Gas Emissions, GDP, and Carbon Intensity, 1990–2019	63
2.38	Share of Manufacturing Carbon Emissions and GDP, 2005–19	63
2.39	Annual Growth Rate of the Carbon Intensity of Energy Use, by Manufacturing Sector	64
3.1	Structure and Evolution of Enterprises, by Size, Republic of Korea, 2000–18	71
3.2	Birth Rate of Enterprises, Selected Countries, 2016	72
3.3	Structure of Enterprises, by Size, Republic of Korea and OECD Average, 2018	73
3.4	GVC Participation of Manufacturing Enterprises, Republic of Korea, 2010–14	74
3.5	Trends in the Adoption of Digital Technologies, Republic of Korea, 2010–17	75
3.6	Robot Density in the Manufacturing Sector, Selected Economies, 2019	76
3.7	Technology Adoption, by Sector and Firm Size Group (General Business Functions), Republic of Korea	77
3.8	Trajectory toward Impartial Administration and Predictable Enforcement Laws, UMICs, OECD, and the Republic of Korea, 1900–2015	78
3.9	Relative Strength of Elite Actors, Republic of Korea, 1904–2015	79
3.10	Debt-to-Equity Ratio in the Manufacturing Sector, Republic of Korea, 1963–2007	80
3.11	Number of Major Financial Institutions, Republic of Korea, 1990–2020	82
3.12	Corporate Bond Offerings, Republic of Korea, 1980–2005	83
3.13	Assets of Major Financial Institutions, Republic of Korea, 1995–2017	86
3.14	Bank Profitability and Soundness, Republic of Korea, 1997–2018	86
3.15	Composition of Bank Loans, Republic of Korea, 1990–2017	87
3.16	Leverage, by Firm Size: Audited Firms, Republic of Korea, 1990–2019	88
3.17	Actual Inflation and Inflation Targets, Republic of Korea, 2001–20	90
3.18	Contrasting Monetary Policy Responses: Policy Rates around the AFC and GFC, Republic of Korea	90
3.19	Foreign Reserves and External Debt, Republic of Korea, 1994–2020	91

3.20	Product Market Regulation Scores of OECD Countries, 1998–2018	95
3.21	Burden of Government Regulation, Rank, Selected Countries and World Median, 2007–17	96
3.22	Law Enforcement by the Korea Fair Trade Commission, 1981–2019	97
3.23	Targeting of Beneficiaries for Innovation Support, by Ministry, Republic of Korea, 2018	104
3.24	Entrepreneurial Framework Conditions, Selected Countries	106
3.25	Venture Capital Investment, Selected Countries, 2010–21	108
4.1	Global FDI Trend and China's Integration, 1970–2020	123
4.2	Trade Performance, by Country, 1970–2019	125
4.3	Compositional Changes in Korean Merchandise Trade	126
4.4	Structural Changes in Merchandise Exports, Republic of Korea, 1980–2010	127
4.5	Export Share of Large Firms across Countries, 2015	127
4.6	Services Trade and Relative Performance of Exports of Services, Republic of Korea and across Countries, 1980–2019	128
4.7	Services Trade Restrictiveness Index, by Sector, Republic of Korea and OECD	130
4.8	Foreign Direct Investments, Republic of Korea, China, and Other Countries, 1982–2018	131
4.9	Inward FDI Stock across Countries, 2018	132
4.10	Global Shares of Gross and Value-Added Exports and Imports, Republic of Korea, 1995–2011	132
4.11	VAX Ratios, Selected Economies, 1995 and 2011	133
4.12	Accounting Framework for Global Value Chains	134
4.13	Value-Added Composition of Manufacturing and Nonmanufacturing GVCs, Republic of Korea and Rest of the World, 1995–2011	136
4.14	Employment Composition of Manufacturing and Nonmanufacturing GVCs, Republic of Korea and Rest of the World, 1995–2011	137
4.15	Change in the VAX Ratio and Economic Performance, Selected Economies, 1995–2011	139
4.16	Revealed Comparative Advantage, by Industry, Republic of Korea, 1995–2011	141
4.17	Effectively Applied Weighted Tariff Rates, Republic of Korea, 1989–2019	144
4.18	Trade Finance by Public Export Credit Agencies, Germany, Japan, Republic of Korea, and United States, 2014	145
4.19	Financial Closedness: World versus the Republic of Korea, 1990–2018	148
4.20	Financial Closedness Indexes: Aggregate Level, Republic of Korea, 1990–2018	149
4.21	Financial Market Openness in the Republic of Korea	150
4.22	Capital Flows during the Global Financial Crisis, Republic of Korea	151
B4.3.1	International Reserves and Global Imbalances, Selected Countries and Regions, 1990–2014	152
4.23	Impact of Global Real Trade Shocks on the Macroeconomy, Republic of Korea	155
4.24	Impact of Global Real Trade Shocks on the Republic of Korea and Other Countries	156
4.25	Impact of Global Output Decline on Economic Growth in Asian Economies	156
4.26	Role of Fiscal and Monetary Policies, Republic of Korea and Country Groups	157

5.1	European Innovation Scoreboard, 2020	167
5.2	Change in Global Performance since 2012	167
5.3	Innovation Inputs versus Outcomes for the Republic of Korea and Selected Countries	168
5.4	Top 10 Countries in Patent Cooperation Treaty Applications, 2019	169
5.5	Metrics for the Quality of Innovation: Top 10 High-Income Economies, 2019	169
5.6	R&D Investment in Israel, the Republic of Korea, Sweden, and Switzerland, 1996–2020	170
5.7	Sources of Research and Development Spending: Private and Public Sectors, 2015–20	171
5.8	Direct Government Funding and Government Tax Support for Business R&D, 2006 and 2020	171
5.9	R&D Expenditures, by Firm Size, 1995–2019	172
5.10	Concentration of Enterprise R&D, 2018 (percent of total)	173
B5.1.1	Outlook for the Republic of Korea's Semiconductor Industry, 1997–2019	177
5.11	Development Patterns of Concept Design Capability and Implementation Capability, 1995–2015	180
5.12	Fixed Broadband Subscriptions of Speed Tier over 100 Mbps, 2019	181
5.13	ICT Sector Value Added, 2020	182
5.14	Distribution of R&D Expenditures, by Research Stage: GERD and BERD, 2002–19	183
5.15	Composition of the Policy Mix across Selected Ministries, by Instrument, 2018 (percent of total)	187
5.16	Innovation Support Programs, by Responsible Ministry, 2018	189
5.17	Budget Applications for Direct and Indirect Support Instruments	192
5.18	R&D Spending and TFP Growth, Selected Countries, 2009–18 Average	192
5.19	Firms Engaged in International Collaboration for Innovation, Selected Countries	193
5.20	R&D in Services, 2015	194
6.1	Changing Trends in Gross Enrollment Rates, by Level of Education, Republic of Korea, 1975–2020	207
6.2	Ratios of the Ministry of Education Budget to the Government Budget and GDP, Republic of Korea, 1963–2019	208
6.3	Share of Private School Students, by Level of Education, Republic of Korea, 1965–2020	208
6.4	Wage Premium, by Level of Education, Republic of Korea, 1980–2016	208
6.5	Ratio of Research and Development Budget in Higher Education to Gross Domestic Product, Selected Countries, 1997–2018	210
6.6	Share of Tertiary Graduates in STEM Fields, Selected Countries, 2015	211
6.7	High School System in the Republic of Korea	216
6.8	Employment Rate of Specialized Vocational High School Graduates, Republic of Korea, 2007–19	217
6.9	Trainees, by Type of Training, Republic of Korea, 1998–2019	219
6.10	The Expanding Labor Market, Republic of Korea, 1970s–1987	220
6.11	Balancing Labor Demand and Supply in an Expanding Labor Market, Republic of Korea, 1987–97	221

6.12   Labor Market Challenges, Republic of Korea, 1997–2016   223

6.13   Transition from an Aging Society to an Aged Society, Selected Countries, 1860–2020   223

6.14   Poverty Rate among Individuals Ages 65 and Older, Selected Countries, 2018   225

6.15   Mandatory and Involuntary Retirement, Republic of Korea, 2005–19   225

6.16   Unemployment Rate and Number of Nonregular Workers, Republic of Korea, 1995–2014   226

6.17   Effect of Nonregular (Temporary) Status on the Probability of Standard Employment, Selected Countries   227

6.18   Relative Wage, by Firm Size, Republic of Korea   227

6.19   Relative Wage of Nonregular to Regular Workers, by Firm Size, Republic of Korea   228

6.20   Relative Wage of Nonregular Workers, by Firm Size, Republic of Korea   229

6.21   Unemployment Rate among Youth and Young Adults, Republic of Korea, 2000–20   229

6.22   Job Search Difficulties among Youth and Young Adults, Republic of Korea, 2007 and 2018   229

6.23   Active Labor Market Programs to Support Youth Employment, Republic of Korea   230

6.24   Labor Force Participation Rate, by Gender, Republic of Korea, 2000–20   231

6.25   Gender Pay Gap in Average Annual Earnings, Republic of Korea, 2019 and 2020   232

6.26   Career Challenges for Well-Educated Women, Republic of Korea   232

6.27   Policies to Promote Female Labor Force Participation during the COVID-19 Crisis, Republic of Korea   233

6.28   Health Expenditures in OECD Countries, 2019   236

6.29   Consultations with Doctors per Year, Selected Countries   237

6.30   General Government Spending on Social Protection, Republic of Korea, 1970–2018   238

6.31   Total Tax Revenue, Republic of Korea, 1972–2019   238

Tables

2.1   Young Plants' Effects on Productivity Growth, 1995–2013 (percent)   54

2.2   Evolution of TFPR Dispersion, 1986–2016   56

3.1   External Financing of Nonfinancial Firms in the Pre-Crisis Era, Republic of Korea, 1976–95, (five-year average, percent)   84

3.2   Major Policy Actions and Events to Support Startups, Republic of Korea   102

3.3   Birth and Death Rates of Businesses in Selected Countries, 2018 (percent)   107

4.1   Reduction of General Tariff Rates, Republic of Korea (average tariffs, percent)   124

4.2   GVC Income, Republic of Korea and Rest of the World, 1995 and 2011   135

4.3   GVC Employment, Republic of Korea and Rest of the World, 1995 and 2011   137

4.4   Labor Productivity, Republic of Korea and Rest of the World, 1995 and 2011   139

4.5   Chronology of Korean Free Trade Agreements   142

B4.2.1   Timeline of the Republic of Korea-US FTA   143

4.6   Main Activities of Korean Export Promotion Agencies (as of 2020)   146

4.7   Timeline of Key Trade Facilitation Reforms, Republic of Korea, 1989–2010   147

5.1   Evolution of R&D Expenditure, by Firm Size, 1997–2006   173
5.2   Comparison of Large-Scale R&D Projects Conducted by Korean Government,
      1980s and 1990s   175
5.3   Changes in Policy for the Development and Promotion of Innovative Growth Drivers   179
5.4   Broadband Investment Program, 1995–2014 (US$, millions and percent)   180
5.5   Selected Innovation Policy Instruments, 2019   186
5.6   Innovation Support Instruments, Republic of Korea, OECD, and Developing Countries   191
6.1   PISA Scores and Rank, Republic of Korea, 2000–18   206
6.2   Linkage between the Labor Force and National Economic Development Strategies   209
6.3   Paradigm Shift in University-Industry Collaboration in the Republic of Korea   214
6.4   Paradigm Shift of Korea's Vocational Training System   218
6.5   Strictness of Employment Protection: Individual and Collective Dismissals
      (Regular Contracts), Selected Countries, 1990–2019   235

Foreword

The rise of the Republic of Korea from postwar hardship to prosperity within a lifetime is a story of remarkable economic success. The past six decades witnessed Korea transform itself from one of the world's poorest countries into a global powerhouse—from a GDP per capita of just US$158 in 1960 to US$34,998 today. This transformation required resilience and reinvention, effective public policy, and entrepreneurial spirit.

The World Bank has been a partner of Korea since the start of its modern development, providing policy advice as well as US$15 billion in financing between 1962 and 1999. Over time, the partnership has progressed into one of mutual support and an exchange of ideas on how to achieve development outcomes. The present report is a testament to this productive relationship.

Innovative Korea: Leveraging Innovation and Technology for Development, is a joint effort by the World Bank and the Korea Development Institute (KDI), a leading economic and social policy think tank. The report explores the economic drivers of Korea's ascent to become the world's 10th largest economy and the lessons other developing countries may draw from it.

In the early decades, Korea succeeded by focusing on the foundations of long-run growth—promoting manufacturing exports, upgrading technology, and investing in infrastructure and human capital. The economy rapidly industrialized, while the country's increasingly educated population provided the skills needed to climb the technological ladder. Industrial policy played a pivotal role as the government partnered with large conglomerates to drive growth.

Korea's development path, however, was not without hurdles. In the early 1980s, Korea suffered an economic contraction, and the Asian Financial Crisis in the late 1990s underlined the urgency of reforms to avoid a "middle-income trap." Korea responded with a decisive shift away from its earlier economic paradigm, moving from state-led to more market-driven growth, introducing more competition, overhauling its financial sector, and prioritizing small and medium-size enterprises and technology innovation. Deeper integration into global value chains and foreign investment led to booming exports, and Korea bolstered its human capital focus with an expanded social safety net and more market-oriented education. This successful reinvention offers important lessons to other countries facing their own development challenges.

Today, Korea is at a crossroads again: Growth has slowed, and the population is aging rapidly. Korea will need to find a way to reverse declining productivity growth by improving service sector efficiency while maintaining its manufacturing edge in a shifting competitive environment. Korea is also poised to play a significant role in global efforts to transition to greener, more sustainable and inclusive growth. As this report shows, Korea can face these challenges with confidence based on its remarkable track record of innovation, reform, and economic success.

Innovative Korea will provide useful insights to those interested in Korea's development story, as well as practical lessons for public policy. We hope this report also will inform the next phase of the partnership between the World Bank and Korea to assist developing economies in catalyzing sustainable growth through sound public policy and green innovation.

Dongchul Cho   *Manuela V. Ferro*
President   Vice President
Korea Development Institute   East Asia and Pacific Region
Sejong   World Bank
                                                              Washington, DC

Acknowledgments

This report was prepared jointly by the World Bank and the Korea Development Institute (KDI). Preparation of the report was managed by World Bank South Asia practice manager (and former World Bank Korea office country manager) Hoon Sahib Soh, KDI vice president Youngsun Koh, and World Bank senior private sector specialist Anwar Aridi. The core team included Chanwoo Lee (former first senior deputy governor, Financial Supervisory Service), Indae Yoon (director general, Ministry of Economy and Finance, Republic of Korea), Minseok Hong (World Bank senior operations officer), Tae Hoon Kim (World Bank operations officer), and Yoon Jung Lee (World Bank consultant). Excellent research support was provided by Yoon Jung Lee, Kyeyoung Shin, Ryo Sun Jang, Daein Kang, Deyun Ou, and Yahui Zhao (World Bank staff and consultants). The work was carried out under the guidance of Manuela Ferro (World Bank East Asia and Pacific regional vice president), Martin Raiser (World Bank South Asia regional vice president and former World Bank country director for China, Korea, and Mongolia), Mara Warwick (current World Bank country director for China, Korea, and Mongolia), and Jason Allford (World Bank Korea office country manager).

The team is grateful for peer review comments provided by Bert Hofman (director of the East Asian Institute at the National University of Singapore), Marina Wes (World Bank country director for the Arab Republic of Egypt), Mark Andrew Dutz (World Bank consultant and former lead economist), and Andrew Mason (World Bank lead economist). The project benefited from upstream guidance from key advisors Philippe Aghion (INSEAD), Barry Eichengreen (University of California, Berkeley), Martin Raiser (World Bank South Asia regional vice president), and William Maloney (World Bank Latin America and the Caribbean region chief economist).

The joint World Bank–KDI team prepared the six chapters through a series of workshops and consultations with Korean and international experts. In addition, the team utilized data, analysis, and expertise from universities and relevant ministries and agencies in Korea. The team is grateful for the generous support provided by Korea's Ministry of Economy and Finance.

The Overview was prepared by Hoon Sahib Soh.

Chapter 1, "The Foundation of Korea's Long-Run Growth," was prepared by Hoon Sahib Soh and Youngsun Koh. Yoon Jung Lee contributed on investments in infrastructure.

Chapter 2, "Korea's Transition to a High-Income Economy," was prepared by Luan Zhao and Yusha Li (World Bank) and Jungsoo Park and Yoonsoo Lee (Sogang University). Youngsun Koh contributed on inclusive growth; Mary C. Hallward-Driemeier (World Bank) on services-led development; Hyungna Oh (Kyunghee University) and Hyoung Gun Wang (World Bank) on green growth; Gene Kindberg-Hanlon (International Monetary Fund) on global productivity trends; and Katelyn Jison Yoo on the impact of COVID-19.

Chapter 3, "Transformation of Korea's Growth Paradigm," was prepared by Anwar Aridi, Kyeyoung Shin, and Yoon Jung Lee (World Bank); Namhoon Kwon (Konkuk University); and Hyunbae Chun (Sogang University). Inseok Shin (Chung-ang University) contributed on financial sector development; Jungwoo Lee (Science and Technology Policy Institute [STEPI]) on Korean unicorns; Dongchul Cho (KDI) on macroeconomic developments since the global financial crisis; Jurgen Rene Blum (World Bank) on governance reforms (impartial administration and predictable enforcement of laws); Hwa Ryung Lee (KDI) on the platform economy; Minkyung Kim (World Bank) on Pangyo Techno Valley; and Youjin Choi (World Bank) on financing for small and medium enterprises.

Chapter 4, "Leveraging Global Integration and International Trade," was prepared by Ekaterine T. Vashakmadze, Jongrim Ha, Daisuke Fukuzawa, and Juncheng Zhou (World Bank); Woo Jin Choi (University of Seoul); Sunghoon Chung (KDI); and Ju Hyun Pyun (Korea University). Ruth Banomyong (dean, Thammasat Business School, Thammasat University) contributed on trade facilitation.

Chapter 5, "Promoting Innovation and Technology," was prepared by Marcin Piatkowski (World Bank), Shahid Yusuf (Growth Dialogue), and ChiUng Song and Ji Hyun Kim (STEPI).

Chapter 6, "Investing in Human Capital and Strengthening the Labor Market," was prepared by Soonhwa Yi, Aija Maarit Rinkinen, Hayeon Kim, and Ryo Sun Jang (World Bank); Yong-seong Kim (KOREATECH); and Sung Joon Paik (KDI School of Public Policy and Management). Kangyeon Lee (World Bank) provided review comments.

Soyoun Jun and Min Jae Kang provided excellent administrative and logistics support. Patricia Katayama and Caroline Polk managed the publication of the report. William Shaw was the principal editor, Sandra Gain was the copy editor, and Ann O'Malley was the proofreader.

About the Editors

Anwar Aridi is a senior private sector specialist in the World Bank's Finance, Competitiveness, and Innovation (FCI) Global Practice in the East Asia and Pacific Region based in Seoul, Republic of Korea. Previously, he was in the Europe and Central Asia Region, based in Sofia, Bulgaria, and prior to that, in Washington, DC. He joined FCI's Global Practice as a Young Professional in 2015. Aridi specializes in science, technology, and innovation policy; private sector development; technology entrepreneurship; and technology transfer. He previously worked as an economic and technology policy analyst at SRI International Center for Science, Technology, and Economic Development and as a junior professional associate in the World Bank's Middle East and North Africa Country Management Unit. His latest books include *Europe 4.0: Addressing the Digital Dilemma and Innovation Agencies: Cases from Developing Economies* (World Bank). Aridi holds a PhD in science and technology policy from the Trachtenberg School of Public Policy and Administration at George Washington University.

Youngsun Koh is a senior research fellow at the Korea Development Institute (KDI). He also serves as senior vice president and chief research officer at KDI. After joining KDI in 1993, he initially focused his research on fiscal policy, covering issues in macroeconomics and the financial management system. Later, his interests expanded to other areas, including economic development, inequality, labor, and education. His most recent publication is about the reform of the higher education sector in the Republic of Korea. Throughout Koh's career, he has held various positions at KDI: director for the Department of Macroeconomic and Financial Policy (2006–07), director for the Department of Public Finance and Social Policy (2007–11), chief economist (2011–13), executive director of the Center for International Development (2018–19), and executive director of the Global Knowledge and Exchange Development Center (2019–21). He also worked for the Government of Korea as the second vice minister of the Office for Government Policy Coordination (2013–14) and as vice minister of the Ministry of Employment and Labor (2014–17). Koh studied economics at Seoul National University and holds a PhD in economics from Stanford University.

Hoon Sahib Soh is an economist and manager with more than 23 years of experience at the World Bank. He is currently the World Bank Macroeconomics, Trade, Investments and Public Sector practice manager for the South Asia Region. He manages a large and diverse portfolio of lending projects and analytical and technical assistance engagements in Bangladesh, Bhutan, and India. Previously, he was the special representative (country manager) of the World Bank Korea Office. Soh oversaw the transformation of the Korea Office to a Global Innovation and Technology Center for Sustainable Development. Soh was previously at the World Bank's Beijing Office, as the World Bank program leader for the Equitable Growth, Finance and Institutions Practice Group, responsible for supervising work related to economic policy and institutions in China and Mongolia. His publications include *Innovative China: New Drivers of Growth* and *China Systematic Country Diagnostics: Towards a More Inclusive and Sustainable Development.* Soh joined the World Bank in 2000 as a Young Professional. Since then, he has worked in regional departments (Africa, East Asia and the Pacific, and Latin America and the Caribbean) as an economist and in the corporate policy unit. Before joining the World Bank, he worked in Korea at the POSCO Research Institute and the Arthur D. Little consulting firm. Soh holds a PhD in economics from Stanford University.

Overview

Introduction

The Republic of Korea is one of the few low-income economies that has successfully developed into a high-income economy in recent history, making it a valuable case study. Korea today is a highly industrialized, global innovation and technology leader and the 10th largest economy in the world, with per capita income approaching the average of Organisation for Economic Co-operation and Development (OECD) countries. However, in the 1950s, Korea was one of the poorest countries in the world, with decidedly bleak prospects, making the country a well-known case study of successful development.

This report summarizes the sources of Korea's remarkable growth performance and the policies and institutional reforms that made it possible. This overview is organized into three sections: Key Drivers of Korea's Remarkable Growth Performance, Policy and Institutional Transformation, and Lessons for Developing Countries. The report focuses on Korea's successful transition from middle income to a high-income economy in the 1990s and its economy and policies since then. The report highlights its escape from the "middle-income trap" by leveraging innovation and technology for development. Although the universality of the middle-income trap concept has been debated, it draws attention to the difficulty of sustaining growth over the long run, which is required to become a high-income economy.

The foundations of Korea's growth over the past 50 years have been high levels of investments in physical and human capital, expansion of manufacturing exports, and industrialization and the resulting structural transformation of the economy. In the earlier to middle decades of its modern development, Korea's growth was led by a "developmental state" model that guided private investment through targeted industrial policies. To succeed in the transition from middle to high income that has eluded so many other countries, Korea had to transform its growth model. It had reached the limits of relying on government promotion and guidance of investment, which drove growth at a lower income level, and instead needed to shift to a more private sector–led growth model with a greater emphasis on productivity and innovation-led growth.

The need to evolve became urgent when the shortcomings of the developmental state model were exposed by the Asian Financial Crisis (AFC) in 1997–98. Along with the transition to a democracy in the 1980s, the AFC was a defining moment in Korea's modern development history that built a national consensus on the need to take decisive actions on much-needed reforms of the country's growth paradigm, to increase the emphasis on promoting markets and the development of frontier innovation and technologies. The focus of industrial policies was transformed from targeting large firms and industries to prioritizing support for small and medium-size enterprises (SMEs) and technology entrepreneurs. Exports increased significantly through greater integration into global value chains (GVCs) facilitated by expanding overseas direct investments (ODIs). Investment in human capital development contin-ued, complemented by an expanded social safety net and a more integrated, market-based and demand-oriented approach to education and training.

Key Drivers of Korea's Remarkable Growth Performance

Korea sustained 29 years of rapid growth (greater than 6 percent) from 1962 to 1991 as it transitioned from low to middle income, a relatively rare accomplishment. In comparison, the median duration of rapid growth in other countries was nine years. Korea's annual real growth of gross domestic product (GDP) averaged 7.3 percent in the 1990s, significantly narrowing the difference in income with the OECD coun-tries and the United States (figures O.1 and O.2). Korea crossed the World Bank's gross national income per capita threshold for high-income economies, calculated using the World Bank's Atlas method, in 1995 and joined the OECD also in 1995.[1] Korea was reclassified as an upper middle-income country from 1998 to 2000, as its economy contracted by 5.1 percent in 1998 during the AFC, but it quickly rebounded and again became a high-income economy in 2001 and grew by an average annual rate of 5.0 percent from 1998 to the global financial crisis (GFC) in 2008. Korea's growth slowed to an average of 3.1 percent per year after the GFC, but this was still higher than the OECD average of 1.8 percent.

Korea's remarkable sustained growth over the past five decades was due to a commitment to strengthen-ing the key foundations of long-term development of macroeconomic stability, promotion of manufactur-ing exports, and investments in infrastructure and human capital. This commitment was sustained from the 1960s when it was a low-income economy and across successive government administrations representing different political parties. The foundations of long-term growth enabled the later stages of the country's development when Korea successfully transitioned from middle income to a high-income economy.[2]

Korea's growth benefited from contributions from both investments and productivity improvements. Investments in physical and human capital were the largest contributor to Korea's development from the 1960s to the 1990s (figure O.3). Korea sustained high rates of physical capital investment even after

FIGURE O.1 **Gross Domestic Product per Capita in the Republic of Korea, the OECD, and EMDEs, 1960–2020**

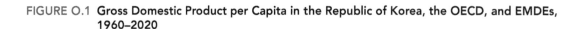

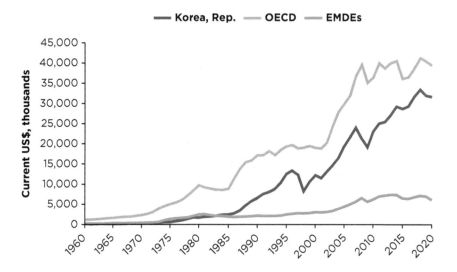

Source: Calculations based on data from World Development Indicators, World Bank (https://databank.worldbank.org/source/world-development-indicators).
Note: EMDEs = emerging markets and developing economies; OECD = Organisation for Economic Co-operation and Development.

FIGURE O.2 Relative Income Dynamics, OECD Countries, 1960–2019

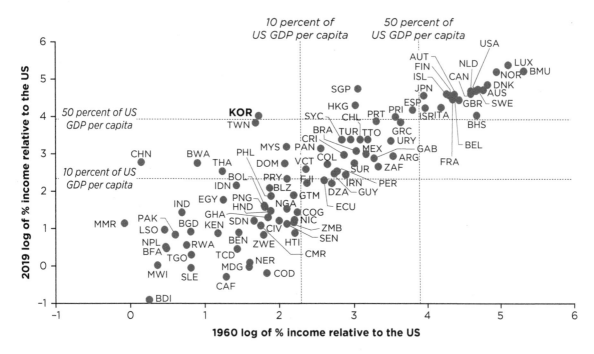

Sources: World Development Indicators, World Bank (https://databank.worldbank.org/source/world-development-indicators); National Statistics, Republic of China (Taiwan, China) (http://statdb.dgbas.gov.tw/pxweb/Dialog/statfile1L.asp?lang=1&strList=L).
Note: The horizontal and vertical lines indicate 10 and 50 percent levels of the US gross domestic product per capita. For a list of country codes, go to https://www.iso.org/obp/ui/#search. OECD = Organisation for Economic Co-operation and Development.

FIGURE O.3 Capital Formation and Its Contribution to Gross Domestic Product Growth

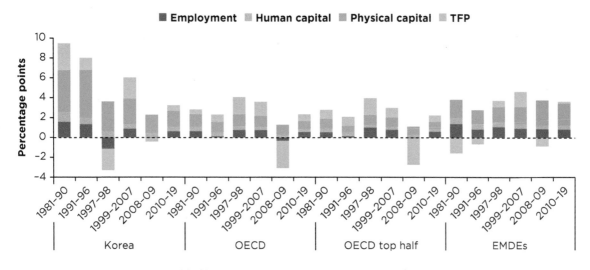

Source: Calculations based on Penn World Table 10.0.
Note: EMDEs = emerging markets and developing economies; OECD = Organisation for Economic Co-operation and Development; TFP = total factor productivity.

FIGURE O.4 **Gross Capital Formation, 1960–2020**

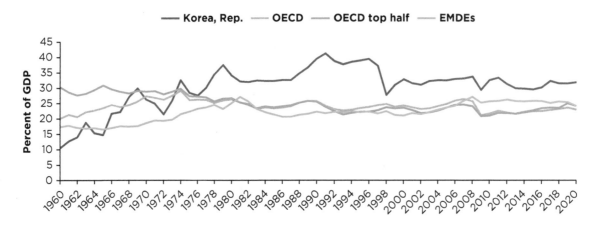

Source: Calculations based on data from World Development Indicators, World Bank (https://databank.worldbank.org/source/world-development-indicators).
Note: EMDEs = emerging markets and developing economies; GDP = gross domestic product; OECD = Organisation for Economic Co-operation and Development.

achieving relatively high per capita income levels, at rates higher than most other countries at similar income levels. Between 1990 and 1997, when Korea transitioned to a high-income economy, its gross capital formation averaged 38 percent of GDP, significantly higher than the average of 22 percent among OECD countries (figure O.4). Korea's high investment rates were mainly driven by private investment, which accounted for 83 percent of total investment and above 80 percent in subsequent decades.

However, the contribution of capital to growth declined after the 1990s. This reflected both declining investment (as a share of GDP), from the very high levels in the 1990s, and diminishing returns to investment due to the higher stock of investment.[3] Korea is also experiencing declining marginal returns on investments because it has accumulated a large stock of capital and therefore additional investments have less of an impact. Both the public and private stocks of capital per capita in Korea today are comparable to those in OECD countries (2017).[4]

Korea has accumulated significant human capital since the early decades of its development, resulting in average years of schooling increasing from 5.4 years in 1970 to 12.1 years in 2015. The net enrollment rate in primary schools reached close to 100 percent by the 1970s, and subsequently the enrollment rates in secondary and tertiary schools increased. In addition, the number of health care facilities expanded, public health programs successfully addressed communicable diseases, and a nationwide network of public health centers was established to serve low-income households. As a result, Korea attained the average level of human capital of OECD countries by the 1990s (Penn World Table) when it was still a middle-income country. In 2020, Korea was ranked fourth globally in the World Bank's Human Capital Index.

Large investments in physical and human capital were complemented by rapid growth in total factor productivity (TFP) (figure O.5). TFP measures the level of outputs that can be produced by a given level of inputs (productive efficiency) in the economy. Many fast-growing emerging markets and developing economies have generated growth through capital accumulation. Korea combined high rates of capital accumulation with relatively large TFP contributions to growth. TFP growth has been a significant factor in Korea's rapid convergence to the per capita income levels of advanced economies.

The contribution of TFP to growth declined in the 1990s leading up to the AFC, following the country's over-investment in the heavy and chemical industries in the previous decade. The contribution of TFP picked up in the 2000s in the years immediately following the AFC, becoming nearly equivalent to the contribution of physical capital (figure O.3). Productivity improved following the significant structural reforms carried out in response to the AFC, which opened markets, promoted market competition,

FIGURE O.5 Total Factor Productivity, 1960–2019

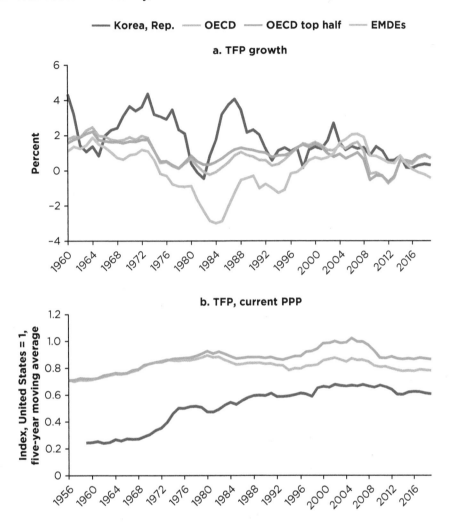

Source: Calculations based on data from Penn World Table 10.0.
Note: EMDEs = emerging markets and developing economies; OECD = Organisation for Economic Co-operation and Development; PPP = purchasing power parity; TFP = total factor productivity.

and improved financial intermediation through a complete overhaul of the financial sector. The reorientation of government support to SMEs, technology startups, and innovation and technology promoted the wider adoption of information and communications technology (ICT), which also contributed to productivity growth.

Since the GFC, the contributions of both capital and TFP to overall growth have declined. Various measurements indicate that TFP growth in Korea has declined to around zero since the GFC (figure O.5, panel a). The declining growth since the GFC has been associated with the growth slowdown of the capital-intensive manufacturing industries, which experienced a slowdown in export growth. Due to declining global trade, Korea's export growth fell significantly, from an annual average of 10 percent in 2007–12 to an annual contraction of 0.5 percent in 2013–20, before picking up to an annual average of 15.9 percent in 2021–22 during the COVID-19 pandemic. As Korea's major manufacturing industries are heavily export oriented, the decline in exports impacted the performance of those industries. Korea has not been alone in experiencing declining productivity growth. Productivity growth in most high-income economies has declined steadily since the 1980s, plunged during the GFC, and subsequently has not fully recovered. The convergence of Korea's TFP level to the global frontier (US level) has halted since the 2000s, as has that of other OECD countries (figure O.5, panel b).

STRUCTURAL TRANSFORMATION OF THE ECONOMY AND EXPORT GROWTH LED BY MANUFACTURING

Korea's economy has undergone significant structural transformation over the past decades (figure O.6). The share of agriculture in the economy declined rapidly and the industry sector expanded, particularly in the 1970s and 1980s when its share increased from around 27 percent in 1970 to 40 percent in 1990. However, the service sector has remained the largest share of the economy, increasing from 44 percent in 1970 to 51 percent in 1990 and 60 percent 2010. The share of employment in industry peaked in the early 1990s and has declined since then, but the share of value-added in industry has remained relatively stable, gradually declining from 40 percent in 1990 to 35 percent in 2022. Korea has so far largely delayed the "deindustrialization" experienced by many economies by maintaining a relatively high share of value added in industry, but the share of employment in manufacturing has been declining.

FIGURE O.6 Changes in Industrial Economic and Employment Structure, 1970–2018

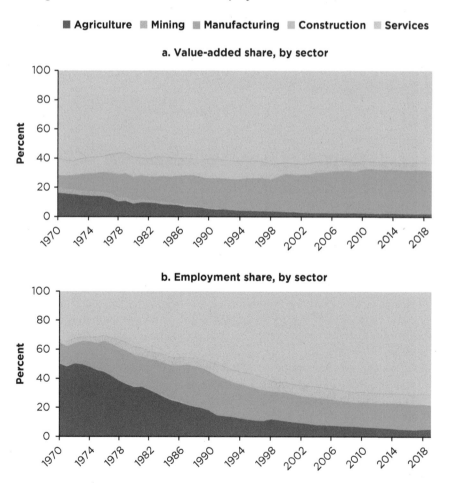

Source: Productivity Database, Asian Productivity Organization.

Until the 1990s, the contribution of between-sector productivity growth (structural transformation of the economy) to overall labor productivity growth was greater than the contribution of within-sector productivity growth (figure O.7), reflecting the impact from the reallocation of excess labor from the agriculture sector to the manufacturing and service sectors, which have higher levels of productivity. The labor productivity of manufacturing began to increase sharply in the 1990s, subsequently increasing to 73 percent of the OECD average level of productivity in 2000 and then to above the OECD average in 2018 (figure O.8).

By the 1990s when Korea transitioned from middle income to a high-income economy, between-sector productivity growth (structural transformation) began to play a smaller and declining role compared to

FIGURE O.7 **Within- and Between-Sector Labor Productivity Growth, 1980–2017**

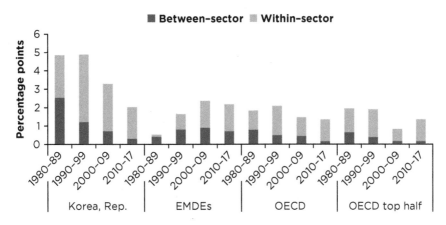

Source: Calculations based on data from the Global Productivity Database, World Bank.
Note: EMDEs = emerging markets and developing economies; OECD = Organisation for Economic Co-operation and Development.

FIGURE O.8 **Sectoral Labor Productivity, Republic of Korea, 1970–2018**

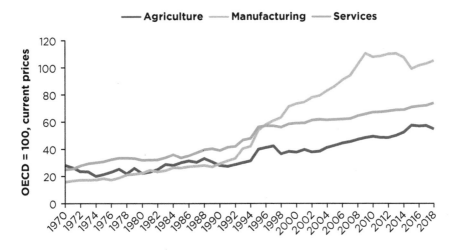

Source: Calculations based on data from OECD STAN Industrial Analysis Database.
Note: OECD = Organisation for Economic Co-operation and Development.

FIGURE O.9 **TFP Growth Decomposition Based on Enterprise Data, 1991–2018**

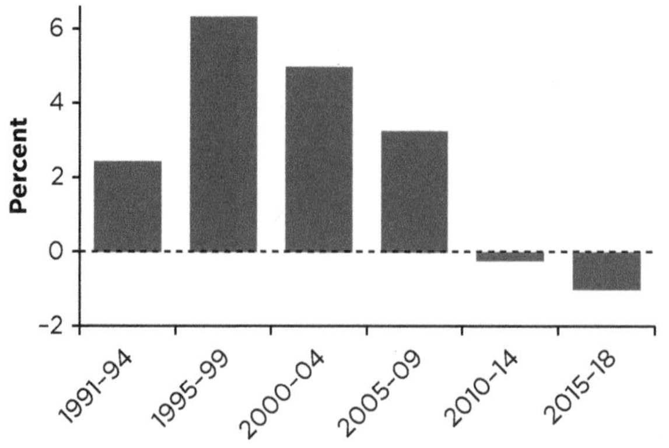

Source: Calculations based on data from the Mining and Manufacturing Survey, Statistics Korea (https://kosis.kr).
Note: TFP = total factor productivity.

within-sector productivity growth. Within-sector productivity growth was generated primarily by the manufacturing sector, which has been the primary source of labor productivity growth in Korea since the 1990s. The manufacturing sector accounted for 1.7 percentage points of aggregate productivity growth in Korea during 1980–2010. In contrast, excluding China, manufacturing has contributed 0.2 percentage points to aggregate growth in emerging markets and developing economies since the 1980s.

Analysis of enterprise data[5] in Korea shows that TFP growth rates in manufacturing were relatively high in the 1990s until the AFC and have declined since then (figure O.9). Most of the TFP growth in the manufacturing industry has been due to productivity growth within existing firms (within effect) as opposed to reallocation of resources to more productive firms (between effect) and entry and exit of firms (J. Lee 2020). The between effect has accounted for only about 5 percent of total productivity growth. Korea also has large and increasing dispersion in productivity, further indicating that there is considerable potential to improve allocative efficiency (Kim, Oh, and Shin 2017; Y. Lee 2020).[6] In part, the widening productivity dispersion may reflect the expansion of large business groups following the deregulation policies after the AFC.

The net entry effect has accounted for only about 10 percent of total TFP growth, although entry and exit rates have been relatively high in Korea, especially in fast-growing industries. However, young firms (younger than three years) are important sources of productivity growth. Their impact is captured as a within effect, accounting for about one-third of the contribution to productivity from the within effect in the 1990s and a slightly smaller share in the 2000s. The productivity growth of young firms declined significantly after the GFC and was a major contributor to the substantial slowdown in overall productivity growth (Y. Lee 2020).

Korea's manufacturing productivity growth has been closely associated with export growth. Exports have been the primary focus of industrial policies since the 1960s when Korea's growth strategy was reoriented from import substitution to export promotion. Korea's trade volume started to increase rapidly in the 1990s by taking advantage of the accelerated globalization of trade and expansion of the GVCs. Global trade and investments benefited from the establishment of the World Trade Organization in 1995, the spread of ICT, and China's global integration (figure O.10). By 2020, Korea's exports and imports approached nearly 80 percent of GDP. Along with the expanding volume of trade, Korea's share of high-technology exports has increased since the mid-1990s. Korea's ranking on Harvard University's Economic Complexity Index increased from 21st in 1995 to fourth in 2020, reflecting the increasing number and complexity of its export products. Korea's top manufacturing exports now consist of high-technology products, such as semiconductors, electronics, automobiles, ships, and refined petroleum products.

FIGURE O.10 **Trade Openness, 1970–2018**

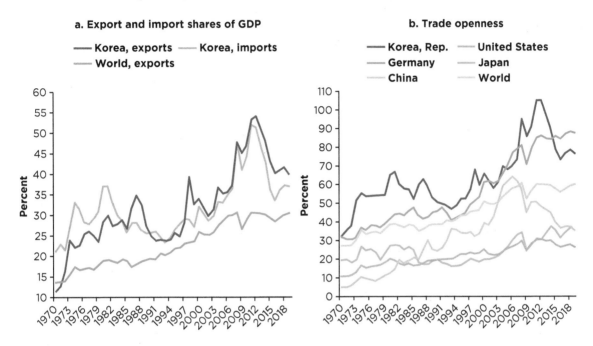

Source: World Development Indicators, World Bank (https://databank.worldbank.org/source/world-development-indicators).
Note: Trade values include both goods and services. GDP = gross domestic product.

Along with the acceleration of the expansion of international trade, Korea's ODI started to take off in the mid-1990s. Prior to 1990, the stock of ODI was close to zero (figure O.11, panel a). The number of foreign affiliates of Korea's firms began to increase in the mid-1990s, mainly driven by investments in China for manufacturing facilities (figure O.11, panel b). In 1994, approximately three-quarters of Korea's new foreign affiliates were established in China, of which more than 80 percent were in manufacturing. In the 2000s, China still accounted for most of Korea's new ODI, but the destination of Korea's ODI has diversified significantly since the GFC.

In contrast to ODI, foreign direct investment (FDI) into Korea has been relatively low. In the earlier decades of Korea's modern development, the government discouraged FDI, preferring licensing and imported equipment to absorb foreign technologies. Companies used debt rather than equity financing, to retain corporate control. Korea started to liberalize FDI in the 1980s when it converted a positive list of industries in which FDI was allowed to a negative list of industries that restricted or prohibited FDI. The negative list is generally considered a more transparent and predictable approach to FDI restrictions. FDI reforms accelerated after the AFC, including the removal of restrictions on cross-border mergers and acquisitions and land ownership. Spurred also by the depreciation of the won, FDI sharply increased, especially in the financial sector. However, subsequently FDI has declined and has remained relatively modest. Korea's stock of FDI was only 12.4 percent of GDP in 2018, the second lowest among OECD member countries.

The expansion of ODI since the mid-1990s promoted Korea's integration into GVCs. Korea's GVC integration resulted in a V-shaped trend in the foreign content of its exports, with a declining share up to 1995 and a rapid increase since then (figure O.12). Korea's manufacturing sector has been globalizing significantly through forward and backward participation in GVCs. Prior to the 1990s, Korea's participation was mostly limited to forward integration into GVCs, by supplying inputs to the supply chains organized

FIGURE O.11 Foreign Direct Investments of Republic of Korea, China, and Other Countries, 1982–2018

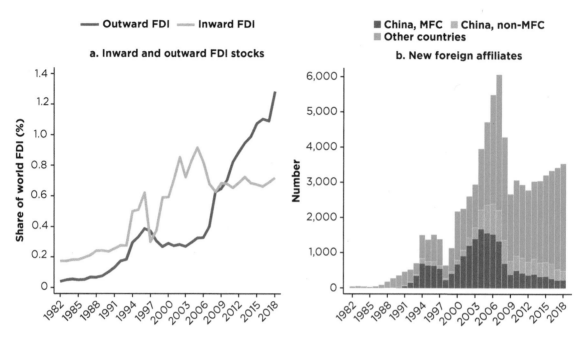

Sources: For panel a, UNCTAD Data Center; panel b, Korea Export-Import Bank.
Note: FDI = foreign direct investment; MFC = manufacturing.

FIGURE O.12 Structural Changes in Korean Merchandise Exports, 1980–2010

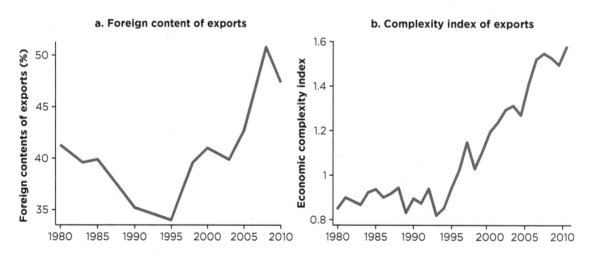

Sources: For panel a, calculations using the input-output tables from the Bank of Korea (for available years); for panel b, Observatory of Economic Complexity V3.0 (https://legacy.oec.world/en/rankings/country/eci/).

by foreign firms. As a share of total income, Korea's value-added contribution from supplying foreign industries increased from 24.5 percent in 1995 to 39.6 percent in 2011. Since the 1990s, firms in Korea have expanded their backward linkages in GVCs, sourcing foreign inputs for their own exports of final products. As a result, the share of foreign value-added contributions in Korea's final outputs increased from 25.4 percent in 1995 to 42.3 percent in 2011. Both forward and backward linkages in GVCs have helped firms in Korea to enhance their productivity, focus on their comparative advantages, and access foreign knowledge and expertise.

Korea's integration into GVCs has been led by the country's large firms, in particular family-owned and controlled business conglomerates called "chaebols." Samsung, Hyundai, SK, LG, and Lotte are among the largest chaebols. Many of the chaebols have been focused on manufacturing exports, benefiting from the government's industrial policy support. In the 1970s, the government initiated a major program to develop the heavy and chemical industries, which accelerated the growth of the chaebols. The heavy and chemical industries drive was a "moonshot" attempt to upgrade the country's industrialization trajectory. The chaebols that were selected to invest in the heavy and chemical industries experienced tremendous growth by gaining preferential access to subsidized credit and lower tax rates. The drive helped to expand the investments and outputs of targeted industries, such as the iron and steel, petrochemicals, machinery, and shipbuilding industries, but it has also been criticized for inefficient and excessive investments, significant debt accumulation, and engendering the market dominance of the chaebols.

The large firms' integration into GVCs has widened the productivity gap between the large and small firms in Korea. The ratio of the average labor productivity of large to small firms increased from 174 percent in 1980 to 265 percent in 2000 and further to 291 percent in 2019. This productivity gap between large firms and SMEs in Korea is one of the largest among OECD countries (OECD 2020). The productivity gap is greater in the manufacturing sector than in the service sector. The manufacturing sector is dominated by large exporting enterprises, which has contributed to the larger productivity gap. In contrast, the service sector has a large share of small, self-employed businesses.

Korea faces a structural challenge of having a large share of employment in small firms with lower levels of productivity. Micro, small, and medium-size enterprises (MSMEs) accounted for 85 to 88 percent of total employment in 2000–18, compared to the average of around 70 percent in OECD countries in 2015. The employment share of MSMEs (enterprises with fewer than 299 employees) is similar to the OECD average, but Korea's employment share of small firms (10-49 employees) is the highest among OECD countries in the manufacturing sector and selected traditional service sectors, such as the wholesale and retail and accommodation and food service sectors. The large share of workers in small firms with lower productivity growth prospects has contributed to a widening wage gap, with significant implications for income inequality.

Compared to the manufacturing sector, Korea has been less successful in leveraging the service sector for growth and development. Korea's labor productivity in the service sector remains at only around 60 percent of the OECD average and 30 to 40 percent of the US levels (figure O.8). Along with manufacturing exports, Korea's services trade has also significantly expanded since the 1990s. However, Korea's services exports have not experienced the more rapid growth seen in other high-income economies as they transitioned to a service-based economy. This reflects Korea's overall strategy to focus mainly on building its comparative advantage in manufacturing and take advantage of foreign providers for services. It also reflects the overall lower productivity of Korea's service sector and hence the relative lack of international competitiveness of its services exports.

A key challenge for Korea is to reduce the concentration of employment in low-productivity and low-wage service sectors, including wholesale and retail trade, transportation and storage, and accommodation and food service activities, which account for a higher share in services than in most other OECD countries. Going forward, Korea can take greater advantage of opportunities to promote services-led growth, including through new digital technologies and "servicification" of manufacturing.

GLOBAL INNOVATOR AND TECHNOLOGY LEADER

Korea converged to the global manufacturing productivity frontier by continuously upgrading its industrial technologies. As a result, it has become a highly competitive, capital- and research and development (R&D)–intensive high-technology manufacturing exporter. The value-added share of capital-intensive industries increased from 50 percent of total industry outputs in 1991 to 68 percent in 2011 and remained above 60 percent throughout the 2010s. The share of the high-technology sector in real manufacturing value added rose from 22 percent in 1990 to 44 percent in 2018, and the share of low- and medium-technology sectors fell from 37 and 48 percent to 11 and 44 percent, respectively (figure O.13).

Korea's successful development into a high-technology manufacturing exporter has been the result of decades of prioritized investments in science and technology (S&T). The country's R&D has been focused on deepening the technological capability of manufacturing industries to support a continuous series of industrial technology upgrading, from light industries in the 1960s, to heavy and chemical industries in the 1970s and 1980s, and to high-technology industries in the 1990s and beyond. Korea initially took advantage of catch-up growth by absorbing and adopting existing foreign technologies and knowledge but then subsequently focused on building domestic capabilities to produce new innovations at the global technology frontier and transition into a high-income and knowledge-based economy.

As a result, Korea succeeded in becoming a global technology and ICT manufacturing leader, with the second highest spending on R&D as a percentage of GDP in the world, world-class digital infrastructure, and among the highest levels of digital adoption (figure O.14). The Bloomberg Innovation Index 2020 ranked Korea second globally, behind Germany. IMD's World Competitiveness Ranking has consistently ranked Korea among the top 20 countries over the past decade, and third on innovation capacity and 13th on S&T infrastructure competitiveness. Korea was ranked 10th in the 2020 Global Innovation Index and achieved the top rank on human capital and research.

Korea is at the forefront or among the top three countries in the world in terms of tertiary school enrollment, expenditure on R&D (as a percentage of GDP), and number of researchers per capita. The number of researchers increased from about 3,000 per million population in 1996 to 9,800 per million in 2018, significantly higher than the 6,900 OECD average. In 2019, Korea was ranked fifth globally in the number of Patent Cooperation Treaty applications and first relative to the size of its GDP. Samsung and LG, two of the largest firms in Korea, had the third and 10th largest numbers of Patent Cooperation Treaty applications among global companies, respectively.

The adoption of digital technologies in Korea has been associated with higher levels of TFP (Chung and Aum, 2021). In 2020, the ICT sector accounted for 11.7 percent of GDP, the highest share among OECD countries (figure O.15). The foundation for Korea's remarkable digital development over the past four decades was established in the 1980s when the country was still a middle-income economy. Government research institutes (GRIs) played an instrumental role in developing key digital technologies for the telecommunication and semiconductor industries. Korea initiated investments in digital government in the 1980s, when it was still a lower-middle-income country. The various government information

FIGURE O.13 **Value-Added Share, by Level of Technology, Republic of Korea, 1980–2018**

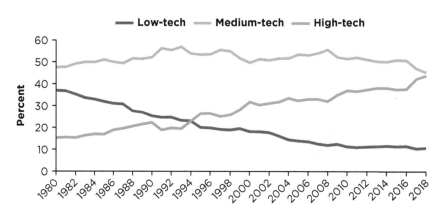

Source: Calculations based on data from OECD STAN Industrial Analysis Database.

FIGURE O.14 **Digital Adoption Index, OECD Countries, 2021**

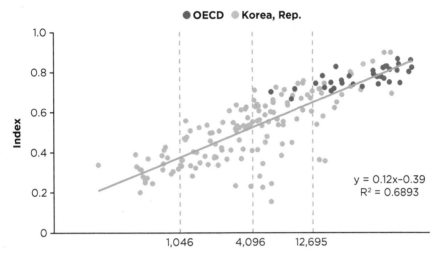

Source: Calculations based on data from World Bank 2017, updated for 2021.
Note: OECD = Organisation for Economic Co-operation and Development.

FIGURE O.15 **Value Added of the ICT Sector, 2020**

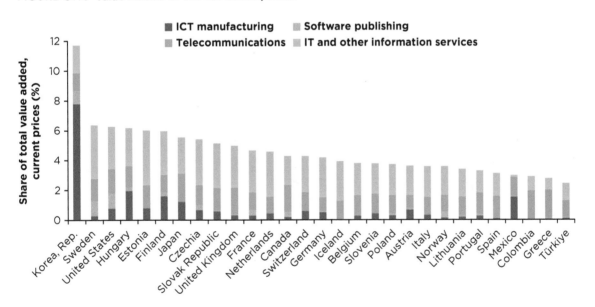

Source: STAN structural indicators (iSTAN), 2022 edition, Organisation for Economic Co-operation and Development (https://stats.oecd.org/Index.aspx?DataSetCode=STANI4_2020#).
Note: ICT = information and communications technology; IT = information technology.

technology systems have now been integrated into a common e-government platform to improve public service delivery and transparency. Anticipating the critical role of ICT, from 1995 to 2015 the government embarked on a major program to build a broadband infrastructure network. Today, Korea's ICT infrastructure is ranked second in the 2017 ICT Development Index of the International Telecommunication Union, and Korea ranked first among 29 OECD countries in the 2019 OECD Digital Government Index and third in the 2022 United Nations E-Government Survey.

INCLUSIVE AND SUSTAINABLE GROWTH

Korea successfully combined sustained rapid economic growth with significant poverty reduction. The poverty rate declined from 21.5 percent of urban households in 1975 to 7.4 percent in 1996 (World Bank 2004). Major land reforms in the 1940s and 1950s helped equalize the distribution of land, which provided the basis for more inclusive growth. At the time, land was the major asset in the economy, given that 71 percent of the population was in the agriculture sector (Kim 2006) and much of the country's industrial assets had been destroyed during the Korean War (1950–53). Rapid export-led growth since the land reforms significantly reduced poverty and mobilized broad support for Korea's growth policies. Economic growth created manufacturing jobs. Large and systematic investments in basic education were a critical driver of poverty reduction and inclusive growth by facilitating socioeconomic mobility and widening access to the jobs created by the rapid industrialization of the economy. As a result, economic growth in the earlier decades of Korea's modern development was relatively inclusive, despite the relatively low reliance on redistributive welfare policies.

During Korea's rapid growth, the estimated Gini coefficient deteriorated modestly or improved marginally (World Bank 2004). However, the estimated Gini coefficient has deteriorated in the 2000s (figure O.16). The deteriorating Gini coefficient could have been driven by the widening wage disparity between small and large firms and regional disparity and the concentration of growth and resources in Seoul, the capital city. Korea's expanded policy support for SMEs since the AFC could be understood as a policy response to address the disparity between small and large firms. The growing number of double-income households could have also contributed to the worsening of household income inequality, due to the earnings disparity between single-income and double-income households.

Income inequality improved in the 2010s, reversing the deteriorating trend in the previous decade. The estimated decline of the Gini coefficient is greater for estimates based on market income than for disposable income, reflecting the expansion of the government's income redistribution policy since the AFC. Today, Korea's income inequality is higher than the OECD average, but it is in line with the level of inequality of lower-income OECD countries. Most of the lower-income OECD countries with income inequality greater than Korea's are countries that were previously central planning, socialist economies.

FIGURE O.16 Gini Coefficients, 1990–2016

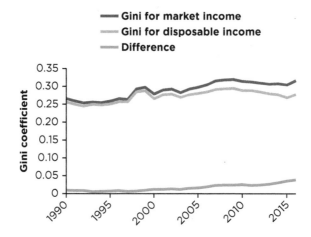

Source: Statistics Korea (https://kosis.kr).
Note: The data are for urban households with two or more members.

In the earlier decades of its modern development, Korea prioritized economic growth rather than redistributive polices to promote poverty reduction, taking a "Growth First, Distribution Later" approach. However, in the 1970s Korea began to establish its social safety net system, which would serve as a building block for its redistributive policies. The National Health Insurance was introduced in 1977 for workers in large firms and subsequently expanded to cover the entire population by 1989. Hence, universal health care coverage was attained within only a dozen years. The National Pension Scheme was launched in 1988 for large firms and expanded in the subsequent years. The pension system was complemented by the Employment Insurance System (EIS), which was introduced in 1995 to support the unemployed with income support and various active labor market policies (ALMPs).

Despite this progress, the massive unemployment and widespread poverty during the AFC exposed the inadequacy of the country's social safety net. In 1999, about 2 million people received some form of social assistance benefits, but half of the poor still were not covered. In response, social protection programs were significantly expanded. The government introduced the National Basic Livelihood Security program, which provides income support to the poor and encourages beneficiaries to participate in the labor market. The coverage of the National Pension Scheme was expanded by removing previous restrictions on beneficiaries based on employment categories. The EIS was expanded in 1998 to cover all businesses. New social protection programs were added in the 2000s, including Emergency Welfare Support (2006), Earned Income Tax Credit (2007), Basic Old-age Pension (2007), and Long-term Care Insurance (2008). Subsequently, student loan programs (2010) and scholarship programs (2012) were introduced to support low-income households, and childcare allowances (2012) were introduced for children younger than six years. The existing minimum wage system was extended to all industries.

Balanced regional development was also a key priority of the government to address inequality across regions. Korea urbanized from 25 percent of the population living in urban areas in 1970 to 75 percent by 1990. As the country urbanized, the government expanded efforts to extend key infrastructure and social services to underserved, rural areas. Access to electricity in rural areas grew from 12 percent in 1965 to over 90 percent in 1975. Significant investments in transport connectivity reduced the economic distance between urban and rural areas. Coordinated planning and infrastructure investments helped to integrate rural areas and secondary cities with the main urban centers.

As Korea became a high-income economy, social concerns for the environment, pollution, and the quality of life became a greater priority. Korea adopted a national green growth strategy in 2008 as a new growth strategy, to transform its economy from a carbon-intensive to a low-carbon growth model. The Framework Act on Low Carbon, Green Growth in 2010 outlined national goals for low-carbon green growth and the associated institutional framework and mitigation and adaptation policies. The Korea Emissions Trading Scheme was introduced in 2015. It is one of the earliest and largest carbon emissions trading schemes outside the United States and the European Union.

Despite such progress, there are concerns in Korea that a low-carbon transition could undermine the international competitiveness of the manufacturing sector if it must bear the cost of decarbonization. Korea started to decouple GDP growth from carbon emissions in the 2010s. The country's average annual growth of real GDP and carbon emissions from fuel combustion were 3.3 and 1.6 percent, respectively, in 2010–19 (figure O.17). However, during the same period, the United States and Japan reduced their emissions by 1.3 and 0.7 percent annually, respectively. The contribution of Korea's manufacturing sector to GDP has been maintained at about 25 percent, but its proportion of carbon emissions has been smaller and decreasing over time. In 2018, Korea accounted for 1.86 percent of total carbon emissions in the world. It was the sixth largest carbon emitter and the 15th largest per capita emitter (Stangarone 2020; World Bank 2022).

FIGURE O.17 **Greenhouse Gas Emissions, GDP, and Carbon Intensity, 1990–2019**

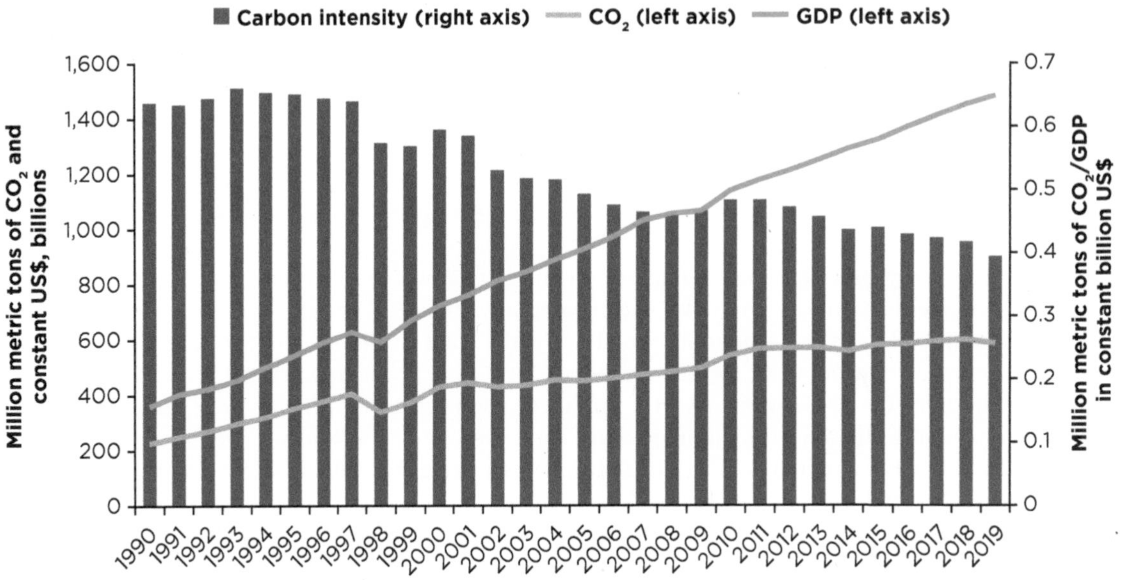

■ **Carbon intensity (right axis)** — **CO$_2$ (left axis)** — **GDP (left axis)**

Sources: For emissions from combustion, IEA 2021; World Development Indicators, World Bank (2005–20) (https://data.worldbank.org); for GDP, World Bank data.
Note: GDP = gross domestic product; CO$_2$ = carbon dioxide.

Policy and Institutional Transformation

TRANSFORMATION OF KOREA'S GROWTH PARADIGM

Until the 1990s, Korea's growth model was based on a government–big business coalition that was led by a "developmental state" that actively coordinated, organized, guided, and intervened in the market. The government used targeted industrial policies that provided preferential access to resources to large manufacturing exporters, in particular family-owned conglomerates called chaebols. The government bureaucracy oversaw the allocation of preferential access to credit to chaebols through its control over the financial system ("financial repression"). A competent and effective bureaucracy worked closely with the private sector to elicit information on key market constraints, through an "embedded autonomy" (Evans 1989; Evans and Rauch 1999). The strategic alliance between the government and big businesses helped to mobilize and concentrate resources and address coordination externalities. However, the arrangement undermined the full development of markets, inhibited market competition, constrained access to resources for stakeholders outside the coalition, and risked capture by rent-seeking private interests and political elites.

This government–big business coalition successfully drove Korea's growth for more than three decades. Direct interventions in the market and deals-based relationships were the "glue" that held together the state and big business coalition. But this deals-based management became increasingly difficult as Korea's economy expanded and became more complex and globalized. For its next stages of development, Korea had to transition from deals to market-based impartial rule of law to realize its full economic and social potential. There were signs that the necessary changes were already beginning to take place in the 1980s, in terms of greater impartiality of public administration and more transparent laws and predictable enforcement (figure O.18).

Reforms of the growth paradigm became necessary because Korea's transition to a high-income economy needed to draw from the entrepreneurial energy and innovation of a wider segment of the economy

FIGURE O.18 Impartial Administration and Predictable Enforcement of Laws, Republic of Korea, 1900–2015

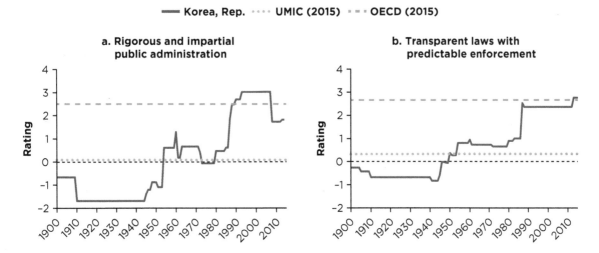

Source: Calculations by World Bank staff based on data from Varieties of Democracy (V-Dem), 2015, database hosted by Gothenburg Institute and Kellogg Institute (https://www.v-dem.net/en/).
Note: OECD = Organisation for Economic Co-operation and Development; UMIC = upper-middle-income country.

and society. However, such reforms threatened powerful political and business vested interests that had enjoyed preferential access to resources. Two major events provided the impetus that was necessary to overcome entrenched vested interests and transform Korea's political economy and institutional landscape—the transition to democratic national presidential elections in 1987 and the AFC in 1997–98.

The democratic reform in 1987 was the culmination of decades of popular protests for a fully democratic political system. It fundamentally altered the bargaining strength of the bureaucracy and big business and strengthened stakeholders outside the coalition, such as the media, national legislators, and civil society organizations (figure O.19). The emergence of new stakeholders and institutional checks and balances expanded accountability and rules-based contestability. Greater scrutiny by the media and civil society helped to combat corruption and created a more level playing field.

The AFC in 1997–98 was the second watershed moment that significantly altered the balance of power between the government, big business, and emerging stakeholders. The AFC had a devastating impact on the country's outputs and jobs and exposed Korea's structural flaws and the shortcomings of its development model. Real GDP contracted by 5.7 percent in 1998, foreign exchange reserves were nearly depleted, about half of the 30 largest chaebols went bankrupt, and the top five commercial banks had to be recapitalized with public funds.

The AFC accelerated the transformation of Korea's growth paradigm. Despite the emergence of new political stakeholders after the transition to free elections, the influence of the government–business coalition remained significant. The dominance of large business groups in the economy and their reckless borrowing and expansion were viewed as major causes of the AFC. As a result, the AFC strengthened the society-wide support for the reform of the government-business coalition. The crisis accelerated many of the important market oriented structural reforms that had been initiated before the crisis, helping the country to rebound quickly to a real GDP growth rate of 10.7 percent in 1999. The preexisting state-market paradigm was fundamentally transformed, from the developmental state model to a greater reliance on markets. Instead of guiding, controlling, and directly intervening in the market through industrial policies, the state increasingly focused on promoting the development of markets and strengthening market competition. The focus of industrial policy was reoriented from large firms to SMEs and technology startups and from specific firms and industries to broader support for innovation and technology. The reforms can be organized into two major areas: (a) promotion of markets, and (b) transformation of industrial policies.

FIGURE O.19 **Relative Strength of Elite Actors, Republic of Korea, 1904–2015**

- **Bureaucratic actors**
- **Economic actors (national)**
- **International economic actors and organizations**
- **Local government leaders**
- **Media**
- **National legislators**
- **Civil society organizations**
- **Foreign governments**
- **Judicial actors**
- **Military actors**
- **National chief executive**
- **Political party elites**

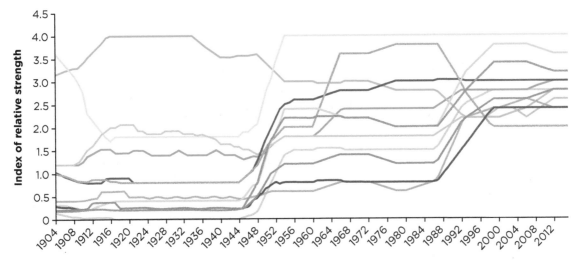

Sources: World Bank 2017.
Note: The relative strength of elite actors is measured on a 0–4 scale, ranging from 0 (no power to influence decision-making) to 4 (the group has a lot of power to influence decision-making on many issues). For more information on specific variables and survey methodology, see World Bank and V-Dem (2016) and Coppedge et al. (2015).

PROMOTION OF MARKETS

Financial Sector and Corporate Restructuring

In the earlier decades of Korea's development, the government believed that the financial sector lacked the capacity to support the development of the real economy. Therefore, it intervened heavily to mobilize and manage the allocation of financial resources to support the expansion of manufacturing exports. The government controlled the interest rates and channeled financial flows to selected industries through the state-controlled central bank, state-owned commercial banks, and state-dominated regulatory bodies (Shin 2006). The Bank of Korea had been under the direct control of the Ministry of Finance, and commercial banks were nationalized in the 1960s. The government also intervened in the managerial decisions of private financial institutions, by utilizing regulatory bodies and the market infrastructure. The heavy repression of the financial sector left it underdeveloped and allowed the significant accumulation of debt in the nonfinancial corporate sector, which left the country vulnerable to the external shocks of the AFC.

The financial sector reforms in response to the AFC were part of a big-bang approach to monetary policy reforms, capital market liberalization, and financial sector globalization. A fully floating exchange rate system was introduced, interest rate controls were liberalized, corporate and government bonds and money markets were opened to foreign investors, and the ceiling on foreign investments in equities was lifted. The government replaced the restrictive "Foreign Exchange Management Act" with the "Foreign

Exchange Transaction Act," which fundamentally transformed the foreign exchange regulatory regime from a positive to a negative list system. As a result, foreign financial transactions had to be reported but no longer required authorization from the government.

The restructuring of the commercial banking sector was central to the resolution of the AFC in Korea. A consolidated approach to financial sector regulation and supervision was at the core of Korea's comprehensive restructuring of the financial regulatory framework. Shortly after the outbreak of the AFC, the new Financial Services Commission Act was introduced to consolidate the ad hoc and fragmented financial regulatory system and supervisory framework. The Financial Services Commission Act established the Financial Services Commission as a new, unified agency governing all the regulated financial institutions. It also established the Financial Supervisory Service, which consolidated existing financial supervisory institutions across the banking, insurance, and securities sectors into a unified operational body. The focus of the Financial Services Commission and Financial Supervisory Service has been financial sector stability and soundness.

The government introduced the Prompt Corrective Action program, modeled on the US Federal Deposit Insurance Improvement Act, to restructure financial institutions under distress rapidly and transparently and mandate capitalization for failing financial institutions. The number of banks declined from 25 before the AFC to 14 in 2005. The ratio of nonperforming loans to total loans declined from 8.3 percent in 1999 to 6.6 percent in 2000 and further to 1.9 percent in 2002. Recapitalization of banks raised the average capital ratio of commercial banks from 7.0 percent in 1997, which was below the minimum 8 percent requirement, to 10.8 percent in 1999, but at a cost of approximately 18 percent of GDP to the government. The AFC fundamentally transformed the composition of the commercial loan portfolio, from corporate to household loans and from large firms to SMEs. The share of household loans increased to 52 percent in 2015–17. The leverage of the largest firms declined significantly, and SMEs significantly increased their leverage ratios. Policy loans to SMEs have continuously increased since the AFC. As a result, Korea has the highest ratio of policy loans to GDP among OECD countries (Kim 2014).

The AFC also resulted in significant restructuring of the nonbank financial institutions, which by 1995 had grown to 38.5 percent of the total assets of the financial sector. As a result of the AFC, more than 771 nonbank financial institutions closed, and many others underwent restructuring. The number of merchant banks, which had been a major source of financing for the chaebols, fell dramatically, from 30 to just two (J. H. Lee 2017). The regulatory framework for investment trust companies was restructured to align with the global standards for collective investment schemes, adopt international standards, and prevent managerial interference from the government.

The reforms of the financial sector significantly strengthened Korea's financial sector stability and resilience by introducing market-oriented reforms. As a result, the country relatively successfully managed the impact of the GFC two decades later, although the size of the external shock was greater than the AFC. Korea experienced net capital outflow of US$25.5 billion in October 2008 during the GFC, which was more than 3 percent of GDP and far larger than the US$6.4 billion outflows in December 1997, the worst month during the AFC. Export demand declined by approximately 40 percent from September to December 2008 during the GFC, compared to the relatively sustained export demand during the AFC. Despite the much larger shocks, Korea's corporate and financial sectors remained relatively stable during the GFC and domestic demand contracted far less. In contrast to the AFC, no large conglomerates failed and no major banks needed to be rescued by the government during the GFC.

An ambitious corporate restructuring program in the aftermath of the AFC complemented the comprehensive restructuring of the financial sector. The five largest chaebols were subjected to a Big Deals program, which required them to exchange business lines to streamline and prioritize their businesses. For the sixth through 64th conglomerates, firms were required to implement restructuring workout programs in return for debt reduction and rescheduling. The workout programs were led by the creditor banks, but the financial supervisory authorities and the newly established Corporate Restructuring Coordination Committee oversaw and coordinated the workouts. Failure to implement restructuring successfully would lead to insolvency of the firms. Altogether, 104 firms participated in the workout program. Of the 30 largest business groups in 1996, 14 went bankrupt or entered workout programs by the end of 1999, including Daewoo, one of the largest chaebols.

FDI restrictions were significantly loosened to mobilize foreign capital for the corporate restructuring. A new Foreign Investment Promotion Act (1998) streamlined investment procedures and strengthened incentives for foreign investments. Cross-border mergers and acquisitions were allowed, the ceiling on foreign equity ownership in the stock market was eliminated, restrictions on foreign land ownership were liberalized, and foreign exchange controls were liberalized. More than 30 sectors were liberalized after the AFC. Under the Foreign Exchange Transaction Act, restrictions on foreign ownership remained for 30 industrial sectors,

Corporate restructuring was complemented by corporate governance reforms to promote prudent management and strengthen the transparency and accountability of corporate management. Before the AFC, corporate governance in Korea fell short of international standards. In particular, the chaebols were tightly controlled by their founding families such that the control rights of the family owners far exceeded their shareholdings. In 1996, a typical controlling shareholder of a chaebol owned 23 percent of the shares outstanding but controlled 68 percent of the votes, through cross and circular holdings of shares among affiliates (Kim and Kim 2007). The board of directors was relatively ineffective in monitoring and disciplining management. Minority shareholder rights were weak, and few firms in Korea had outside directors. The chaebols drew on internal financing among the affiliates, which allowed them to avoid having to disclose the financial and operational information that is typically necessary to access external financing. The disciplining mechanism of the capital market was relatively poorly developed in the absence of hostile takeover threats through mergers and acquisitions.

As a result of the AFC, a consensus emerged that weak corporate governance was a major cause of the corporate over-indebtedness and excessive risk taking that had led to the crisis. Thus, ambitious corporate and financial restructuring programs included reforms to strengthen corporate governance and enhance the managerial transparency of corporations. The Securities and Exchange Act and the Commercial Codes were amended to relax requirements on exercising minority shareholder rights. It became easier for minority shareholders to file derivative suits, inspect accounting records, make a motion to dismiss directors, and file shareholder proposals (Nam 2004). The requirements for accounting, reporting, auditing, and disclosure of financial statements were strengthened. The chaebols were required to produce consolidated and combined financial statements. The amendment to the Monopoly Regulation and Fair Trade Act (MRFTA) required large, chaebol-affiliated firms to disclose information on large-scale transactions with specific firms and obtain approval from their board of directors for the transactions. The amended Securities and Exchange Act strengthened the role of outside directors, requiring large public firms to appoint at least half of the board members from outside and form a mandatory audit committee of which at least two-thirds of the members must be outside directors. To promote mergers and acquisitions, the minimum purchase requirement for tender offers was abolished and restrictions on mergers and acquisitions by foreign investors were loosened.

The corporate governance reforms have contributed to significant improvements in the quality of corporate governance in Korea, as reflected in the Corporate Governance Index (Black, Jang, and Kim 2005), which measures shareholder rights, board structure, board procedure, disclosure, and ownership parity. The improvements in the Corporate Governance Index also reflected the large-scale privatization post-AFC, which expanded the number of firms managed by professionals and with majority foreign shareholders (Kim and Kim 2007). Five years after the AFC, most of the listed firms had outside directors. The share price of firms in Korea with 50 percent or more outside directors has been 40 percent higher than firms without outside directors (Black, Jang, and Kim 2005). However, although progress on corporate governance is generally acknowledged, the control of the chaebols by the family owners remains debated today.

Market Competition, Deregulation, and Chaebol Policies

Competition policies and institutions were introduced in Korea when it was still a middle-income economy. The Korea Fair Trade Commission (KFTC) was launched in 1980 with the enactment of the MRFTA. The MRFTA was a symbol of political commitment to fairness, competition, and economic efficiency, but it allowed exemptions for cartels and anticompetitive mergers if they were deemed necessary to support industrial policies. As a result, competition policy was at times superseded by industrial policy objectives.

To strengthen competition policy, in 1996 KFTC was separated from the government and established as an independent agency (KFTC 2011). Subsequently, KFTC's role was greatly expanded in response to the AFC. The introduction of the leniency program in 1997 for voluntary reporting of collusion and a further amendment in 2005 greatly increased the effectiveness in discovering cartels. In 1999, the Omnibus Cartel Repeal Act removed legal exemptions for cartels and mergers from competition policy, and the legal standard for antitrust penalties was strengthened from "substantial" to "unreasonable" restraint of competition, which made it easier to prove antitrust cases. The growing importance of KFTC is reflected in the increasing number of enforcements and the size of the fines (figure O.20). In 2016 and 2017, KFTC received the top rating in the global assessment of competition authorities conducted by the *Global Competition Review*, a leading antitrust journal in the United Kingdom.[7]

A unique feature of MRFTA is the focus on chaebols. The MRFTA contained provisions to suppress aggregate concentration, although the intensity of regulatory enforcement has fluctuated over the decades. It also included restrictions on the total shareholding that chaebol affiliates can hold in other companies; prohibition on reciprocal shareholding and limits on debt guarantees among affiliated companies; and restrictions on transactions among affiliated companies to prevent undue benefits to related parties.

Efforts to reduce the economic dominance of large firms have been complemented by policy measures to protect SMEs, given concerns that large firms have enjoyed entrenched market power and raised barriers to entry for new SMEs. MRFTA and its companion statutes include provisions to protect SMEs against the abuses of large enterprises in transactions. In addition, Korea has had policies to restrict the entry of large enterprises into sectors where SMEs are active, given strong political and social pressure to protect SMEs. One of the most notable entry barriers was the "Products Reserved for SMEs" regulation, which was introduced in 1979 and was gradually reduced and completely abolished in 2006 for hindering competition and for nonconformity with the World Trade Organization. However, entry barriers were revived in response to the deteriorating business conditions due to the GFC, including through voluntary agreements between small and large enterprises.

A major deregulation drive in response to the AFC complemented efforts to strengthen market competition. Excessive regulations were perceived as a source of inefficiency and corruption that contributed to the AFC. In response, the government prioritized business deregulation to support the economic

FIGURE O.20 **Legal Enforcement by the KFTC, 1981–2019**

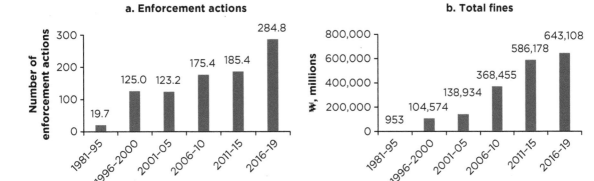

Source: KFTC 2019.
Note: Panel a shows the annual average number of enforcement actions for the abuse of market dominance, merger enforcement, and cartel behaviors. Panel b shows the annual average fines for all types of violations. KFTC = Korea Fair Trade Commission.

recovery. The Framework Act on Administrative Regulation, which was enacted in 1997, mainstreamed the monitoring and review of regulations in the government by requiring quality control of regulations in government institutions, laws, rights, and courts and by introducing mechanisms for citizen feedback. The Regulatory Reform Committee, co-chaired by the prime minister and a private sector expert, was established under the president's office in 1998 to lead a major deregulation drive. The Regulatory Reform Committee was an independent agency with the authority to oversee the quality of regulations and the regulation-making process. To make regulations more transparent, predictable, and effective, the government adopted requirements for information disclosure, independent reviews, impact analysis, and stakeholder consultations.

The deregulatory drive reduced the number of regulations from 10,372 in 1998 to 7,294 in 1999. However, since then the number of regulations has steadily increased to 15,182 in 2014 as the urgency for regulatory reforms waned. The deregulatory drive was not sustained due to lack of incentives and cooperation on regulatory reforms within the government and insufficient focus on producing tangible results for businesses and citizens. It has been criticized for excessively focusing on quantitative targets without sufficient attention to the qualitative impact. Foreign businesses have indicated the need to make business regulations less complicated and opaque.

Korea's business regulations and barriers to market competition remain relatively significant. Its OECD Product Market Regulation score deteriorated from the 72nd percentile in 2003 to the 92nd percentile in 2018 as other countries made greater progress on relevant reforms, worsening Korea's ranking. According to the Product Market Regulation score, regulations are particularly restrictive in retail price controls and regulation, command and control regulation, barriers in network sectors, and trade barriers. Korea also has had a relatively low global ranking on "burden of government regulation" in the World Economic Forum's Global Competitiveness Index, ranking 33rd of 38 OECD countries in 2018 (WEF 2019).

In 2019, the government introduced the regulatory sandbox program, an innovative program to address regulatory restrictions on entrepreneurship. The program temporarily grants business permits if a new technology or business model conflicts with existing regulations or if the relevant regulations are ambiguous or deemed inadequate. The regulations are then reviewed and updated as required. The United Kingdom's Financial Conduct Authority created the regulatory sandbox for the financial sector in 2014. Since then, regulatory sandboxes have been adopted in other countries to promote financial technology firms. The innovation of Korea's regulatory sandbox program is that it covers nonfinancial sectors in addition to the financial sector.

Promotion of Exports

Until the 1980s, Korea's tariff rates were relatively high to protect domestic industries from foreign competition. However, intermediate and capital goods imported to produce goods for export were provided tariff exemptions. Subsequently, imports were liberalized through a major tariff reduction program that lowered the simple average tariff rate from 23.7 percent in 1983 to 8 percent in 1994, similar to the levels in major developed economies. In addition, the previous multiple tariff rates were replaced with a uniform tariff rate of 8 percent for most manufactured goods. By 2019, the weighted tariff rates fell further to below 5 percent for consumption goods and 3 percent for other goods.

Since the 1990s, tariff reductions have been pursued through bilateral free trade agreements (FTAs) to expand trade with partner countries. As of January 2021, Korea had 17 FTAs with more than 50 countries, including with the Association of Southeast Asian Nations (2007), the European Union (2011), the United States (2012), and China (2015). Industries that were relatively heavily protected in the 1990s, such as the food and textile industries, experienced significant reduction of tariff rates as a result of the FTAs (figure O.21).

Korea complemented tariff reductions with major trade facilitation reforms and investments in trade infrastructure. Import clearance was transformed from a permit system to a self-declaration system in 1996,

FIGURE O.21 **Effectively Applied Weighted Tariff Rates, Republic of Korea, 1989–2019**

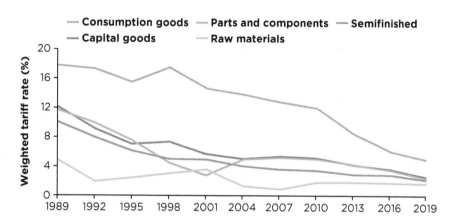

Source: Calculations based on data from the Korea Trade Statistics Promotion Institute.
Note: Tariff rates are weighted by the product import shares.

and post-entry investigation for cargo clearance was adopted. An "on-dock" immediate delivery system was introduced in 1998, which allowed importers to unload and release imported goods simultaneously at the time of entry. These measures provided the basis for the development of e-customs and e-trade in the 2000s. In partnership with the Korea International Trade Association, a private organization composed of traders, the government launched the uTradeHub in 2007, an internet-based services platform that provides real-time tracking of cargo and electronic submission and monitoring of associated paperwork. As a result of these reforms and investments, Korea was ranked first in the 2021 Global Survey of Digital and Sustainable Trade Facilitation. Korea's overall logistics cost was estimated to be a comparatively low 9 percent of GDP (in 2016) and it is ranked 17th of 139 countries in the World Bank's 2023 Logistics Performance Index.

Korea also promoted trade through export credit agencies (ECAs) and export promotion agencies. In Korea, public ECAs have been the dominant providers of trade finance, in contrast with the larger role of private ECAs in most high-income countries. The dominance of public ECAs can hinder the overall development of the market, but the public ECAs in Korea played an important role in providing trade finance in the earlier decades of Korea's development when private trade financing was constrained by a relatively underdeveloped financial sector. During the GFC, public ECAs in Korea expanded their credit supply, which compensated for the reduced supply of private trade finance. Korea also has a long history of utilizing export promotion agencies. The government established the Korea Trade-Investment Promotion Agency in 1962 to help exporters connect with foreign trading partners. This was critical because the cost of searching for trading partners can be as large as half of all trade costs (Allen 2014).

TRANSFORMATION OF INDUSTRIAL POLICIES

Science and Technology Industrial Policy

Post-AFC, industrial policies were reoriented from supporting large firms to promoting innovation and technology and SMEs and entrepreneurship. The two transitions are interrelated, as the support for SMEs emphasizes strengthening their innovation and technology capabilities.

Korea focused on building its science and technology capabilities from the beginning of its modern development. The Science and Technology Promotion Act (1967) laid the initial legislative framework for the national S&T policies. The act outlined national R&D planning and programs and prioritized S&T investments, related human resource capacity building, and foreign technology imports and cooperation. The government established new ministries and institutions, including the Ministry of Science and Technology; the

Korea Advanced Institute of Science and Technology, an S&T focused university; a range of GRIs, including the multidisciplinary Korea Institute of Science and Technology; and the Daedeok Science Town, a technology hub that is home to numerous GRIs and private research institutes. The early reliance on GRIs was unlike the typical approach of other countries that focused on building research capacity in leading universities.

Korea had the foresight to recognize early on the potential of digital technology to drive the country's economic growth and development. The foundation for Korea's digital development over the past four decades was established in the 1980s when it was still a middle-income economy. In the 1980s through the 1990s, GRIs, such as the Electronics and Telecommunication Research Institute and the Korea Institute of Electronics Technology, made significant contributions to the development of critical telecommunication and semiconductor technologies for the domestic industries. Today, there are 11 GRIs for fundamental research and 14 GRIs for applied research, in diverse fields such as ICT, aerospace and aviation, nuclear power, marine engineering, energy, natural resources, and information and data processing technology.

By the 1990s, Korea was approaching the technology frontier and began to reorient its policy focus from promoting technology adoption to generating frontier innovation. The government, industry, academia, and research institutes worked together to advance the country's technology innovation system, strategically pursue national R&D projects, and develop promising technologies of the future. Korea's spending on R&D jumped from 0.5 percent of GDP in 1980 to 1.6 percent in 1990 when Korea was still an upper-middle-income country (figure O.22). Its R&D spending as a percentage of GDP in 1990 was significantly greater than that in other upper-middle-income countries and approached the EU average of 2.2 percent of GDP two decades later in 2019.

By the 1990s, the center of Korea's R&D shifted from the public to the private sector. The chaebols started to invest significantly in domestic R&D, and private R&D expenditures increased by an

FIGURE O.22 **R&D versus GDP per Capita, across Countries, 1965–2020**

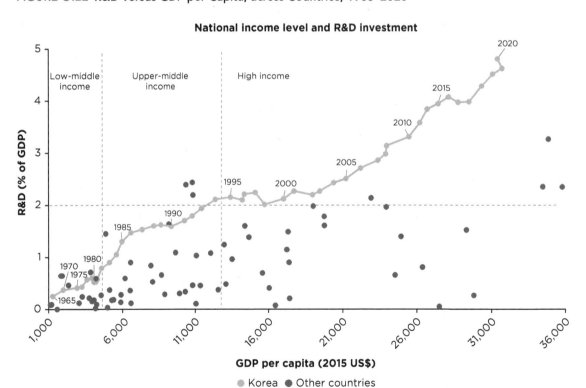

Sources: Hong, Choi, and Kim 2020, based on World Bank 2020.
Note: GDP = gross domestic product; R&D = research and development.

unprecedented 26 times from 1980 to 1990 and exceeded 80 percent of total R&D spending by the end of the 1990s. As the country strengthened its domestic innovation and technology capabilities, the ratio of technology imports to business R&D fell from about 90 percent in the mid-1970s to 30 percent in the mid-1980s (Chung 2011). The number of corporate R&D centers skyrocketed from 46 in 1981 to 42,155 in 2020, and they increasingly focused on developing new technologies, products, and services, expanding beyond the previous focus on absorbing foreign technologies.

Subsequently, Korea's total R&D spending increased from 1.6 percent of GDP in 1990 to 2.1 percent in 2000 (figure O.22), when the country transitioned to a high-income economy. The Ministry of Science and ICT (formerly the Ministry of Science and Technology) and the Ministry of Knowledge Economy began reorienting research toward high-technology industries. The Five-Year S&T Principal Plan and the National R&D Program managed by the Ministry of Science and Technology launched funds to support research to develop frontier technologies in areas such as semiconductors, satellites, and bioscience. Technology development programs included the Creative Research Initiative in 1997, the National Technology Roadmap and the 21st Century Frontier R&D Program in 1999, the Biotech 2000 Plan, and the Nanotechnology Development Plan in 2001.

In 2001, the government enacted the Framework Act on Science and Technology to provide long-term support for S&T development. In the same year, the government also introduced the G7 Project, a national R&D mega-program to develop new innovations and technologies. The G7 Project was a more top-down, government-led initiative compared to previous public R&D projects that had a more bottom-up approach, designed and planned by researchers from the GRIs. In 2003, the government issued the Science and Technology Master Plan, the first in a series of five-year plans to improve the capacity and funding for R&D, focused on developing the R&D workforce and increasing funding for basic research. In 2010, the government issued the "Long-Term Vision for Science and Technology Development and a Future Vision for S&T: Towards 2040," which further shifted the center of the national innovation system from the government to the private sector.

Since the 2000s, there has been another significant jump in national R&D spending, from 2.1 percent of GDP in 2000 to 3.3 percent in 2010 and to 4.8 percent in 2020 (figure O.22), the second highest in the world after Israel. The increase in R&D spending was driven by the increase in the share of business enterprise R&D (BERD) spending (figure O.23). Korea's BERD was 3.6 percent of GDP in 2018, more than

FIGURE O.23 **Sources of R&D Expenditure, Republic of Korea, 1995–2018**

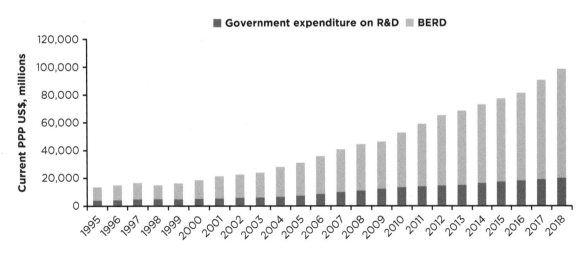

Source: Organisation for Economic Co-operation and Development (https://stats.oecd.org/).
Note: BERD = business enterprise research and development; PPP = purchasing power parity; R&D = research and development.

twice the OECD average of 1.7 percent. Over time, the government has expanded its support for BERD. By the early 2000s, Korea led all other OECD countries in fiscal incentives provided for private sector R&D, totaling 0.3 percent of GDP and 46 percent of government support for BERD. In 2019, Korea's total government support for BERD was fourth among OECD countries.

As the center of Korea's research shifted from the public sector to the private sector, the government began shifting its focus to basic and fundamental research to complement private spending on applied research and product development. The government increased funding for universities to carry out basic research and encouraged the chaebols to expand upstream research. Basic research's share of the government R&D budget increased from 19.4 percent in 2003, to 25.4 percent in 2008, and to about 33 percent in 2012. The government launched several Big Science programs and established national core research centers to encourage joint research in frontier S&T fields. The government also built innovation clusters, most notably Pangyo Techno Valley near Seoul, which is equivalent to Silicon Valley in the United States. Pangyo today is home to close to 1,300 high-technology firms and approximately 65,000 employees.

From 1995 to 2015, the government embarked on a major program to build the broadband infrastructure network. The construction of the ICT network was carried out in two phases. In the first phase, from 1995 to 2005, US$32.5 billion was invested to build the national information highway and connect the major urban areas. In the second phase, from 2005 to 2014, US$2.6 billion was invested in the remaining smaller urban and rural areas. The construction of the ICT infrastructure was a public-private partnership that combined the government's policy direction and the private sector's capacity for project management and execution. Financing was shared, 5 percent by the government and 95 percent by the private sector. Korea's ICT infrastructure is now considered among the best in the world, ranking first on the 2016 ICT Development Index of the International Telecommunication Union and second in 2017.

Today, Korea's science, technology, and innovation system is vast and complex, with more than 20 government agencies that allocate the R&D budget. It consists of more than 300 R&D management regulations, 60 research support systems, and more than 400 support instruments covering the entire spectrum of innovation policy instruments, including loans, grants, technical assistance, and indirect instruments, such as tax incentives and credit guarantees (Frias et al. 2021). Indirect support instruments represent almost 40 percent of the overall spending; loans and credit guarantees account for 29 percent; grants account for almost 25 percent; and the remaining spending is on technology extension services, technology transfer offices, and technology parks. Basic research accounts for 14 percent of total research, which is comparable to the 17 percent OECD average.

There are three key remaining challenges for Korea's innovation system. One, Korea has a relatively low level of international collaboration in science and innovation among OECD countries. Two, Korea devotes less to R&D in services than any other OECD country, although the returns to R&D in services can be as high as in manufacturing (Audretsch et al. 2018). Three, promoting R&D innovation in SMEs remains a challenge. Technological capabilities and rates of successful commercialization of R&D among SMEs in Korea remain lower than in other developed countries (KISTEP 2019).

Support to SMEs

Korea's large firms, in particular the chaebols, have clearly played a major role driving Korea's economic growth. However, there have been concerns that the dominance of the chaebols resulted in entrenched market power and barriers to entry for new competitors. In response, since the 2000s industrial policies have been significantly reoriented from supporting large firms to supporting SMEs and entrepreneurship. To prioritize the promotion of SMEs, the Small and Medium Business Administration was established in 1996 and subsequently elevated to the Ministry of SMEs and Startups in 2017. By the 2000s, SMEs were the largest beneficiaries of government support for innovation (Frias et al. 2021). The government introduced policy instruments that systematically targeted SMEs in different stages of growth, for example, proof-of-concept, commercialization, scale-up, and restructuring (Jang 2009). By 2018, only 11 percent of public policy support for enterprises was allocated to large firms, 58 percent to MSMEs, and 31 percent to "middle-market" firms (figure O.24).

FIGURE O.24 Targeting of Beneficiaries by Ministry as Share of Total Resources Allocated, 2018

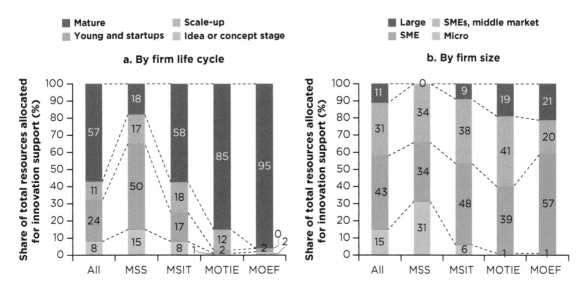

a. By firm life cycle

b. By firm size

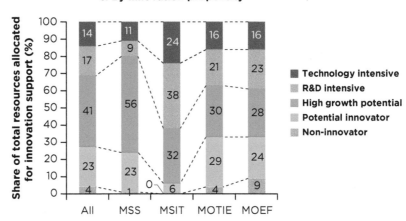

c. By innovation propensity

Sources: Frias et al. 2021, based on data from MOEF 2017; ministry budget and planning documents.
Note: MOEF = Ministry of Economy and Finance; MOTIE = Ministry of Trade, Industry, and Energy; MSIT = Ministry of Science and ICT; MSS = Ministry of SMEs and Startups; R&D = research and development; SMEs = small and medium-size enterprises.

Korea's MSME support program today is comprehensive and diverse. The government budget for SME support programs increased by 57.7 percent between 2017 and 2020 (Noh 2020). In 2020, there were 439 central government programs and 1,313 local government programs, for a total of 1,754 programs covering the entire spectrum of policy instruments. Financial support accounted for 57 percent, followed by 17 percent for technical support, 9 percent for human resource development support, and 8 percent for managerial extension programs.

Public financial support for SMEs consists of policy loans, credit guarantees, and equity investment. The main sources of policy loans are development banks (the Korea Development Bank and the Industrial Bank of Korea) and the Korea SMEs and Startups Agency. Korea has been active in using credit guarantees to support SMEs, provided through the Korea Credit Guarantee Fund, the Korea Technology Finance Corporation, and the Korea Regional Credit Guarantee Foundation. For SMEs that have limited access to financing due to lack of collateral, the Korea Technology Finance

Corporation provides credit guarantees based on assessments of their technologies. The Bank of Korea incentivizes SME lending through its Bank-Intermediated Lending Support Facility. SMEs account for over 80 percent of all bank loans (figure O.25). However, SMEs receive only 2.4 percent of total corporate direct financing (in 2020), indicating that equity financing has been allocated mainly to large firms.

SMEs also benefit from substantial tax incentives. The Special Tax Reduction for SMEs reduces corporate and income tax by 5 to 30 percent, depending on the region, type of business, and company size. Corporate tax, income tax, and local tax are reduced for three to five years for SME startups. In addition, there are tax credits for general investment, R&D and human resources development expenses, and employment increases. To promote startups, there are tax exemptions for capital gains of venture capital firms and tax breaks for angel investment. Many tax incentives for SMEs have sunset rules, but many are extended. The tax incentives could be more performance oriented by incorporating a greater focus on promoting growth potential and requiring improvements in the performance and profitability of the beneficiary firms.

At the core of the reorientation of industrial policies to SMEs has been a greater focus on promoting their R&D and technology upgrading. The Korea Small Business Innovation Research program was introduced in 1998 to support SME R&D. The program, which is modeled after the US Small Business Innovation Research Program, required a minimum share of government and public agencies' R&D budgets to be allocated to SMEs. By 2018, 17.4 percent of government R&D was invested in SMEs. By 2020, up to 54 percent of policy support was allocated to technology-intensive firms and potential innovators (figure O.24).

With regards to technology support programs for SMEs, Korea has a strong focus on promoting digital innovation. Digital innovation accounts for 15 percent of the total number of SME support programs, more than the OECD average and three times more than in developing countries. Korea has among the highest levels of digital adoption globally (figure O.14), but there is a significant technology gap between large and small firms (figure O.25) and the adoption rates vary considerably by the type of digital technology. The share of firms using advanced Fourth Industrial Revolution technologies is especially low among lagging SMEs. There are concerns that the low technology adoption rates have contributed to the large productivity gap between large and small firms in Korea. To facilitate SMEs' access to public R&D resources, the government established the National Science and Technology Information Service, a portal that provides information on national R&D programs and projects, human resources, research equipment, and facilities.

To promote research collaboration, the government established research clusters and supported the networking of R&D institutes, S&T parks, incubators, and research universities. It also established joint international R&D centers and international exchange programs for researchers and engineers (Hwang et al. 2002). In 2003, the New Technology Purchasing Assurance Program was introduced to create demand for technologies produced by SME R&D through government procurements. By 2019, SMEs accounted for 77 percent of the public procurement market (Statistics Korea 2020). There is evidence that these programs have contributed to the growth of SMEs (Lee and Jung 2018) and the product innovation of venture firms (Choi et al. 2014).

Technology and business extension programs have been used to address the large gap in managerial quality between SMEs and large firms. In the 1980s, the government began to build an extensive network of public and nonprofit technology extension providers for SMEs. In 2005, the SME Consulting Service Program was introduced to strengthen and expand business extension services for SMEs, through innovation vouchers, training programs, and a consultancy evaluation system to ensure the quality standards of consultants (Kim 2007). Specialized technology diffusion agents were promoted, such as engineering consulting firms, capital goods producers, and researchers.

Ensuring the effectiveness of government R&D support programs for SMEs remains an ongoing challenge. There is evidence that the programs helped increase the sales, assets, employment, and R&D expenditure of SMEs but the impacts were not always significant (Oh and Kim 2018). Korea's SMEs

FIGURE O.25 **Estimated Technology Sophistication in Manufacturing, Selected Countries**

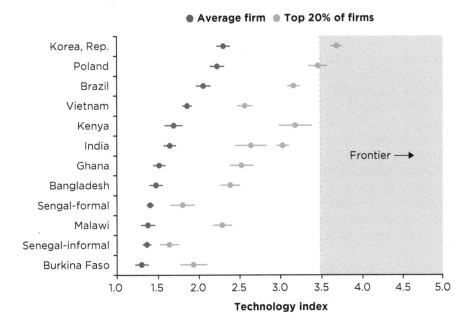

Sources: Cirera, Comin, and Cruz 2022; data from Firm-level Adoption of Technology (FAT) surveys for various countries.

continue to have less developed technological capabilities and lower rates of successful commercialization compared to peers in other developed countries (KISTEP 2019). R&D by SMEs is concentrated in the low-R&D-intensive service sector, whereas large firms dominate the R&D-intensive manufacturing sectors. The proliferation of SME support programs has resulted in significant duplication of government support,[8] allowed poorly performing SMEs to survive on government support, and encouraged SMEs to remain small to retain eligibility for public support. Hence, SME policies would benefit from a greater emphasis on promoting growth and productivity (World Bank 2021). There are also concerns that the significant expansion of policy support to SMEs reduced incentives for financial institutions to improve their capacity for credit evaluation of SMEs, thus hindering the development of a private market for SME financing (Jones and Kim 2014).

Promotion of Technology Entrepreneurship

Since the 1990s, the promotion of technology entrepreneurship and the strengthening of the entrepreneurial ecosystem have been central to Korea's SME policies to promote technology upgrading (Sohn 2006). The Act on Special Measures for the Promotion of Venture Businesses (1997) provided subsidies and tax exemptions to venture capital companies and liberalized relevant regulations. The government's financial support for entrepreneurial technology businesses was expanded, and the Korean Securities Dealers Automated Quotations (KOSDAQ), modeled after the National Association of Securities Dealers Automated Quotations (NASDAQ) stock market, was established in 1996 as a stock market for technology businesses.

Since the 2000s, there has been a significant increase in the number and size of venture businesses, the venture capital market, KOSDAQ listings, and merger and acquisition venture deals. The venture boom in the early-to-mid 2000s produced the first generation of technology-based venture firms, three of which, Kakao, Naver, and Celltrion, are now among the largest companies in Korea by market capitalization.

Korea's venture capital investments increased from 0.05 percent of GDP in 2010 to 0.16 percent in 2019, the largest increase and in 2021, fifth largest among OECD countries at 0.258 percent (OECD 2023). The number of venture capital funds increased from 101 in 2013 to 165 in 2020. In 2021, Korea had 11 unicorns (privately owned companies valued at more than US$1 billion), which was the 10th largest number globally, although far less than the 157 in China and the 388 in the United States. Technology-based venture firms are making outsized contributions to total R&D. Venture firms account for 11.5 percent of the total R&D business and about 50 percent of SMEs' R&D, although venture firms make up only 1 percent of the total number of SMEs (KISTEP 2018).

Korea's startup environment has improved over the past decades and in 2018 was ranked 24th of 137 countries on the Global Entrepreneurship Index and ninth of 44 countries on the Global Entrepreneurship Monitor's National Entrepreneurship Context Index (GEDI 2018). Korea has the highest rate of startups but also the lowest survival rates among comparators. Korea's total early-stage entrepreneurship activity rate increased from 6.7 in 2016 to nearly 15 in 2019 (Korea Entrepreneurship Foundation 2019), significantly higher than the rates of China (8.7) and Japan (5.4). However, the one- and two-year survival rates were 64 and 53 percent, respectively, which were lower than all comparators. The relatively low survival rates suggest that there are significant challenges for startups to grow.

The government provides targeted support for technology startups with high growth potential, through government-backed venture capital funds, business incubators and accelerators and innovation centers, public procurement of R&D, and innovation clusters and networking support for R&D cooperation. In 2005, the government established the Korea Venture Investment Corporation (KVIC), a venture capital fund-of-funds, to mobilize private financing for startups. In December 2022, KVIC leveraged US$8.2 billion in total funding invested in 1,125 partnership funds to generate investments in SMEs and startups nearly 3.5 times the size of the fund, thereby significantly crowding in private financing. The government provides the capital and professional management specialists handle the investment decisions, overseen by an investment management committee. The government has also supported the rapid growth of angel investments through tax benefits and support programs for accelerators.

Despite its successes, Korea's entrepreneurial ecosystem faces several challenges, including the low survival rates of startups, difficulty of scaling up, lack of diversification of venture capital investors, and continued reliance on government support. There has been a decline in the ratio of high-growth startups to total firms in almost all industries (Lee, Im, and Han 2017). Among companies with 10 or more regular workers, the proportion of gazelle companies, which are young, high-growth companies, fell from 2.6 percent in 2009 to 1.6 percent in 2015.

PRODUCING AN EDUCATED AND SKILLED WORKFORCE

Investments in Education and Skills

Investing in human capital development has always been a top priority for Korea, from the earliest days of its modern development history. As a result, Korea has among the highest levels of human capital, ranking fourth of 173 countries on the World Bank's Human Capital Index (in 2020). Korea attained the average level of human capital of OECD countries by the 1990s (Human Capital Index of the Penn World Table), when it was still a middle-income economy. Korea's 15-year-olds have consistently been among the top ranks in reading, science, and math on the Program for International Student Assessment test since its inception in 2000. Korea ranked fourth in higher education achievement and 11th in graduates in sciences in the IMD World Digital Competitiveness ranking in 2020.

Korea expanded its education system by first focusing on primary education and then secondary and finally tertiary education. The primary school gross enrollment rate reached 96 percent by 1959, less than a decade after the Korean War, and mass adult literacy campaigns in 1945–48 and 1954–58 successfully reduced the illiteracy rate from 78.2 percent in 1948 to 4.1 percent in 1958 when Korea was still a low-income economy. The enrollment rates in lower and upper secondary schools started to increase rapidly in the 1970s and reached the levels of high-income economies by the mid-1980s, when Korea was a middle-income economy. In the 1990s, Korea shifted its focus to tertiary education to support the country's ambition to become a global technology leader, and the enrollment rates in tertiary schools increased from 24 percent in 1990 to 66 percent in 2005 (figure O.26). By 2019, 70 percent of 25-to-34-year-olds had tertiary education, significantly higher than the OECD average of 45 percent.

The expansion of Korea's education system reflected sustained, long-term public investments in education. The Ministry of Education's share of the government budget steadily increased from 14.3 percent in the early 1960s to 22.8 percent in the mid-1990s and subsequently has remained in the 15 to 20 percent range, or approximately 3 to 4 percent of GDP. The investment more than doubled the number of primary and secondary schools, from approximately 4,600 in 1950, to 10,500 in 1990, and to 11,700 in 2020. The average class size halved from around 60 students in 1965, to 53 in 1990, and to 23 in 2020. The number of teachers grew from approximately 56,000 in 1950, to 142,000 in 1970, 285,000 in 1990, and 433,000 in 2020. High-quality teachers were recruited through relatively high salaries, job security, and social status, which made the profession relatively attractive. A national curriculum and textbooks, high-quality teachers with university education, and parents' prioritization of their children's education contributed to the high quality of education in Korea.

Significant private spending complemented public spending on education. Private spending on education has remained relatively high. As a result, the combined public and private education expenditures have been estimated to be the highest among the OECD countries, at 7.1 percent of GDP in 2000 (OECD 2003), reflecting the relatively high shares of private schools and also significant spending on private tutoring, which is a large industry in Korea. Korea's education spending was 5.3 percent of GDP in 2019, public and private education taking 4.0% and 1.3%, respectively (OECD 2022). The share of private high school students has been declining since peaking at 61.9 percent in 1993, but the share of students in private tertiary institutions has remained between 70 and 80 percent.

In the earlier decades, foreign development aid complemented domestic financing of education. Foreign aid contributed to the financing of the construction of education facilities, teacher training, modernization of vocational and technical education, and scholarships for overseas education. US foreign aid financed technical assistance provided by the University of Minnesota from 1955 to 1960 to Seoul National University, one of the preeminent universities in Korea, to modernize the university.

FIGURE O.26 **Changing Trend in Gross Enrollment Rates, by Level of Education, Republic of Korea, 1965–2019**

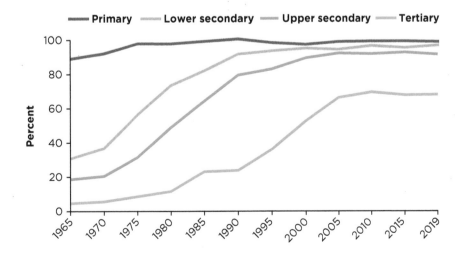

Sources: Koh et al. 2010; Ministry of Education and Korean Educational Development Institute (various years).

The World Bank financed 10 education-related projects in Korea over several decades. Korea has also been sending significant numbers of students overseas for education. It currently has the third largest foreign student population in the United States, after China and India.

There have been strong incentives to obtain a higher education due to the economy's increasing demand for an educated and skilled labor force. The government systematically linked national economic planning and human capital planning, to ensure coordination of the supply of and demand for skilled labor. Education development plans accounted for the skilled labor force that was necessary for national economic development. The strong demand for educated and skilled labor was reflected in significant returns to investments in education (Koh 2018). In the 1980s, the premium for tertiary education was estimated to be more than 40 percent. After subsequently declining, the premium started to rise again in the 2000s, driven by demand from expanding high-technology industries and deeper integration into the global production network (Koh 2019).

To promote innovation- and technology-led development, Korea has prioritized science, technology, engineering, and mathematics (STEM) education. The government prepared Five-Year Science and Technology Development Plans from the 1960s until the early 2000s, which emphasized expanding the supply of the S&T workforce. The budget for R&D in higher education continuously increased, and the government established new S&T universities, including the Korea Advanced Institute of Science and Technology and the Gwangju Institute of Science and Technology. In the 2000s, the government emphasized expanding research grants, subsidizing programs for strengthening industry-academia collaboration, and developing a comprehensive information technology platform for scientists and engineers. Major programs launched at that time, such as the Brain Korea 21 Project to finance the upgrading of research capacity of universities and researchers, remain active today.

As a result of the emphasis on STEM education, Korea has a high share of STEM tertiary graduates. In 2015, 29 percent of the country's tertiary school graduates were in the STEM fields, significantly higher than the OECD average and the third highest after Germany (37 percent) and Austria (30 percent). More recently, the government launched integrated STEAM (STEM combined with Arts) programs in schools to promote multidisciplinary thinking, creative problem solving, and real-world applications of S&T. In 2016, more than 50 percent of elementary schools, 48 percent of middle schools, and 32 percent of high schools implemented STEAM programs. However, the efforts to prioritize critical thinking and creative problem solving remain an unfinished agenda in Korea's education system, given the emphasis on preparing for college entrance exams. The extreme competition for college entrance has been criticized for placing a heavy burden on students and their families.

Given the strong preference for higher academic education, it has been challenging to ensure that technical and vocational education is viewed as an attractive alternative education track. The government has aimed to promote balanced development of academic and vocational education, to supply the skilled labor demanded by the expanding industries. However, demand for higher academic education increased as the country transitioned to a higher income level, and the proportion of vocational high school students declined from 45.0 percent in 1980 to 35.5 percent in 1990 and 23.8 percent in 2010. Subsequent efforts to increase the share of vocational high school graduates were largely unsuccessful, and the government's priorities were adjusted in the 2000s to focus on addressing the skills mismatch of high school graduates, the rising unemployment among university graduates, and the sharply declining student population as the country started to experience a declining overall population and rapid aging.

The government introduced several reforms in response to the declining share of vocational high school students. One, it introduced Meister high schools as a new model of vocational high school to prepare students for high-skilled, high-technology jobs. Meister high schools collaborate closely with industry on the curriculum and training, and internships are provided to ensure a high level of employment after graduation. Two, the government restructured and downsized the vocational high school system, reducing the number of vocational high schools from 692 in 2010 to 400 by 2015 (50 Meister high schools and 350 specialized vocational high schools). Financial support was provided to transform vocational high schools into general academic high schools and to retrain the teachers. Three academic and vocational educational pathways were further integrated to provide an open pathway for vocational school graduates to access academic and higher education schools. Vocational school graduates who worked after graduation were provided greater opportunities to pursue higher education, to address concerns that vocational education limited their options for future education.

Nonformal vocational training (employee training) has complemented formal vocational training in Korea. Korea established a nonformal vocational training system in 1967 and has since implemented a mandatory training system and a variety of vocational training programs for SMEs. In 1995, the government introduced the EIS, which uniquely combined unemployment benefits with financial support for vocational training and job search. The Vocational Competency Development Program under EIS provides financial support for training and is demand driven, allowing employers and individuals to select vocational training institutes and programs based on their training needs. EIS is financed by employment insurance fees collected from employers. The integration of formal and nonformal vocational training with academic education is the basis for the lifetime learning system in Korea that supports workers to maintain and enhance their productivity and employability through reskilling and upskilling throughout their career.

Labor Market Reforms

From the mid-1970s to the mid-1980s when the country transitioned to a middle-income economy, the previous excess labor supply became a labor shortage as the demand for skilled workers increased but the supply of qualified labor was constrained. The government invested in the labor market infrastructure to facilitate more efficient allocation of labor, including by expanding public employment services and improving long-term workforce projections. As the labor market tightened, workers demanded higher wages, greater rights, and fairer treatment. In response, the government enacted a minimum wage in 1986 and severance payments[9] and passed legislation to protect disadvantaged groups such as women, the disabled, and the elderly.

Globalization in the 1990s and the AFC fundamentally changed the terrain of Korea's labor market. Massive layoffs followed the closures and reorganizations of firms and banks during the AFC, and the unemployment rate spiked to 9 percent, an unprecedented level for Korea. The massive layoffs provided the impetus for decisive labor market reforms that were necessary for employment adjustments, but this required a national consensus among key stakeholders. In 1998, a tripartite committee of representatives of businesses, labor unions, and the government was established that agreed to legalize collective dismissals and the use of temporary nonregular workers to enhance labor market flexibility. In return, the political participation of unions was legalized and the rights of civil servants and teachers to unionize were enhanced.

Since the AFC, Korea has been expanding ALMPs to promote employment, including employment services, subsidized employment (public works projects and subsidies to firms that employ targeted groups, such as youth), skills training, and entrepreneurship promotion (figure O.27). However, Korea spends only 0.6 percent of GDP on ALMPs, less than many OECD countries, with half of the spending on direct job creation. Of the various programs, the Employment Success Package Program for Vulnerable Groups (youth and the elderly) is unique in that it combines employment services, vocational skills training, internship opportunities, and income support. Program evaluation indicates that it has been relatively effective in promoting employment among vulnerable groups.

Korea has developed an integrated approach to employment services and labor market infrastructure to promote employment. The Employment Welfare Plus Center provides support for registering for unemployment, claiming employment insurance, and assisting in employment search and career development. The Labor Market Information System provides labor-related data on job search, career planning, skills development, and labor supply and demand. The Korea Employment Information Service, a public agency, uses the Labor Market Information System to monitor labor market developments and evaluate policies.

FIGURE O.27 **Labor Market Development since the AFC, Republic of Korea, 1997–2016**

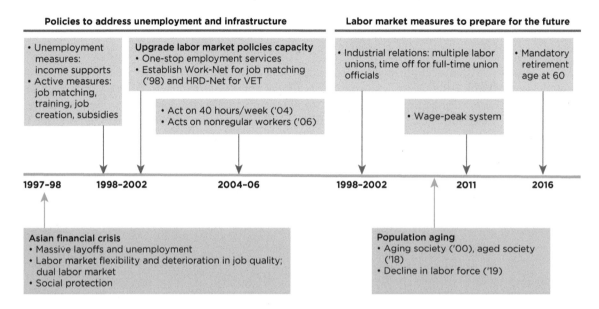

Source: Based on Keum et al. 2017.
Note: HRD = human resources development; VET = vocational education and training.

Today, Korea faces several labor market challenges. First, the nonregular workers introduced during the AFC now account for more than one-third of total employment, which is the highest share in the OECD, including workers in the "gig economy." Nonregular employment has been criticized for widening the disparity in job security and quality, working hours, social insurance coverage, and access to vocational education and training. The government has introduced laws to ensure fair treatment and prevent the abuse of nonregular workers by regulating nonregular contracts, but there is evidence that these acts have reduced the overall employment of nonregular workers.

Second, the population is aging rapidly due to the significant increase in life expectancy and sharp decline in the fertility rate, which is the lowest in the world. Population aging significantly affects the size and composition of the labor force and increases the importance of older workers. In the 2010s, two important initiatives were introduced, the wage-peak system, which provides wage subsidies if employers and employees agree on extending employment of older workers at reduced wages, and mandatory retirement, which entitles workers to work until age 60.

Third, youths in Korea face a lower employment rate and longer time finding employment, compared to youths in other OECD countries. The government is addressing youth unemployment by providing tailored job matching services, skills training, and subsidies for hiring and employment continuity. Coordination between education providers and employers is critical to address rising youth unemployment, by ensuring that education and training are responsive to the skills demanded by potential employers.

Fourth, the female employment rate in Korea remains significantly lower (52.8 percent) than in other OECD countries (more than 70 percent). However, the labor force participation rate of younger women has increased significantly, to 76.3 percent, and is now essentially equivalent to the rate of their male counterparts. Nevertheless, about half of women with young children do not work, indicating that they face significant challenges in combining work with childcare responsibilities. Korea's high gender pay gap of 36 percent, which is much higher than the OECD average of 12.8 percent, further discourages female labor force participation. In response, the government has rolled out a combination of ALMPs; inclusive, gender-neutral workplace policies; and childcare-related support.

Lessons for Developing Countries

THE FOUNDATIONS OF LONG-RUN SUCCESS

Korea's successful escape from the "middle-income trap" was possible because the country has continuously invested in the basic foundation of long-term success for decades since it was a low-income economy. Developing countries can learn from Korea's experience in sustaining a long-term focus on maintaining macroeconomic stability, promoting manufacturing exports by the private sector, and investing in physical infrastructure and human capital. Korea's long-term success was based on a close public-private partnership that helped to address the enormous hurdles and investments required for industrialization.

Korea maintained a relatively stable macroeconomic environment, which provided firms the confidence to plan and invest for the long term. However, the economy experienced periodic financial sector instability, in 1972 and the early 1980s, when the government had to intervene to address high levels of corporate debt, particularly short-term foreign debt. Government interventions temporarily averted a full-blown crisis, but the excessive demand for debt was not fundamentally addressed and the economy remained vulnerable to future crises. AFC contagion became a major macroeconomic crisis in Korea due to mismanaged foreign reserves, excessive levels of corporate debt, and a financial sector that was weakened by financial repression. It was a major crisis, but the economy quickly recovered and, most importantly, Korea used the crisis to carry out major reforms that have allowed it to sustain growth since the AFC. Developing countries need to be able to recognize the signs of increasing macroeconomic vulnerability and take the necessary decisive actions, which could be costly in the short term but would strengthen the resilience of the economy to a far costlier major crisis in the medium to long term.

Korea's successful growth strategy has been centered on the promotion of manufacturing exports. In the earlier decades of its development, Korea actively used targeted and interventionist industrial policies to support specific firms and industries. However, such policies have been phased out and are considered contrary to global trade and investment rules. There are also many country examples of ineffective, unsuccessful, and harmful industrial policies. Instead, what countries can learn from Korea's relatively successful experience with industrial policies is to ensure that policies to support the private sector have clear and measurable objectives and are disciplined through objective performance criteria, such as export targets in the case of Korea's industrial policies.

Korea's promotion of manufacturing exports also benefited from focused and sustained political commitment, government leadership, and a competent and motivated bureaucracy and public institutions that avoided the worst excesses of rent-seeking abuses. Annual export targets were monitored in Export Promotion Meetings that were chaired by the president and highly publicized. Close consultations between the government and private enterprises, through an "embedded autonomy," helped Korea to identify major market constraints and opportunities. Policy making benefited from an emphasis on quantitative targets and data-driven analysis. Local capacity for policy research and analysis was strengthened through research institutes and policy think tanks, such as the Korea Development Institute, which was established in 1971.

Developing countries can learn from Korea's policy choices that supported the rapid expansion of its exports from the 1990s, when the country transitioned from a middle-income to a high-income economy. Import liberalization programs from the 1970s through the 1990s had opened the economy to international competition. The loosening of restrictions on overseas investments in the 1990s encouraged private firms to invest in overseas production facilities, which accelerated Korea's integration into GVCs. Subsequently, Korea reduced trade barriers by expanding FTAs, which opened previously protected industries, such as food and textiles, to greater competition. It complemented the tariff reductions with investments in trade facilitation and infrastructure, in particular the digitalization of the trade infrastructure. As a result, Korea ranked first in the 2021 Global Survey of Digital and Sustainable Trade Facilitation and 17 out of 139 countries in the 2023 Logistics Performance Index. For developing countries, Korea's experience highlights the importance of lowering tariffs, an efficient duty drawback system, and bilateral and multilateral trade agreements to promote exports; and investments in trade facilitation and digitalization of the trade infrastructure to complement the policy reforms.

Korea's successful development was based on manufacturing exports. However, going forward, opportunities for developing countries to leverage manufacturing exports may be more constrained. Therefore, developing countries will need to leverage growth through both manufacturing and services. Korea has been less successful in leveraging services for growth, but since the 1990s globally the labor productivity growth of services has matched the productivity growth of industries in many regions. Promoting both manufacturing and services would take advantage of the increasing "servicification" of manufacturing. Developing countries can promote trade in services and the dissemination and adoption of new technologies for services, enhance the skills needed to apply new technologies to services, and promote intersectoral linkages between manufacturing and services.

Korea successfully built world-class infrastructure from the devastation of the Korean War. Korea is sixth among 141 economies in the infrastructure pillar of the Global Competitiveness Report (WEF 2019). Developing countries can learn from Korea's experience with long-term planning that supported comprehensive and coordinated development of roads, railways, ports, and airports to enhance multimodal connectivity. Public enterprises were established in the road, railway, water, and telecommunication sectors to build the specialized skills and expertise necessary to manage investments in the sectors. Investments in industrial complexes were a key feature of infrastructure investments, including the Ulsan Industrial Complex, which became a major industrial center. Korea strengthened project management capacity and mobilized public and private financing for infrastructure investments. Dedicated domestic sources of financing were set aside for infrastructure investments, such as a special consumption tax on gasoline and diesel for investments in the transportation sector. Since the AFC, public-private partnerships have been expanded in infrastructure investments, resulting in most investments in transport infrastructure being financed through public-private partnerships and expanded private investments in other sectors.

Korea's sustained prioritization of human capital development resulted in relatively high levels of educational attainment at each stage of its development. In 1960, Korea already achieved nearly universal primary school enrollment, when the norm for countries at a similar level of development was around 60 percent. Investments in school facilities and teachers were a major priority under the Five-Year Economic and Social Development Plans initiated in 1960, which supported rapid and sequential expansion of first primary, subsequently secondary, and finally tertiary education. Korea was already spending a substantial share of GDP on education in the 1960s and increased it further in the following decades. Private schools supplemented public schools in secondary and tertiary education. Although the shares of private secondary schools have been declining, private tertiary institutions have remained dominant at around 70 to 80 percent of all tertiary schools. High-quality professionals were recruited into the teaching profession by providing high salaries, job security, and high social status.

The expansion of basic health care services complemented the investments in education. In the earlier decades of Korea's modern development, the government focused on expanding health care facilities and nationwide public health programs, such as on communicable disease prevention and deworming. The nationwide network of public health centers served mostly low-income households and implemented public health programs. However, in Korea much of the health care has been provided by private providers. The public sector owns only around 10 percent of the general hospitals, less than 5 percent of the specialized hospitals, and few of the clinics (Koh 2010). Private providers depend on disbursements from the National Health Insurance in addition to patients' out-of-pocket payments. The introduction of the National Health Insurance and the requirement for hospitals to accept its patients have greatly expanded access to health care.

Korea's experience highlights the importance of the government taking a strong leadership role and sustaining commitment to designing and implementing human resources development policies over the long term. Investments in primary education, adult literacy, and basic health services can both reduce inequality and generate huge dividends in terms of future productivity. Korea also provides a successful example of transitioning education and training policies from a government-controlled and supply oriented approach to a more market-based and demand oriented approach, which has helped it to respond more effectively to the changing demand for labor. Its experience highlights the importance of coordination between human resources development and national economic planning and policies, to ensure adequate supply of skilled labor for rapid growth.

TRANSITIONING FROM A STATE-LED TO A MARKET-LED GROWTH PARADIGM

Developing countries can learn from Korea's experience in using a crisis to overcome a political economy bottleneck and catalyze major reforms of its growth paradigm. In the decades leading up to the AFC, large-scale investments by private conglomerates, particularly the chaebols, drove Korea's growth and technology upgrading, but the promotion of the large conglomerates also resulted in excessive risk taking and borrowing and conglomerates that were "too-big-to-fail." Korea's history highlights the risks to the financial system and the overall economy from subsidizing large firms without sufficient market discipline, which can encourage excessive risk taking.

In response to the AFC, Korea transitioned to a more market-driven economy. Developing countries can learn from Korea's experience in pursuing major corporate, financial, public sector, and labor market reforms that helped to impose stronger market discipline, strengthened corporate governance, and introduced a modern system of financial sector regulations and supervision and more flexible labor market practices. By allowing the bankruptcy of some of the largest chaebols during the AFC, Korea's government signaled that not even the largest firms would be protected by the "too-big-to-fail" principle. Post-AFC reforms that promoted greater independence of the monetary authority and strengthened the management of external risks enabled Korea to be more resilient to the subsequent macroeconomic shocks of the GFC. Korea's experience demonstrated that as the economy becomes more sophisticated, management through targeted industrial policies and direct interventions in markets become less effective and tenable. It is therefore important to have a blueprint for the transition to a more market-driven economy for the transition to higher income levels.

Korea has consistently prioritized enterprise support throughout its modern development history. Post-AFC, the government adjusted and recalibrated its enterprise support policies to focus on MSMEs and entrepreneurship. There are four major lessons from Korea's enterprise policy support. First, post-AFC the government's policy support emphasized the promotion of new growth industries by expanding support to high-technology R&D and technology startups. The improved entrepreneurial ecosystem and expanded access to entrepreneurial financing over the past two decades contributed to the high rate of technology startups. New post-AFC technology startups grew to become among the largest companies in Korea today. Korea's experience demonstrates that the government can play a critical role in fostering the development of a dynamic entrepreneurial ecosystem, through a diverse set of direct and indirect support policies that target both the demand and supply sides of the entrepreneurial ecosystem. Nevertheless, technology startups in Korea face low survival rates and difficulties in growing and globalizing.

Second, post-AFC Korea has promoted market competition by expanding the role of the Korean Free Trade Commission, regulating perceived unfair trade practices in transactions between large enterprises and SMEs, and limiting the entry of large enterprises into specific markets. Addressing the perceived unfair competitive advantage of large firms vis-à-vis MSMEs through regulations has been a consistent priority, but there are also concerns that this has constrained market competition. Korea's experience highlights the difficulties in achieving long-term and sustained reductions in the business regulatory burden. After initial progress post-AFC in deregulating the economy, business regulations have increased as the complexity of the economy and various social demands expanded. Korea's experience with increasing productivity growth in the retail sector by lowering entry barriers for big-box stores and chain supermarkets highlights the importance of promoting market competition for aggregate productivity improvement. Lowering entry barriers can introduce new services and technologies that can spur productivity growth.

Third, the government's policies to support MSMEs expanded and became diverse and comprehensive. These policies included R&D support programs, financing schemes, tax benefits, and regulatory reforms for improving the business environment. The policy mix has included instruments less commonly used by peer countries, such as public procurement and credit guarantees that focus on supporting technology-intensive SMEs. The pivot to MSMEs succeeded in significantly expanding MSMEs' access to financing and support services. However, Korea's experience also indicates that as the portfolio of policy instruments expands, so can inefficiencies, redundancies, coordination costs, and the risk of market distortion. To promote policy coordination and selectivity, Korea centralized administrative data on SME innovation support programs through the National Science and Technology Information Service portal and expanded evaluation of policy effectiveness. From the standpoint of developing economies that have limited resources, it is important to ensure the selectivity and effectiveness of policy instruments by clearly defining policy goals, ensuring policy ownership and accountability, and justifying the selection of policy instruments through an effective monitoring and evaluation framework.

Fourth, Korea's SME policies have emphasized support for digitalization and promotion of the digital economy. The early focus on building the ICT infrastructure produced a platform for SMEs to participate in the digital economy. Support for digital innovation accounts for 15 percent of SME support programs in Korea, more than the OECD average and three times more than developing countries. However, the significant digital gap between large and small firms, in particular with regards to advanced technologies such as cloud computing and big data, remains an important challenge. The low adoption of digital technologies by MSMEs could be due to the lack of managerial capabilities and complementary R&D that enable the efficient use of digital technologies. Policies to support digital adoption in developing economies must account for the importance of complementary enabling factors for digital adoption among MSMEs.

REORIENTING INDUSTRIAL POLICIES TO FOCUS ON PROMOTING INNOVATION AND TECHNOLOGY

Korea's economic success was driven by the pursuit of technology upgrading to build manufacturing capabilities, improve productivity, and boost global competitiveness. Korea's experience demonstrates that developing countries can reap tremendous returns from early, sustained, and focused investments in innovation and technology. Korea's successful technology upgrading was based on getting the development basics right—infrastructure, human capital development, and macroeconomic stability—and absorbing and disseminating existing technologies from abroad to its light and medium technology manufacturing sector. Expanding tertiary education institutions produced the highly educated and skilled workforce necessary to drive R&D and adopt technologies in manufacturing industries. The government established GRIs, which developed key technologies for the telecommunication and semiconductor industries, when the private sector lacked R&D capacity. The government also embarked on major investments in the broadband infrastructure network and the digitalization of the government, which helped to establish Korea's world-class ICT infrastructure.

Much of the research conducted during the first three decades of Korea's industrialization was applied, downstream research taking advantage of existing technologies to innovate incrementally, improve manufacturing efficiency, and develop new products. This approach yielded substantial dividends and is suited to the needs and capabilities of most low- and middle-income countries. As Korea transitioned from a middle income to a high-income economy, it reoriented its policies from the adoption of foreign technologies to the domestic generation of frontier technologies. Private sector R&D expanded and largely supplanted the GRIs and, accordingly, the government focused on incentivizing and supporting private firms to expand their R&D to enhance their competitiveness. Hence, public-private partnerships have been central to building Korea's science, technology, and innovation capabilities.

Korea's experience suggests that innovation and technology promotion policies in developing countries need to be designed according to the country's capabilities and distance from the technology frontier. As the gap with the technology frontier narrowed and the government's administrative capacity matured, Korea deployed a broader range of policy instruments of increasing complexity. This became possible as the country accumulated capabilities in policy analysis, planning, execution, and evaluation. However, the proliferation of innovation and technology promotion policies has resulted in the duplication of government support and has allowed poorly performing firms to survive on government support. Hence, Korea's experience highlights the importance of coordination among policy instruments and conditioning policy support on firm performance and growth potential.

Developing countries can learn from Korea's comprehensive approach to promoting technologies, including subsidies for firms to invest in research and innovations, direct investments in basic research, and support for technical education in high schools and tertiary education institutes. The government, industry, academia, and research institutes worked together to advance the country's technology innovation system, develop promising technologies of the future, and strategically pursue national R&D projects. Developing countries can also learn from Korea's high level of investments in R&D throughout each phase of its development. Korea's R&D investments (as a percentage of GDP) increased rapidly and reached the average level of EU countries when it was an upper-middle-income country. However, across countries, the returns to R&D tend to decline as income rises, and at higher income levels, significant R&D investments do not necessarily translate into significant increases in productivity. It indicates that higher R&D alone is insufficient to improve productivity and that complementary reforms to promote market competition and human capital investments are needed to ensure the impact of R&D.

PRODUCING AN EDUCATED AND SKILLED WORKFORCE

The success of Korea's S&T policies was made possible by the parallel accumulation of education and skills, reflecting Korea's sustained commitment to human capital development. Korea systematically linked human capital development planning with national economic development planning, so that policies to increase the supply of human capital, through tertiary education and technical and vocational training, were coordinated with the projected demand for skills in the economy. The relatively high quality of education and the focus on STEM education were critical. As a result, the number of researchers in R&D in Korea increased from 2,173 per million in 1996 to 7,980 per million in 2018, the second largest in the world after Denmark (World Bank 2020). The government promoted the repatriation of foreign-trained Korean scientific researchers from abroad with ample job opportunities in public and corporate research institutes and GRIs. Korea's successful technology upgrading benefited from its focused attention on STEM education, complementary vocational skills development, and absorption of Korean scientific talent from the global diaspora.

Korea focused on STEM education and building S&T capabilities when it was still a low-income economy. Its experience indicates that even low-income economies can start building S&T knowledge and research capabilities. Sustained and early investments in STEM education and R&D infrastructure are critical to produce future scientists and researchers. Korea's special purpose S&T universities, such as the Korea Advanced Institute of Science and Technology and the Gwangju Institute of Science and Technology; special purpose science high schools; and STEM programs can be examples to benchmark for developing countries. Korea's Meister high schools are considered a successful case study of industry-academia cooperation that has helped to enhance the attractiveness of vocational education and produced graduates with high employability. Korea's experience highlights the importance of collaboration with industries in designing and implementing education and training programs and research projects.

Korea carried out a series of reforms to meet the rapidly changing demand for high-skilled labor in the economy. Over the decades, the focus of education and training policies in Korea shifted from a government-controlled and supply oriented approach to a more market-based and demand oriented approach. The academic and vocational education tracks were integrated to help make vocational education a more attractive option and promote lifetime learning. Korea also actively promoted nonformal vocational training to respond flexibly to the changing skills demanded by the market. Korea's experience with the compulsory vocational training system (1976–98) and the Employment Insurance System (1995–present) indicates that nonformal training systems could play a significant role in complementing formal education and training systems, to supply skilled workers to the economy by retraining incumbent workers and the unemployed.

Developing countries can learn from Korea's experience in pursuing difficult labor market reforms through society-wide consensus building. In response to the AFC, Korea carried out difficult labor market reforms through a tripartite committee of businesses, labor unions, and government representatives, to build support for a new social contract that legalized collective dismissals and temporary nonregular workers in return for greater workers' union rights. Although these reforms enhanced labor market flexibility, they also resulted in labor market duality between regular and nonregular workers. In response, Korea sought to regulate and thereby protect nonregular workers, but there are concerns that this has raised labor costs for SMEs and reduced the quality of nonregular jobs, as large firms switched to employment contracts, such as subcontractors, with even less job security.

Since the AFC, the government has expanded ALMPs—employment services, direct job creation, skills development, and entrepreneurship promotion—to reduce unemployment. Korea's experience indicates that social protection programs integrated with ALMPs can help support targeted vulnerable groups. For example, Korea's Employment Success Package Program promotes the employment of vulnerable young and old workers by integrating social protection with labor market activation measures. In addition, Korea's EIS combines income assistance with skills development and employment services for unemployed workers. It has expanded training opportunities through a combination of vocational training programs, unemployment benefits, and financial support for targeted groups. By creating demand for training, EIS has helped expand the supply of professional trainers.

Korea's experience highlights the benefits of investing in the labor market information infrastructure for job seekers, employers, and the government. The Labor Market Information System has helped to improve the monitoring and evaluation of labor market policies and programs and enhanced evidence-based policy making. All government agencies, such as the national statistics agency (Statistics Korea), are required to share relevant labor market data. This has enabled the government to develop and operate several support networks—Work-net, HRD-net, and the Employment Insurance Network—and to provide integrated support for employment and welfare.

INCLUSIVE AND SUSTAINABLE GROWTH

Korea's experience highlights the importance of promoting growth as a key driver of poverty reduction and shared prosperity. Major land redistribution reforms carried out at the beginning of the country's modern development, when land was the major asset in the economy, helped to create initial conditions conducive for inclusive growth. Large and systematic investments in primary and secondary education were central to addressing poverty, by expanding access to the jobs generated by the rapid industrialization of the economy. Developing countries can learn from Korea's experience in combining the promotion of growth and expansion of access to education and jobs to promote poverty reduction and shared prosperity.

Korea began establishing the key elements of its social safety net—the National Pension Scheme, Employment Insurance System, and National Health Insurance—in the 1970s when the country was a low-income economy. However, the social safety net initially had relatively limited coverage and benefits as Korea took a "Growth First, Distribution Later" approach to poverty reduction. As a result, the social safety net was inadequate to address the massive unemployment and widespread poverty during the AFC. Learning from Korea's experience, developing countries can put greater emphasis on expanding the social safety net system in the early stages of their development, to complement a growth-first policy.

Korea recognizes that its next challenge is to transition to greener, low carbon intensive, and environmentally sustainable growth. Korea's approach to transitioning to a greener economy has emphasized the promotion of green innovations and technologies as potential new drivers of growth. The transition to a low-carbon economy will be challenging for a manufacturing-based economy such as Korea, but it began decoupling GDP growth from carbon emissions growth in the 2010s.

Notes

1. In calculating gross national income (GNI—formerly referred to as GNP) in U.S. dollars for certain operational and analytical purposes, the World Bank uses the Atlas conversion factor instead of simple exchange rates. See https://datahelpdesk.worldbank.org/knowledgebase/articles/378832-what-is-the-world-bank-atlas-method.
2. Chapter 2 covers Korea's key foundations of growth.
3. Chapter 2 shows that since the AFC Korea's incremental capital output ratio (ICOR) surpassed the average ICOR of Emerging Markets and Developing Economies and has been approaching the OECD average. A higher ICOR indicates a lower impact of additional investment in capital on growth.
4. The stock of capital is estimated based on both public and private capital stock per capita, using the World Bank's World Development Indicators and International Monetary Fund data. See chapter 2 for details.
5. Korea lacks enterprise surveys that go back to the earlier years. Therefore, historical plant-level data were used to carry out the enterprise-level analysis of TFP growth.
6. Productivity dispersion is a measure of resource misallocation (Hsieh and Klenow 2009).
7. In 2017, the top rating was shared with France, Germany, and the United States.
8. From 2012 to 2016, 28,075 firms received R&D projects, of which about 5,776 received duplicate support from the Korea Small Business Innovation Research program and the Ministry of SMEs and Startups (Oh and Kim 2018).
9. Severance payments in Korea are retirement lump sum payments that increase with employment duration.

References

Ahn, S. 2019. "How Will the Government Design the SME R&D Strategy?" KISTEP Issue Paper 2019-16 (Vol. 274). KISTEP, Chungcheongbuk-do, Republic of Korea. https://www.kistep.re.kr/board.es?mid=a10306010000&bid=0031&act=view&list_no=35405. (Korean).

Allen, T. 2014. "Information Frictions in Trade." *Econometrica* 82 (6): 2041–83.

Audretsch, D., M. Hafenstein, A. Kritikos, and A Schiersch. 2018. "Firm Size and Innovation in the Service Sector." DIW Berlin Discussion Paper, IZA DP No. 12035, Institute of Labor Economics, Bonn, Germany.

Black, B., H. Jang, and W. Kim. 2005. "Does Corporate Governance Predict Firms' Market Values? Evidence from Korea." Working Paper No. 86/2005, ECGI Working Paper Series in Finance, European Corporate Governance Institute, Brussels, Belgium.

Choi J., K. H. Lee, J. Y. Seo, S. Kim, S. Lee, and B. G. Kim. 2014. "Improvement Strategies of Public Procurement Market Policy for Fostering Technology Based Innovative SMEs." Science and Technology Policy Institute, Sejong City, Korea.

Chung, S. 2011. "Innovation, Competitiveness, and Growth: Korean Experiences." *Annual World Bank Conference on Development Economics 2010, Global Lessons from East Asia and the Global Financial Crisis*, edited by J. Yifu Lin and B. Pleskovic. Washington, DC: World Bank. https://doi.org/10.1596/978-0-8213-8060-4.

Chung, S., and S. Aum. 2021. "Organizing for Digitalization at the Firm Level." *SSRN*, October 29, 2021. https://ssrn.com/abstract=3976386.

Cirera, X., D. Comin, and M. Cruz. 2022. *Bridging the Technological Divide: Technology Adoption by Firms in Developing Countries*. Washington, DC: World Bank.

Coppedge, M., J. Gerring, S. I. Lindberg, J. Teorell, D. Altman, M. Bernhard, M. S. Fish, and others. 2015. *Varieties of Democracy: Codebook v4.* Gothenburg, Sweden: Varieties of Democracy (V-Dem) Project, V-Dem Institute, University of Gothenburg; and Notre Dame, Indiana: Helen Kellogg Institute for International Studies, University of Notre Dame. https://www.v-dem.net/en/.

Evans, P. 1989. "Predatory, Developmental, and Other Apparatuses: A Comparative Political Economy Perspective on the Third World State." *Sociological Forum Special Issue: Comparative National Development: Theory and Facts for the 1990s* 4 (4): 561–87.

Evans, P., and J. E. Rauch. 1999. "Bureaucracy and Growth: A Cross-National Analysis of the Effects of 'Weberian' State Structure on Economic Growth." *American Sociological Review* 64 (5): 748–65.

Frias, J., H. Lee, M. A. Lee, and R. Balbontin. 2021. "The Korean Innovation Policy Mix: Lessons from Building Technological and Innovation Capabilities and Implications for Developing Countries." World Bank, Washington, DC.

GEDI (Global Entrepreneurship and Development Institute). 2018. *Global Entrepreneurship Index.* Washington, DC: GEDI. http://thegedi.org/2018-global-entrepreneurship-index-data/.

Hong, S., Y. Choi, and S. Kim. 2020. "Technology Innovation and Development Cooperation: Focusing on the ICT Sector." In *International Cooperation and Knowledge Sharing 2020: Innovation and International Development Cooperation,* edited by S. Ahn. Series No. 2020-05. Sejong City, Korea: Korea Development Institute. https://www.kdi.re.kr/research/reportView?pub_no=17071. (Korean).

Hsieh, C.-T., and P. J. Klenow. 2009. "Misallocation and Manufacturing TFP in China and India." *Quarterly Journal of Economics* 124 (4): 1403–48. https://doi.org/10.1162/qjec.2009.124.4.1403.

Hwang, Y., Y. Bae, J. Park, H. Cho, Y. Chang, and N. S. Vornortas. 2002. "Techno-Economic Paradigm Shift and Evolution of STI Policy in Korea and the United States." Research Report 2002-12, Science and Technology Policy Institute, Seoul, Republic of Korea.

Jang, J. H. 2009. "Review of Consistency of SME Policy: Application of Disparity Theory on the Institutional Discourse." *Korean Public Management Review* 23 (2): 191–214. (Korean).

Jones, R. S., and M. Kim. 2014. "Promoting the Financing of SMEs and Start-ups in Korea." OECD Economics Department Working Papers No. 1162, OECD Publishing, Paris. http://dx.doi.org/10.1787/5jxx054bdlvh-en.

Keum, H.-S., S.-J. Kim, W.-B. Kim, H.-S. Kim, J. T. Song, G.-S. Yoo, K.-Y. Lee, J.-H. Lee, C.-S. Lee, S.-H. Jang, B.-S. Chung, and D.-S. Hwang. 2017. *Labor Market Policy in Korea.* Seoul, Republic of Korea: Seoul National University Press.

KFTC (Korea Fair Trade Commission). 2011. *Trace of Market Economy Development: Korea Fair Trade Commission, History of 30 years.* Sejong City, Republic of Korea: KFTC.

KFTC (Korea Fair Trade Commission). 2019. *Statistical Yearbook of 2019.* Sejong City, Republic of Korea.

Kim, E. H., and W. Kim. 2007. "Corporate Governance in Korea: A Decade after the Financial Crisis." Research Paper 123, University of Texas School of Law, Austin, TX.

Kim, I. Y. 2006. "Deconstructing the Myth about Land Reform." In *Reexamining Korea's History in the Period around Its Liberation,* edited by J. H. Park, C. Kim, I. Y. Kim, and Y. H. Rhee, 295–344. Seoul, Republic of Korea: Chaeksesang.

Kim, J. Y. 2007. "SME Innovation Policies in Korea." In *The Policy Environment for the Development of SMEs,* 129–50. Singapore: Pacific Economic Cooperation Council.

Kim, M., J. Oh, and Y. Shin. 2017. "Misallocation and Manufacturing TFP in Korea, 1982-2007." *Federal Reserve Bank of St. Louis Review* 99 (2): 233–44.

KISTEP (Korea Institute of S&T Evaluation and Planning). 2018. "Survey of Research and Development in Korea." KISTEP, Chungcheongbuk-do, Republic of Korea.

Koh, Y. 2010. "The Growth of Korean Economy and the Role of Government." In *The Korean Economy: Six Decades of Growth and Development,* edited by I. Sakong and Y. Koh, 7–82. Sejong City, Republic of Korea: Korea Development Institute.

Koh, Y. 2018. "The Evolution of Wage Inequality in Korea." Policy Study 2018-01. Korea Development Institute, Seoul.

Koh, Y. 2019. "Wage Inequality in Korea: How and Why It Has Changed over the Decades." *KDI Policy Forum*, 274 (3). https://doi.org/10.22740/kdi.forum.e.2019.274.

Koh, Y., S. K. Kim, W. K. Chang, Y. Kim, Y. Lee, J. S. Kim, S. Y. Lee, and Y. O. Kim. 2010. "Social Policy." In *The Korean Economy: Six Decades of Growth and Development*, edited by I. Sakong and Y. Koh, 227–310. Sejong City, Republic of Korea: Korea Development Institute.

Korea Entrepreneurship Foundation. 2019. "Global Entrepreneurship Monitor (GEM) 2019 Korea." Korea Entrepreneurship Foundation, Seoul, Republic of Korea. https://www.gemconsortium.org/economy-profiles /south-korea-2/policy.

Lee, J. 2020. "Effects of Small Business Support Projects: Evidence from Korea." *KDI Journal of Economic Policy* 42 (1): 1–30.

Lee, J. H. 2017. *Government Reform to Develop Entrepreneurship Ecosystem*. Sejong, Republic of Korea: Korea Development Institute. (Korean).

Lee, K., B. Im, and J. Han. 2017. "The National Innovation System (NIS) for the Catch-up and Post-Catch-up Stages in South Korea." In *The Korean Government and Public Policies in a Development Nexus*, vol. 2, edited by J. Choi, H.-J. Kwon, and M. G. Koo, 69–82. Springer.

Lee, M., and T. Jung. 2018. "The Effects of Public Procurement on the Growth of Small and Medium Enterprises." *Asia Pacific Journal of Small Business*. 40 (4): 33–50.

Lee, Y. 2020. "Long-Term Shifts in Korean Manufacturing and Plant-Level Productivity Dynamics." Policy Research Working Paper 9279, World Bank, Washington, DC. http://hdl.handle.net/10986/33940.

Lee, Y., W. Kim, and J. Park. 2020. "Export and Productivity: An Analysis of Plant-level Data." BOK Working Paper N2020-19, Bank of Korea, Seoul, Republic of Korea. https://www.bok.or.kr/imerEng/bbs/B0000196/view.do?nttI d=10060085&menuNo=600341&pageIndex=2.

MOE and KEDI (Ministry of Education and Korean Educational Development Institute). Various years. *Korea Education Statistics Service*. Chungcheongbuk-do, Republic of Korea: KEDI. https://kess.kedi.re.kr/eng/index.

MOEF (Ministry of Economy and Finance of the Republic of Korea). 2017. "2018 Tax Expenditure Budget Report 2017." MOEF, Sejong City, Republic of Korea.

Nam, I. C. 2004. "Corporate Governance in the Republic of Korea and its Implications for Firm Performance." ADB Institute Discussion Paper No. 10, Asian Development Bank, Tokyo, Japan.

Noh, M. 2020. "A Plan to Improve Aggregation and Coordination of SME Polices." *Korea Small Business Institute SME Focus*. 12 (1): 20–24.

OECD (Organisation for Economic Co-operation and Development). 2021. "Productivity in SMEs and Large Firms," in *OECD Compendium of Productivity Indicators 2021*. Paris: OECD Publishing. https://doi .org/10.1787/54337c24-en.

OECD (Organisation for Economic Co-operation and Development). 2022. "What Proportion of National Output Is Spent on Educational Institutions?" in *Education at a Glance 2022: OECD Indicators*, 254–65. Paris: OECD Publishing. https://doi.org/10.1787/3197152b-en.

OECD (Organisation for Economic Co-operation and Development). 2023. "Venture Capital Investments." *OECD. Stat*. Paris, France. https://stats.oecd.org/Index.aspx?DataSetCode=VC_INVEST.

Oh, S., and S. Kim. 2018. "The Achievements and Direction of R&D Support for Small and Medium-sized Enterprises." *STEPI Insight* 224. Sejong City, Republic of Korea: STEPI. https://www.stepi.re.kr/site/stepiko /report/View.do?reIdx=226&cateCont=A0501. (Korean).

Shin, I. 2006. "Evolution of Korean Financial Regulations." In *Regulatory Reforms in the Age of Financial Consolidation*, edited by J. C. Lee and J. K. Kim. Sejong City, Republic of Korea: Korea Development Institute.

Sohn, D. 2006. "The Advancement and Evolution of the Venture Ecosystem of Korea." Science and Technology Policy Institute, Sejong City, Republic of Korea. https://nkis.re.kr:4445/subject_view1.do?otpId=STEPI00011541&otpSeq=0&popup=P#none.

Stangarone, T. 2020. "South Korea's Green New Deal." *The Diplomat*, May 29. https://thediplomat.com/2020/05/south-koreas-green-new-deal/.

Statistics Korea. 2020. "Statistics on Public Procurement." Statistics Korea, Daejeon, Republic of Korea. https://kosis.kr/statisticsList/kosis.kr.

Statistics Korea. 2023. "Income Distribution Index." Household Financial Welfare Survey. Statistics Korea, Daejeon, Republic of Korea. https://kosis.kr/statHtml/statHtml.do?orgId=101&tblId=DT_1HDLF05&conn_path=I3.

WEF (World Economic Forum). 2019. *Global Competitiveness Report 2019*. Geneva: WEF. https://www.weforum.org/reports/how-to-end-a-decade-of-lost-productivity-growth.

World Bank. 2004. *Republic of Korea: Four Decades of Equitable Growth*. Washington, DC: World Bank. https://documents.worldbank.org/en/publication/documents-reports/documentdetail/307551468752966588/republic-of-korea-four-decades-of-equitable-growth.

World Bank. 2017. *World Development Report 2017: Governance and the Law*. Washington, DC: World Bank.

World Bank. 2020. *World Development Indicators*. Washington, DC: World Bank. https://databank.worldbank.org/source/world-development-indicators.

World Bank. 2021. *The Innovation Imperative for Developing East Asia*. Washington, DC: World Bank.

World Bank. 2022. *World Development Indicators*. Washington, DC: World Bank. https://databank.worldbank.org/source/world-development-indicators.

World Bank and V-Dem. 2016. "Codebook: Measuring Elite Power and Interactions." Background paper, WDR 2017, World Bank, Washington, DC.

Abbreviations

₩	Korean won
AFC	Asian Financial Crisis
ALMPs	active labor market policies
APO	Asian Productivity Organization
ASEAN	Association of Southeast Asian Nations
ATQ	autonomous tariff quota
BERD	business enterprise research and development
BIS	Bank for International Settlements
BK21	Brain Korea 21
BOK	Bank of Korea
CO_2	carbon dioxide
CPI	Consumer Price Index
DRAM	Dynamic Random Access Memory
EAP	East Asia and the Pacific
ECA	export credit agency
EDI	Electronic Data Interchange
EFTA	European Free Trade Association
EIF	Employment Insurance Fund
EIS	Employment Insurance System
EMDEs	emerging markets and developing economies
EPA	export promotion agency
ERP	enterprise resource planning
ESPP	Employment Success Package Program
ETS	emissions trading system
FDI	foreign direct investment
FSC	Financial Services Commission
FSS	Financial Supervisory Service
FTA	free trade agreement
GATT	General Agreement on Tariffs and Trade
GDP	gross domestic product
GEM	Global Entrepreneurship Monitor
GERD	gross expenditure on research and development
GFC	global financial crisis

GGGI	Global Green Growth Institute
GHG	greenhouse gas
GNI	gross national income
GRI	government research institute
GVC	global value chain
HCIs	heavy and chemical industries
HRD	human resources development
HUNIC	Hub University/College for Industrial Collaboration Project
HVDC	high voltage direct current
ICOR	incremental capital output ratio
ICT	information and communications technology
IFR	International Federation of Robotics
IIP	international investment position
ILO	International Labour Organization
IMD	International Institute for Management Development
IMF	International Monetary Fund
IP	intellectual property
IPCC	Intergovernmental Panel on Climate Change
IT	information technology
ITC	investment trust company
KAIS	Korea Advanced Institute of Science
KAIST	Korea Advanced Institute of Science & Technology
KDI	Korea Development Institute
KEDI	Korean Educational Development Institute
KEIS	Korea Employment Information Service
KERIS	Korea Education and Research Information Service
KETS	Korea's emissions trading system
KFTC	Korea Fair Trade Commission
KICCE	Korea Institute of Child Care and Education
KIET	Korea Institute for Industrial Economics & Trade
KIPO	Korean Intellectual Property Office
KISDI	Korea Information Society Development Institute
KIST	Korea Institute of Science and Technology
KISTEP	Korea Institute of S&T Evaluation and Planning
KLI	Korea Labor Institute
KOFAC	Korea Foundation for the Advancement of Science & Creativity
KONEX	Korea New Exchange
KOSBI	Korea Small Business Institute
KOSDAQ	Korean Securities Dealers Automated Quotations
KOSIS	Korean Statistical Information Service
KOTEC	Korea Technology Finance Corporation
KRIVET	Korea Research Institute of Vocational Education and Training
KRX	Korea Exchange
KTNET	Korea Trade Network
KVCA	Korean Venture Capital Association
KVIC	Korea Venture Investment Corporation
LED	light emitting diode
LINC	Leaders in Industry-University Cooperation
LMIS	Labor Market Information System
Mbps	megabits per second

MES	manufacturing execution system
MFC	manufacturing
MOE	Ministry of Education, Republic of Korea
MOEF	Ministry of Economy and Finance, Republic of Korea
MOEL	Ministry of Employment and Labor, Republic of Korea
MOLIT	Ministry of Land, Infrastructure and Transport, Republic of Korea
MOSF	Ministry of Economy and Finance, Republic of Korea
MOST	Ministry of Science and Technology, Republic of Korea
MOTIE	Ministry of Trade, Industry and Energy, Republic of Korea
MPM	Ministry of Personnel Management, Republic of Korea
MRFTA	Monopoly Regulation and Fair Trade Act
MSIT	Ministry of Science and ICT
MSMEs	micro, small, and medium-size enterprises
MSS	Ministry of SMEs and Startups, Republic of Korea
NASDAQ	National Association of Securities Dealers Automated Quotations
NIA	National Information Society Agency
NMFC	nonmanufacturing
NTIS	National Science and Technology Information Service
ODI	overseas direct investment
OECD	Organisation for Economic Co-operation and Development
OPC	Office of Government Policy Coordination, Republic of Korea
OT	operating technologies
PCA	Prompt Corrective Action program
PISA	Programme for International Student Assessment
PPP	public-private partnership
PPP	purchasing power parity
PTV	Pangyo Techno Valley
PWT	Penn World Table
R&D	research and development
RCA	revealed comparative advantage
RCEP	Regional Comprehensive Economic Partnership Agreement
ROA	return on assets
ROE	return on equity
S&T	science and technology
SMEs	small and medium-size enterprises
SOC	social overhead capital
SOE	state-owned enterprise
STEAM	science, technology, engineering, arts, and mathematics
STEM	science, technology, engineering, and mathematics
STEPI	Science and Technology Policy Institute
STI	science, technology, and innovation
SVAR	structural vector autoregression
SW	software
TFP	total factor productivity
TFPR	revenue-based total factor productivity
UMIC	upper-middle-income country
UNESCAP	United Nations Economic and Social Commission for Asia and the Pacific
UNESCO	United Nations Educational, Scientific and Cultural Organization
VAX	ratio of value-added exports to gross exports
VC	venture capital

VCDP	Vocational Competency Development Program
VET	vocational education and training
VHS	vocational high school
VLSI	Very Large Scale Integration
VRCA	value-added revealed comparative advantage
VT	vocational training
WEF	World Economic Forum
WIPO	World Intellectual Property Organization
WTO	World Trade Organization

CHAPTER 1

The Foundation of Korea's Long-Run Growth

Introduction

The Republic of Korea is one of the few countries in recent history that successfully transitioned from a middle- to high-income economy, making it a valuable case study. Korea crossed the World Bank's threshold to become a high-income economy around the mid-1990s before the country's growth was temporarily derailed by the Asian Financial Crisis (AFC) in 1997. This turned out to be a watershed in the country's development, as the crisis accelerated many of the important market oriented reforms that were already under way, helping the country to recover quickly from the AFC and continue on its growth trajectory to put itself firmly among the high-income economies.

This report focuses on the past three decades, during which Korea transitioned from a middle- to high-income economy. This chapter introduces Korea's preceding decades of development from a low- to middle-income economy, to provide the historical context necessary to understand the country's successful transition to a high-income economy. The basic foundation of its sustained rapid growth was built during the earlier decades, when Korea invested in infrastructure and human capital development and promoted industrialization and exports.

Korea's Rapid Development

Korea's transition from a low- to middle- and then high-income economy was achieved by sustained, relatively high rates of growth over several decades. Countries typically fail to develop not necessarily because of the lack of rapid growth but rather because of the failure to sustain rapid growth (Pritchett and Summers 2014). Episodes of sustained, very rapid growth (greater than 6 percent) are rare. Korea experienced 29 years of very rapid growth from 1962 to 1991. In comparison, the median duration of very rapid growth periods is nine years. Only two other economies have recently experienced similarly long periods of very rapid growth: China, from 1977 to 2018 (41 years), and Taiwan, China, from 1962 to 1994 (32 years). Moreover, Korea's very rapid growth was followed by a period of still relatively high (greater than 4 percent) rates of economic growth.

As a result, Korea was one of the few low-income economies in 1960 that joined the ranks of high-income economies by 2019 (figure 1.1).[1] Its global ranking in per capita income[2] reached the

This chapter was prepared by Hoon Sahib Soh (World Bank) and Youngsun Koh (Korea Development Institute). Yoon Jung Lee (World Bank) contributed on investments in infrastructure.

FIGURE 1.1 Relative Income Dynamics, 1960–2019

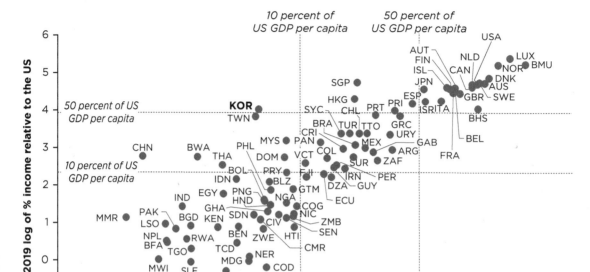

Sources: World Development Indicators, World Bank (https://databank.worldbank.org/source/world-development-indicators); National Statistics, Republic of China (Taiwan, China) (http://statdb.dgbas.gov.tw/pxweb/Dialog/statfile1L.asp?lang=1&strList=L).
Note: Figure 1.1 is based on Agénor and Canuto (2012) and Bulman, Eden, and Nguyen (2017), using data from the World Development Indicators for 1960–2019. Hong Kong SAR, China (HKG) on the horizontal axis refers to 1961 instead of 1960. For a list of country codes, go to https://www.iso.org/obp/ui/#search. GDP = gross domestic product.

19th percentile in 2019. Only a handful of economies made the transition from low- or middle-income to high-income between 1960 and 2009 (Bulman, Eden, and Nguyen 2017). They include Korea and the other East Asian "Tigers"—Singapore (SGP in figure 1.1), Hong Kong SAR, China (HKG), and Taiwan, China (TWN)—and Puerto Rico (PRI) and Spain (ESP).[3]

Korea's long-run growth pattern has been similar to that of other countries that have successfully transitioned to high-income economies. Figure 1.2 shows the average growth rate of gross domestic product (GDP) per capita over the next 20 years, at each level of GDP per capita. Korea's 20-year average growth rate was highest in 1967, indicating that 1967–87 was the fastest growing 20-year period in Korea's development history. Its GDP per capita growth rates have since been declining as its income (GDP per capita) levels have increased. The inverted U-shaped relationship between growth rate and income level closely follows the growth trajectories of other economies that have transitioned to high income.

The growth trajectories of the countries that successfully transitioned to high income have been quite similar to each other (figure 1.2). China joined this trajectory around 1991. In comparison, most developing countries, such as Brazil, India, Malaysia, Türkiye, and Vietnam, have recorded substantially lower growth of GDP per capita, relative to their income levels. As a result, they have so far failed to attain high-income status. This has led to concerns about a "middle-income trap" for some countries that have not transitioned to high income (box 1.1).

Middle-income countries experience growth slowdowns mainly due to productivity slowdowns (Agénor and Canuto 2012; Eichengreen et al. 2014). Intersectoral resource reallocation (the release of unskilled labor from agriculture) and foreign technology adoption drive the growth of low-income

FIGURE 1.2 Income Level and Long-Run Economic Growth in Subsequent Years

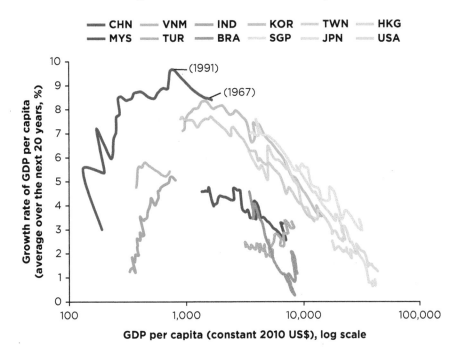

Sources: World Development Indicators, World Bank (https://databank.worldbank.org/source/world-development-indicators); Statistics Korea (https://kosis.kr).
Note: The horizontal axis refers to GDP per capita in 1960–99, and the vertical axis refers to average growth over the next 20 years. The rightmost point for each country denotes the income level in 1999 on the horizontal axis and the average growth in 1999–2019 on the vertical axis. The data start in 1961 for Hong Kong SAR, China, and in 1984 for Vietnam. For a list of country codes, go to https://www.iso .org/obp/ui/#search. GDP = gross domestic product.

BOX 1.1 The Middle-Income Trap

The term "middle-income trap" was introduced in *An East Asian Renaissance: Ideas for Economic Growth* (Gill and Kharas 2007) and has since become popular among policy makers and researchers. The concept was drawn from the observation that rapid growth had allowed a significant number of countries to achieve middle-income status, but few made the additional leap to become a high-income economy. Discussions of the middle-income trap contrasted the experience of the stagnation of growth among countries in Latin America and the Middle East and North Africa and the sustained rapid growth of countries in East Asia. However, even in East Asia, there were concerns that middle-income economies, such as Malaysia, the Philippines, and Thailand, were being squeezed between the low-wage, low-income competitors that dominate in mature industries and the high-income innovators that dominate in industries undergoing rapid technological change. This was also a concern in Korea, despite its higher income level.

However, there is an ongoing debate about the existence of the middle-income trap. Researchers have disputed its existence (Felipe et al. 2017; Han and Wei 2017; Im and Rosenblatt 2013) and consider the debate anachronistic, given that middle-income countries have been growing faster than other countries since the mid-1980s (Patel et al. 2021). Yet, middle-income countries are disproportionately likely to experience growth slowdowns (Aiyar, Shekhar, et al. 2018), and the growth slowdowns are most likely to occur in the per capita income ranges of US$10,000 to US$11,000 and US$15,000 to US$16,000 in 2005 purchasing power parity US dollars (Eichengreen et al. 2014). These growth slowdowns may be temporary, and it has been challenging

Continued

BOX 1.1 Continued

to estimate their magnitudes econometrically and identify the precise turning points and other empirical regularities (Agénor 2016). Regression to the mean and the difficulty of sustaining rapid growth, regardless of the income level, could provide a better explanation for the economic data than the middle-income trap (Pritchett and Summers 2014). Furthermore, the evidence for the middle-income trap may depend on whether it is defined in absolute or relative (to the US income level) terms.

Rather than being limited by the middle-income trap, economies may simply differ in the speed of their transition from middle to high income and the resulting convergence to high-income economies (Felipe et al. 2017). Hence, researchers have focused on identifying the policy and institutional factors that could explain the difference in the speed of convergence and whether those factors differ between middle-income and other economies. Also, the focus on policy choices in middle-income countries was the intention of the original authors of the term (Gill and Kharas 2015). The contention is that growth slowdowns in middle-income countries result from bad policies that have proven to be difficult to change.

It has been challenging to identify the most critical causes of growth slowdowns in middle-income economies because a large number of factors have been identified, including (a) low levels of infrastructure, (b) poor macroeconomic and debt management, (c) lack of access to finance for innovation, (d) large governments (significant government involvement in the economy) and excessive regulations, (e) low level of innovation and low share of high-technology exports, (f) weak enforcement of contracts and property rights, (g) inefficient labor markets, (h) limited regional integration, (i) unfavorable demographic trends, and (j) vulnerability to banking or currency crises (Agénor and Canuto 2012; Aiyar et al. 2018; Cavallo et al. 2018; Han and Wei 2017). Many of these factors are consistent with the view that productivity slowdowns are the main cause of the middle-income trap.

---

economies to middle income, but this strategy may be insufficient for the transition to high income. Countries experience diminishing returns to physical capital investments, and the poor quality of human capital constrains the absorption of advanced foreign technologies and expansion of innovative activities. The necessary shift from input-led growth to productivity- and innovation-led growth makes the transition from middle to high income challenging. Diversification and technology upgrading of production and exports—supported by human capital upgrading, structural reforms, and innovation—help to accelerate the transition to high income (Felipe et al. 2017).

THE FOUNDATION OF KOREA'S RAPID DEVELOPMENT

Korea built the foundation of its rapid and sustained development on six key building blocks: (a) macroeconomic stability underpinned by relatively prudent fiscal and monetary policies, (b) promotion of manufacturing exports through industrial policies, (c) expansion of the private sector, (d) an effective bureaucracy, (e) investments in infrastructure, and (f) human capital development. These key factors were also present in many of the East Asian countries that developed successfully (Balassa 1985, 1988; Gereffi 1989; Jenkins 1991; Kay 2002; Lin 1988; Ranis and Orrock 1985; World Bank 1993). Like Korea, much of the foundation for sustained rapid growth in the East Asian Tigers was established before the 1980s.

The importance of these six success factors is not without controversy, in particular Korea's relatively heavy-handed approach to industrial policies in the early years of development (Lall 2004). Debates remain on whether Korea would have attained comparative advantages in higher value-added activities without interventionist industrial policies. Even export promotion invites differing interpretations, with some stressing the free trade regime offered to exporters, such as through tax breaks for imported intermediate goods, and others stressing the protection of domestic markets that was granted until exporters gained international competitiveness.

BUILDING BLOCK ONE: MACROECONOMIC STABILITY

Korea maintained a relatively stable macroeconomic environment during its rapid growth takeoff. It experienced a significant macroeconomic crisis during the AFC, due to the lack of macroprudential discipline in the financial sector and the high corporate debt accumulation that this had engendered. However, the country quickly recovered and has since maintained prudent macroeconomic management.

Korea experienced relatively high annual average inflation rates of 13.2 percent in the 1960s and 15.2 percent in the 1970s, but inflation then declined to 8.4 percent in the 1980s, 5.7 percent in the 1990s, 3.1 percent in the 2000s, and 1.7 percent in the 2010s (OECD 2022). Although in the earlier decades inflation was relatively high, often it still remained far lower than what was frequently observed in other regions.

Korea has generally maintained prudent fiscal policies, particularly since the 1980s. Central government spending[4] as a percentage of GDP fell from 22.9 percent in 1982 to 15.3 percent in 1987, to control inflation. As a result, the fiscal balance went from a large deficit in 1982 (-4.2 percent of GDP) to a small surplus in 1987 (0.2 percent of GDP). Since then, the balance has remained largely neutral, and public debt as a percentage of GDP continued to decline before increasing sharply during the AFC (figure 1.3). The fiscal consolidation in the 1980s helped to create fiscal space to finance the financial sector reform programs post-AFC.

The exchange rate has been broadly stable in Korea, again with the AFC period being a major exception. In 1964, the multiple exchange rate system was abolished and the base rate was nearly doubled, from ₩130 to ₩255 per US dollar, to promote exports. Except for a few instances of excessive undervaluation (for example, in 1964 and 1998) or overvaluation (1979), the real exchange rate mostly stayed within the ±20 percent band around its average during 1970–2019.

Over the decades, Korea has avoided significant current account imbalances. The current account deficits on average amounted to 2.3 percent of GDP in the 1970s and 1.8 percent in the 1980s, and since the 1990s, Korea has had current account surpluses. Nonetheless, the moderate but persistent deficits in the 1960s and 1970s, which were caused by a rapid increase in industrial investments, led to a buildup of large external and domestic liabilities (figure 1.4). However, expanding exports and large trade surpluses in the second half of the 1980s sharply reduced the country's external debt.

FIGURE 1.3 Central Government Financial Balance, 1970–2019

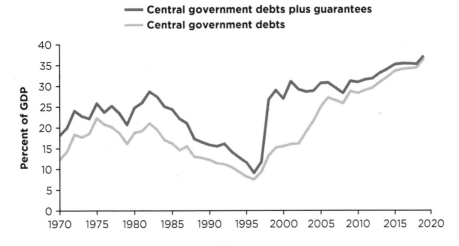

Sources: Koh 2010; Open Fiscal Data (https://www.openfiscaldata.go.kr).
Note: The figure shows jumps in debts and guarantees in the aftermath of the Asian Financial Crisis. The guarantees were given to the deposit insurance and public asset management agencies that issued bonds to recapitalize banks and buy up their nonperforming loans. GDP = gross domestic product.

FIGURE 1.4 **Outstanding Stock of External Assets and Liabilities, 1965–2019**

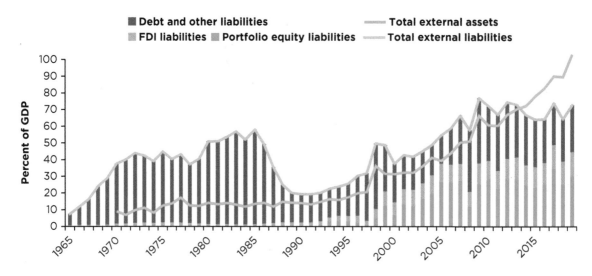

Sources: Koh 2010; Bank of Korea (http://ecos.bok.or.kr).
Note: FDI = foreign direct investment; GDP = gross domestic product.

Until the 1990s, Korea had tightly controlled capital flows and limited domestic economic agents' access to foreign financing. Responding to the private sector's demand for low-cost capital in the 1990s, the government loosened restrictions on foreign borrowing by bank and nonbank financial institutions. In addition, liberalization of the capital markets was a requirement for joining the Organisation for Economic Co-operation and Development (OECD) in 1996.[5] However, the expanded access to foreign borrowing in the 1990s led to significant accumulation of external debt, which made the country vulnerable to the AFC.

The AFC was not the first time Korea experienced the risks of a corporate and financial sector crisis. The government intervened when high levels of debt threatened the stability of the corporate and banking sectors in 1972, converting all curb market loans to low-interest, long-term loans from public banks (Koh 2010). In the 1980s, the government sought to address overcapacity and over-indebtedness in the heavy and chemical industries (HCIs), with a series of government coordinated rationalization programs. Government interventions temporarily averted a full-blown crisis, but the excessive demand for debt was not addressed and, as a result, the economy remained vulnerable to future adverse shocks.

BUILDING BLOCK TWO: PROMOTION OF MANUFACTURING EXPORTS THROUGH INDUSTRIAL POLICIES

Toward the end of the 1960s, Korea reoriented from an import substitution to an export promotion development strategy. The multiple exchange rate system was unified, eliminating privileged access to foreign exchange. The near doubling of the Korean won-to-US dollar exchange rate in May 1964 further incentivized productive exporting activities (Jones and Kong 1980). Concessional export credits and tariff exemptions on imported intermediate goods for exports were automatically extended. Annual export targets were established, monthly Export Promotion Meetings were organized and chaired by the president of Korea, and highly publicized awards were announced for the best performing exporters on the annual Day of Exports. Export volumes began to grow rapidly, and the annual growth rate of exports averaged 30 to 40 percent between the mid-1960s and the mid-1970s (figure 1.5).

Compared to exports, Korea took a more gradual and cautious approach to import liberalization. Import barriers were used strategically to protect domestic producers in the early stages of industrialization.

FIGURE 1.5 **Imports and Exports, 1955–2019**

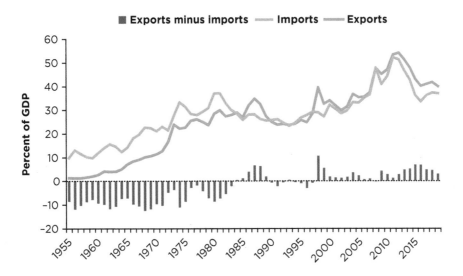

Source: Bank of Korea (http://ecos.bok.or.kr).
Note: GDP = gross domestic product.

The government remained cautious in opening up the domestic market, due to concerns about persistent current account deficits and the weak competitiveness of domestic firms. However, exporters enjoyed exemptions from high tariffs and other import restrictions, essentially carving out a free trade regime for exporters (Radelet 1997). The quantitative restrictions on imports were relaxed in the latter half of the 1970s, and import liberalization accelerated in the 1980s and continued in the 1990s (figure 1.6), exposing domestic manufacturers to international competition.

Korea's export drive coincided with the rapid globalization of international trade and investments, expanding opportunities for exports. The integration of Korea's economy into the global value chains accelerated in the 1990s through the launch of the World Trade Organization in 1995, the rapid diffusion of information and communications technology (ICT), and China's efforts to attract foreign direct investment to jumpstart its economic growth (see chapter 4). Imports, exports, and overseas direct investment increased rapidly in the 1990s, and Korea's economy underwent structural change toward higher value-added industries as it further integrated into global value chains.

Before the AFC, Korea actively used targeted industrial policies to promote manufacturing exports (box 1.2). The focus in the 1950s was on import substitution and promoting upstream industries to produce intermediate goods for downstream industries. In the 1960s, the focus was reoriented to promoting exports, and in the 1970s to building high value-added industries. Throughout, promotion of manufacturing industrialization remained at the core of the country's development strategy. Korea's industrial policies featured close consultation between the government and private enterprises, through an "embedded autonomy," which aimed to identify major market constraints and opportunities (Rodrik 2004).

Korea's Five-Year Economic Development Plans focused on industrial modernization. The Five-Year Plans specified targets for economic growth and identified key industries to be promoted. In particular, the Second Five-Year Plan (1967–71) emphasized the HCIs, including the steel, machinery, and petrochemical industries. The HCI drive was representative of Korea's "moonshot" approach to industrial policies, which sought radical change of the country's comparative advantages. Laws were introduced to provide financial support and tax incentives to selected sectors, including machinery (1967), shipbuilding (1967), steel (1969), electronics (1969), petrochemicals (1970), and nonferrous metals (1971). Construction started on a petrochemical complex in 1969 and an integrated iron and steel mill in 1970.

FIGURE 1.6 **Trend in Import Liberalization, 1955–99**

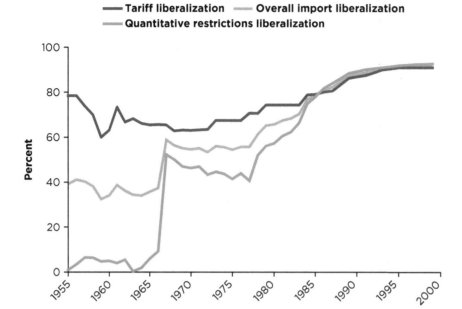

Sources: Kim 1988, 2001; Koh 2008.
Note: Import liberalization is measured as the number of freely imported items divided by the number of total items, expressed as a percentage.

BOX 1.2 Industrialization and the Industrial Policy Debate

The efficacy, efficiency, and necessity of industrial policy has been long debated. Active and discretionary industrial policies were an essential part of the growth strategies of successful East Asian economies. The successful East Asian economies also focused on promoting technology-intensive industries (Lall 2004). The extent to which active industrial policies contributed to the region's remarkable growth and development has been debated (Stiglitz and Yusuf 2001; World Bank 1993). Successful industrial policies require strong institutions that can prevent rent-seeking abuses, institutional mechanisms with clear performance criteria for selective interventions, and a bureaucracy that can pull back on the interventions when they become excessive. Most developing countries may not possess these requirements for implementing industrial policy effectively. In addition, changes in global economic governance since the late twentieth century have introduced restrictions on the use of market interventions and constrained the use of discretionary industrial policy instruments that East Asian countries previously used.

Views on industrial policies can be organized into two groups. The neoliberal group believes that policies to promote conducive markets are sufficient to promote economic growth. In contrast, the structuralist group believes that this is insufficient and selective industrial policies are necessary to correct market failures (Lall 2004). Market failures include information and coordination externalities (Rodrik 2004). Information externalities occur when entrepreneurs keep few of the gains from the discovery of new opportunities because competitors have access to information on the new opportunities and can therefore take advantage of the same opportunities. This reduces incentives for entrepreneurial activities in developing countries (Hausmann and Rodrik 2003). Coordination failures arise when large-scale investments in multiple areas are required for investments to become profitable.

Continued

THE FOUNDATION OF KOREA'S LONG-RUN GROWTH | 9

> **BOX 1.2 Continued**
>
> There are many examples of ineffective and unsuccessful industrial policies in Africa, Latin America, South Asia, and Southeast Asia. However, these industrial policy failures cannot be assessed in isolation from the country's overall economic policies. To be successful, industrial policies often need to be complemented by an open trade regime, prudent macroeconomic management, flexible exchange rates, expansion of public education, investment in economic infrastructure, and property rights protection.
>
> Industrial policies have typically been associated with support for the manufacturing sector. Manufacturing has been the main driver of growth for many countries that have experienced successful economic development (Felipe, Mehta, and Rhee 2014; Hausmann, Hwang, and Rodrik 2007; Rodrik 2013). In recent years, the "premature deindustrialization" observed in developing countries has generated pessimism about their potential to leverage manufacturing industrialization for development. Although the manufacturing share of an economy typically rises and then falls with increasing income, deindustrialization has been observed at lower levels of income compared to economies that developed earlier. As a result, services are now proposed as an alternative to manufacturing as an engine of growth for developing countries (IMF 2018; Nayyar, Hallward-Driemeier, and Davies 2021).
>
> Despite the concerns raised by premature deindustrialization, countries that have recently achieved rapid economic growth and convergence with advanced economies generally did so through the manufacturing sector. Manufacturing has been essential for convergence because labor productivity in manufacturing has exhibited unconditional convergence across economies (Rodrik 2013). Generally, countries with a larger manufacturing sector have converged to high-income levels faster than countries with a smaller manufacturing sector. However, not all manufacturing subsectors are the same. Countries that can produce and export the sophisticated manufactured goods that high-income, high-productivity countries export can expect higher rates of growth (Hausmann, Hwang, and Rodrik 2007).

The country pursued the drive for HCIs throughout the 1970s until the focus was shifted to stabilization in 1979 to control inflation.

The Five-Year Plans, including the HCI drive, focused on promoting exports. The goal was to move to higher value-added segments of the export market and increase export volumes. The enormous hurdles and investments required for the industrialization drive required public-private partnerships (PPPs). The government determined the industrial and export targets, and the private sector implemented the targets by building factories and exporting manufactured products. Even in sectors such as shipbuilding, which had a state-owned enterprise (Korea Shipbuilding Corporation), the government requested Hyundai, one of the major chaebols, to carry out the investments and industrial upgrading.

Despite its achievements, the HCI drive has been criticized for creating serious overcapacity in the late 1970s, which led to a government-led rationalization program in the 1980s. The government addressed the excessive and overlapping investments by directing the consolidation of industries, facilitated by debt write-offs, new concessional loans, and tax relief. Large volumes of directed credit and foreign lending increased corporate debt, heightening Korea's vulnerability to economic shocks. Financial repression, as reflected in the official lending rates hovering below inflation and well below the curb market rates, was used to mobilize large volumes of credit for the chaebols. However, this hampered the development of financial markets and the healthy growth of the banking industry.

BUILDING BLOCK THREE: EXPANSION OF THE PRIVATE SECTOR

Korea's extraordinary export growth was driven by large, family-owned and -controlled business conglomerates called "chaebols" (box 1.3). According to Korea's Federal Trade Commission's definition (firms with total assets of more than ₩5 trillion), 76 large conglomerates control 2,108 subsidiaries. The top five business groups account for 50.5 percent of assets and 54.8 percent of the total profits of all business groups in Korea and collectively employ more than half a million workers (*The JoongAng* 2020; Korea

Fair Trade Commission 2022). The five largest business conglomerates are Samsung, Hyundai, SK, LG, and Lotte (box 1.3).

The chaebols grew from the enterprises established in the early years of Korea's modern development, when private sector entrepreneurs faced enormous challenges. The abject poverty, extensive destruction of infrastructure during the Korean War (1950–53), massive political and social dislocation, and widespread informality in the earlier decades in Korea made the eventual rise of chaebols highly improbable. Korea's early entrepreneurs had to contend with a poor business environment and extensive informality. These are the same adverse conditions typically faced by entrepreneurs in low-income economies, which have prevented their growth and expansion. This makes the stories of the successful first-generation entrepreneurs that grew into the chaebols all the more remarkable.

BOX 1.3 Korea's Five Largest Chaebols

Samsung Group, the Republic of Korea's largest and most profitable chaebol, was founded in 1938 as a small trading company exporting goods such as fruit, dried fish, and noodles. After first expanding into sugar refining and the wool mill business in the 1950s, Samsung gradually broadened its portfolio over the years to include electronics, insurance, shipbuilding, aviation, automobiles, chemicals, luxury resorts, hospitals, and an affiliated university. Semiconductor manufacturing, which was established in the late 1970s, initially accumulated huge losses and was thought to be a failure. However, eventually it propelled Samsung Electronics into a global leader in semiconductors and consumer electronics, accounting for 14 percent of Korea's gross domestic product in the past decade. Currently, the group is led by second- and third-generation descendants of the founder, Lee Byung-Chul, and the family is the second wealthiest family in Asia according to Forbes.

Hyundai Group started as a small construction company in 1947. Its construction of the first major highway in Korea was one of the group's early achievements and contributed to Korea's industrialization. Hyundai Group's early growth was driven by heavy industries such as automobiles and shipbuilding, which were established in 1967 and 1973, respectively. Today, Hyundai Motor Group is the third largest carmaker in the world, and Hyundai Heavy Industries is the world's largest shipbuilding company. Hyundai continued to expand beyond heavy industries with numerous subsidiaries, including in finance and electronics. However, the Asian Financial Crisis and the death of Hyundai's founder, Chung Ju-Yung, led to the group breaking into five separate firms in 2003.

SK Group. Founder Chey Jong-Gun's acquisition of Sunkyung Textiles in 1953 was the beginning of the SK Group, also known as SK Holdings. It expanded its business in the textile and chemical industries before acquiring Korea Oil Corporation in 1980 to add the petrochemicals business. With more than 144 subsidiaries, SK group operates in diverse fields such as energy, chemicals, telecommunications, and semiconductors. SK Telecom is the largest wireless carrier in Korea, and SK Hynix is the second largest memory chip manufacturer in the world. In May 2022, its total assets surpassed that of Hyundai Motor Group to become the second largest company in Korea after Samsung Group.

LG. Lucky was co-founded by Koo In-Hoe and Huh Man-Jung in 1947 and expanded into consumer electronics, cosmetics, televisions (displays), and telecommunications. LG Corporation derives its name from the merger of Lucky with GoldStar in 1995, expanding the business to the consumer electronics, chemicals, and plastics industries. In 2005, the families split and the Hoe family established GS Holdings, which included subsidiaries in retail, construction, and energy. LG Display is the world's largest display company, and LG Energy Solution is the second largest electric vehicle battery manufacturer.

Lotte. The founder of Lotte Group, Shin Kyuk-Ho, established Lotte as a chewing gum company in Tokyo, Japan, in 1948. After relations between Japan and Korea were restored in 1965, he established Lotte Confectionary in Korea in 1967. The business group expanded into other food products and the hotel industry. Today, Lotte Group's businesses include department stores, theme parks, entertainment, construction, alcoholic beverages, finance, and retail in both Japan and Korea. Unlike the other top five chaebols, Lotte mostly focuses on domestic markets and the service sector.

The chaebols were key beneficiaries of the government's industrial policies, which provided them preferential access to low-cost credit in return for meeting export targets. The HCI drive in the 1970s accelerated the expansion of the chaebols, which worsened the monopolistic market structure of the industries and the "economic entrenchment" and concentration of economic power in the chaebols (Morck, Wolfenzon, and Yeung 2005).

Many of the chaebols focused on export oriented manufacturing, unlike in other developing countries, where business groups were often engaged in banking, retail trade, property development, and other domestic market activities. Therefore, the chaebols faced foreign competition in the export markets and had to invest heavily in innovation to improve their competitiveness. Private sector spending on research and development (R&D) amounted to 0.3 percent of GDP in 1980, but it rose in the following decades to 1.3 percent in 1990, 2.4 percent in 2010, and 3.5 percent in 2018. Today, Korea has one of the highest levels of R&D spending as a percentage of GDP, and the private sector accounts for about three-quarters of all R&D spending. This contrasts with developing countries where domestic R&D activities are relatively weak and the role of the private sector is significantly smaller.

In Korea, the large private conglomerates had room to grow and expand because state-owned enterprises (SOEs) had a relatively limited role in the competitive and commercial sectors. By the 1960s and 1970s, the government had established SOEs in key utility and network sectors, such as energy, water supply, railroads, and expressways, which invested in the country's infrastructure. SOEs were also established in more commercial sectors, such as mining, fertilizer, machinery, shipbuilding, steelmaking, chemicals, construction, and banking, but they were gradually privatized over time. The small number of commercial SOEs that remained at the time of the AFC played a relatively minor role in their respective sectors. The exceptions were the banking and steel manufacturing sectors, in which the SOEs played significant roles. SOEs in those sectors were privatized in response to the AFC.

Until the 1990s, the chaebols continued to expand and diversify their businesses, benefiting from the government's industrial policy support. The number of subsidiaries of the 10 largest chaebols increased from 242 in 1980 to 306 in 1996, and the paid-in capital of the 30 largest chaebols doubled from ₩35.2 trillion in 1980 to ₩70.6 trillion in 1997. The "Big Five"—Samsung, Hyundai, LG, Lotte, and SK—refrained from diversification, but their total size grew as some of their subsidiaries turned into conglomerates (Lee 2010). As the size of the chaebols grew, they were perceived as "too big to fail" for the economy. However, this notion was weakened during the AFC when Daewoo and other chaebols were allowed to go bankrupt. The crisis offered a chance to roll back the implicit government protection and expose the chaebols to stronger market discipline.

Clearly, the chaebols played a central role in driving Korea's economic growth, but their dominance and influence on the economy have been controversial. The chaebols' debt-fueled expansion was identified as a fundamental cause of the AFC in Korea. Critics have contended that the close relationship between the government and the chaebols fostered a culture of political-business collusion that allowed excessive debt accumulation. Chaebols have also been criticized for leveraging their market power to gain unfair advantages, stifling the development of small and medium-size enterprises in Korea.

Chaebols have also attracted criticism for corporate governance shortcomings. Chaebols typically had a large number of subsidiaries that were often closely interlinked through cross shareholdings, vertical transactions, and exchange of employees between member firms. The owner families enhanced their control through cross shareholdings and pyramidal ownership structures and direct participation in management. The unique corporate governance of the chaebols emerged as a solution to various market failures and institutional deficiencies that prevailed in the early decades of Korea's development. However, the development and maturation of markets and institutions since the earlier decades has reduced the relevance of the chaebol corporate governance structure.

Family-owned business conglomerates are not unique to Korea. Similar forms of business conglomerates can be found in developed and developing countries. Korea is in the middle of a range of 27 comparator countries in terms of the balance between family-owned versus publicly traded firms, with 35 percent of the large firms in Korea owned by families and 40 percent publicly held in 1984 (La Porta,

Lopez-De-Silanes, and Shleifer 1999). Widely dispersed ownership is the norm in the United States and the United Kingdom, but in other countries, firms are more typically held by families or the state. Like in Korea, many firms across countries also employ various control-enhancing mechanisms for their owners, including pyramids, managerial participation, and dual share classes, enabling the owners to exercise control of the firms to a greater degree than their equity ownership (Carney and Child 2013; Claessens et al. 2000; Faccio and Lang 2002).

BUILDING BLOCK FOUR: EFFICIENT AND EFFECTIVE BUREAUCRACY

The term "developmental state" was used to describe the state-led development planning and active state interventions in Korea and other countries in East Asia in the late twentieth century (Haggard 2018). Korea's bureaucracy was described as having an "embedded autonomy" (Evans 1989, 1995), which required a competent and strong bureaucracy that elicited information from the private sector on key market constraints but was sufficiently insulated from rent-seeking private interests and potentially predatory state elites. Such an institutional setting is considered a key contributing factor to a successful industrial policy (Rodrik 2004).

State capacity is positively associated with economic prosperity (figure 1.7). State capacity can be defined and measured in various ways. Fiscal capacity enables the state to levy tax revenues to implement its policies, and legal capacity enables it to enforce rules and regulations (Hoffman 2015; Johnson and Koyama 2017). Limited government, through constitutional constraints on the arbitrary exercise of state power (North and Weingast 1989), can be considered another aspect of state capacity that contributes to economic growth (Dincecco and Katz 2016). A public sector characterized by meritocratic recruitment and predictable, long-term career rewards is conducive to economic growth (Evans and Rauch 1999).

Public revenue collection is a key measure of state capacity. The government in Korea has made continuous efforts to rationalize the tax structure and strengthen tax administration to increase revenues. As foreign aid started to dry up, the government organized a centralized tax collection agency (the predecessor of today's National Tax Service) in 1966, with a clear mission to raise revenues. A comprehensive

FIGURE 1.7 Relationship between Government Effectiveness and per Capita Income

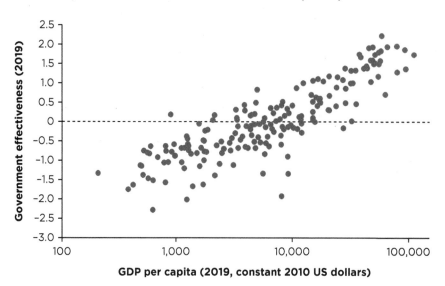

Source: Worldwide Governance Indicators, World Bank.
Note: GDP = gross domestic product.

income tax was introduced in 1974 and a value-added tax in 1977. In the 1990s, social security contribu-tions began to increase rapidly as pension, health, and other social insurance programs were introduced or expanded. Korea's current level of tax revenue as a percentage of GDP is comparable to that of low–tax revenue countries in the OECD, including the United States.

Given the central role of the government in the "developmental state" model, talent recruitment and management of the civil service were critical. Until the early 1960s, recruitment of civil servants was beset by widespread corruption and cronyism. In 1963, the Civil Servant Law was overhauled and writ-ten examinations became mandatory for recruitment and promotion. The examinations were highly competitive. Between 1965 and 1985, about 157,000 applicants took the civil service examination and approximately 2,600 were selected, or 1.7 percent of the applicants (Kim and Leipziger 1997). On-the-job training and education were strengthened, salaries and pension benefits were increased substantially, and obligations were imposed on civil servants to maintain integrity and political neutrality. The amended Civil Servant Law established a merit-based recruitment and promotion system and higher ethical and technocratic standards for civil servants. The new recruitment system remains largely intact today.

A capable bureaucracy must be supported by a conducive overall governance environment to be effec-tive. Korea was under an authoritarian regime from the 1960s through the mid-1980s. Despite wide-spread corruption in the earlier decades of Korea's development, political accountability was enforced to a degree necessary to ensure prioritization of the country's overall development goals and prevent the government from deteriorating into a predatory rent-seeking state. Mass participation in voting and popular protests pressured the incumbent powers to legitimize their rule by prioritizing national devel-opment and improving the livelihoods of the population. Opposition political parties were effective in mobilizing popular opposition to the incumbent regime. Finally, despite political suppression, the media played a critical role in putting pressure on the regime.

BUILDING BLOCK FIVE: INVESTMENTS IN INFRASTRUCTURE

Korea was able to maintain very high rates of savings and investment (figure 1.8). Some have contended that the Asian Miracle has been due to high saving and investment rates (Noland and Pack 2003) and that industrial policy succeeded by promoting an investment boom, not an export boom (Rodrik 1995). Korea was also generally successful in managing public investments and avoiding the scale of corruption that undermined the productivity of investments in other countries. This was critical in the early years given that Korea was recovering from enormous political and economic dislocations and public investments were urgently needed to rebuild the nation. The public investments in infrastructure in the 1950s and 1960s made future private investments profitable (Bhagwati 1999).

Korea's infrastructure half a century ago was a major obstacle to economic development because it had been decimated during the Korean War (1950–53). From the 1960s, expanding the country's physi-cal infrastructure became a key priority for national development. Land, water supply, transportation, power, and communications infrastructure were prioritized for development. Large and sustained invest-ments were made and a significant part of the public infrastructure was established by the early 1980s and subsequently continued to expand in quantity and quality. As a result, Korea ranked sixth among 141 economies in the infrastructure pillar of the *Global Competitiveness Report 2019* (WEF 2019).

Access to electricity was considered a key priority for industrial development. In 1960, only 19.9 percent of households had access to electricity (Kim and Lee 1997). Electricity capacity and demand expanded quickly with industrialization in the 1960s. The Five-Year Electricity Source Development Plans estab-lished seven thermal power plants and two hydroelectric power plants by 1967. Initially, access to elec-tricity was prioritized in urban and industrialized areas. By the end of 1965, 51 percent of urban areas had access to electricity, but only 12 percent of rural areas had access. The Rural Electrification Project (1965–91) started to reduce the gap between the two areas, raising rural access to electricity to over 90 percent by 1975. Access to electricity was virtually universal by the end of the 1970s.

FIGURE 1.8 **Gross Capital Formation, 1960–2020**

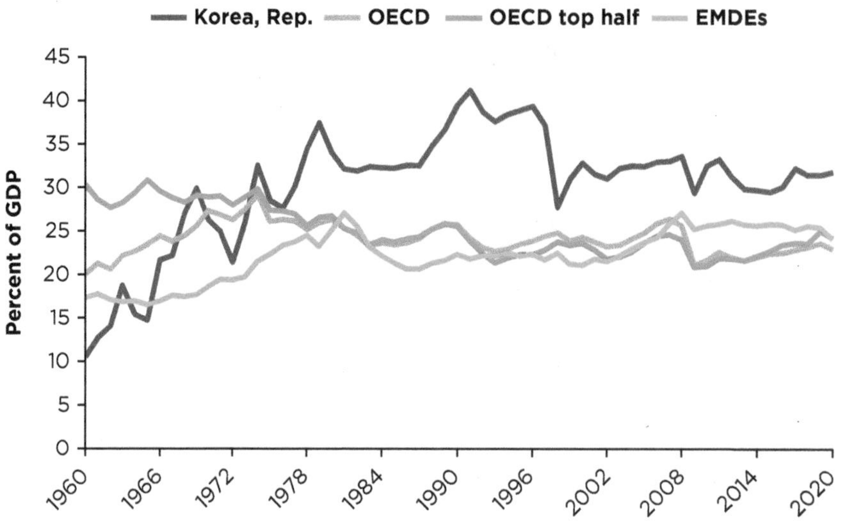

Source: World Development Indicators, World Bank (https://databank.worldbank.org/source/world-development-indicators).
Note: EMDEs = emerging markets and developing economies; OECD = Organisation for Economic Co-operation and Development.

Transportation infrastructure was expanded to keep pace with Korea's rapid industrialization. Roads, railways, ports, and airport facilities were developed simultaneously to enhance connectivity in the mountainous country. The first expressway of 29.5 kilometers was built in 1968, and by 1977 the total length of expressways was 1,224 kilometers (Academy of Korean Studies n.d.). Total railway track length in 1965 was 4,897 kilometers, which extended to 6,007 kilometers in 1980. Port traffic increased from 2.0 million tons in 1962 to 9.3 million tons in 1971, an average annual increase of 16.6 percent (Republic of Korea, MOLTM and KDI 2012). The government took the lead in constructing transportation infrastructure, and road and railway construction was managed by public enterprises. The Korea Expressway Corporation was established in 1969 for road construction and maintenance, and Korea National Railway was established in 1963 to manage the railways.[6]

In the early years, international foreign aid was a vital source of financing for the transportation sector, including from the US government agency, the International Cooperation Administration; its successor, the United States Agency for International Development; and the US EXIM Bank and the World Bank until the late 1970s. From the early 1990s, a series of laws were enacted to fund investments in the transportation sector by establishing the Special Accounts for Traffic Facility. The account was financed by a special consumption tax on gasoline and diesel, tariff on imported cars, and airport fees.

To improve water infrastructure, the government established the Korea Water Resources Corporation in 1967 and formulated the Ten-Year Comprehensive Water Resource Development Plan (1966–75), the first comprehensive plan for water resource management in the country. Water supply per capita increased from 106 liters per day in 1965 to 256 liters per day in 1980 (Republic of Korea, MOLIT and KDI 2013). International aid agencies supported water infrastructure investments immediately after the Korean War, but from the 1960s, the government led the investments in water infrastructure. The government reinvested income from water infrastructure and gradually increased government investments. The investment costs of the multipurpose dams were borne by the government until 1991. After that, they were financed by revenues from existing dams.

Starting in the 1960s, the government established industrial complexes to support its export promotion strategy. The government invested 10.7 percent of total funds allocated to the first Five-Year

Economic Development Plan (1962–66) to build industrial complexes. The first complex, the Ulsan Industrial Complex, was established in 1962 to develop the HCIs, but most of the industrial parks built in the 1960s targeted light industry. Ulsan went on to become a major center of industrialization in Korea, and it now has the world's largest automobile assembly plant, operated by Hyundai Motor Company; the world's largest shipyard, operated by Hyundai Heavy Industries; and the world's third largest oil refinery, owned by SK Energy. In the 1970s, large-scale coastal industrial complexes were built for the HCIs to take advantage of the easy access to water and ports.

Building a world class telecommunications network was a major priority for the government. The telephone network was limited until the early 1960s, with only 123,000 telephone lines. Phone lines expanded nearly 300 times by 1981, to 3.5 million, but demand far exceeded supply with industrialization. Imported landline equipment was a major bottleneck in the expansion. Therefore, the government successfully promoted the development of the technology to produce the landline equipment domestically. Landline accounts grew 16.9 percent annually between 1981 and 1990, exceeding the average annual economic growth rate of 10.1 percent. The backlog in telephone lines was completely cleared by 1987 and the number of telephone landlines reached 13.3 million by 1990 (Republic of Korea, MSIT and NIA 2021). Anticipating the critical role of ICT, in the mid-1990s, the government embarked on a major program to build a broadband infrastructure network. As a result, today, Korea's ICT infrastructure is considered among the best in the world. The ICT Development Index of the International Telecommunication Union ranked Korea first in the world in ICT infrastructure in 2016 and second in 2017.

To mobilize private financing for public infrastructure, Korea introduced PPPs through the Private Capital Inducement for Social Overhead Capital Act in 1994. Previously, investments in public infrastructure were largely financed by the government. As a result of the Act, the majority of investments in transport infrastructure are now through PPPs, and PPPs have been adopted for investments in the public water and sewer systems, city parks, public rental housing, and schools (Republic of Korea, MOSF and KDI 2013).

BUILDING BLOCK SIX: HUMAN CAPITAL DEVELOPMENT

Human capital development has been a central pillar of Korea's development strategy. Korea has prioritized education from the beginning of its modern development history. The Education Law of 1949 stipulated six years of compulsory schooling. After the Korean War (1950–53), a six-year plan (1954–59) was prepared and implemented to expand primary education. The gross enrollment rate reached 96 percent in 1959. The enrollment rates in lower and upper secondary schools started to increase rapidly in the 1970s, followed by the rapid increase of enrollment in tertiary schools in the 1990s (figure 1.9). In parallel, the Five-Year Plan (1954–58) to eradicate adult illiteracy was highly successful. The illiteracy rate plummeted from 78.2 percent in 1948 to 4.1 percent in 1958.

The rising educational levels raised the quality of the labor force. Approximately 60 percent of workers did not have a high school diploma in 1980, but the share declined to 4 percent in 2016. Similarly, only 9 percent of the labor force had a tertiary education degree in 1980, but the share increased to 41 percent in 2016. Throughout its modern development, Korea's labor force has tended to be more educated than would be predicted by the income level. In 1960, Korea already had near universal primary school enrollment, when the norm for countries at a similar income level was around 60 percent. Its secondary school enrollment rate was nearly triple what would have been expected for its income level, 27 percent versus 10 percent; and its literacy rate was more than double the expected literacy rate, 71 percent versus 31 percent (Rodrik 1995).

Policy reforms played an important role in expanding secondary and tertiary education. In the 1960s and 1970s, entrance exams for secondary schools were discontinued to expand access to secondary education. In the 1980s, the government-controlled quotas on new students for tertiary institutions were significantly increased. In the mid-1990s, the government moved from a discretion-based to a rules-based

FIGURE 1.9 **Gross Enrollment Rate, by Level of Education, 1965–2019**

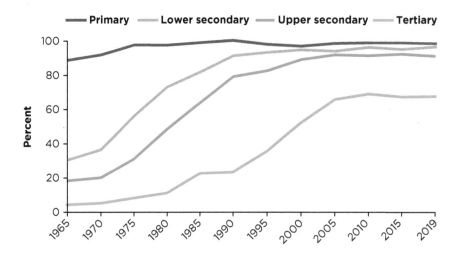

Sources: Koh et al. 2010; Republic of Korea, MOE and KEDI, various years.

FIGURE 1.10 **Wage Premium Compared to High School, by Level of Education, 1980–2016**

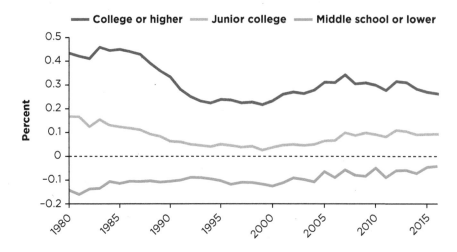

Source: Koh 2018.
Note: The figure illustrates the higher returns to education against the baseline (for example, 0.1 represents a premium of 10 percent). The wage premiums are estimated using Mincer-type wage equations that control for workers' sex, age, work experience, firm tenure, establishment size, occupation, and industry. The left-hand-side variable in the wage equations is log of hourly wage. The data are from the Wage Structure Survey by the Ministry of Employment and Labor, Republic of Korea, and cover establishments with 10 or more workers.

mechanism for authorizing the establishment of new colleges. The number of colleges and students rose rapidly. Entrance exams administered individually by colleges were replaced by a centralized high school graduation exam. The goal was to reduce the burden on high school students. These reforms contributed to the rapid increase in demand for higher education in the 1980s and 1990s.

The increasing demand was driven by significant returns to investment in higher education (Koh 2018). The premiums were very high in the 1980s (figure 1.10). Compared to high school education, the premium for junior college (two or three years) education was around 10 percent, and the premium for workers with four years of college or higher levels of education was more than 40 percent. These premiums reflected industries' increasing demand for skills. The subsequent transition of the economy to more sophisticated and value-added industries increased the demand for a more skilled and educated workforce. The premiums on education slowly declined as the supply of skills increased, but the premiums remained substantial throughout the 1980s and 1990s (Koh 2018).

The increase in the demand for education was addressed by a rapid expansion of the supply of school facilities and teachers. Investments in education increased rapidly under the Five-Year Plan initiated in 1962, expanding the facilities and the number of teachers for compulsory education (Korea Development Institute 2010). Education remained a top priority in public spending in the following decades. Spending on education has remained around 20 percent of total government spending and nearly 5 percent of GDP. The number of primary and secondary schools more than doubled, from approximately 4,600 in 1950, to 10,500 in 1990 and 11,700 in 2020. The average class size fell from around 60 students in 1965, to 53 in 1990, and 23 in 2020. The number of teachers also grew rapidly, from approximately 56,000 in 1950, to 142,000 in 1970, 285,000 in 1990, and 433,000 in 2020. Teachers enjoyed relatively high salaries, job security, and social status and respect, making the profession attractive.

Private institutions supplemented government efforts to expand secondary and tertiary education (figure 1.11). They provided diversity and competition in service provision. For primary education, almost all students attend public schools and only a very small portion attend private schools. The share of students attending private schools is much higher for secondary education. However, the shares have been falling since the 1970s for lower secondary schools and since the 1990s for upper secondary schools. This decline may have been driven by the discontinuation of entrance exams and the random assignment of students to nearby schools, including to private schools, which expanded access to education but undermined the ability of private schools to differentiate themselves from public schools by requiring higher entrance requirements. In contrast to secondary education, tertiary education has remained predominantly private. The share of students in private tertiary institutions has remained between 70 and 80 percent.

Human capital development also benefited from expanded access to basic health care services. The number of health care facilities increased rapidly, and the government rolled out nationwide public

FIGURE 1.11 Share of Students Attending Private Institutions, 1965–2019

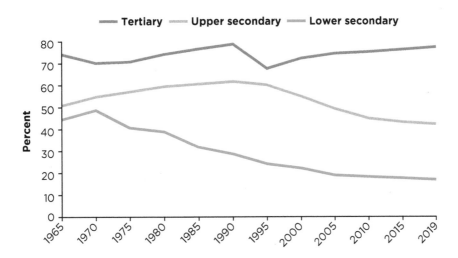

Sources: Koh et al. 2010; Republic of Korea, MOE and KEDI, various years.

health programs, such as for communicable disease prevention and de-worming. The government maintained a nationwide network of public health centers that served mostly low-income households and implemented public health programs. However, much of the health care in Korea is provided by private providers. The public sector owns only around 10 percent of the general hospitals, less than 5 percent of the specialized hospitals, and few of the clinics (Koh 2010). Private providers depend on disbursements from the National Health Insurance in addition to patients' out-of-pocket payments. The introduction of National Health Insurance and the requirement to accept National Health Insurance patients have greatly expanded access to health care.

As a result of the improvements in public health and the overall quality of life, Korea experienced significant improvements in national health indicators. Infant mortality declined from 45 deaths per 1,000 live births in 1970 to 17 deaths in 1980 (figure 1.12), and life expectancy at birth increased from 56.3 years in 1965, to 65.0 years in 1980 (figure 1.13).

FIGURE 1.12 **Infant Mortality Rate, 1970–2018**

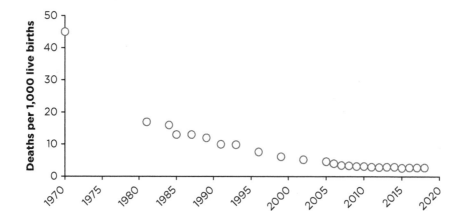

Source: Statistics Korea (https://kosis.kr).

FIGURE 1.13 **Life Expectancy at Birth, 1965–2020**

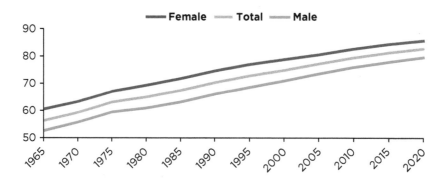

Source: Statistics Korea (https://kosis.kr).

Conclusions and Implications for Developing Countries

From the ashes of the Korean War, Korea embarked on nation building and industrialization that built the foundation of its eventual transition to a high-income economy. The land reforms of the late 1940s and the expansion of basic education helped dismantle the existing class structure and united the population under a belief in common history and destiny. Industrialization started in the 1950s with import substitution of basic consumer goods, but the approach was decisively changed to export promotion in the 1960s, and the economy started to expand rapidly in the 1970s with the growth of capital-intensive sectors.

Different explanations have been offered for the outstanding performance of Korea and other East Asian economies. From a neoliberal point of view, these economies succeeded by getting the basics right, by keeping inflation moderate, maintaining competitive exchange rates, emphasizing basic education, investing in physical infrastructure, promoting exports, and building an efficient bureaucracy. From a structuralist viewpoint, however, these economies did not stop at getting the basics right but used targeted government interventions to diversify their industrial composition and push selected domestic firms into higher value-added sectors.

Despite a large volume of research, it is difficult to find clear-cut evidence for either of these views. Developing countries around the world have promoted specific sectors, hoping to jumpstart economic growth. They are in effect adopting the structuralist approach. For them, the question is not about whether to pursue targeting industrial policies but about how best to implement them.

In the early decades of its development, Korea succeeded by focusing on both getting the basics right and using targeted industrial policies. However, its interventions relied on private sector entrepreneurs to realize its goals. Entrepreneurs had to secure foreign loans, import equipment and technology, build factories, manufacture the products, and find and sell to foreign buyers. The government largely succeeded in channeling the entrepreneurs' ambition and resourcefulness away from zero-sum, rent-seeking activities and toward value-creating activities by rewarding them according to their export performance. The strategy helped the chaebols build international competitiveness in manufacturing exports. They have since continuously diversified into high-technology sectors and powered Korea's rise to a high-income economy.

However, the strategy has not been without controversy. The chaebols came to dominate the economy and were criticized for unfairly crowding out smaller firms. Their heavy reliance on debt financing, and the financial suppression that facilitated preferential access to credit, increased the vulnerability of the economy to the AFC. In response to the AFC, Korea embarked on wide-ranging reforms to transform its growth model and address its deep-rooted economic challenges.

Notes

1. "Low-income" economy is defined as gross domestic product (GDP) per capita below 10 percent of the US level, "middle income" as between 10 and 50 percent, and "high income" as above 50 percent. In figure 1.1, Taiwan, China's GDP per capita in 2019 was slightly below 50 percent of the US level.

2. In terms of gross domestic product per capita in constant 2010 US dollars. The data are from World Development Indicators, World Bank (https://databank.worldbank.org/source/world-development-indicators).

3. The definition of high income is slightly different from that used in World Bank publications. If the threshold for high income were slightly lower, Portugal (PRT) and Greece (GRC) would qualify as having successfully transitioned to a high-income economy by 2019.

4. In terms of consolidated expenditure and net lending. Data are from Open Fiscal Data (https://www.openfiscaldata.go.kr/portal/service/openInfPage.do?mId=C020).

5. "Korea's position on the OECD codes of liberalization of capital movements and current invisible operations, international investment and multinational enterprises" (OECD 1996).

6. In 2005, Korea National Railway was split into two public enterprises, Korea Railroad Corporation, which is responsible for railway operations, and Korea National Railway, which is responsible for railway construction and maintenance.

References

Academy of Korean Studies. n.d. "Seoul-Incheon Expressway." In *Encyclopedia of Korean Culture*. Seoul, Republic of Korea: Academy of Korean Studies and DongBang Media Co. https://encykorea.aks.ac.kr/Article/E0002745.

Agénor, P. 2017. "Caught in the Middle? The Economics of Middle-Income Traps." *Journal of Economic Surveys* 31 (3): 771–91.

Agénor, P.-R., and O. Canuto. 2012. "Middle Income Growth Traps." Policy Research Working Paper 6210, World Bank, Washington, DC.

Aiyar, S., R. Duval, D. Puy, Y. Wu, and L. Zhang. 2018. "Growth Slowdowns and the Middle-income Trap." *Japan and the World Economy* 48: 22–37. https://doi.org/10.1016/j.japwor.2018.07.001.

Balassa, B. 1985. "Exports, Policy Choices, and Economic Growth in Developing Countries after the 1973 Oil Shock." *Journal of Development Economics* 18 (1): 23–35.

Balassa, B. 1988. "The Lessons of East Asian Development: An Overview." *Economic Development and Cultural Change* 36 (3): S273–90.

Bhagwati, J. 1999. "The 'Miracle' That Did Happen: Understanding East Asia in Comparative Perspective." In *Taiwan's Development Experience: Lessons on Roles of Government and Market*, edited by E. Thorbecke and H. Wan, Jr., 21–39. New York: Springer Science+Business Media.

Bulman, D., M. Eden, and H. Nguyen. 2017. "Transitioning from Low-Income Growth to High-Income Growth: Is There a Middle-Income Trap?" ADBI Working Paper Series No. 646, Asian Development Bank Institute, Tokyo.

Carney, R. W., and T. B. Child. 2013. "Changes to the Ownership and Control of East Asian Corporations between 1996 and 2008: The Primacy of Politics." *Journal of Financial Economics* 107 (2): 494–513.

Cavallo, E., B. Eichengreen, and U. Panizza. 2018. "Can Countries Rely on Foreign Saving for Investment and Economic Development?" *Review of World Economics* 154: 277–306. https://doi.org/10.1007/s10290-017-0301-5.

Claessens, S., S. Djankov, and L. H. P. Lang. 2000. "The Separation of Ownership and Control in East Asian Corporations." *Journal of Financial Economics* 58 (1-2: 81–112).

Dincecco, M., and G. Katz. 2016. "State Capacity and Long-Run Economic Performance." *Economic Journal* 126 (590): 189–218.

Eichengreen, B., D. Park, and K. Shin. 2014. "Growth Slowdowns Redux." *Japan and the World Economy* 32: 65–84. https://doi.org/10.1016/j.japwor.2014.07.003.

Evans, P. 1989. "Predatory, Developmental, and Other Apparatuses: A Comparative Political Economy Perspective on the Third World State." *Sociological Forum* 4 (4, special issue): 561–87.

Evans, P. 1995. *Embedded Autonomy: States and Industrial Transformation*. Princeton, NJ: Princeton University Press.

Evans, P., and J. E. Rauch. 1999. "Bureaucracy and Growth: A Cross-National Analysis of the Effects of 'Weberian' State Structure on Economic Growth." *American Sociological Review* 64 (5): 748–65.

Faccio, M., and L. H. P Lang. 2002. "The Ultimate Ownership of Western European Corporations." *Journal of Financial Economics* 65 (3): 365–95.

Felipe, J., A. Mehta, and C. Y. Rhee. 2014. "Manufacturing Matters . . . But It's the Jobs That Count." ADB Economics Working Paper Series No. 420, Asian Development Bank, Manila, Philippines.

Felipe, J., U. Kumar, and R. Galope. 2017. "Middle-income Transitions: Trap or Myth?" *Journal of the Asia Pacific Economy* 22 (3): 429–53. https://doi.org/10.1080/13547860.2016.1270253.

Gereffi, G. 1989. "Rethinking Development Theory: Insights from East Asia and Latin America." *Sociological Forum* 4: 505–33.

Gill, I., and H. Kharas. 2007. *An East Asian Renaissance: Ideas for Economic Growth.* Washington, DC: World Bank.

Gill, I. S., and H. Kharas. 2015. "The Middle-Income Trap Turns Ten." Policy Research Working Paper 7403. World Bank, Washington, DC.

Haggard, S. 2018. *Developmental States.* Elements in the Politics of Development Series. Cambridge, England: Cambridge University Press.

Han, X., and S. Wei. 2017. "Re-examining the Middle-Income Trap Hypothesis (MITH): What to Reject and What to Revive?" *Journal of International Money and Finance* 73 (A): 41–61. https://doi.org/10.1016/j.jimonfin.2017.01.004.

Hausmann, R., J. Hwang, and D. Rodrik. 2007. "What You Export Matters." *Journal of Economic Growth* 12: 1–25.

Hausmann, R., and D. Rodrik. 2003. "Economic Development as Self-Discovery." *Journal of Development Economics* 72 (2): 603–33.

Hoffman, P. 2015. "What Do States Do? Politics and Economic History." *Journal of Economic History* 75 (2): 303–32.

Im, F. G., and D. Rosenblatt. 2013. "Middle-Income Traps: A Conceptual and Empirical Survey." Policy Research Working Paper 6594. World Bank, Washington, DC.

IMF (International Monetary Fund). 2018. "Manufacturing Jobs: Implications for Productivity and Inequality." *World Economic Outlook: Cyclical Upswing, Structural Change,* 129–71. IMF: Washington, DC.

Jenkins, R. 1991. "Learning from the Gang: Are There Lessons for Latin America from East Asia?" *Bulletin of Latin American Research* 10 (1): 37–54.

Johnson, N. D., and M. Koyama. 2017. "States and Economic Growth: Capacity and Constraints." Explorations in Economic History 64: 1–20.

Jones, L. P., and I. S. Kong. 1980. *Government, Business, and Entrepreneurship in Economic Development: The Korean Case.* Cambridge, MA: Harvard University Press.

The JoongAng. 2020. "Conglomerates Employ 800k, the Largest Increase by LG Electronics." https://www.joongang.co.kr/article/23745555#home.

Kay, C. 2002. "Why East Asia Overtook Latin America: Agrarian Reform, Industrialisation and Development." *Third World Quarterly* 23 (6): 1073–1102.

Kim, K. S. 1988. "The Economic Effect of Import Liberalization and the Industrial Adjustment Policies." Korea Development Institute, Sejong City, Republic of Korea (Korean).

Kim, K. S. 2001. "Korea's Industrial and Trade Policies." Institute for Global Economics, Seoul, Republic of Korea (Korean).

Kim, K., and D. Leipziger. 1997. "Korea: A Case of Government-Led Development." In *Lessons from East Asia,* edited by D. Leipziger. Ann Arbor, MI: University of Michigan Press.

Kim, S. H., and K. Y. Lee. 1997. "The Mechanization of Housework: Focused on Diffusion Process and Influencing Factors." *Journal of Korea Home Management Association* 15 (3): 73–82. https://www.koreascience.or.kr/article/JAKO199711920655924.pdf.

Koh, Y. 2008. *Korea's Economic Growth and the Role of Government: Past, Present, and Future.* Seoul: Korea Development Institute. (Korean).

Koh, Y. 2010. "The Growth of Korean Economy and the Role of Government." In *The Korean Economy: Six Decades of Growth and Development,* edited by I. Sakong and Y. Koh, 7–82. Sejong City, Republic of Korea: Korea Development Institute.

Koh, Y. 2018. "The Evolution of Wage Inequality in Korea." Policy Study 2018-01. Korea Development Institute, Sejong City, Republic of Korea.

Koh, Y., S. K. Kim, W. K. Chang, Y. Kim, Y. Lee, J. S. Kim, S. Y. Lee, and Y. O. Kim. 2010. "Social Policy." In *The Korean Economy: Six Decades of Growth and Development*, edited by I. Sakong and Y. Koh, 227–310. Sejong City, Republic of Korea: Korea Development Institute.

Korea Development Institute. 2010. *The Korean Economy: Six Decades of Growth and Development*, vol. V. Sejong City, Republic of Korea: Korea Development Institute. (Korean).

Korea Fair Trade Commission. 2022. "Designation of Large Conglomerates in 2021." Korea Fair Trade Commission, Sejong City, Republic of Korea. https://www.ftc.go.kr/www/selectReportUserView.do?key=10&rpttype =1&report_data_no=9061.

La Porta, R., F. Lopez-De-Silanes, and A. Shleifer. 1999. "Corporate Ownership around the World." *Journal of Finance* 54 (2): 471–517.

Lall, S. 2004. "Reinventing Industrial Strategy: The Role of Government Policy in Building Industrial Competitiveness." G-24 Discussion Paper Series, United Nations, New York and Geneva.

Lee, H.-G. 2010. *History of Korea's Chaebol*, revised edition. Gyeonggido, Republic of Korea: Daemyung Publishing Company.

Lin, C.-Y. 1988. "East Asia and Latin America as Contrasting Models." *Economic Development and Cultural Change* 36 (3): S153–S197.

Morck, R., D. Wolfenzon, and B. Yeung. 2005. "Corporate Governance, Economic Entrenchment, and Growth." *Journal of Economic Literature* 43 (3): 655–720.

Nayyar, G., M. Hallward-Driemeier, and E. Davies. 2021. *At Your Service? The Promise of Services-Led Development*. Washington, DC: World Bank Group.

Noland, M., and H. Pack. 2003. *Industrial Policy in an Era of Globalization: Lessons from Asia*. Washington, DC: Institute for International Economics.

North, D., and B. Weingast. 1989. "Constitutions and Commitment: The Evolution of Institutions Governing Public Choice in Seventeenth-Century England." *Journal of Economic History* 49 (4): 803–32.

OECD (Organisation for Economic Co-operation and Development). 1996. "Multilateral Agreement on Investment." OECD CIME/CMIT DAFFE/INV/IME(96)13, DAFFE/INV/IME (96) 31. OECD, Paris.

OECD (Organisation for Economic Co-operation and Development). 2022. "Prices: Consumer Prices." Main Economic Indicators (database). OECD, Paris. https://doi.org/10.1787/0f2e8000-en.

Patel, D., J. Sandefur, and A. Subramanian. 2021. "The New Era of Unconditional Convergence." *Journal of Development Economics* 152. https://doi.org/10.1016/j.jdeveco.2021.102687.

Pritchett, L., and L. H. Summers. 2014. "Asiaphoria Meets Regression to the Mean." Working Paper 20573, National Bureau of Economic Research, Cambridge, MA. doi:10.3386/w20573.

Radelet, S. 1997. *Economic Growth in Asia*. Cambridge, MA: Harvard Institute for International Development.

Ranis, G., and L. Orrock. 1985. "Latin American and East Asian NICs: Development Strategies Compared." In *Latin America and the World Recession*, edited by E. Durán, 48–66. Cambridge, UK: Cambridge University Press.

Republic of Korea, MOE and KEDI (Ministry of Education and Korean Educational Development Institute). Various years. *Brief Statistics on Korean Education*. Sejong City, Republic of Korea: Ministry of Education.

Republic of Korea, MOLIT and KDI (Ministry of Land, Infrastructure and Transport and Korea Development Institute). 2013. "Korea's River Basin Management Policy 2012." Economic Development Experience Modulation. MOLIT and KDI, Sejong City, Republic of Korea.

Republic of Korea, MOLTM and KDI (Ministry of Land, Infrastructure and Transport and Korea Development Institute). 2012. "Korean Port Development Policy." Modulation of Land Maritime Development Experience. MOLTM, Sejong City, Republic of Korea.

Republic of Korea, MOSF and KDI (Ministry of Economy and Finance and Korea Development Institute). 2013. *Public-Private Partnerships: Lessons from Korea on Institutional Arrangements and Performance, 2012*. Modulation of Korea's Development Experience, Knowledge Sharing Program. Sejong City, Republic of Korea: MOSF and KDI.

Republic of Korea, MSIT and NIA (Ministry of Science and IT and National Information Society Agency). 2021. "History of Korean Information and Communication Network Development." Daegu, Republic of Korea: NIA. https://www.korea.kr/archive/expDocView.do?docId=39683.

Rodrik, D. 1995. "Getting Interventions Right: How South Korea and Taiwan Grew Rich." *Economic Policy* 20: 55–107.

Rodrik, D. 2004. "Industrial Policy for the Twenty-First Century." SSRN. http://dx.doi.org/10.2139/ssrn.617544.

Rodrik, D. 2013. "Unconditional Convergence in Manufacturing." *Quarterly Journal of Economics* 128 (1): 165–204.

Stiglitz, J. E., and S. Yusuf. 2001. *Rethinking the East Asian Miracle*. Washington, DC: World Bank and Oxford University Press.

WEF (World Economic Forum). 2019. *Global Competitiveness Report 2019*. Geneva: WEF. https://www3.weforum.org/docs/WEF_TheGlobalCompetitivenessReport2019.pdf.

World Bank. 1993. *The East Asian Miracle: Economic Growth and Public Policy*. New York: Oxford University Press.

CHAPTER 2

Korea's Transition to a High-Income Economy

Introduction

The Republic of Korea is one of the few developing countries in the past century that has successfully transitioned from a middle-income to a high-income economy within just a few decades. This chapter identifies key features of Korea's successful transition to a high-income economy. The chapter analyzes the main sources of Korea's economic growth during this transition, the associated structural transformation of its industries, and the evolution of firm dynamics. The chapter also highlights the remaining challenges for Korea to sustain its growth and development.

In the past three decades, Korea's economy has undergone a major transformation as it transitioned to a high-income economy. The transformation was a continuation of the economic transformation that took place in the 1970s and 1980s, when successful industrialization and rapid expansion of the manufacturing sector fueled Korea's growth. Industrial policies in the 1970s to promote the heavy and chemical industries resulted in rapid accumulation of capital and helped the country reach middle-income status by the early 1980s. In the 1990s, Korea recognized the need to evolve and started to increase the emphasis of its support policies toward the promotion of research and development (R&D)–intensive and high-technology industries. Despite the temporary setback of the Asian Financial Crisis (AFC), Korea's economy quickly adjusted and recovered. It has sustained growth over the past two decades by strengthening its global competitiveness in high-technology industries.

This chapter focuses on Korea's economic development since the 1990s, when it transitioned from a middle- to a high-income economy. The next section explains changes in the macroeconomic fundamentals and major sources of Korea's economic growth from the 1990s. The chapter then analyzes the sectoral transformation and industrialization of the economy, assesses the economy from the firm dynamic perspective, and analyzes the inclusivity and sustainability of Korea's growth.

This chapter was prepared by Luan Zhao and Yusha Li (World Bank) and Jungsoo Park and Yoonsoo Lee (Sogang University). Mary C. Hallward-Driemeier contributed on services-led growth, Katelyn Jison Yoo (World Bank) contributed on the impact of COVID-19, Hyungna Oh (Kyunghee University) and Hyoung Gun Wang (World Bank) contributed on green growth, and Gene Kindberg-Hanlon (International Monetary Fund) contributed on global productivity trends.

Macroeconomic Performance and Key Sources of Growth

Korea's development since the 1990s can be organized into three distinct phases. In phase one, from 1990 to the AFC (1990–97), Korea succeeded in transitioning from middle to high income, based on the World Bank's threshold for high income. In phase two, from the AFC to the global financial crisis (GFC) (1998–2008), Korea's growth paradigm transitioned from input-based growth to productivity-based growth. In phase three, the post-GFC period (2009 to the present), Korea has been experiencing a growth slowdown as its per capita income approached the Organisation for Economic Co-operation and Development (OECD) average, although its real gross domestic product (GDP) growth rate remained above the OECD average.

PHASE ONE: FROM 1990 TO THE AFC (1990–97)

Up to the AFC, Korea sustained its rapid economic growth of the earlier decades. Its annual real GDP growth rate averaged 7.3 percent in the 1990s, when it transitioned from middle income to a high-income economy (figure 2.1). During this period, Korea's gross national income (GNI) per capita grew at an average annual rate of 7.7 percent, well above the OECD countries. Korea crossed the World Bank's GNI per capita threshold for high-income economies, calculated using the World Bank's Atlas method, in 1995 and joined the OECD in the same year, which symbolized the country's entry into the ranks of advanced economies.[1]

Korea's rapid growth prior to the AFC benefited from contributions from all facets of the economy, encompassing capital, labor, and productivity, with the latter measured by total factor productivity (TFP). The largest contribution came from capital accumulation. Capital contributed about 60 percent of GDP growth between 1990 and 1997 (figure 2.2, panel a). Compared to many other economies, Korea was able to maintain high investment rates even after achieving high per capita income levels. Between 1990 and 1997, gross capital formation accounted for 38 percent of GDP, which was significantly higher than the average of 22 percent across OECD countries (figure 2.2, panel b). Korea's high investment rate was mainly driven by private investment (figure 2.2, panel c).

Human capital has been critical for Korea's growth and transition to a high-income economy. Korea's average years of schooling increased from 7.6 in 1980 to 9.8 in 1990, and further to 10.8 in 1995 (figure 2.3, panel a). The rapid rise in educational attainment contributed to significant accumulation of human capital. According to the Human Capital Index published by the Penn World Table, Korea quickly caught up with the advanced economies and surpassed the average level of human capital of the OECD countries in 1991 (figure 2.3, panel b). On average, human capital explains about 10 percent of Korea's growth during 1990 to 1997. Despite a decline from the 1980s, human capital still contributed more to growth than in many OECD countries.

Employment contributed around one-sixth of Korea's growth between 1990 and 1997, benefiting from a demographic dividend. Following a rise in the 1980s, Korea's working-age population (ages 15 to 64) increased from 29.7 million in 1990 to 32.8 million in 1997, providing the labor force to support rapid growth. Furthermore, employment grew faster than the working-age population between 1990 and 1997, driven by a low unemployment rate and steady rise in labor participation rates.

TFP also played a key role in supporting growth in the decades before Korea transitioned to a high-income economy (figure 2.2, panel a). Similar to other rapidly growing emerging markets and developing economies (EMDEs), capital accumulation is a significant source of growth for Korea. In addition, Korea benefited from the exceptionally large contribution from TFP growth, complementing the contribution to growth from capital accumulation. To a significant extent, the high TFP growth allowed Korea to converge rapidly to the income levels of high-income economies.

PHASE TWO: FROM THE AFC TO THE GFC (1998–2008)

The AFC had a devastating impact on the country's output and jobs and exposed Korea's structural flaws and the shortcomings of its development model. The economy contracted by 5.1 percent in 1998, and

FIGURE 2.1 **GDP and GDP per Capita, 1960–2020**

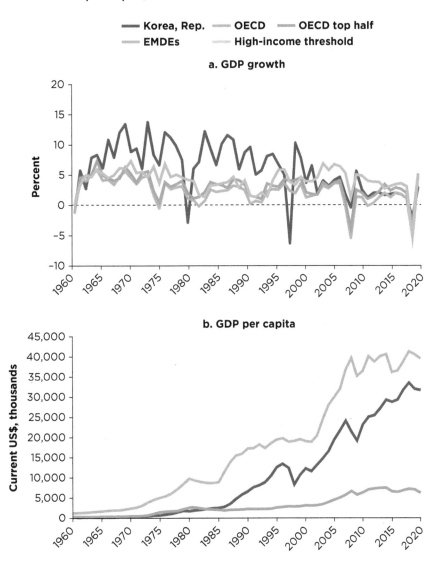

Source: Calculations based on data from World Development Indicators, World Bank (https://data.worldbank.org).
Note: OECD represents the OECD average, and EMDEs represents the EMDE average, unless otherwise specified. EMDEs = emerging markets and developing economies; GDP = gross domestic product; GNI = gross national income; OECD = Organisation for Economic Co-operation and Development.

Korea was reclassified as an upper middle-income country from 1998 to 2000, according to the World Bank's high-income economy threshold. However, the growth rate rebounded to 11.5 percent in 1999, and Korea again became a high-income country in 2001. Thereafter, until the GFC, GDP growth slowed to an annual average rate of 5.0 percent, which was still higher than the OECD average of 3.5 percent. Sustained growth allowed Korea to continue to close the income gap with the OECD countries. In 1998, Korea's per capita GNI in current US dollars equaled 42 percent of the OECD average. This ratio increased to 56 percent in 2008.

TFP growth increased in the years following the AFC, in response to the significant reforms carried out to address the structural flaws exposed by the crisis (figure 2.2, panel a, and figure 2.4, panel a). From

FIGURE 2.2 Capital Formation and Its Contribution to GDP Growth

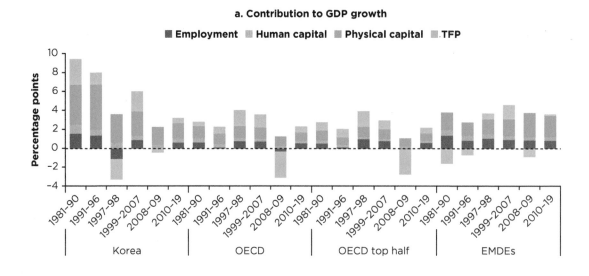

a. Contribution to GDP growth

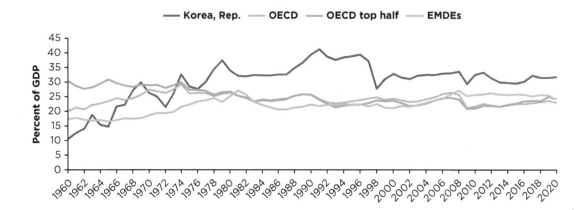

b. Gross capital formation

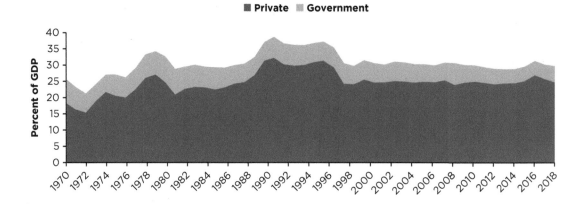

c. Share of private and public investment

Source: For panel a, calculations based on data from Penn World Table 10.0; for panel b, World Development Indicators, World Bank (https://data.worldbank.org); for panel c, capital stock database, International Monetary Fund.
Note: EMDEs = emerging markets and developing economies; GDP = gross domestic product; OECD = Organisation for Economic Co-operation and Development; TFP = total factor productivity.

FIGURE 2.3 Human Capital

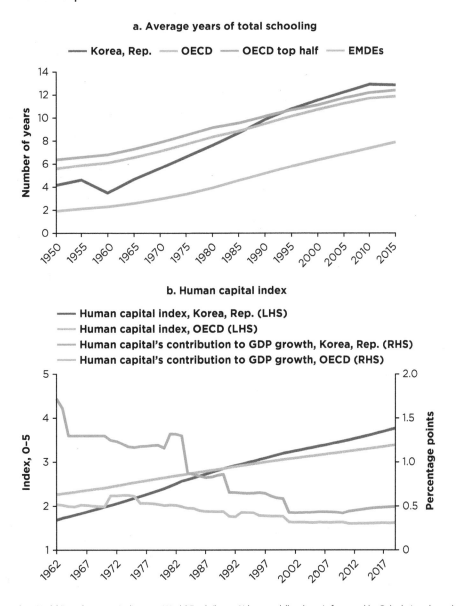

a. Average years of total schooling

— Korea, Rep. — OECD — OECD top half — EMDEs

b. Human capital index

— Human capital index, Korea, Rep. (LHS)
— Human capital index, OECD (LHS)
— Human capital's contribution to GDP growth, Korea, Rep. (RHS)
— Human capital's contribution to GDP growth, OECD (RHS)

Source: For panel a, World Development Indicators, World Bank (https://data.worldbank.org); for panel b, Calculations based on data from Penn World Table 10.0.
Note: EMDEs = emerging markets and developing economies; LHS = left-hand side; OECD = Organisation for Economic Co-operation and Development; RHS = right-hand side.

1999 to 2008, the relative contribution of TFP to real GDP growth was nearly equivalent to the contribution of physical capital. As a result of higher TFP growth, Korea's TFP level continued to converge toward that of the OECD countries (figure 2.4, panel b).

The increase in TFP growth after the AFC is consistent with findings from firm-level data (Baek, Kim, and Kwon 2009; Jung et al. 2013). Firms appeared to respond to changing comparative advantages in Korea, focusing on raising productivity in response to rising wages and income levels and diminishing returns to capital investments. The increased importance of productivity was accompanied by

FIGURE 2.4 **Total Factor Productivity, 1960–2019**

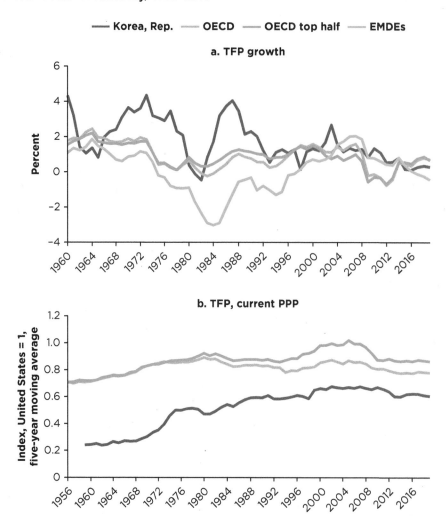

Source: Calculations based on data from Penn World Table 10.0.
Note: EMDEs = emerging markets and developing economies; OECD = Organisation for Economic Co-operation and Development; PPP = purchasing power parity; TFP = total factor productivity.

a rising share of high-technology and R&D-intensive industries. The sustained technological progress in information and communications technology and its diffusion across industries contributed to improved productivity (Hur, Lee, and Hyun 2013; Kim 2004). Furthermore, the TFPs of non-chaebol firms (chaebols are family-owned conglomerates in Korea) increased in chaebol dominated industries that were liberalized after the AFC to promote competition (Aghion, Guriev, and Jo 2021).

Since the AFC, capital's contribution to growth has steadily declined (figure 2.5, panel a), primarily reflecting two factors. First, Korea's investment as a share of GDP declined from the extraordinarily high levels in the 1990s, to around 30 percent in phase two, which was still greater than the OECD average. Second, Korea's investment has shown signs of diminishing returns (figure 2.5, panel b). Since the AFC, the incremental capital-output ratio has risen to a level in line with the OECD average, suggesting

FIGURE 2.5 **Capital Contribution to Growth and Capital Returns**

a. Contribution of physical capital to growth

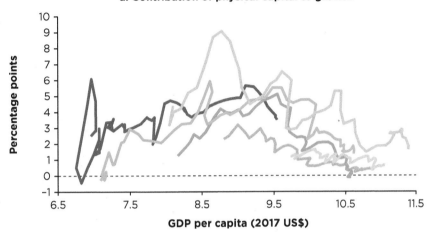

b. Incremental Capital Output Ratio (ICOR)

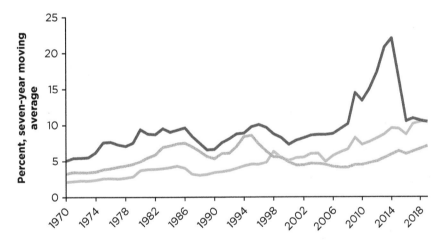

Source: For panel a, calculations based on data from Penn World Table 10.0; for panel b, calculations based on data from World Development Indicators, World Bank (https://data.worldbank.org).
Note: In panel b, the spike in ICOR in the early 2010s reflects the sharp decline of GDP growth, and hence the denominator of the ICOR, during the GFC. EMDEs = emerging markets and developing economies; GDP = gross domestic product; GFC = global financial crisis; OECD = Organisation for Economic Co-operation and Development.

deteriorating investment efficiency (figure 2.5, panel b). Although capital deepening can still explain a significant part of the higher labor productivity growth in Korea compared to the OECD average, capital's contribution has reached its limit due to the high stock of capital accumulated over the decades of high rates of capital investment. Both public and private capital stock per capita in Korea are now comparable to the OECD countries (figure 2.6).

FIGURE 2.6 **Public and Private Capital Stock per Capita, 2017**

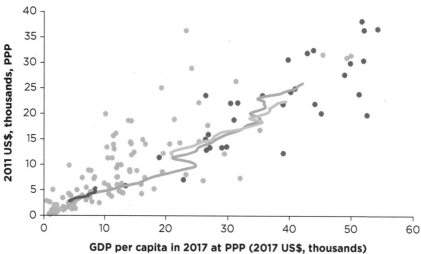

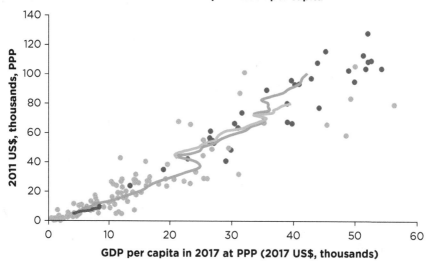

Sources: Calculations based on data from World Development Indicators, World Bank (https://data.worldbank.org); IMF investment and capital stock database, International Monetary Fund.
Note: EMDEs = emerging markets and developing economies; GDP = gross domestic product; OECD = Organisation for Economic Co-operation and Development; PPP = purchasing power parity.

PHASE THREE: POST-GFC (2009 TO THE PRESENT)

Korea's growth slowed further after the GFC, but it continued to exceed that of the OECD countries. From 2009 to 2019, Korea's real GDP growth averaged 3.1 percent, above the OECD average of 1.8 percent. Korea's labor productivity growth has mirrored the secular decline of labor productivity in high-income economies that preceded the AFC and continued thereafter (box 2.1). However, Korea's higher labor productivity growth rate has enabled the country to continue to converge to the average labor productivity of OECD countries.

The growth contributions of both capital and TFP have declined since the GFC. Moreover, the impact of investment on growth further moderated in phase three (figure 2.5, panel b), highlighting the need to sustain growth of TFP going forward. Although there has been a global slowdown in TFP growth across countries in the past decade, Korea's TFP growth performance has been weaker than that of the OECD countries. Various measurements indicate that TFP growth in Korea has declined to around zero since the GFC (figure 2.7). As a result, the convergence of Korea's TFP level to that of the United States, which can be considered the global frontier, has slowed over the recent decade (figure 2.4, panel b).

Along with the rest of the world, Korea faces the challenge of recovering from the sizable economic disruptions of the COVID-19 pandemic. Yet, the country's initial rapid and effective health and economic response has to a large extent mitigated the short-term impact. After the economy contracted by 1.0 percent in 2020 due to the pandemic, Korea's real GDP surpassed its pre-pandemic level in early 2021. By comparison, in high-income economies, GDP contracted on average by 4.5 percent in 2020 and had not reached the pre-pandemic level by the end of 2021. In the early COVID-19 waves, the government had controlled the transmission of the virus through early and aggressive testing and contact tracing; transparent risk communication to the public; promotion of transmission-reducing behaviors, including wearing a mask, washing hands, and social distancing; and expansion of available spare hospital beds

FIGURE 2.7 **Total Factor Productivity Growth, 1974–2019**

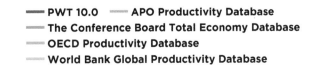

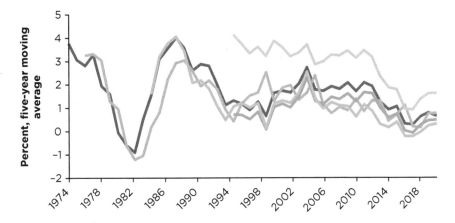

Sources: Calculations based on data from Penn World Table 10.0; APO Productivity Database; The Conference Board Total Economy Database; OECD Productivity Database; World Bank Global Productivity Database.
Note: APO = Asian Productivity Organization; OECD = Organisation for Economic Co-operation and Development; PWT = Penn World Table.

BOX 2.1 How Have Global Productivity Trends Evolved?

Globally, labor productivity growth has declined since the global financial crisis (GFC) (Eichengreen 2015). The decline in advanced economies' labor productivity growth since the GFC continues a longer term trend and is mirrored in Korea's declining labor productivity growth. Labor productivity growth in emerging markets and developing economies (EMDEs) has declined since the GFC, but it remains above the long-term average growth.

Advanced economies. The labor productivity growth of advanced economies has been steadily declining since the 1980s, but the rate of decline accelerated following the GFC. The slowdown previous to the GFC has been attributed to a declining contribution from information and communications technology (ICT)–intensive sectors in the United States, slow adoption of ICT technologies, restrictive product market regulations, and sectoral misallocation in parts of Europe.[a] During the GFC, labor productivity growth in advanced economies plunged and never recovered to pre-crisis rates. On average during 2013–18, annual labor productivity growth was 0.7 percent in the median advanced economy, half the previous average in the runup to the GFC, and over 1 percentage point below the rates in the 1980s. Since 2008, investment growth has slowed sharply in response to weak and highly uncertain growth prospects, heightened policy uncertainty, and credit constraints in the aftermath of the GFC (Dieppe, Kilic-Celik, and Kindberg-Hanlon 2020). In addition to the negative effects on capital deepening, reduced investments and weaker demand due to the GFC are likely to have reduced the pace of innovation, further dragging down productivity growth (Adler et al. 2017; Anzoategui et al. 2019).

EMDEs. Within EMDEs, the labor productivity growth slowdown since the GFC has been particularly pronounced in China, where a policy-guided decline in public investment growth has been underway for several years, and in commodity exporters, which were hit hard by the commodity price plunge of 2014–16. In contrast to advanced economies, weak post-GFC productivity growth follows on the heels of a major productivity surge during 2003–08, when EMDEs' productivity growth more than doubled from the averages in the 1990s. The slowdown following the GFC only partially reversed a rising trend in labor productivity growth since the 1980s.

Ahead of the GFC, EMDEs' productivity growth was boosted by reforms that allowed greater foreign direct investment inflows in the 1990s and China's accession to the World Trade Organization in 2001, which unleashed a productivity boom in China and its trading partners. A decade of service sector oriented reforms boosted productivity in other major EMDEs, such as India in the 1990s and 2000s (Bosworth and Collins 2008; Tuan, Ng, and Zhao 2009). The rapid productivity improvements were also associated with improved educational attainment, working-age population growth, and increased participation in value chains driven by trade liberalization (Dieppe, Kilic-Celik, and Kindberg-Hanlon 2020). Since the GFC, the rate of improvements in many of these productivity covariates has slowed in the majority of EMDEs alongside productivity growth, as educational systems matured, global value chain growth stagnated, and the demographic dividend faded.

a. For a summary of the effects of the ICT slowdown on US productivity in the 2000s, see Jorgenson, Ho, and Stiroh (2008). In Europe, the decline in productivity has been ascribed to sectoral misallocation due to cheap credit in Southern Europe (Gopinath et al. 2017), failure to adopt ICT and associated technology to the same extent as the United States (van Ark, O'Mahony, and Timmer 2008), and restrictive product market regulations (Haltiwanger, Scarpetta, and Schweiger 2014).

---

and community treatment centers. The government has lifted most of the quarantine measures since April 2022. There has been a subsequent surge in COVID-19 cases, but the cumulative fatality rate has remained low compared to other countries.

Korea's economic resilience to the pandemic also benefited from its timely economic response to the initial outbreak and the robust trade performance that followed. The authorities loosened monetary policy and implemented a wide range of fiscal and financial measures to support growth in response to the outbreak of COVID-19. The Bank of Korea cut its policy rate by 75 basis points to a historic low of 0.5 percent in May 2020 and injected significant liquidity to stabilize financial markets and support small and medium-size enterprises and sectors that were significantly impacted. Following a sharp contraction at the beginning of the pandemic, Korea's export activity picked up quickly, driven by strong global demand for electronic goods in response to increased remote work. The strong rebound in export growth contributed to Korea's pandemic recovery.

Structural Transformation of the Economy

The evolution of Korea's economic and employment structures has broadly followed the development paths of other high-income economies. In the 1970s and 1980s, agriculture's contribution to total value added declined rapidly and in parallel the industry sector expanded significantly. However, the service sector remained the largest sector, accounting for approximately 60 percent of total value added and a rapidly increasing share of employment as the employment share of agriculture sharply declined (figure 2.8). Excess labor in the agriculture sector was migrating to the service sector and, to a lesser extent, to the industry sector.

FIGURE 2.8 **Changes in Industrial Economic and Employment Structure, 1970–2018**

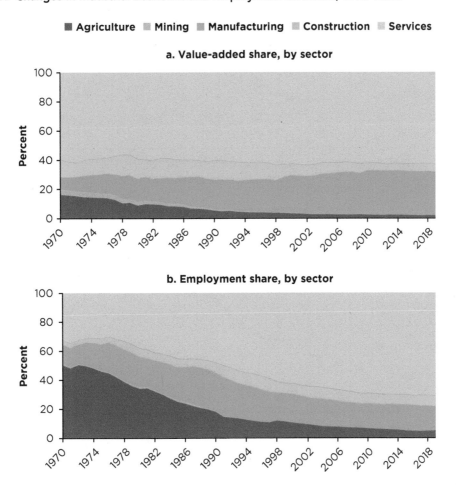

Source: Productivity Database, Asian Productivity Organization.

Many economies have experienced "deindustrialization" as they have matured and grown to high income. However, in Korea, the value-added share of industry has remained relatively stable at around 25 to 30 percent since the mid-1980s, although the employment share of the sector peaked in the early 1990s and has declined steadily since then. Hence, Korea has reduced the pace of deindustrialization to a far greater extent than in comparator countries (figure 2.9). The decline in the industrial labor share could be due to Korea's high adoption rate of industrial robots, the second highest in the world after Singapore, which has allowed capital to substitute for labor. The decline in labor share also reflects increases in the shares of capital- and technology-intensive industries in the manufacturing sector. ·

The manufacturing sector has been a significantly larger driver of aggregate productivity growth in Korea than in other countries (figure 2.10, panel a). The sector accounted for 1.7 percentage points of

FIGURE 2.9 International Comparison of Industrial Structural Transformation

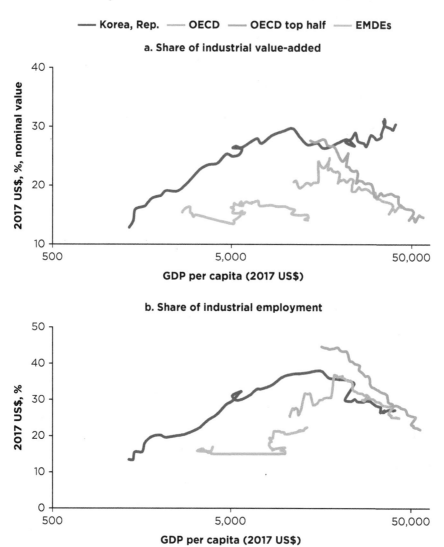

Source: Calculations based on data from the Global Productivity Database, World Bank.
Note: EMDEs = emerging markets and developing economies; GDP = gross domestic product; OECD = Organisation for Economic Co-operation and Development.

FIGURE 2.10 Labor Productivity, Republic of Korea, by Sector

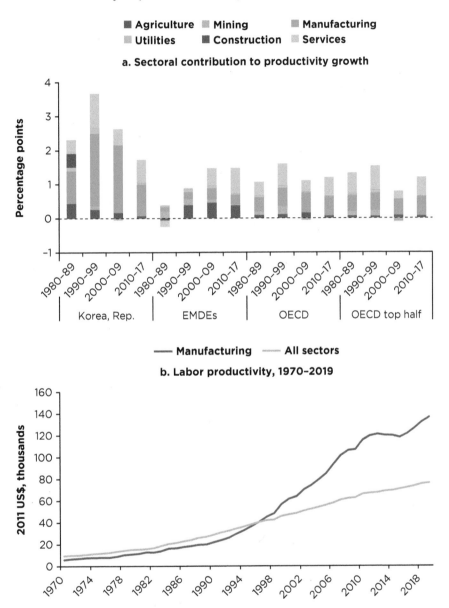

Sources: For panel a, calculations based on data from the Global Productivity Database, World Bank; for panel b, calculations based on data from the Productivity Database, Asian Productivity Organization.
Note: EMDEs = emerging markets and developing economies; OECD = Organisation for Economic Co-operation and Development.

aggregate productivity growth in Korea during 1980–2010. Except in China, manufacturing has contributed only 0.2 percentage point to productivity growth in EMDEs since the 1980s. Manufacturing productivity in Korea was low in the early decades but began to grow rapidly in the early 1990s as the sector globalized and surpassed the average productivity level of the entire economy in the mid-1990s (figure 2.10, panel b).

Since then, Korea's manufacturing productivity has improved further, as its share of total employment declined but its value-added share remained relatively stable. By 2019, labor productivity in the manufacturing sector was about twice the overall productivity of the economy. Korea's productivity level has rapidly converged toward the OECD average, primarily driven by the manufacturing sector. By 2000, Korea's labor productivity in the manufacturing sector was already about 73 percent of the OECD average (figure 2.11, panel a). In 2018, Korea's labor productivity level in the manufacturing sector already surpassed the OECD average, although it remained lower than the US level, which can be considered the global frontier (figure 2.11, panel b).

In contrast to manufacturing, Korea's labor productivity in the service sector is still far from the level of OECD countries (figure 2.11). Korea's service sector consists of a mix of modern and legacy sectors, with significant differences in labor productivity. High-productivity service sectors include

FIGURE 2.11 Sectoral Labor Productivity Compared to Global Frontiers, 1970–2018

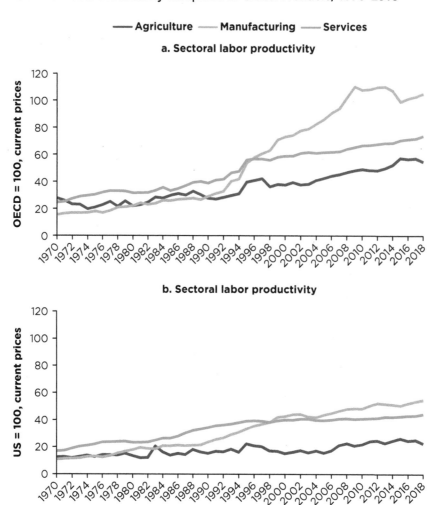

Source: Calculations based on data from the STAN Industrial Analysis Database, OECD.
Note: OECD = Organisation for Economic Co-operation and Development.

telecommunications; finance, insurance, and real estate; and information technology. Low-productivity sectors include wholesale and retail, accommodation and food services, and other services. The high-productivity sectors (high-productivity services and manufacturing sectors) have an average labor productivity that is approximately four and a half times that of the low-productivity sectors (low-productivity services and agriculture sectors).

Korea benefited greatly from labor moving from the lower to higher productivity sectors, but its effect has diminished over time (figure 2.12, panel a). Labor reallocation contributed most to productivity growth

FIGURE 2.12 Productivity Growth and Structural Transformation, 1980–2017

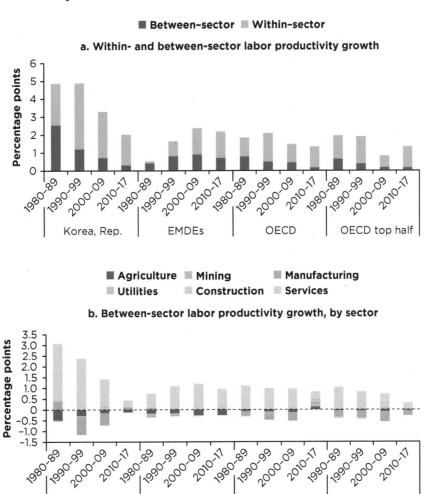

Source: Calculations based on data from the Global Productivity Database, World Bank.
Note: Following the methodology in McMillan, Rodrik, and Sepulveda (2017), the change in labor productivity can be decomposed into changes in productivity within sectors and movement of workers across sectors: $\Delta P_t = \sum_{i=1}^{n} \theta_{i,t-k} \Delta p_{i,t} + \sum_{i=1}^{n} p_{i,t} \Delta \theta_{i,t}$, where ΔP_t is the change in economywide labor productivity, $\Delta p_{i,t}$ is the change in labor productivity in industry I, $\theta_{i,t}$ is the employment share of industry i at time t, and Δ denotes change between periods t and t-k. The first component in the equation is the sum of productivity growth within individual sectors weighted by the employment share of each sector at the beginning of the period. The second term—the "structural change" component—is the inner product of sectoral productivity levels at the end of the period and the change in sectoral employment shares. EMDEs = emerging markets and developing economies; OECD = Organisation for Economic Co-operation and Development.

in Korea in the 1980s, when the share of workers employed in agriculture declined by about 16 percent and the shares in manufacturing and services increased by 5 and 10 percent, respectively. In the 1990s and 2000s, the share of employment in manufacturing steadily declined, resulting in a negative contribution to labor productivity growth (figure 2.12, panel b). Labor was instead moving from the agriculture sector into services, which had a lower productivity level compared to manufacturing. This contributed to the weaker contribution from labor reallocation to aggregate labor productivity growth and an overall slowdown of the aggregate labor productivity growth in recent decades. By the 2010s, labor productivity growth was almost entirely driven by within-sector productivity growth.

MANUFACTURING SECTOR

In addition to the changes in the sectoral composition of the economy, there have been significant structural changes within the manufacturing sector. Since the 1990s, the value-added shares of key capital-intensive industries with higher labor productivity increased, while those of light industries declined. The value-added shares of Korea's key capital-intensive industries increased from 50 percent in 1991 to 68 percent in 2011 and subsequently declined modestly to 63 percent in 2019 (figure 2.13, panel a). The employment shares increased from 37 percent in 1991, peaked at 52 percent in 2013, and declined slightly to 49 percent in 2019. The expansion of key capital-intensive industries is also evident in the rising export shares of electronics, automobiles, and ships, and in parallel the declining export shares of light manufacturing industries (figure 2.13, panel b).

FIGURE 2.13 **Key Capital-Intensive Industries, Republic of Korea**

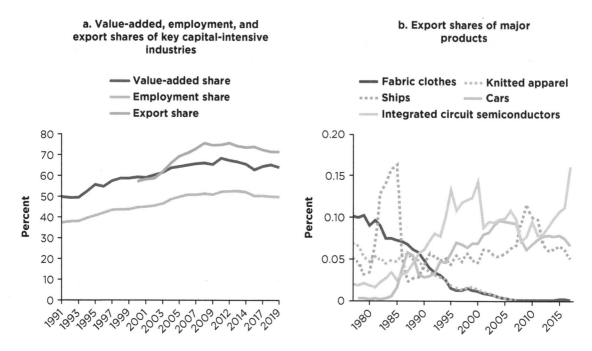

a. Value-added, employment, and export shares of key capital-intensive industries

- Value-added share
- Employment share
- Export share

b. Export shares of major products

- Fabric clothes
- Knitted apparel
- Ships
- Cars
- Integrated circuit semiconductors

Sources: Mining and Manufacturing Survey, Statistics Korea (https://kosis.kr); for panel b, Lee 2020.
Note: Key capital-intensive industries include (a) coke, briquettes, and refined petroleum products; (b) chemicals and chemical products; (c) basic metals; (d) electronic components, computers; (e) visual, sound, and communication equipment; (f) other machinery and equipment; (g) motor vehicles, trailers, and semitrailers; and (h) other transport equipment.

The composition of the manufacturing sector experienced a transformation from low-technology to high-technology industries. The share of the high-technology sectors in real manufacturing value added increased from 22 percent in 1990 to 44 percent in 2018, while the shares of the low- and medium-technology sectors fell from 37 and 48 percent to 11 and 45 percent, respectively (figure 2.14, panel a). The share of high-technology sectors in total employment increased from 21 percent in 1990 to 30 percent in 2018, and the employment share of low-technology sectors declined from 51 to 21 percent (figure 2.14, panel b).

Within manufacturing, the electrical manufacturing sector has expanded particularly rapidly since the 1990s. The share of the electrical sector in manufacturing value-added increased from 11 percent

FIGURE 2.14 **Shares of Technology (Research and Development)–Intensive Manufacturing Industries, 1980–2018**

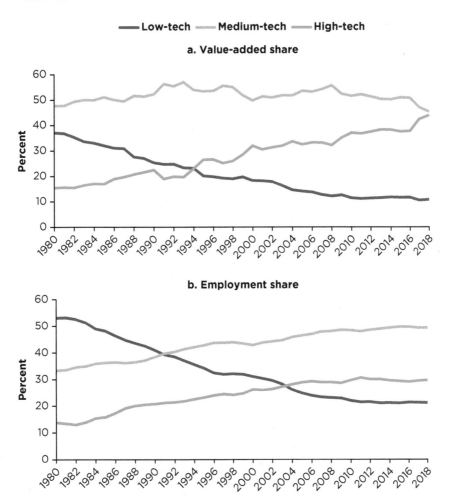

Source: Calculations based on data from the STAN Industrial Analysis Database, Organisation for Economic Co-operation and Development.
Note: The low-tech sector includes food products, beverages, tobacco products, manufacturing of wood and products of wood and cork, manufacturing of paper, paper products, printing, and publishing. The medium-tech sector includes chemicals, rubber, plastics, fuel products, other nonmetallic mineral products, manufacturing of basic metals and fabricated metal products, manufacturing of transport equipment, and manufacturing of furniture. The high-tech sector includes machinery and equipment and manufacturing of electrical, electronic, and optical equipment.

in 1980 to 35 percent in 2018, and the employment share rose from 10 to 18 percent (figure 2.15, panel a). Korea's labor productivity in electrical manufacturing increased sharply relative to non-electrical manufacturing and reached more than twice the level of non-electrical manufacturing by 2018 (figure 2.15, panel b).

The rapid productivity convergence of Korea's industry sector was primarily driven by capital- and R&D-intensive manufacturing sectors (figure 2.16, panel a). Productivity convergence toward the global frontier has been more advanced in manufacturing of electronics, machinery and equipment, and metals (figure 2.16, panel b). The rapid growth of these high-performing sectors explains a large part of Korea's catch-up in productivity growth.

FIGURE 2.15 **Electrical Manufacturing, Republic of Korea**

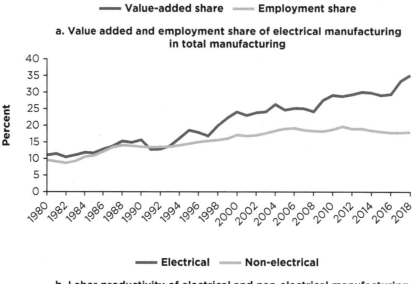

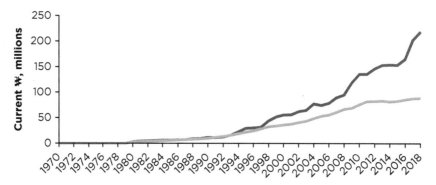

Source: Calculations based on data from the STAN Industrial Analysis Database, Organisation for Economic Co-operation and Development.

FIGURE 2.16 **Labor Productivity of Manufacturing Subsectors, 1970–2018**

a. Sectoral labor productivity, manufacturing, current ₩

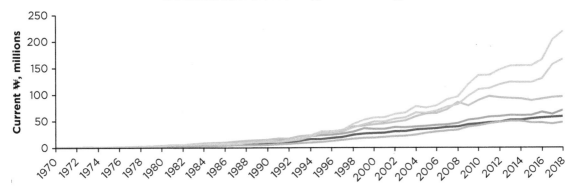

b. Sectoral labor productivity, manufacturing standardized to US productivity levels

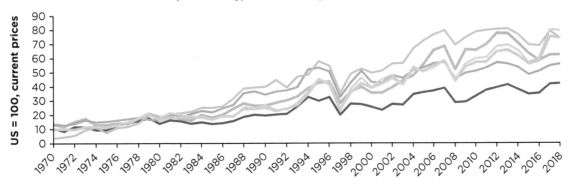

Source: Calculations based on data from the STAN Industrial Analysis Database, Organisation for Economic Co-operation and Development.

Since the GFC (phase three), there has been a significant slowdown in growth of the key capital-intensive industries. The average annual growth of the capital-intensive industries fell from 5.8 percent in 2007–12 to 0.3 percent in 2012–17 (figure 2.17, panel a). If the semiconductor industry is excluded, the capital-intensive industries contracted annually by 2.3 percent. Employment growth also declined significantly, from 3.0 percent in the pre-GFC period to 0.7 percent in the post-GFC period (figure 2.17, panel b). The weaker performance of the key capital-intensive industries has translated into lower labor productivity growth, which fell from 2.8 percent annual growth in the former period to an annual contraction of 0.4 percent in the latter period (figure 2.17, panel c). Excluding the semiconductor industry, the growth rate drops to an annual contraction of 2.8 percent in the latter period.

The growth slowdown of the key capital-intensive industries has been associated with the slowdown in export growth in the post-GFC period (figure 2.17, panel d). In Korea, declining export growth has typically reduced productivity growth, especially in input-inelastic sectors in which inputs are not flexibly adjusted as export growth decreases (Kim, Lee, and Shin 2021). Due to the global slowdown of

FIGURE 2.17 **Key Industries versus Non-Key Industries, Republic of Korea, 2002–17**

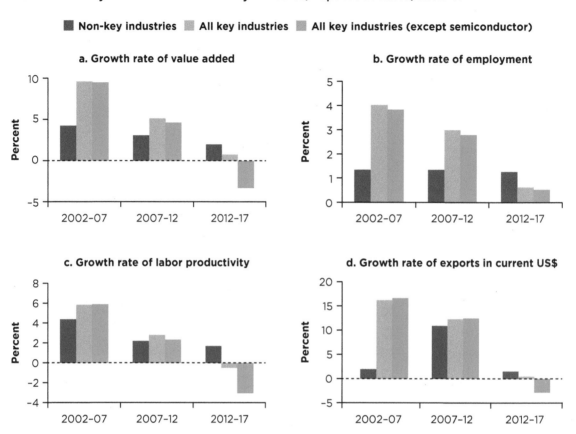

■ **Non-key industries** ■ **All key industries** ■ **All key industries (except semiconductor)**

Source: Mining and Manufacturing Survey, Statistics Korea (https://kosis.kr).

international trade since the GFC, Korea's export growth in key capital-intensive industries fell significantly, from 12.7 percent in 2007–12 to 0.5 percent in 2012–17. The decline in exports resulted in the poor performance of the capital-intensive industries, which are heavily export oriented.

SERVICE SECTOR

The productivity of the service sector has been stagnant and lagging far behind other OECD countries. By 2018, Korea's labor productivity in the service sector was only 74 percent of the OECD average (figure 2.11). Korea's labor productivity represents less than half the US level in each major service sector (figure 2.18, panel a). Labor productivity is especially low in wholesale and retail trade, transportation and storage, and accommodation and food service activities (figure 2.18, panel b).

Although the advanced service sectors have expanded, the traditional low-productivity services continue to dominate the service sector and their share remains higher compared to those in most other OECD countries. In Korea, employment in services has been concentrated in the low-productivity service industries. Their employment share in total services has been falling, but it remains higher than that in most other OECD countries (figure 2.19).

FIGURE 2.18 Labor Productivity of the Service Sector, 1998–2018

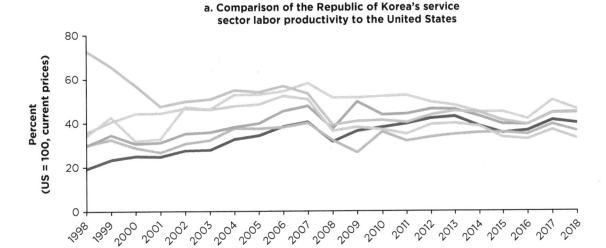

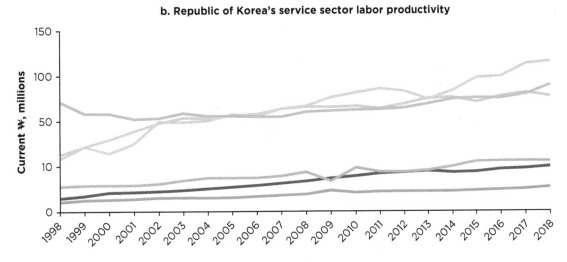

Source: Calculations based on data from the STAN Industrial Database, Organisation for Economic Co-operation and Development.

A key challenge for Korea is to reduce the concentration of employment in low-productivity and low-wage service industries and improve overall service sector productivity. This challenge is becoming more critical given that manufacturing jobs have been gradually contracting. Korea can take advantage of expanding the potential for services-led growth, including new digital technologies and innovations and spillovers from manufacturing, reflecting the increasing value-added shares of services in manufacturing (box 2.2).

FIGURE 2.19 Employment Share of Traditional Services in Total Services

- Accommodation and food service
- Transportation and storage
- Wholesale and retail trade
- Real estate

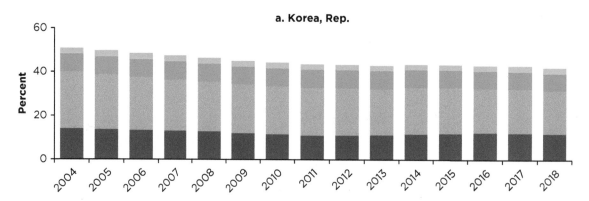

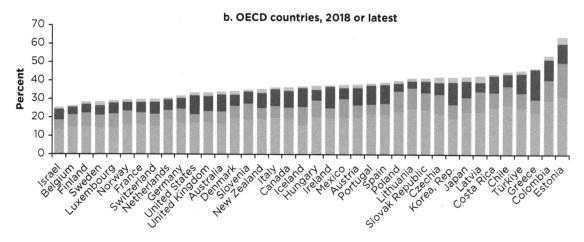

Source: STAN Industrial Database, OECD.
Note: OECD = Organisation for Economic Co-operation and Development.

BOX 2.2 Is Korea Capturing the Promise of Services-Led Growth?

The Republic of Korea is one of the best examples of manufacturing-led development. Its success in entering and moving up manufacturing value chains to pursue an export-led development path is considered a model for other countries. In contrast, Korea has not taken advantage of the increasing role of services in driving productivity growth and labor market changes.

As in most high-income countries, services are the dominant sector in Korea. Globally, employment shares in agriculture have declined and industry shares have been largely flat or declining slightly, while services have absorbed all the increase. Korea characterizes this pattern. While manufacturing receives much of the attention of policy makers, services are a bigger driver of structural change. Understanding the scope of the

Continued

BOX 2.2 Continued

service sector for productivity growth and job creation is important in shaping policy priorities to ensure that its potential is fully realized.

Labor productivity growth in services has matched labor productivity growth in industry in many regions since the 1990s (figure B2.2.1, panel a). East Asia and the Pacific (EAP) has enjoyed labor productivity growth rates in both industry and services that have been significantly higher than in other regions. Within EAP, Korea's particularly high rate of productivity growth in industry has enabled it to catch up and join the ranks of high-income countries. However, it has not performed as well in the service sector. Korea's rate of growth of value added in services has been half the EAP average and much lower than China's service sector productivity growth (figure B2.2.1, panel b).

The potential for services-led growth has expanded due to several factors. First, digital technologies are enabling greater economies of scale in services, particularly those that can be delivered remotely. Breaking the simultaneity of production and consumption of services means they can be traded, expanding the potential market for firms. Second, there is greater innovation and investment in intangible capital and automation, which can raise the productivity of workers in services, including that of low-skilled workers. Information and accounting apps and electronic transfers of funds can improve the quality of services and expand access to markets. Third, the increase in intersectoral linkages means that benefits can have multiplier effects that affect a larger set of firms and activities. The potential for spillovers has expanded through the "servicification" of manufacturing, agriculture, and other services.

FIGURE B2.2.1 Compound Annual Growth Rate of Value Added per Worker in the Service and Industry Sectors, 1991–2019

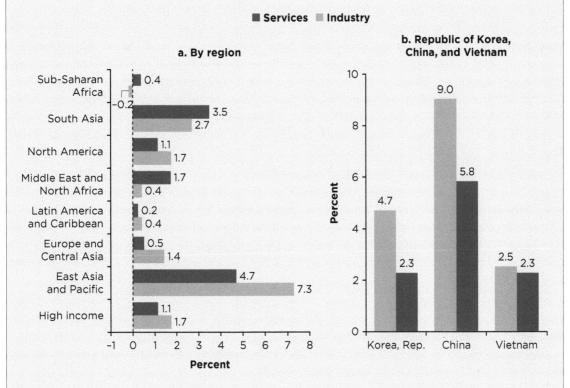

Source: Calculations based on data from World Development Indicators, World Bank (http://data.worldbank.org).

Continued

BOX 2.2 Continued

Developing countries that are still in the process of becoming industrialized can take advantage of opportunities to increase productivity in the service sector. For Korea, success in manufacturing increasingly depends on access to complementary services. Services represent an increasing share of value added in goods as inputs such as research and development and services embedded in goods (for example, apps on a phone) or after-sale services (for example, repair services).

To take advantage of these new opportunities for scale, innovation, and spillovers, actions in four policy areas are needed. One, governments can promote access to and adoption of new technologies. Two, governments can enhance the skills needed to use new technologies. Not everyone must have high-level digital skills. Rather, non-digital skills that complement automation, such as interpersonal skills, are growing in importance. The ability to be adaptable and manage change is also important. Three, governments can promote trade—making what is increasingly tradable actually traded. The agenda for services trade often involves easing domestic regulations and standards for sectors that restrict foreigners from investing or providing services. Four, governments can improve the degree of linkages between sectors. Given that Korea has a fairly high degree of intersectoral linkages, there remains potential to realize even greater productivity gains from opening up restrictions on services trade.

Source: Nayyar, Hallward-Driemeier, and Davis (2021).

Firm Dynamics

Korea's sustained rapid growth was driven by the strong performance of large manufacturing firms. In the early stages of its development, Korea's export promotion policies favored firms with large-scale production to achieve cost efficiency. With the rapid growth in scale during the 1980s, these large firms began to gain international competitiveness. The large firms played a central role in Korea's subsequent transition to a high-income economy and have driven growth throughout all three phases, although their relative shares have gradually declined. The value-added shares of large firms (300+ workers) were 65 percent of total value added in 1980, gradually declining to 52 percent in 2009, and have been stable since then (figure 2.20, panel a). The employment share of large firms was 53 percent in 1980 and subsequently declined to 29 percent in 2009 and 26 percent in 2019 (figure 2.20, panel b).

The significantly larger decline of the employment share compared to the value-added share reflects the improving labor productivity of the large firms. This has also resulted in a growing labor productivity gap between large and small firms. The ratio of the average labor productivity of large firms (300 or more workers) to small firms (10 to 299 workers) increased from 174 percent in 1980 to 265 percent in 2000, and further to 291 percent in 2019. The labor productivity of small firms was only 36 percent that of large firms in the manufacturing sector in 2019 (figure 2.20, panel c). The productivity gap between large firms and small and medium-size enterprises in Korea is one of the largest among OECD countries (OECD 2020).

Korea faces the structural challenge of having a large share of employment in low-productivity, small firms. Korea's employment share of small firms (1–49 workers) is the highest among OECD countries in the manufacturing sector and traditional service sectors, such as the wholesale and retail, accommodations, and food service sectors (figure 2.21). The dominance of low-productivity small firms in Korea's economy affects not only aggregate growth but also income inequality, as the growing productivity gap between small and large firms leads to a widening wage gap.

The transformation of Korea's industrial structure was achieved through the active entry, exit, and growth of firms. High rates of entry and exit were observed in fast-growing industries. During phase one (1990–97), when manufacturing shifted from light to capital-intensive industries, the entry rates were relatively high for capital-intensive industries such as machinery and equipment, electronic and electrical

FIGURE 2.20 **Performance of Manufacturing Firms, by Size, 1980–2019**

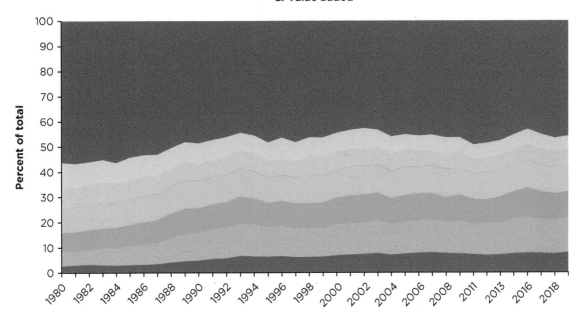

a. Value added

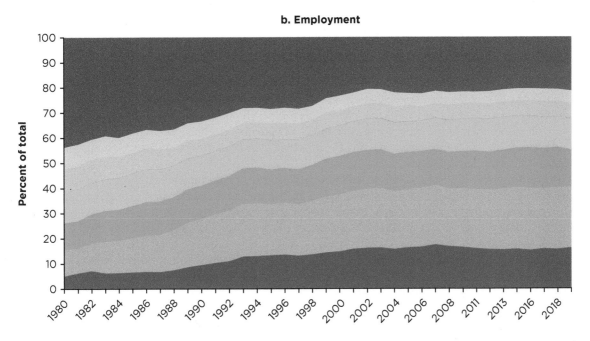

b. Employment

Continued

FIGURE 2.20 Continued

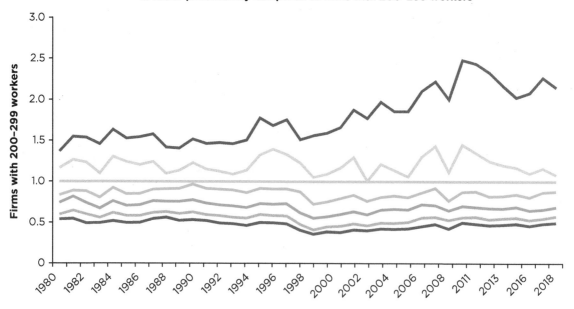

c. Labor productivity compared to firms with 200–299 workers

Source: Mining and Manufacturing Survey, Statistics Korea (https://kosis.kr).

equipment, motor vehicles, trailers, semitrailers, and chemicals. More than 30 percent of manufacturing plants in the late 1980s and early 1990s were new. Despite the relatively high exit rates, which are typically observed in growing industries, net entry rates (entries minus exits) were remarkably high in phase one. The net entry rates of capital-intensive industries steadily declined but remained relatively high until phase three (2009–present), reflecting the sustained growth of these industries through continuous upgrades of plants and products.

In contrast, the net entry rates declined more significantly in light industries. The entry rates for textiles were high in the late 1980s when the industry maintained a relatively high rate of growth. After the AFC, however, as the textiles industry shrank, the entry rates declined and the exit rates increased, leading to negative net entry rates. In food and beverages, the entry and exit rates have been consistently low since the late 1980s.

Investment rates were high in the fast-growing industries with high entry and exit rates. The investment rates in the electronic and electrical equipment and motor vehicles industries were very high, at over 20 percent in the late 1980s. In later years, the investment rates in these industries declined but remained higher than those in the textile and food industries.

TFP growth is an important source of economic growth. Productivity growth can result from between-firm reallocations of resources, among existing firms and through the entry and exit of firms, and from within-firm productivity growth. The "between" effect improves aggregate productivity by reallocating resources from less to more productive firms. The reallocation of resources can also occur through the entry of more productive firms and the exit of less productive firms. The "within" effect reflects improved productivity of existing firms, without accounting for the contributions from resource reallocation.

FIGURE 2.21 **Employment Shares, by Firm Size: Manufacturing and Selected Services across Countries**

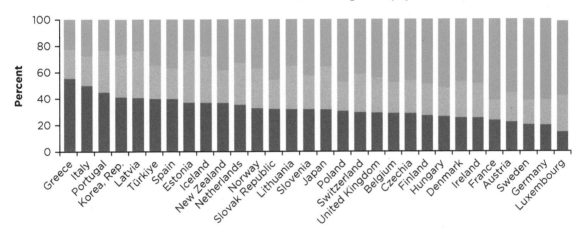

■ Small (1–49) ■ Medium (50–249) ■ Large (250+)

a. Share of labor in the manufacturing sector, by firm size

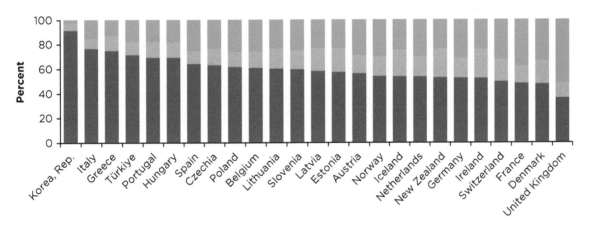

b. Share of labor in selected traditional service sectors, by firm size

Source: Structural and Demographic Business Statistics, Organisation for Economic Co-operation and Development, 2016, 2017 (https://stats.oecd.org).
Note: The selected traditional service sectors include the wholesale and retail, accommodations, and food service sectors.

Analysis of plant-level data[2] in Korea shows that TFP growth rates in manufacturing were relatively high in phase one (1990–97) and steadily declined in phases two (1998–2008) and three (2009–present) (figure 2.22). In addition, the analysis indicates that most of the TFP growth in the manufacturing industry has been due to the within effect of productivity growth in existing plants as opposed to the between effect or the effect of entry and exit (Lee 2020).[3] The between effect has been relatively small, accounting for only about 5 percent of total productivity growth. Firm entry and exit rates have been relatively high in Korea, but the net entry effect has accounted for only about 10 percent of total productivity growth.

TFP decomposition analysis of two-digit Standard Industrial Classification industries suggests that within-plant productivity growth is the most important source of total productivity growth for most industries.

FIGURE 2.22 TFP Growth Decomposition, 1991–2018

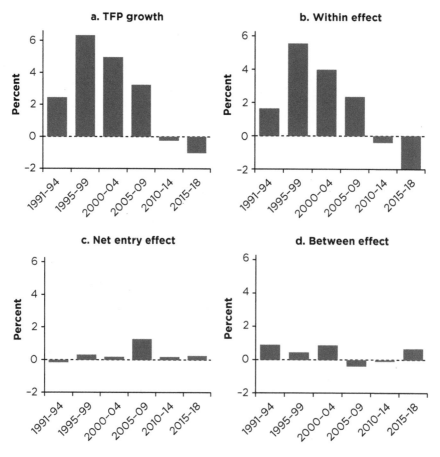

Source: Calculations based on data from the Mining and Manufacturing Survey, Statistics Korea (https://kosis.kr).
Note: TFP = total factor productivity.

The between effect played an important role in some industries, such as the food industries in the early 1990s, motor vehicles in the late 1990s, and electronics in the 2000s. However, in most industries, productivity growth was driven by the productivity growth of existing plants. Furthermore, productivity growth was uneven across industries. For example, productivity growth was exceptionally low in the chemicals industry in the early 1990s, reflecting the overinvestments in the earlier period as a result of the government-led heavy and chemical industries drive.

Analysis of the productivity decomposition indicates that the contribution of entry and exit to productivity growth has been relatively small in Korea, despite the relatively high rates of entry and exit. However, it would be misleading to conclude that new firm entries are not important sources of productivity growth. The productivity growth of a plant occurs in the early stages of the plant's life cycle, which would be measured as within-plant productivity growth. Therefore, assessing only the impact of firm (plant) entries would potentially underestimate the impact of new firms. Conditional on their survival, young plants in Korea show high rates of productivity and employment growth. In contrast, both productivity and employment growth rates decline significantly for older plants. Employment growth rates are negative for older plants (figure 2.23).

FIGURE 2.23 **Total Factor Productivity and Employment Growth, by Plant Age**

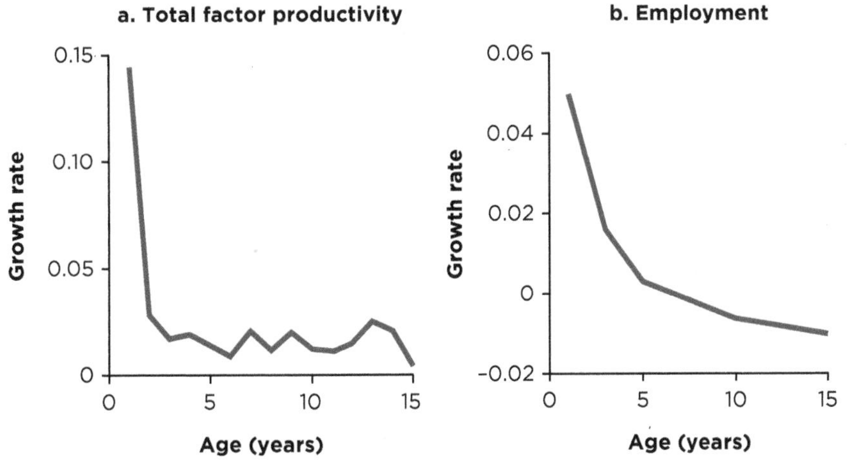

Source: Calculations based on data from the Mining and Manufacturing Survey, Statistics Korea (https://kosis.kr).

Active young manufacturing plants are critical for sustaining productivity growth in Korea. To account for the early growth effects of entrants, the within effect components of plants can be decomposed into the contributions of three age groups: 0 to 3 years, 4 to 7 years, and 8 or more years (figure 2.24). Young plants with fewer than 3 years accounted for about one-third of the contribution to productivity from the within effects in the 1990s and a slightly smaller share in the 2000s. These findings suggest that the rapid growth of entrants has been an important driver of productivity growth in phases one (1990 to AFC) and two (AFC to GFC). After the GFC, however, the contribution of young plants dramatically declined, leading to the substantial slowdown in productivity growth.

TFP growth in Korea fell in phase three (post-GFC). The slowdown in TFP growth has been part of a global phenomenon observed across countries. Recent studies find that the decline in firm dynamism and the lack of startups are important challenges facing the United States after the GFC (for example, Decker et al. 2016). In Korea, the rates of job creation and destruction have declined since the mid-2000s, although net job creation rates did not decline (Choi and Kim 2019). The entry rates of startups in Korea have declined since the GFC but remain relatively high. However, new entrants have suffered from low survival rates.

The decline in productivity growth has been pronounced in young plants. Lower contributions from both net entries and existing young plants contributed to the decline in young plants' productivity growth, more so the latter compared to the former (Kim 2017) (table 2.1). The productivity growth of young plants has been declining since the GFC, resulting in the declining contribution of young plants to within-plant productivity growth. This is important because in Korea, young plants have had an outsized impact on productivity growth, accounting for nearly half of aggregate productivity growth although their value-added share has been on average only about 15 percent. The sharp decline in the productivity growth of young plants in high-technology industries is particularly worrisome (Kim 2017; Lee, Kim, and Park 2020) (figure 2.25).

The productivity slowdown in the early 2010s was not limited to young plants. Within-plant productivity growth declined for older plants as well (Lee, Kim, and Park 2020). Both young and old plants (8 years and older) experienced a dramatic decline in productivity growth after 2011 (figure 2.26).

The within-plant productivity growth slowdown was likely driven by the productivity slowdown of large, export oriented firms, due to the decline in global trade since the GFC. Overall, productivity

FIGURE 2.24 **Productivity Decomposition of Within Effects, by Plant Age, 1991–2018**

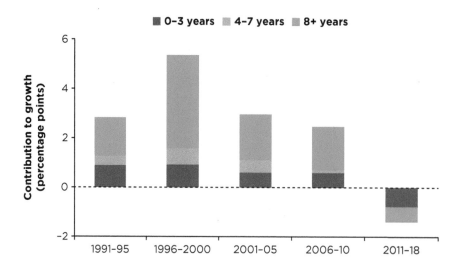

Source: Calculations based on data from the Mining and Manufacturing Survey, Statistics Korea (https://kosis.kr).

TABLE 2.1 **Young Plants' Effects on Productivity Growth, 1995–2013 (percent)**

Period	Mean (standard deviation)		
	All	Continuing	Net entrants
1995–2013	2.8 (1.5)	1.8 (1.3)	1.0 (0.7)
1995–2004	3.2 (1.8)	2.3 (1.5)	0.9 (0.6)
2004–13	2.3 (1.1)	1.3 (0.8)	1.0 (0.8)
2011–13	0.9 (0.2)	0.7 (0.1)	0.2 (0.1)

Source: Kim 2017.

growth is positively correlated with export growth in Korea (Kim, Lee, and Park 2020) (figure 2.27). Since the GFC, the decline in export growth has greatly impacted large plants that are heavily involved in export activities.

Korea's productivity growth has been accompanied by substantial productivity dispersion (Kim, Oh, and Shin 2017; Lee 2020). Based on plant-level data from the Mining and Manufacturing Survey, Statistics Korea, the estimated standard deviation of log revenue-based TFP (TFPR) for all manufacturing plants increased steadily, from 0.664 in 1991–95 to 0.83 in 2011–16 (Lee 2020). An increase in the dispersion of TFPR is observed across industries (table 2.2). In textiles, the standard deviation of log TFPR increased from 0.620 in the early 1900s to 0.884 in the mid-2010s, and in electronics, it increased from 0.757 to 1.100. Based on data from a survey of manufacturing plants in Korea from 1991 to 1998, research shows that productivity dispersion is significant in both capital and labor, with the former three times greater than the latter (Virgiliu and Yi 2009).

A large dispersion in productivity suggests that there is considerable room for improving efficiency, given that productivity dispersion is considered a measure of resource misallocation. The degree of allocative efficiency can be measured by comparing current output to hypothetical output in the absence of distortions when resources are optimally allocated to equalize the marginal

FIGURE 2.25 Productivity Decomposition into Different Tech Sectors, 1995–2013

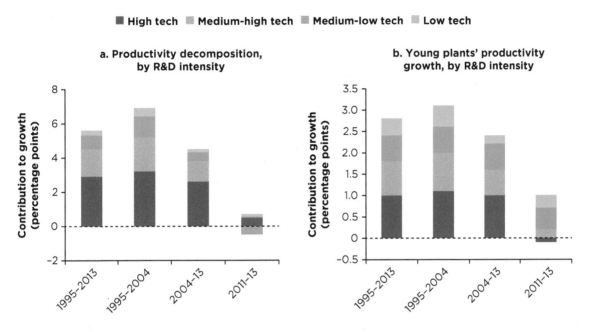

Source: Calculations based on data from Kim 2017.
Note: The contributions to growth have been averaged over different time frames, as specified on the x axis. R&D = research and development.

FIGURE 2.26 Average TFP Growth of Young Plants and Productivity Decomposition by Age, 1991–2018

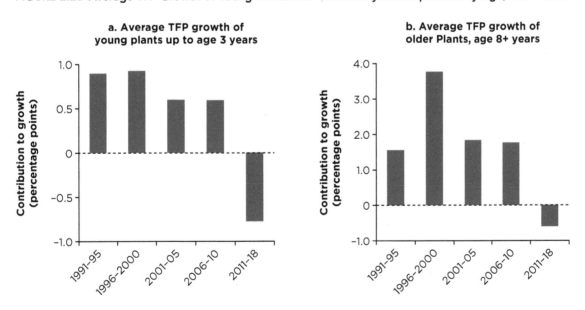

Source: Calculations based on data from the Mining and Manufacturing Survey, Statistics Korea (https://kosis.kr).
Note: TFP = total factor productivity.

FIGURE 2.27 **Productivity and Export Growth in Manufacturing, 2000–17**

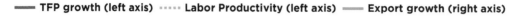

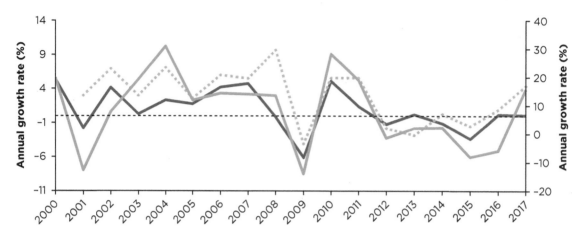

Source: Kim, Lee, and Park 2020.

TABLE 2.2 **Evolution of TFPR Dispersion, 1986–2016**

Sector	Standard deviation of log TFPR					
	1986–90	1991–95	1996–2000	2001–05	2006–10	2011–16
Manufacturing	0.696	0.664	0.714	0.759	0.830	0.830
Textiles and leather	0.653	0.620	0.668	0.743	0.847	0.884
Chemical products	0.705	0.671	0.687	0.717	0.784	0.793
Electronic and electrical equipment	0.797	0.757	0.851	1.001	1.098	1.100
Transportation equipment	0.569	0.565	0.649	0.686	0.825	0.900

Source: Lee 2020.
Note: TFPR = revenue-based total factor productivity.

productivity of firms (Hsieh and Klenow 2009). Using this approach, Korea's allocative efficiency from 1990 to 2012 was lower than that of the United States but similar to that of Japan and higher than that of China (Oh 2015).

The relatively high firm productivity dispersion is consistent with the finding that between-firm reallocation of resources in Korea have made relatively small contributions to overall productivity growth. It indicates that resource allocation has been less than efficient. In addition, empirical analysis reveals that the economy has been in a state of overinvestment, and the interindustry allocation of capital and land has been biased toward industry, compared to efficient levels (Jeong 2020).

Inclusive Growth

Korea's remarkable growth performance over the past several decades has been accompanied by a dramatic reduction in poverty, and equity and inclusivity have become increasingly important to public policies.

Korea's rapid economic growth has resulted in a continuous and significant reduction in poverty. At the beginning of its modern development period, Korea was among the poorest countries in the world. The government carried out major land reforms in the 1940s and 1950s, which helped equalize the distribution of land. At the time, land was the major asset in the economy, given that 71 percent of the population were in the agriculture sector (Kim 2006) and much of the country's industrial assets had been destroyed by the Korean War (1950–53). Subsequently, Korea's success in reducing poverty was due to its sustained and rapid growth, resulting in rising income and welfare gains that were broadly distributed. Korea focused on economic growth and expansion of public education as the main drivers of poverty reduction and inclusive growth.

Korea has combined rapid growth and poverty reduction with relatively moderate levels of inequality,[4] thereby achieving relatively inclusive development. However, the estimated Gini index for Korea increased from the AFC to the GFC (figure 2.28).[5] Widening wage disparities due to diverging performance between small and large firms may have contributed to worsening inequality. In addition, rising female labor participation rates led to a growing number of double-income households, which could have contributed to the worsening of household income inequality due to the widening disparity between single-income and double-income households.

However, income inequality has been improving since the GFC, reversing the earlier trend. The estimated decline in the Gini index is much greater for estimates based on disposable income than for market income. The gap between the disposable and market income Gini indexes has visibly widened since 2010, reflecting the expansion of the government's income redistribution policies. Currently, Korea's income inequality is higher than the OECD average, but it is in line with the level of inequality in lower-income OECD countries. Most of the lower-income countries with income inequality lower than Korea's are former centrally planned, socialist countries.

A key driver of inequality has been the large productivity gaps between large and small firms, which have led to large wage gaps (figures 2.29 and 2.30). The average wage in establishments with 5–9 workers is currently only 65 percent of the average wage in establishments with 300–499 workers. Wage gaps began to widen in the 1990s and only recently stopped widening. Workers in large firms tend to enjoy not only higher earnings, but also better working conditions and more generous benefits. Employees in large firms have little difficulty taking maternity and childcare leaves (figure 2.31). In contrast, employees in small firms, which account for the largest share of employment, face serious challenges even though such leaves are guaranteed by law.

The difficulty of taking maternity and childcare leaves among smaller firms could be one of the reasons for the significantly lower employment-to-population ratio of women of childbearing age (30–44 years) compared to other age groups (figure 2.32). As a result, the employment ratio of working-age (25–54) women in Korea is significantly lower than in most OECD countries (figure 2.33). It appears that many women in Korea have reduced their participation in the labor market, finding it difficult to balance work and childcare responsibilities. Others are postponing or forgoing childbearing, as indicated by Korea's low fertility rate, which is currently the lowest in the world (figure 2.34). The low fertility rate and longer life expectancy are

FIGURE 2.28 **Gini Coefficients, 1990–2016**

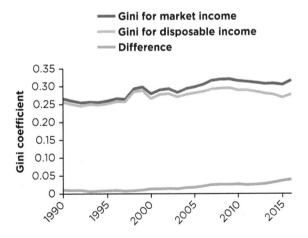

Source: Statistics Korea (https://kosis.kr).
Note: The data are for urban households with two or more members.

FIGURE 2.29 **Wage, by Establishment Size, 1980–2019**

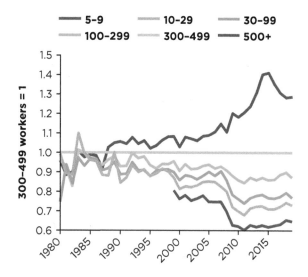

Sources: Ministry of Employment and Labor, Survey of Working Conditions by Employment Type; data from Statistics Korea (https://kosis.kr).

driving Korea's rapid population aging (figure 2.35). Creating jobs with better working conditions would help to ease female labor market participation, increase the fertility rate, and delay population aging.

Unfortunately, jobs in large enterprises, which often have better benefits and working conditions, are becoming increasingly scarce. The share of workers in establishments with 300 or more workers fell from 45 percent in 1980 to 22 percent in 2016. The share of workers in enterprises with 250 or more workers stands at 27 percent, which is lower than in most OECD countries (59 percent in France, 55 percent in Germany, and 44 percent in the United Kingdom). The decline in employment in large firms has been accompanied by rising automation in Korea's industries. In 2020, Korea had one of the highest industrial robot densities in manufacturing in the world. Increasingly, jobs are concentrated in high-skilled occupations or high-technology sectors.

With rapid aging, a major concern has been the high rate of relative poverty among the elderly (65 years and older) (figure 2.36), due to a combination of factors. The elderly in Korea have a relatively low level of educational attainment, which tends to limit earnings. Approximately 70 percent of the younger age group (25–34 years) has a college diploma, compared to approximately 25 percent of the older age group (55–64 years). Relatively low

FIGURE 2.30 **Labor Productivity of Small and Medium-Size Manufacturing Firms Relative to Large Firms, OECD Countries, 2017 or Most Recent Year**

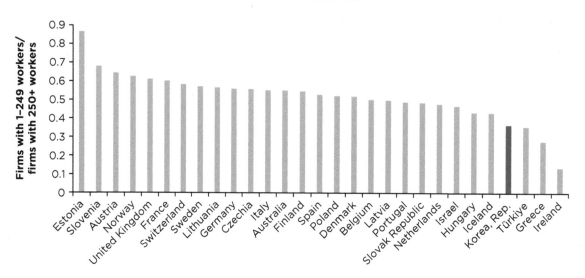

Source: Structural and Demographic Business Statistics Dataset, OECD (https://stats.oecd.org).
Note: OECD = Organisation for Economic Co-operation and Development.

FIGURE 2.31 **Use of Maternity and Childcare Leaves, by Firm Size, 2018**

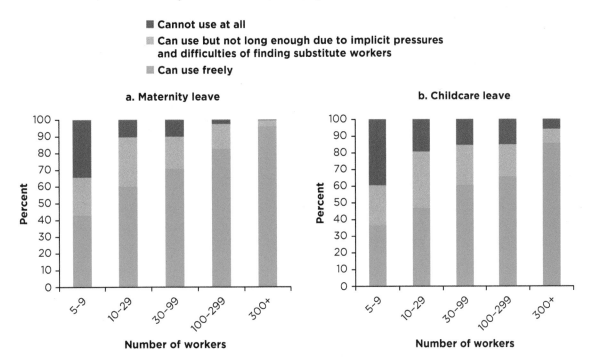

Source: Republic of Korea, MOEL 2019.

earnings due to lower educational attainment have made it difficult for the elderly to accumulate the necessary retirement savings. As a result, the elderly are more likely to have to work into retirement age in relatively low earning occupations, to avoid poverty.

The prevalence of poverty among the elderly also reflects the relatively underdeveloped public pension programs. The National Pension Scheme was launched in 1988, much later than in other advanced countries, and it still covers only approximately 70 percent of employees. Often excluded are the self-employed, who account for about a quarter of total employment and for whom participation in the scheme is not mandatory, and also those employed in the informal sector. Those without sufficient pension benefits are partly assisted by the National Basic Livelihood Security Program and the National Basic Old-Age Pension.

FIGURE 2.32 **Employment-to-Population Ratio, by Sex and Age, Republic of Korea, 2020**

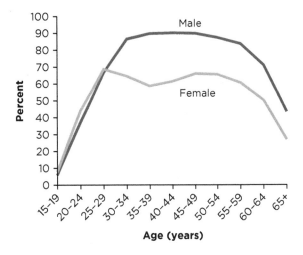

Source: Statistics Korea (https://kosis.kr).

FIGURE 2.33 **Employment-to-Population Ratio for Prime Working-Age (25–54) Women, OECD Countries, 2019**

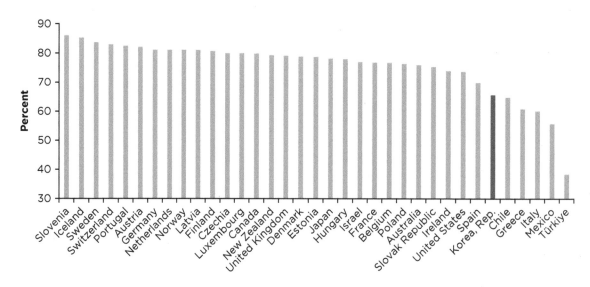

Source: OECD (https://stats.oecd.org).
Note: OECD = Organisation for Economic Co-operation and Development.

FIGURE 2.34 **Total Fertility Rate and GDP per Capita across Countries, 2017**

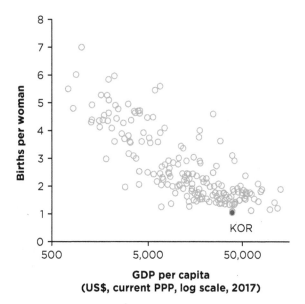

Source: World Development Indicators, World Bank (https://data.worldbank.org).
Note: GDP = gross domestic product; PPP = purchasing power parity.

FIGURE 2.35 **Share of the Elderly (65 years and older) in the Population, 1950–2060**

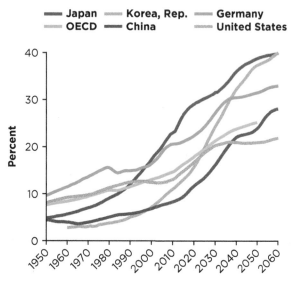

Source: OECD (https://stats.oecd.org).
Note: Values from 2023 to 2060 are projections. OECD = Organisation for Economic Co-operation and Development.

FIGURE 2.36 **Relative Poverty in the OECD Area, 2018 or Most Recent Year**

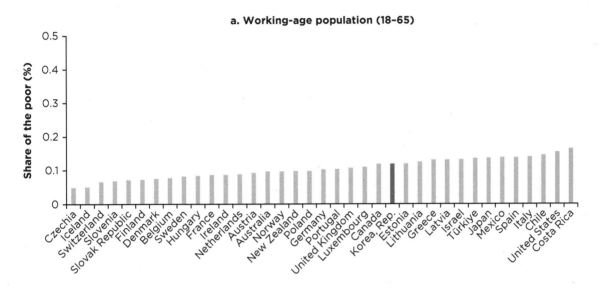

a. Working-age population (18–65)

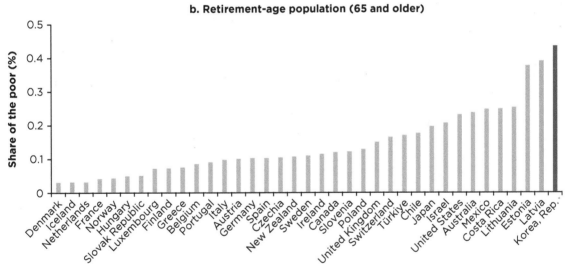

b. Retirement-age population (65 and older)

Source: OECD (https://stats.oecd.org).
Note: The values are the poverty rate after taxes and transfers. The poverty line is 50 percent of the median income. OECD = Organisation for Economic Co-operation and Development.

Green, Sustainable Growth

As Korea reached higher income levels, the deterioration of the environment became a greater national priority. At lower levels of development, environmental sustainability was not a major national policy goal, as attention to environmental concerns was generally seen as an obstacle to rapid economic development. Over time, however, the government placed greater emphasis on the environment. Korea was the first OECD country to adopt a comprehensive green growth strategy in 2008 (Kamal-Chaoui et al. 2011) and introduced the Green New Deal in 2020. Both policies were adopted in the aftermath of crises, the

GFC and the COVID-19 pandemic, respectively. These strategies were intended to support economic recovery and growth with environmental sustainability, with the aim of decoupling growth from carbon emissions and reducing pollution and excessive use of natural resources.

The green growth strategy was seen as a new growth strategy rather than an environmental solution when it was introduced in 2008. The key policy objectives were economic growth and job creation by enhancing the global competitiveness of green industries and transitioning toward a low-carbon economy. The government's contention was that Korea needed to transform its economy from its current carbon-intensive model to a low-carbon growth model to sustain economic growth. However, public support for green growth was relatively weak, due to concerns about whether the decoupling of carbon emissions from growth would be possible without harming growth. Korea's economic growth had been based on the carbon-intensive manufacturing sector, and there were concerns that the low-carbon transition would hamper the international competitiveness of the sector.

Despite the skepticism, green growth was positioned as a national priority. The Presidential Committee on Green Growth was established in 2009 as an advisory committee to the president on the national agenda of green growth, which developed into the 2050 Carbon Neutral Green Growth Committee in 2022. The Presidential Committee on Green Growth was provided the mandate to legislate new laws, propose policy measures to support green projects in the public and private sectors, and coordinate and mediate disagreements among stakeholders. The Framework Act on Low Carbon Green Growth (2010) introduced detailed goals for low-carbon green growth, the institutional framework, and mitigation and adaptation policies, including on the emissions reduction target management system, the emissions trading scheme, green transport systems, low-carbon green buildings, green financing, promotion of a green lifestyle, and green innovation and R&D investments. The Framework Act's long-term goals were to be translated into actionable "Five-Year Green Growth Plans," to be formulated every five years (GGGI 2016).

Korea has gradually started to decouple GDP growth from carbon emissions. Korea's average annual growth of GDP and carbon dioxide emissions from fuel combustion were 3.3 and 1.6 percent, respectively, in 2010–19 (figure 2.37). However, in comparison, during the same period, the United States and Japan reduced their annual emissions by 1.3 and 0.7 percent, respectively. In 2018, Korea accounted for 1.86 percent of the total carbon emissions in the world, and it was the sixth largest carbon emitter and the fifteenth largest per capita emitter (Stangarone 2020; World Bank 2022). The contribution of Korea's manufacturing sector to GDP has been maintained at about 25 percent, but manufacturing's share of carbon emissions has been smaller and decreasing over time (figure 2.38). Korea's manufacturing sector exhibited some of the highest carbon intensity levels in the world in 2005, but its carbon intensity fell by 23.2 percent between 2010 and 2019.

A strong price signal is critical for a successful green transition. Setting an appropriate carbon price would motivate investors to participate actively in the low-carbon transition. Korea's emissions trading system (KETS) provides the market in Korea for carbon pricing. It is one of the earliest and largest carbon emissions trading schemes outside the United States and the European Union. The volume of transactions on KETS has increased since the establishment of the carbon emissions trading market in 2015. The total volume of allowances traded in 2019 was ₩1,083 billion (38 million tons), more than 17 times the 2015 volume of ₩62.5 billion (5.7 million tons). However, KETS suffered from low carbon market liquidity, reflecting the relatively low number of participants. Carbon pricing has also continued to increase, although it dropped sharply during the COVID-19 pandemic. A large share of greenhouse gas emissions in the manufacturing sector has been under KETS carbon pricing. The carbon intensity of energy use in the manufacturing sector has declined only slightly, but that of KETS participants in the manufacturing sector declined significantly from 2015 to 2017 (figures 2.38 and 2.39).

Korea's second major green initiative, the Korean Green New Deal, was announced in July 2020. It was a part of the Korean New Deal, a post-COVID-19 pandemic recovery plan. Growing international pressure to reduce greenhouse gas emissions to net-zero levels by 2050, such as the influential Intergovernmental

FIGURE 2.37 Greenhouse Gas Emissions, GDP, and Carbon Intensity, 1990–2019

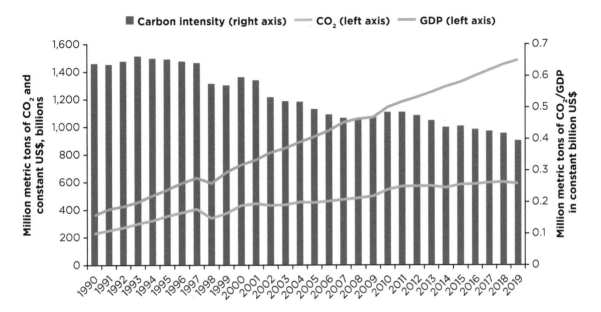

Sources: For emissions from combustion, IEA 2021; World Development Indicators, World Bank (2005–20) (https://data.worldbank.org); for GDP, World Bank data.
Note: GDP = gross domestic product; CO_2 = carbon dioxide.

FIGURE 2.38 Share of Manufacturing Carbon Emissions and GDP, 2005–19

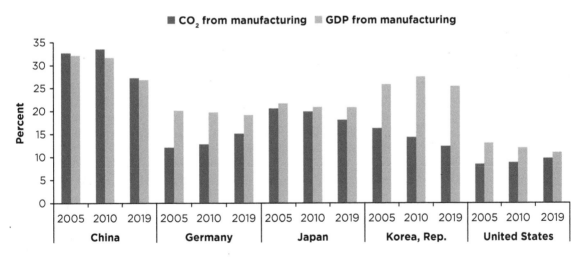

Sources: IEA, 2021; World Development Indicators, World Bank (2005–20) (https://data.worldbank.org).
Note: CO_2 = carbon dioxide; GDP = gross domestic product.

FIGURE 2.39 **Annual Growth Rate of the Carbon Intensity of Energy Use, by Manufacturing Sector**

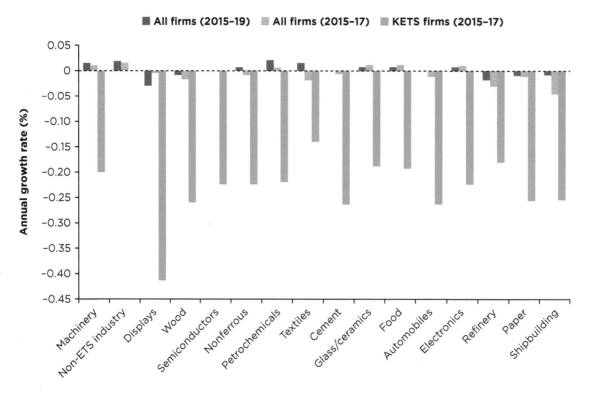

Sources: Korea Energy Agency; NETIS database (2015–19); National GHG Inventory data, Greenhouse Gas Inventory and Research Center (2015–17).
Note: ETS = emissions trading system; GHG = greenhouse gas; KETS = Korea's emissions trading system.

Panel on Climate Change Special Report (IPCC 2019), played an important role in pushing for the Green New Deal. Similar to the green growth strategy of 2008, the Green New Deal was framed as a growth strategy to create 1.9 million jobs by 2025. Low carbonization, eco-compatibility, and creation of high-quality jobs were viewed as critical for the country's competitiveness and sustainability. The Green New Deal highlighted the urban, energy, and industrial sectors. In October 2020, the government increased the country's 2030 Nationally Determined Contribution target from a 24.4 percent reduction by 2030 compared to the 2017 level of emissions to 40 percent of the 2018 level and net carbon neutrality by 2050. This would be achieved through five key transitions, in clean power and hydrogen fuel, energy efficiency, carbon removal and utilization technologies, circular economy for industrial sustainability, and carbon sink technology.

The Green New Deal was revised to the Green New Deal 2.0 a year later, with increased investment and job creation goals. The social and information infrastructure project for carbon neutrality was adopted, which included, for example, the development of environmental impact assessment matrixes, carbon and waste footprints, and climate-related financial information disclosure systems. The Framework Act has evolved into the Climate Change Response Act, which was ratified in August 2021, making Korea the 14th country in the world to legislate a carbon neutrality act (Republic of Korea, MOE 2021). The most significant change in the Green New Deal 2.0 was the addition of the Human New Deal as the third pillar, which called for enhancing the social safety net, investing in human capital, and reducing inequality in education and child and elderly care. The top priority of the Human New Deal was the creation of high-quality jobs. The government allocated ₩61 trillion to the Green New Deal, ₩50 trillion to the Human New Deal, and ₩49 trillion to the Digital New Deal up to 2025.

Private sector engagement in investment and innovation for the green transition is an essential part of a successful green transition (OECD 2021). Korea's National Pension Fund announced its commitment to cut investments in new coal power plants at home and abroad. The manufacturing sector has committed to environmental, social, and governance goals, such as RE100, a global corporate initiative committing to 100 percent renewable electricity (Climate Group 2022).

Conclusions and Implications for Developing Countries

Korea's successful transition from a middle- to high-income economy was built on previous decades of high levels of investments in physical and human capital and promotion of manufacturing exports by large conglomerates. The stock of physical and human capital rapidly reached OECD levels, and the resulting declining marginal returns to investments meant that the search for productivity-led new drivers of growth increasingly became an economic imperative. In response, the government actively promoted the transition to more capital-, technology-, and R&D-intensive manufacturing, which was critical for Korea's transition to a high-income economy and for sustaining its growth rates above the OECD average. Since the GFC, the declining contribution of TFP growth has been a concern. This will need to be addressed for Korea to continue to converge to the productivity levels of the frontier OECD countries.

Korea's experience has five major implications for developing countries. One, sustained investments in physical and human capital are essential for growth. In the earlier decades, Korea's growth into a middle-income economy was driven by investments in physical and human capital that complemented productivity growth. Even after Korea became a high-income country, physical and human capital investments remained critical contributors to growth.

Two, Korea used the AFC as an opportunity to pursue major structural reforms of the economy. The AFC exposed the shortcomings of Korea's growth model and led to significant market reforms to promote market competition and reorient industrial policies from the promotion of industries and firms to the promotion of innovation and technology. These reforms helped Korea to initiate the transition from input-led to productivity-led growth. Overall growth slowed down after the AFC, but contributions from both productivity improvements and investments kept Korea's growth above that of OECD countries and sustained the convergence of its labor productivity to the levels of OECD countries. Moreover, TFP growth increased after major reforms were carried out in response to the AFC, indicating that reforms to promote market competition and innovation and technology helped to facilitate the transition to a more productivity-led growth paradigm.

Three, Korea prioritized the promotion of startups. Growth has been led by large manufacturing exporting firms, which become more productive and more intensive in capital and high technologies. Since the GFC, the overall slowdown in global trade led to the declining performance of key capital-intensive industries, which were export oriented. Growth contributions from capital and TFP have declined further, resulting in a further decline in overall growth. TFP growth declined to around zero based on estimates from macroeconomic and enterprise data. This reflected a substantial weakening of the contribution of within-firm productivity growth of young firms and the continued minimal contribution of the between-firm productivity growth. The latter raises concerns about lack of allocative efficiency.

Four, Korea's successful development was based on manufacturing exports. However, developing countries will need to look for opportunities to leverage growth through both manufacturing and services, given that going forward, opportunities for developing countries to leverage manufacturing exports may be more limited. Labor productivity growth in services has matched the labor productivity growth in industry in many regions since the 1990s. The potential for services-led growth has expanded due to digital technologies and innovations, which have raised the quality and expanded the markets and tradability of services. The expanded potential is also due to greater intersectoral linkages between manufacturing and services ("servicification of manufacturing"). Korea's future growth will equally need to rely more on stimulating productivity growth in the service sector. The country's continued success in manufacturing will increasingly depend on access to complementary services.

Five, Korea's remarkable growth performance over the past several decades has been accompanied by a dramatic reduction in poverty. Korea has combined rapid growth and poverty reduction with relatively moderate levels of inequality, thus resulting in relatively inclusive development. Inequality worsened from the AFC to the GFC, but since then, it has been declining, supported by the expansion of welfare programs. Equity and inclusivity have become increasingly important for public policies. The major land reforms in the 1960s helped equalize the distribution of assets. Subsequently, Korea focused on economic growth and expansion of public education as the main drivers of poverty reduction and inclusive growth. They have been complemented by a major expansion of the government's income redistribution policies since the AFC, which have helped increase the disposable income of the poor.

Notes

1. In calculating gross national income (GNI—formerly referred to as GNP) in U.S. dollars for certain operational and analytical purposes, the World Bank uses the Atlas conversion factor instead of simple exchange rates. See https://datahelpdesk.worldbank.org/knowledgebase/articles/378832-what-is-the-world-bank-atlas-method.

2. Korea lacks enterprise surveys that go back to the earlier years. However, historical plant-level data are available that can be used to carry out plant-level analysis of TFP growth.

3. Lee (2020) follows Foster, Haltiwanger, and Krizan (2001) in the decomposition. In the study, plant-level productivities are estimated using the generalized method of moments estimation developed by Wooldridge (2009). Using the estimated elasticity of each factor at the three-digit industry level, the TFP index for plant j is computed as follows:

$$lntfp_{jt} = lnY_{jt} - \alpha_l lnL_{jt} - \alpha_m lnM_{jt} - \alpha_k lnK_{jt}$$

where Y_{jt} is real gross output, L_{jt} is labor input (employment), M_{jt} is real materials, and K_{jt} is real capital stock. Real gross output is measured as the total value of sales, adjusted for changes in inventories. The two-digit industry-specific deflator from the Bank of Korea was used.

4. Korea's level of inequality has been difficult to verify for the early years of development due to the lack of comprehensive household income data.

5. There are alternative series of household income Gini indexes due to differences in sample and time period coverages. This is because the household income survey (HS1) has expanded its sample coverage over time. The samples for household income survey HS1 were limited to city households with two or more persons until 2006. In 2006, the sample was expanded to all households in all regions. A new household income survey (HS2) was introduced in 2011 to correct for the underrepresentation of high-income households.

References

Adler, G., R. Duval, D. Furceri, S. Kilic Celik, K. Koloskova, and M. Poplawski-Ribeiro. 2017. "Gone with the Headwinds: Global Productivity." IMF Staff Discussion Note 17/04, International Monetary Fund, Washington, DC.

Aghion, P., S. Guriev, and K. Jo. 2021. "Chaebols and Firm Dynamics in Korea." *Economic Policy* 36 (108): 593–626.

Anzoategui, D., D. Comin, M. Gertler, and J. Martinez. 2019. "Endogenous Technology Adoption and R&D as Sources of Business Cycle Persistence." *American Economic Journal: Macroeconomics* 11 (3): 67–110.

Baek C., Y. Kim, and H. Kwon. 2009. "Productivity Growth and Competition across the Asian Financial Crisis: Evidence from Korean Manufacturing Firms." Working Paper Series 2009-12, Center for Economic Institutions, Tokyo, Japan.

Bosworth, B., and S. M. Collins. 2008. "Accounting for Growth: Comparing China and India." *Journal of Economic Perspectives* 22 (1): 45–66.

Choi, H., S. C. Jung, and S. Kim. 2017. "The Effect of Restructuring on Labor Reallocation and Productivity Growth: An Estimation for Korea." KIEP Working Paper 17-04, Korea Institute for International Economic Policy, Sejong City, Republic of Korea.

Choi, K., and J. Kim. 2019. "Decline of Business Growth Dynamism." *Journal of Korean Association of Applied Economics* 21 (4): 5–44.

Climate Group. 2022. "RE100." https://www.there100.org.

Decker, R., J. Haltiwanger, R. Jarmin, and J. Miranda. 2016. "Declining Business Dynamism: What We Know and the Way Forward." *American Economic Review* 106 (5): 203–07.

Dieppe, A., S. Kilic-Celik, and G. Kindberg-Hanlon. 2020. "Global Productivity Trends." In *Global Productivity: Trends, Drivers, and Policies*, edited by A. Dieppe, 49–75. Washington, DC: World Bank.

Eichengreen, B. 2015. "Secular Stagnation: The Long View." *American Economic Review* 105 (5): 66–70.

Foster, L., J. Haltiwanger, and C. Krizan. 2001. "Aggregate Productivity Growth: Lessons from Microeconomic Evidence." In *New Developments in Productivity Analysis*, edited by C. R. Hulten, E. R. Dean, and M. J. Harper, 303–72. University of Chicago Press.

GGGI (Global Green Growth Institute). 2016. "Korea's Green Growth Experience: Process, Outcomes and Lessons Learned." GGGI, Seoul, Republic of Korea. https://gggi.org/report/koreas-green-growth-experienceprocess-outcomes-and-lessons-learned/.

Gopinath, G., Ş. Kalemli-Özcan, L. Karabarbounis, and C. Villegas-Sanchez. 2017. "Capital Allocation and Productivity in South Europe." *Quarterly Journal of Economics* 132 (4): 1915–67.

Haltiwanger, J., S. Scarpetta, and H. Schweiger. 2014. "Cross Country Differences in Job Reallocation: The Role of Industry, Firm Size and Regulations." *Labour Economics* 26 (January): 11–25.

Hsieh, C.-T., and P. J. Klenow. 2009. "Misallocation and Manufacturing TFP in China and India." *Quarterly Journal of Economics* 124 (4): 1403–48.

Hur, J., J. Lee, and H.-J. Hyun. 2013. "Correlation between Sales of Foreign Affiliates and Productivity of Multinational Firms: Evidence from Korean Firm-Level Data." *East Asian Economic Review* 17 (3): 261–79. https://dx.doi.org/10.11644/KIEP.JEAI.2013.17.3.266.

IEA (International Energy Agency). 2021. *Global Energy Review: CO_2 Emissions in 2021*. Fuel Combustion (2021 Highlights). https://www.iea.org/data-and-statistics/data-product/global-energy-review-co2-emissions-in-2021.

IPCC (Intergovernmental Panel on Climate Change). 2019. "Global Warming of 1.5°C. IPCC Special Report." IPCC, Geneva. https://www.ipcc.ch/sr15/download/.

Jeong, H. 2020. "Productivity Growth and Efficiency Dynamics of Korean Structural Transformation." Policy Research Working Paper 9285, World Bank, Washington, DC.

Jorgenson, D. W., M. S. Ho, and K. J. Stiroh. 2008. "A Retrospective Look at the U.S. Productivity Growth Resurgence." *Journal of Economic Perspectives* 22 (1): 3–24.

Jung, H.-J., K.-Y. Na, and C.-H. Yoon. 2013. "The Role of ICT in Korea's Economic Growth: Productivity Changes across Industries since the 1990s." *Telecommunications Policy* 37: 292–310.

Kamal-Chaoui, L., F. Grazi, J. Joo, and M. Plouin. 2011. "The Implementation of the Korean Green Growth Strategy in Urban Areas." OECD Regional Development Working Papers 2011/02, OECD Publishing, Paris. http://dx.doi.org/10.1787/5kg8bf4l4lvg-en.

Kim, I. Y. 2006. "Deconstructing the Myth about Land Reform." In *Reexamining Korea's History in the Period around Its Liberation*, edited by J. H. Park, C. Kim, I. Y. Kim, and Y. H. Rhee, 295–344. Seoul, Republic of Korea: Chaeksesang.

Kim, J. I. 2004. "Information Technology and Firm Performance in Korea." In *Growth and Productivity in East Asia*, vol. 13, edited by T. Ito and A. Rose, 327–49. University of Chicago Press.

Kim, M. 2017. "Aggregate Productivity Growth in Korean Manufacturing." *KDI Journal of Economic Policy* 39 (4): 1–23.

Kim, M., M. Lee, and Y. Shin. 2021. "The Plant-Level View of an Industrial Policy: The Korean Heavy Industry Drive of 1973." Working Paper No. w29252, National Bureau of Economic Research, Cambridge, MA.

Kim, M., J. Oh, and Y. Shin. 2017. "Misallocation and Manufacturing TFP in Korea, 1982–2007." *Federal Reserve Bank of St. Louis Review* 99 (2): 233–44.

Lee, Y. 2020. "Long-Term Shifts in Korean Manufacturing and Plant-Level Productivity Dynamics." Policy Research Working Paper 9279, World Bank, Washington, DC.

Lee, Y., W. Kim, and J. Park. 2020. "Export and Productivity: An Analysis of Plant-level Data." Economic Research Institute (82-2-759-5396). https://www.bok.or.kr/imerEng/bbs/B0000196/view.do.

McMillan, M., D. Rodrik, and C. Sepulveda. 2017. "Structural Change, Fundamentals and Growth: A Framework and Case Studies." NBER Working Paper 23378, National Bureau of Economic Research, Cambridge, MA.

Nayyar, G., M. Hallward-Driemeier, and E. Davis. 2021. *At Your Service? The Promise of Services-Led Development*. Washington, DC: World Bank.

OECD (Organisation for Economic Co-operation and Development). 2020. "OECD Economic Surveys: Korea 2020." OECD, Paris.

OECD (Organisation for Economic Co-operation and Development). 2021. "Private Sector Engagement to Address Climate Change and Promote Green Growth." Private Sector Peer Learning Policy Brief 4, OECD, Paris (accessed August 22, 2021), https://www.oecd.org/dac/peer-reviews/Policy-Brief-4-Private-Sector-Engagement-to-Address-Climate-Change-and-Promote-Green-Growth.pdf.

Oh, J. 2015. "Misallocation between Manufacturing Plants in Korea: Trends and International Comparison." KDI Feature Article, Korea Development Institute, Sejong City, Republic of Korea.

Park, D., and K. Shin. 2012. "Performance of the Service Sector in the Republic of Korea: An Empirical Investigation." ADB Economics Working Paper Series No. 324, Asian Development Bank, Manila, Philippines.

Republic of Korea, MOE (Ministry of Education). 2021. "Carbon Neutrality Act Passed by National Assembly Heralding Economic and Social Transition towards 2050 Carbon Neutrality." Press Release, Republic of Korea, MOE, Sejong City, Republic of Korea. http://eng.me.go.kr/eng/web/board/read.do?menuId=461&boardMasterId=522&boardId=1473610.

Republic of Korea, MOEL (Ministry of Employment and Labor) 2019. "Survey on Family and Work Balance." Employment and Labor Statistics. Sejong City, Republic of Korea: MOEL. http://laborstat.moel.go.kr/hmp/index.do.

Stangarone, T. 2020. "South Korea's Green New Deal." *The Diplomat*, May 29. https://thediplomat.com/2020/05/south-koreas-green-new-deal/.

Tuan, C., L. F. Ng, and B. Zhao. 2009. "China's Post-Economic Reform Growth: The Role of FDI and Productivity Progress." *Journal of Asian Economics* 20 (3): 280–93.

van Ark, B., M. O'Mahoney, and M. P. Timmer. 2008. "The Productivity Gap between Europe and the United States: Trends and Causes." *Journal of Economic Perspectives*, 22 (1): 25–44.

Xu, D. Y., and V. Midrigan. 2009. "Accounting for Plant-level Misallocation." 2009 Meeting Papers 223, Society for Economic Dynamics. https://ideas.repec.org/p/red/sed009/223.html.

Wooldridge, J. 2009. "On Estimating Firm-Level Production Functions Using Proxy Variables to Control for Unobservables." *Economics Letters* 104 (3): 112–14.

World Bank. 2022. World Development Indicators. World Bank, Washington, DC. https://databank.worldbank.org/source/world-development-indicators.

CHAPTER 3

Transformation of Korea's Growth Paradigm

Introduction

Private manufacturing enterprises have been the engine of the Republic of Korea's sustained rapid growth. In particular, Korea's extraordinary export growth was driven by large family-owned and -controlled business conglomerates called "chaebols." In the 1990s when Korea initiated its transition from middle income to a high-income economy, its private manufacturing enterprises focused on upgrading into high-technology exporters. In the 2000s, Korea's large enterprises grew into global companies through the further expansion of exports and globalization of production. The transformation of Samsung Electronics is a prime example of the upgrading of the country's international competitiveness and capabilities. The largest branch of Korea's largest chaebol, Samsung Group, Samsung Electronics became a global electronics exporter in the 1990s and one of the largest semiconductor manufacturers by the 2000s.

The rise of Korea's private manufacturing conglomerates benefited from a symbiotic state-market coalition based on a partnership between the government and big business. The government was a "developmental state" that actively supported private enterprises through targeted industrial policies. It organized, guided, and at times intervened in the markets but relied on the private sector to compete and export. Direct interventions in the market—market "guidance" through targeted financial and other forms of support and import protection—were at the core of industrial policies until the 1970s. By the 1980s, there was a growing recognition of the need to transition to a greater emphasis on private initiatives, external liberalization, and market competition. The growing size and complexity of the economy made these changes necessary.

The Asian Financial Crisis (AFC) was the critical turning point that fundamentally transformed the state-market relationship. The state-market partnership evolved from the state-led "developmental state" model to a state-supported, market-led model. The government took on a more supportive role in the markets by focusing on strengthening the investment climate; providing the necessary public infrastructure; opening up markets; and promoting market competition, innovation, and knowledge accumulation.

This chapter was prepared by Anwar Aridi, Kyeyoung Shin, and Yoon Jung Lee (World Bank); Namhoon Kwon (Konkuk University); and Hyunbae Chun (Sogang University). Inseok Shin (Chung-ang University) contributed on financial sector development; Jungwoo Lee (Science and Technology Policy Institute), on Korean unicorns; Dongchul Cho (Korea Development Institute [KDI]), on macroeconomic developments since the global financial crisis; Jurgen Rene Blum (World Bank), on governance reforms (impartial administration and predictable enforcement of laws); Hwa Ryung Lee (KDI), on the platform economy; Minkyung Kim (World Bank), on Pangyo Techno Valley; and Youjin Choi (World Bank), on financing for small and medium enterprises.

Policy and institutional reforms were introduced to improve the business environment and entrepreneurial ecosystem, strengthen firm capabilities, and discover and nurture new growth industries. Industrial policies shifted from preferential treatment of big firms toward greater emphasis on building the innovation and technology capabilities of small and medium-size enterprises (SMEs). Credit to the chaebols declined and subsidized lending to SMEs rose sharply. The promotion of startups ("venture firms") and technology entrepreneurship became central to the government's agenda. Venture financing has significantly expanded, and Korea's startup environment has improved over the decades, although startups still face significant challenges to growing. More broadly, the economy remains dominated by micro, small, and medium-size enterprises (MSMEs), particularly microenterprises in the service sector, despite the rise of the large manufacturing enterprises. MSMEs have been significantly less competitive and productive than the large enterprises. The growing market dominance of the large firms has raised concerns about entrenched market power and barriers to entry for new competitors.

This chapter examines the contribution of the private sector to Korea's remarkable economic development and the transformation of government policies that promoted private sector development. It begins with an analysis of the evolution of private sector firms and the entrepreneurial ecosystem. Key topics include the structure of enterprises and industries; firm-level productivity trends, including the impact of globalization and market liberalization policies; and the contribution of the enterprise sector to growth and innovation. The chapter then turns to the major reforms that were carried out in response to the AFC and thereafter. It covers the underlying political economy of reforms and outlines the major reforms of macroeconomic policies, restructuring of the financial sector, and policies to promote private sector development. Reforms that opened the economy to trade and foreign direct investment (FDI) flows are discussed in chapter 4. The chapter then traces the reorientation of government industrial policies from targeting large firms to focusing on MSMEs and entrepreneurs. The final section draws lessons from Korea's reform experience for developing countries.

Development of the Private Sector

The main story of the evolution of enterprises in Korea is the growth of large enterprises. Large manufacturing enterprises played a central role in developing Korea's export capabilities into new products and markets (Ciani et al. 2020) and contributed to innovation and technology upgrading, employee training, and adoption of international quality standards at a scale that smaller firms could not have achieved. Large enterprises have led the productivity growth in enterprises in Korea. The total factor productivity (TFP) of large firms significantly outpaced the growth of SMEs' TFP between 1980 and 2019 (see chapter 2), driving Korea's economic growth in the past decades. Hence, large firms were the drivers of Korea's aggregate productivity growth.

The large firms in Korea are concentrated in manufacturing, which accounts for a significant share (27.1 percent) of Korea's gross domestic product (GDP) relative to its peer countries, such as the United States (11.2 percent), Germany (18.2 percent), and Japan (19.7 percent).[1] The top five chaebols (Samsung, Hyundai, SK, LG, and Lotte) are in a dominant position in the manufacturing sector, including the electrical and electronics, chemical and petroleum products, and transportation equipment industries. Their relatively low shares in services partly reflect regulatory restrictions on the entry of the chaebols into some service sectors, for example, the banking sector, and high shares of small, self-employed businesses in several service sectors, including retail trade, restaurants and accommodations, and personal services (Lee 2015).

The growth of Korea's high-technology manufacturing exports after the AFC increased the dominance of the large firms. The growth of large firms' exports was driven by Korea's integration into global value chains (GVCs) and the expansion of Korean firms' overseas direct investments (ODIs) to establish global production networks, particularly in East Asia (see chapter 4). In 2021, the export shares of the top 10 firms and the top 100 firms in Korea were among the highest in the world, at 35.5 and 65.2 percent, respectively (Statistics Korea 2022). Globally, a small number of export "superstars" are often responsible for most exports (Freund and Pierola 2015, 2020). In contrast to the large firms, the export share of SMEs in Korea has declined since the early 2000s and was only 17.6 percent in 2021.

Large firms have been the main driver of economic growth in Korea, but MSMEs are by far the biggest employers in the economy. MSMEs accounted for 99 percent of the number of enterprises and 85–88 percent of total employment from 2000 to 2018 (figure 3.1),[2] significantly higher than the average of Organisation for Economic Co-operation and Development (OECD) countries (around 70 percent in 2015).[3] The employment share of SMEs (excluding microenterprises) was similar to the OECD average, but Korea has had a much higher share of employment in microenterprises. Among the OECD countries, Korea has the third largest share of employment by self-employed business owners with employees, after Greece and Australia (OECD 2022a). In the case of the self-employed without employees, Korea ranked fifth after Chile, Greece, Mexico, and Türkiye (OECD 2022b). MSMEs' share of employment in Korea is significantly larger than their share in value added, indicating that, as in OECD countries, MSMEs have much lower levels of labor productivity than large firms.

The entry of small enterprises is a key driver of employment growth in Korea, and small enterprises account for nearly all net job creation. The average contribution of entrants to net job growth in Korea is significantly higher than that in comparator countries, particularly in the service sector, reflecting the high rates of new entries. In 2016, about 15 percent of enterprises in Korea were started in that year, which was relatively high compared to many peer countries (figure 3.2). However, young enterprises'

FIGURE 3.1 Structure and Evolution of Enterprises, by Size, Republic of Korea, 2000–18

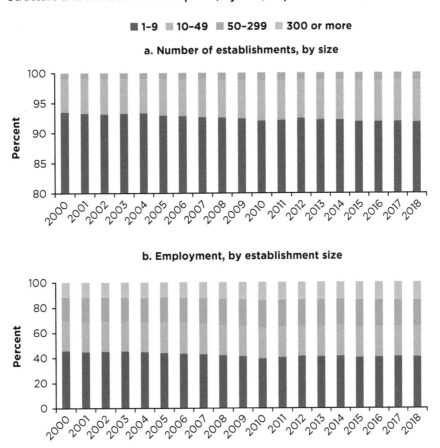

■ 1–9 ■ 10–49 ■ 50–299 ■ 300 or more

a. Number of establishments, by size

b. Employment, by establishment size

Source: Calculations based on data from the Census on Establishments, Statistics Korea, 2010–18 (https://kosis.kr).
Note: The Census on Establishments does not include agricultural farmers or establishments in the public sector.

FIGURE 3.2 **Birth Rate of Enterprises, Selected Countries, 2016**

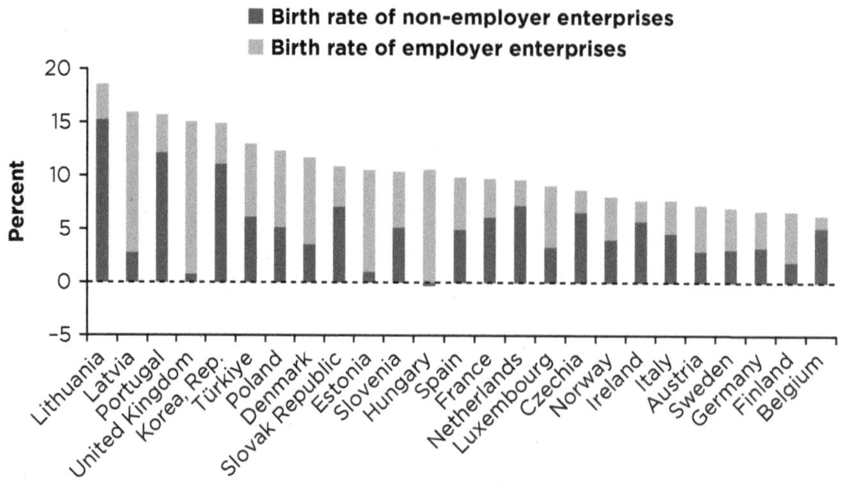

Source: Structural and Demographic Business Statistics, Organisation for Economic Co-operation and Development.

contribution to net job creation is highly negative because of their low survival rate (Cho et al. 2017). Given the high rates of entries and exits, understanding the business dynamism of new firms is critical for developing employment policies.

Self-employed microenterprises (non-employers) accounted for 73 percent of enterprise births (2016), a relatively high share. By contrast, in the United Kingdom, more than 93 percent of new enterprises employed workers (2016). Non-employers have a high exit rate, create relatively insecure jobs, are less likely to grow, and are concentrated in a few low-productivity service sectors. Non-employer entrants differ from entrepreneur startups (venture startups) that have the potential to expand production or provision of services (Lee et al. 2020). To set up a policy to promote startups, therefore, it is crucial to distinguish self-employment from entrepreneurs. Korea has also emphasized promoting the synergy between large firms and SMEs, as large enterprises can provide a production network and outsourcing opportunities that support the growth of SMEs.

Several factors have limited the success and growth of small businesses in Korea (Lee 2020). First, over 80 percent of small businesses are engaged in service industries, with more than 50 percent operating in wholesale and retail and lodging and food services. This concentration stems from the fact that many self-employed business owners choose businesses that do not require a large amount of upfront investment and advanced skill sets, but such businesses tend to exhibit low productivity. As such, there is a significant gap between microenterprises' share of employment and value added relative to the OECD average (figure 3.3). Second, many small businesses are established by necessity because the entrepreneur lacks alternative employment. This is reflected in the sharp increase in the number of small businesses in the five-year periods following the AFC and the global financial crisis (GFC), accounting for 85 percent of the increase over the past two decades. Small businesses that are established during such economic crises are associated with oversupply and profitability challenges. Moreover, necessity-driven entrepreneurs often start their businesses with insufficient preparation. In the 2013 National Small Business Survey, the preparation period of over 60 percent of the respondents was less than six months (Lee 2020).

There is evidence that the share of necessity-driven entrepreneurs has declined. In the 2013 National Small Business Survey, 82.6 percent of the respondents indicated that they did not have alternative career choices other than to start a business, and only 14.3 percent indicated that their motive was the possibility of success. By contrast, in the 2018 to 2020 surveys, less than 20 percent of the respondents selected "lack

FIGURE 3.3 **Structure of Enterprises, by Size, Republic of Korea and OECD Average, 2018**

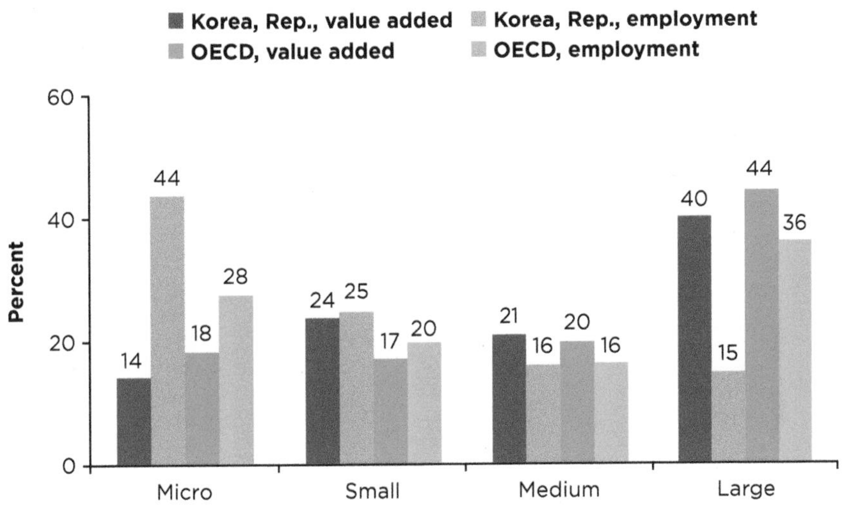

■ **Korea, Rep., value added** ▨ **Korea, Rep., employment**
■ **OECD, value added** ▨ **OECD, employment**

Source: Calculations based on data from Structural and Demographic Business Statistics, OECD.
Note: Micro consists of enterprises with 1–9 employees; small, with 10–49 employees; medium, with 50–249 employees; and large, with 250+ employees. Due to data limitations, not all industries are considered. The manufacturing; utilities; wholesale and retail trade; accommodation and food service activities; information and communication; real estate activities; professional, scientific, and technical activities; and administrative and support service activities are included. Some OECD countries do not have the latest data. The average values were calculated based on countries with complete data. OECD = Organisation for Economic Co-operation and Development.

of employment opportunities" as the reason for starting their business, and over 70 percent of the respondents indicated that they started a business "because they wanted to run their own business" (Han 2020). Similarly, the 2019 Global Entrepreneurship Monitor study indicated that most of the entrepreneurs in Korea did not start their businesses because of a lack of career choice; instead, they were motivated by entrepreneurial opportunities (Korea Entrepreneurship Foundation 2019).

The manufacturing sector has been a significantly larger driver of aggregate productivity growth in Korea, compared to other countries (see chapter 2 for a detailed discussion on productivity). Manufacturing productivity in Korea was low in the early decades, but it began to grow rapidly in the early 1990s as the sector globalized, surpassing the average productivity level of the entire economy in the mid-1990s. By 2019, manufacturing productivity was about twice the average productivity of the economy. Korea's manufacturing sector labor productivity reached about 73 percent of the OECD average in 2000 and surpassed the OECD average by 2018, although it remained lower than the global frontier (the US level).

Participation in GVCs has been an important driver of productivity growth in Korea's manufacturing sector (see chapter 4 for detailed discussion of international trade and globalization). Korea's integration into GVCs accelerated after China joined the World Trade Organization in 2001. As a result, the domestic value-added share in Korea's exports fell from 0.70 in 2000 to 0.59 in 2011, lower than in Germany (0.69), the United States (0.79), and Japan (0.81). GVC participation can enhance production efficiency and promote the productivity growth of enterprises and industries, in particular "intra-trade" sectors such as chemicals and electronics, which trade in both intermediate and final goods (Song 2020).

Large enterprises led the globalization of Korea's manufacturing sector. The GVC participation rate of large firms was on average 62.1 percent between 2010 and 2014, compared to 34.5 percent for SMEs (figure 3.4, panel a). Large enterprises, especially multinational enterprises, can organize global production chains across countries by establishing foreign affiliates and building relationships with arm's length suppliers. In Korea, more than 80 percent of large GVC participants and 50 percent of medium-size

FIGURE 3.4 **GVC Participation of Manufacturing Enterprises, Republic of Korea, 2010–14**

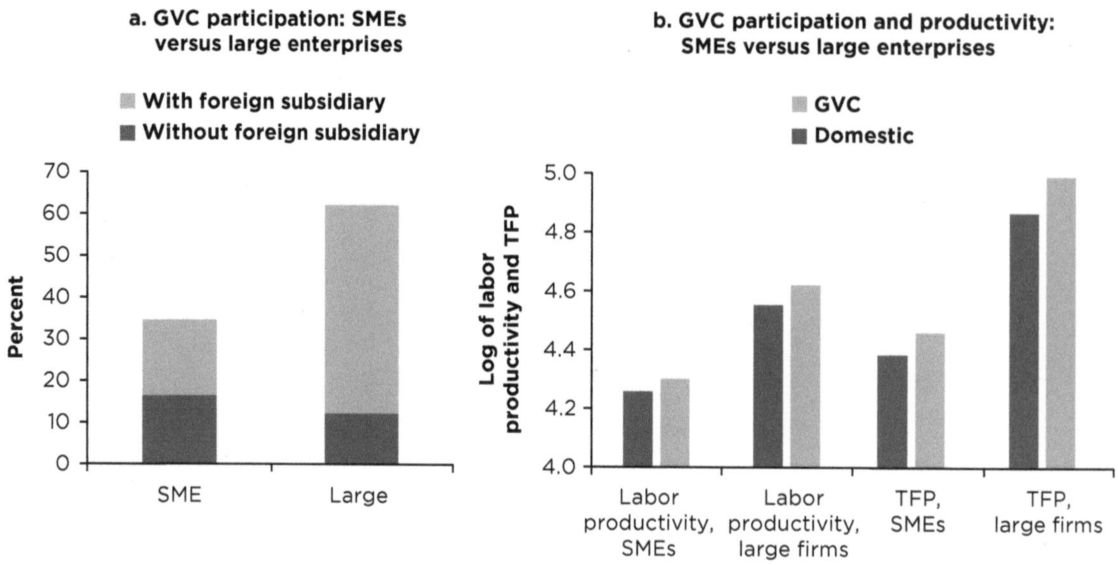

a. GVC participation: SMEs versus large enterprises

■ With foreign subsidiary
■ Without foreign subsidiary

b. GVC participation and productivity: SMEs versus large enterprises

■ GVC
■ Domestic

Sources: Kim, Kim, and Park 2016; Survey on Business Activities (https://kostat.go.kr/menu.es?mid=a20203080000).
Note: Enterprises are defined as GVC participants if they are involved in both exporting and importing, as they are then more likely to trade intermediate goods. GVC = global value chain; SMEs = small and medium-size enterprises; TFP = total factor productivity.

participants have foreign affiliates. As shown in figure 3.4, panel b, GVC participation is associated with greater productivity in Korean manufacturing firms, regardless of their size.

Domestic SMEs have a relatively low rate of participation in GVCs and have faced challenges in maintaining their competitiveness. SMEs can participate indirectly in exporting by supplying parts to the large, exporting enterprises in Korea. However, the expanded GVC participation of large enterprises has implied greater opportunities for large firms to replace domestic suppliers with foreign suppliers of inputs. Hence, there are concerns in Korea that the linkages between the large, exporting enterprises and the SMEs have weakened. Increased concerns about the weakened trickle-down effect resulted in the establishment of the Korea Commission for Corporate Partnership to promote partnerships between large and smaller firms.

In contrast to manufacturing, Korea's labor productivity in the service sector is still far below the average levels in OECD countries. Korea's service sector consists of a mix of modern and legacy sectors with significant differences in labor productivity. The high-productivity service sectors include telecommunications, finance, insurance, real estate, and information technology (IT). The low-productivity service sectors include wholesale and retail and accommodation and food services. Service sectors that typically rely on information and communications technologies (ICT) have exhibited greater productivity gains than the non-ICT service sectors (C. Lee 2019).

DIGITALIZATION OF ENTERPRISES

Firms in Korea are increasingly adopting digital technologies. Although digital technologies do not guarantee better performance (Chung and Kim 2021), they can help enterprises improve their performance by facilitating integration into the global markets and supply chains. According to Statistics Korea's Survey of Business Activities,[4] 12.9 percent of Korean firms were developing or utilizing Fourth Industrial Revolution technologies[5] in 2019, compared to 8.1 percent in 2017. A separate survey of 939 manufacturing plants in Korea found that the adoption rates of all types of digital technologies, including Fourth Industrial Revolution technologies, have increased more rapidly in recent years (Chung and Kim 2021) (figure 3.5). The adoption of digital technologies in Korea has been associated with higher levels of TFP but not with the growth of TFP (Chung and Aum 2021). A possible explanation for this is that digital technology adoption was not adequately followed by relevant learning and training of workers, which are critical for the utilization of the technologies (Chung and Aum 2021).

There are growing concerns that digital transformation could widen the gap between large enterprises and SMEs. Digital platforms that support business transactions could facilitate the entry and growth of SMEs and reduce the productivity gap between large and small enterprises in transaction-related service sectors by reducing the costs of search, verification, and distribution networks (Hallward-Driemeier et al. 2020). However, newer technologies, such as big data, cloud computing, and industrial robots, could favor the large enterprises, which have the capacity necessary to adopt such technologies. The technology adoption rates in Korea vary considerably by the type of digital technology, and the gap between large and smaller firms has grown.[6]

1. *Transactional technologies.* Firms in Korea are active in e-commerce, particularly larger firms. About half of firms with 10 or more employees made purchases via e-commerce in 2019, with the larger firms accounting for a larger share (MSIT and NIA 2020), and about 20 percent made e-commerce sales, compared to 16 percent in Germany and 17 percent in Spain (Bianchini and Kwon 2021).

2. *Informational technologies.* Korea has one of the highest enterprise resource planning software adoption rates among OECD countries (MSIT and NIA 2021), but Korea also has relatively low adoption rates of customer relationship management software, big data, and cloud computing compared to OECD countries (2012–19) (OECD.Stat).[7] There is a persistent digital gap between small and larger firms (Cirera, Comin, and Cruz 2022; MSIT and NIA 2021).

3. *Operational technologies.* Korea has one of the highest numbers of industrial robots per worker in the world, just below Singapore but more than twice the level in Japan and Germany, the next highest countries (figure 3.6). Industrial robots are concentrated in large firms, particularly in the automotive industry.

FIGURE 3.5 **Trends in the Adoption of Digital Technologies, Republic of Korea, 2010–17**

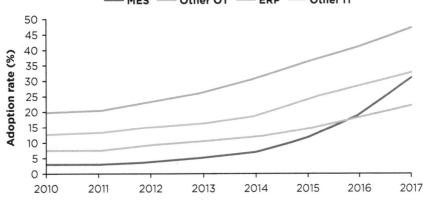

Source: Chung and Kim 2021, 34.
Note: OT includes programmable logit controller, supervisory control and data acquisition, smart sensor (internet of things), and cyber-physical system. IT includes ERP, product lifecycle management, supply chain management, factory energy management system, big data analytics, cloud computing, and artificial intelligence. ERP = enterprise resource planning; IT = information technology; MES = manufacturing execution system; OT = operating technologies.

FIGURE 3.6 **Robot Density in the Manufacturing Sector, Selected Economies, 2019**

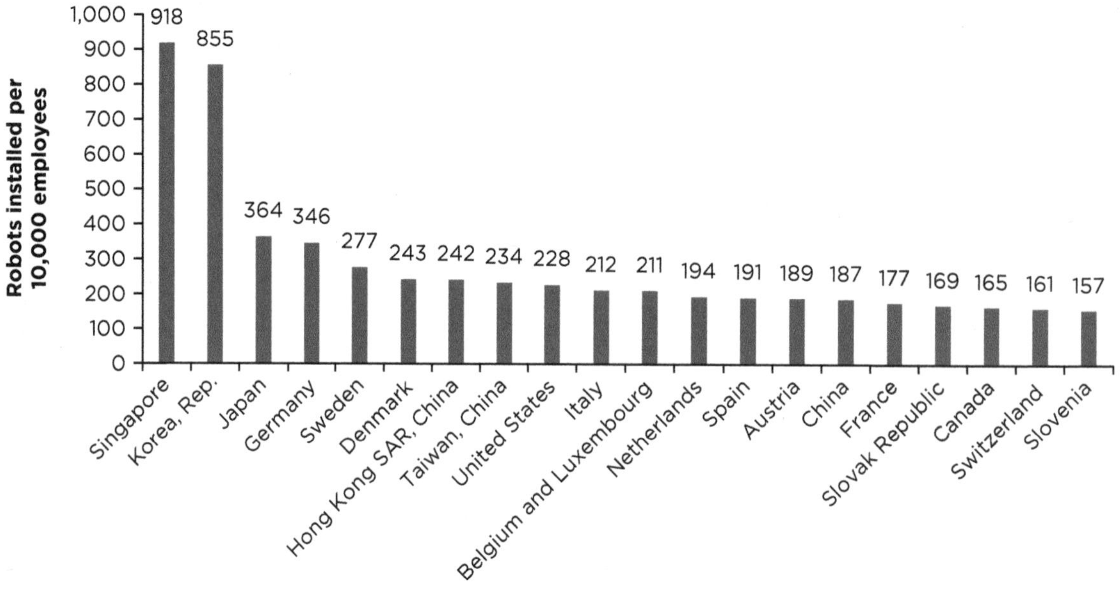

Source: Calculations based on data from IFR 2020.

Despite the increase in the rate of adoption in Korea, the share of firms using Fourth Industrial Revolution technologies is still relatively low, especially among firms that lag in productivity (Cirera et al. 2020). The low technology adoption rates among laggard firms helps to explain the productivity gap between large and smaller firms in Korea as well as the sluggish aggregate productivity performance. The World Bank's recent Firm-level Adoption of Technology survey conducted in Korea[8] indicates that there are sizable differences across industries both in the overall level of technology adoption and the gap between large and small firms in technology adoption.

Although Korea has large firms that are at the global technology frontier, the adoption of advanced technology has been uneven. For example, the adoption of industrial robots is primarily concentrated in large firms in the automotive industry, much like the rest of the world. Sixty-seven percent of large firms in the automotive industry utilize robots for fabrication, compared to only 17 percent in food processing and 9.2 percent in pharmaceuticals. The rate of adoption is considerably lower among SMEs, especially in the pharmaceutical and apparel industries. Overall, 32.8 percent of large firms utilize robots for fabrication, against only 1.3 and 4.2 percent among small and medium-size firms, respectively. The adoption of artificial intelligence is mostly concentrated in large firms, except for a few industries, such as pharmaceuticals, in which SMEs have started to adopt the technology. Large firms in agriculture and manufacturing have adopted advanced production methods at a higher level compared to those in the service (wholesale and retail) sector. The latter exhibits a smaller gap between large and small firms (figure 3.7).

Transformation of the State-Market Paradigm

Large private enterprises were the engine of Korea's sustained economic growth. Leading up to Korea's growth into a middle-income economy, the country's large firms were supported by a strategic alliance between the government and big business, which successfully addressed coordination externalities, promoted economywide resource mobilization, and targeted resource allocation through industrial policies

FIGURE 3.7 **Technology Adoption, by Sector and Firm Size Group (General Business Functions), Republic of Korea**

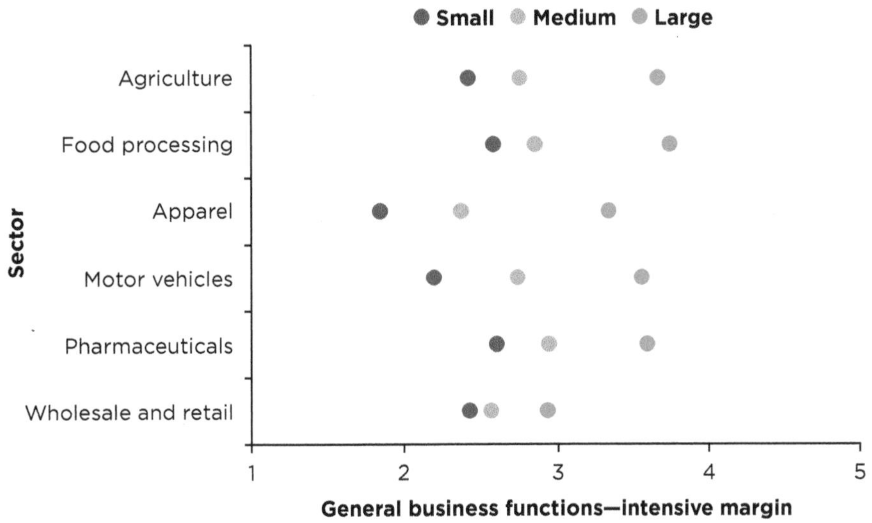

Sources: Cirera, Comin, and Cruz 2022; Cirera et al. 2020.
Note: The figure shows the average intensive margin of technology adoption in general business functions for different sizes of firms in six industries (agriculture, food processing, apparel, motor vehicles, pharmaceuticals, and wholesale or retail). The values are weighted by the sampling weight. Small = 5 to 19 employees; medium = 20 to 99 employees; large = 100 or more employees.

(Doner and Schneider 2016). The government bureaucracy oversaw the allocation of resources through the financial system to the large enterprises, in particular the chaebols, which had preferential access to credit. A close, deals-based relationship between government and big business insiders was the "glue" that was necessary to ensure commitment and coordination between the state and large enterprises. However, it engendered powerful business and political vested interests that opposed greater market competition and wider sharing of scarce resources. This state–big business partnership and the associated "extra-market" arrangements were aligned with the incentives of the political elites and reflected the balance of de facto power in the country.

As Korea's economy grew, markets expanded and supply networks became more complex and globalized. Deals-based relationships were no longer sufficient and needed to be replaced by impersonal, rules-based contract enforcement (Dixit 2004). Korea required a new "political settlement" that mobilized the contributions from a wider range of stakeholders and supported new institutions that promoted market competition and creative destruction. Korea had to transition from deals to rules, and it needed the rule of law to realize its full economic and social potential. It had to introduce more contestable and accountable institutions and impartial rules of the game to constrain arbitrary and discretionary exercise of power and enhance the accountability of policy makers. However, the political elites who helped to drive Korea's growth from low to middle income were powerful enough to block the necessary changes that could threaten their interests.

Korea's transition to a more impartial rule of law was gradually progressing as early as the 1980s. For example, subsidies that had fueled the promotion of the heavy chemical industry in the 1970s were phased out in the 1980s. As its income level rose, Korea began to develop more impartial administration with more predictable enforcement (figure 3.8). OECD country experiences highlight a similar story of decreasing levels of government interventions as their economies expanded and became more complex and their income levels increased. Korea achieved similar improvements

FIGURE 3.8 Trajectory toward Impartial Administration and Predictable Enforcement Laws, UMICs, OECD, and the Republic of Korea, 1900–2015

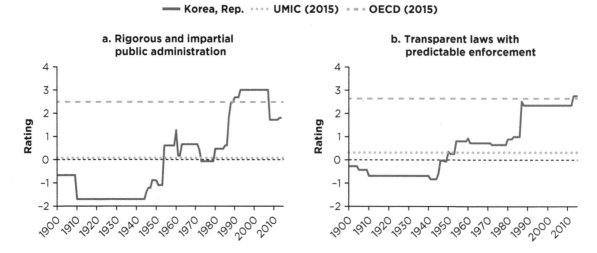

Source: Calculations by World Bank staff based on data from Varieties of Democracy (V-Dem), 2015, database hosted by Gothenburg Institute and Kellogg Institute (https://www.v-dem.net/en/).
Note: EMDEs = emerging markets and developing economies; OECD = Organisation for Economic Co-operation and Development; UMIC = upper-middle-income country.

but more recently. Two significant turning points in the evolution of Korea's political economy and institutional landscape—the transition to democratic national presidential elections in 1987 and the AFC in 1997–98—fundamentally altered the bargaining strength of the bureaucracy and big business and strengthened new stakeholders that changed the political bargaining landscape.

Direct presidential elections were introduced in 1987 in response to decades of popular protests against the autocratic regime. The "political settlement" fundamentally changed as the powerful elites in Korea voluntarily agreed to limit their influence through popular elections, to legitimize their rule. It unlocked new channels of citizen collective engagement and the emergence of new stakeholders, including political parties, legislators, the judiciary, and civil society organizations (figure 3.9).[9] The emergence of new stakeholders and institutional checks and balances expanded accountability and rules-based contestability, which helped to address commitment and collective action challenges. Opposition parties and legislators created political contestability and judicial constraints on the executive, and scrutiny by the media and civil society helped to combat corruption and engender a more level playing field.

Horizontal accountability within the government was strengthened by spreading power across multiple government agencies and independent oversight agencies, such as regulatory and auditing agencies, which reduced the chances of elite capture. The launch of the Korea Fair Trade Commission (KFTC) in 1981 with the enactment of the Monopoly Regulation and Fair Trade Act (MRFTA) represented political commitment to ensuring a level playing field and improving economic efficiency and consumer welfare. Review and oversight of regulatory agencies by other government branches, such as the judiciary, helped to prevent or invalidate regulatory decisions that were not in the public interest. Korea's experience has been consistent with the experience of upper-middle-income countries that transitioned to high-income economies. Compared to upper-middle-income countries that failed to make this transition, those that succeeded had improved their horizontal institutional checks and balances (World Bank 2017).

An increasingly influential media played an important role in the democratic reforms and afterward, enhancing public accountability and government responsiveness. Political engagement must be supported by transparency to help shape political incentives and behavioral norms in the public sector

FIGURE 3.9 **Relative Strength of Elite Actors, Republic of Korea, 1904–2015**

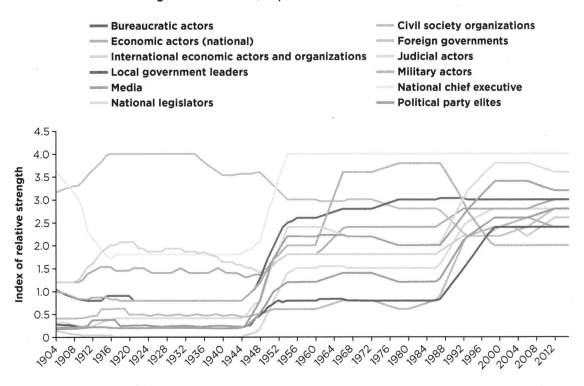

Sources: World Bank 2017.
Note: The relative strength of elite actors is measured on a 0–4 scale, ranging from 0 (no power to influence decision-making) to 4 (the group has a lot of power to influence decision-making on many issues). For more information on specific variables and survey methodology, see World Bank and V-Dem (2016) and Coppedge et al. (2015).

(Campante, Durante, and Sobbrio 2013). A free press contributes to monitoring government officials, informs citizens, and serves as a forum for public debate. Korea benefited from an active media that enhanced transparency and access to information, which facilitated the monitoring of political elites and public service providers. Media coverage helped to reduce special interest groups' capture of and influence on policies.

Civil society organizations and citizen participatory mechanisms have complemented an active media in impacting government policies and regulations by providing less powerful, diffuse interest groups greater influence on policy making. For example, the People's Solidarity for Participatory Democracy, a nongovernmental organization, led the civil campaign that eventually led to the Anti-Corruption Act in 2001. Regulatory bodies have also devised a range of mechanisms that facilitate consumer advocacy. Procedural requirements that government agencies seek diverse inputs during policy design and rollout have countered the influence of powerful interest groups and industry lobbies.

In 1997–98, the AFC was the second watershed moment that significantly altered the balance of power between the state, business, and society. Despite the emergence of new political stakeholders after the transition to free elections, the influence of the state-business coalition remained high. The dominance of large business groups in the economy increasingly became a major concern leading up to the AFC. Their borrowing and expansion were viewed as major contributors to the AFC, thus strengthening the support for reforms to constrain the state–big business coalition and the dominance of big businesses. Chief among the post-AFC reforms was the restructuring of the financial sector that dismantled the preferential credit scheme, which was central to the state–big business coalition (see the next sections for detailed discussion of the reform). Many of the reforms were initiated before the AFC but required decades of gestation and a new political settlement following the AFC for the decisive steps for full implementation of the reforms.

International stakeholders helped to push the post-AFC reforms. Reform-minded domestic stakeholders leveraged international pressure and the exigency for reforms created by the AFC to liberalize and open up the economy and introduce associated institutional reforms. Korea had already experienced the impact of joining the OECD in 1996 on its domestic reform agenda. China's accession to the World Trade Organization was a milestone in the country's reforms and opening up, and the external commitment provided by European Union accession and membership has spurred institutional development for many countries joining the European Union. Similarly, Korea leveraged the AFC to carry out major reforms of its growth paradigm.

The Asian Financial Crisis

The AFC was not the first time Korea experienced the risks of a corporate and financial sector crisis. The government intervened when high levels of debt threatened the stability of the corporate and banking sectors in 1972, converting all curb market loans to low-interest, long-term loans from public banks (Koh 2010). In the 1980s, the government sought to address overcapacity and over-indebtedness in the heavy and chemical industries with a series of government coordinated rationalization programs. These interventions helped to reaffirm the belief in "too big to fail," that the government would bail out the chaebols if they faced serious financial distress. Government interventions temporarily averted a full-blown crisis, but also created excessive demand for debt, which increased the economy's vulnerability to adverse shocks.

A central aspect of the government's support of the chaebols was the targeted industrial policies, which provided preferential access to credit and implicit guarantees for their investments. Such policies supported aggressive investments and entrance into new markets, but the easy access to credit and the moral hazard created by the government's implicit guarantees facilitated undisciplined business expansion and significant debt accumulation (figure 3.10). As credit was allocated to private enterprises based on export targets and industrial policy goals, the financial sector was unable to exert the necessary market discipline to limit access to credit for poorly performing chaebols.

By the 1980s, there was growing recognition that the government needed to move away from direct risk-sharing, eliminate the principle of "too big to fail," and expose the chaebols to market discipline. Market liberalization reforms were initiated in the 1980s and continued into the 1990s. The government

FIGURE 3.10 Debt-to-Equity Ratio in the Manufacturing Sector, Republic of Korea, 1963–2007

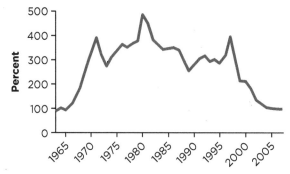

Source: Bank of Korea (http://ecos.bok.or.kr).

was entering unfamiliar territory as it sought to transform the country's growth paradigm gradually, by reducing the role of the state and expanding the role of the markets. Unfortunately, the associated reforms were not always adequately sequenced, and market liberalization reforms were not always matched by institutional reforms to ensure stronger market discipline. The resulting combination of extraordinarily high corporate leverage and "financial repression" made the corporate and financial sectors vulnerable to the AFC contagion.

The AFC started in Thailand in mid-1997, spread to other Southeast Asian countries, and reached Korea in November 1997. The AFC had a devastating impact on the country's outputs and jobs. The economy contracted by 5.7 percent in 1998, about half of the biggest 30 chaebols went bankrupt, and the top five commercial banks had to be recapitalized with public funds. Korea's vulnerability was increased by large current account deficits and deteriorating terms of trade, pressure on the currency under a rigid exchange rate regime, and a slump in corporate profitability leading up to the crisis. Facing national default due to the capital outflows and foreign currency liquidity drain, the Bank of Korea (BOK) increased the policy interest rate to almost 30 percent in December 1997, from the pre-crisis rate of approximately 12 percent, to defend the currency and restrain capital outflows. The contractionary policies significantly aggravated the banking crisis and domestic demand contraction. In response, in December 1997, the government requested a program from the International Monetary Fund, which, along with other international organizations, provided US$55 billion in financing in return for a comprehensive economic and financial restructuring program (IMF 1997; Pollack 1997).

In response to the AFC, the government embarked on major reforms in four areas that fundamentally transformed Korea's growth paradigm. First, the government helped viable private firms to regain financial health, while nonviable firms were restructured or closed. Seventy-three mid-size chaebols and firms underwent bank-led corporate restructuring as a precondition for debt reduction and rescheduling. The five largest chaebols were subject to corporate restructuring to reduce their debt, including a Big Deals program of exchanging business lines to streamline and concentrate their businesses. The government initially played an active role in overseeing and coordinating the workout process due to the weakness of the financial sector, but over time, commercial banks played a more active role. Daewoo, one of the five largest chaebols, was allowed to go bankrupt, debunking the principle of "too big to fail" (Haggard, Lim, and Kim 2003).

Second, the government streamlined and reduced regulations, strengthened corporate governance, and eased restrictions on FDI. Deregulation was used as a tool to free businesses from red tape by reducing the number of regulations, introducing a regulatory impact analysis, and addressing high-impact, multi-ministerial regulations. Corporate governance reforms included strengthening the rights of minority shareholders, imposing more stringent information disclosure requirements, and expanding the role of outside directors. The liberalization of FDI restrictions post-AFC, through the enactment of the Foreign Investment Promotion Act in 1998, resulted in a rapid increase in FDI. However, Korea's FDI inflows remain small relative to GDP compared to other high-income economies. Limits on ODIs were significantly liberalized in 2005, resulting in the rapid expansion of ODIs to establish manufacturing facilities in China and other countries (see also chapter 4).

Third, comprehensive financial sector reforms fundamentally transformed Korea's industrial policies. Financial institutions were restructured to normalize their operations quickly, financial regulations were completely overhauled, and a fully floating exchange rate regime was introduced along with capital account liberalization reforms. Financial regulation was unified under an independent Financial Services Commission (FSC). Failing banks were restructured through the Prompt Corrective Action (PCA) program, which was eventually extended to insurance companies, securities firms, and asset management companies. International standards for capital requirements were adopted and imposed on all financial institutions. Regulatory reforms to mobilize foreign capital allowed foreigners to purchase corporate and government bonds, invest in money markets, and purchase domestic equities. Monetary policy after the AFC was reoriented to inflation targeting, and the BOK transformed into an independent monetary authority with price stability as its policy objective.

Fourth, government ministries and agencies were streamlined, a large-scale privatization of state-owned enterprises (SOEs) was carried out, and a reform of the civil service was undertaken. The government carried out a major privatization program of SOEs to reduce the government's direct role in economic production. Eight SOEs along with many subsidiaries were privatized right after the AFC.[10] However, the further privatization of four SOEs was halted by the next administration.[11] Subsequent administrations tried to revive the privatization drive but were unsuccessful, as public sentiment on privatization became more skeptical. To complement privatization, government functions and services have been outsourced to bring private sector efficiency into the public sector.[12]

The restructuring process was painful, but the AFC engendered strong public support for the necessity of reforms. The economy experienced a V-shaped recovery, with growth rebounding from a 5.7 percent contraction in 1998 to a 10.7 percent expansion in 1999. As a result of the structural reforms, the corporate debt-to-equity ratio dropped from over 400 percent pre-AFC to about 200 percent post-AFC, and the Bank for International Settlements (BIS) capital adequacy ratio increased from 7.0 percent in 1997, to 10.8 percent in 1999, and 12.4 percent in 2005. Significant liberalization of the product and financial markets was complemented by new systems to promote competition, transparency, and stability.

Comprehensive Financial Sector Reforms

THE FINANCIAL SECTOR BEFORE THE AFC

Before the AFC, the banking sector had the largest share of financial intermediation in the economy. State ownership of commercial banks was the cornerstone of Korea's development model in the 1960s and 1970s. In 1962, the government nationalized the five nationwide commercial banks, which subsequently became a conduit through which policy makers directed financial flows to selected industries and firms. In the early 1980s, the four largest national commercial banks were privatized to strengthen market competition (Academy of Korean Studies 2010). Subsequently, the number of commercial banks increased to 15 with new entries. There were also 10 regional banks, for a total of 25 banks leading up to the AFC (figure 3.11). The increasing number of banks reflected the policy makers' emphasis on promoting market competition by facilitating new market entrants.

FIGURE 3.11 **Number of Major Financial Institutions, Republic of Korea, 1990–2020**

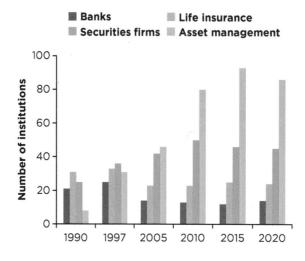

Source: Monthly Financial Statistics, Financial Supervisory Service, Government of the Republic of Korea.

Although commercial banks were the dominant players in the financial sector, capital markets emerged as a stable and significant funding source for firms in Korea in the late 1970s and continued to expand until the AFC. Demand for long-term financing started to increase around the late 1970s with the rise of large manufacturing firms. In response, the government actively promoted the expansion of capital markets, including institutional investors in capital markets. The relevant legal framework and regulatory bodies were established in the late 1960s, and the law and regulations on collective schemes and asset management companies were introduced in the 1970s. Asset management firms, called "investment trust companies (ITCs)," were established under the auspices of the government and capitalized by commercial banks. In the 1980s, the government encouraged banks to engage directly in capital market investment by providing them charters for the trust business. New entrants in the life insurance market were approved in the 1980s and 1990s, and entry restrictions on brokers and dealers in capital markets were liberalized.

By 1995, two years before the AFC, nonbank financial institutions, including investment trusts, bank trust accounts, life insurance firms, merchant banking corporations, and securities firms, had grown to account for 38.5 percent of the total assets of the financial sector, or 47.5 percent of the banking sector.[13] Equity investments accounted for about 17 percent of total external financing by the mid-1990s. In 1972, the government authorized the Korean Investment Corporation, a government agency, to provide guarantees to corporate bonds to promote the corporate bond market. It later chartered the guarantee business to commercial banks and securities firms. Funding by corporate bonds and commercial paper tripled from 8.8 percent of external financing in the late 1970s to 27.7 percent in the early 1990s. The share of corporate bonds with guarantees was around 85 to 90 percent throughout the 1980s and 1990s before the AFC (figure 3.12). Due to the strong growth of bond financing, the share of direct financing surpassed loans in the late 1980s and early 1990s (table 3.1).

Prior to the AFC, the government channeled financial flows toward selected industries through the government's control over the central bank, state-owned commercial banks, and state-dominated regulatory bodies (Shin 2006). The BOK had been under the direct control of the Ministry of Finance. To direct financial flows to selected industries, the BOK had provided "BOK policy loans" as a standing loan facility to support industrial policy. Essentially, these were quasi-government bonds for the purpose of executing industrial policy. Policy loans comprised about 60 percent of the total bank loans on average during the

FIGURE 3.12 **Corporate Bond Offerings, Republic of Korea, 1980–2005**

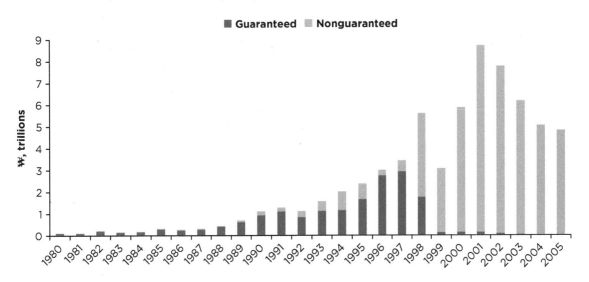

Source: Monthly Financial Statistics, Financial Supervisory Service, Government of the Republic of Korea.

TABLE 3.1 External Financing of Nonfinancial Firms in the Pre-Crisis Era, Republic of Korea, 1976–95, (five-year average, percent)

	1976–80	1981–85	1986–90	1991–95
Direct financing	21.0	31.5	44.3	43.3
Bonds	6.0	12.2	16.3	18.8
Equity	12.2	15.9	21.7	15.6
Commercial paper	2.8	3.4	6.4	8.9
Loans	48.0	41.6	38.9	42.1
Domestic loans	36.3	40.0	35.5	38.3
Foreign loans	11.7	1.6	3.4	3.8
Others	31.1	26.8	16.7	14.6

Source: Bank of Korea, Flow of Funds, various issues.
Note: Values do not add to 100% because of rounding.

1970s and 1980s (Cho and Kim 1997). The BOK policy loans naturally interfered with the BOK's mandate to ensure price stability. Before the AFC, the BOK conducted monetary policy by managing the money supply. To mitigate expansionary effects from policy loans, the BOK issued Monetary Stabilization Bonds to control aggregate liquidity.

The government also directly intervened in the operation of the markets, including the managerial decisions of private financial institutions. The government promoted ITCs and trust accounts of banks, which were "shadow banks" that invested heavily in domestic corporate bonds. The government appointed board members and required regulatory bodies to approve key managerial decisions, such as the introduction of new products, pricing of products, and opening of new branches. In return, retail investors in ITCs believed that their investments in ITC funds were implicitly guaranteed by the government.

RESTRUCTURING OF THE FINANCIAL SECTOR

In mid-November 1997, banks in Korea faced runs on their short-term foreign borrowings, and the foreign exchange reserve of the BOK was depleted toward the end of November. The eruption of the AFC in late 1997 rendered many banks and securities firms bankrupt, and the guarantees provided by financial institutions disappeared virtually overnight. The fraction of guaranteed bonds plunged from 91.5 percent in 1996 to 4.2 percent in 1999. As the first blow from the financial crisis was centered on banks, private corporations in Korea flocked to the corporate bond market in 1998, looking for an alternative source of funding. Issuance of corporate bonds swelled in 1998, resulting in a significant expansion of the ITC industry. When Daewoo, the third largest chaebol and the most active bond issuer in 1998, went bankrupt in August 1999, investors demanded that ITCs redeem their guarantees.[14]

Recognizing the need to consolidate the financial safety net, the new Financial Services Commission Act was enacted shortly after the outbreak of the AFC. During the decades prior to the AFC, an ad hoc system of financial supervision had evolved in Korea. It was a fragmented system with separate supervisory bodies for the banking, insurance, and securities sectors. The FSC Act established the FSC, initially named the Financial Supervisory Commission, as a new regulatory and policy-making body governing all regulated financial institutions. The FSC determines policies and regulations concerning financial supervision, including financial supervisory policies and the licensing of financial institutions. The government also established the Financial Supervisory Service (FSS), which consolidated four existing financial supervisory agencies—the Banking Supervisory Authority, Securities Supervisory Board,

Insurance Supervisory Board, and Non-bank Deposit Insurance Corporation—into a new, unified operational body. The FSS supervises financial institutions and implements the decisions of the FSC. The government quickly built the FSC's human resources and legal authority to carry out urgent restructuring of financial institutions. The FSC rapidly upgraded prudential regulations and led the comprehensive restructuring of the financial industry.

The FSC restructured failing banks through the PCA program introduced in 1997. The PCA program, which is based on the US Federal Deposit Insurance Improvement Act, empowered policy makers to dictate capitalization to failing financial institutions. Although it was initially introduced for banks, over time the PCA program was extended to insurance companies, securities firms, and asset management companies. The PCA proved to be a useful tool for rapid and transparent restructuring of financial institutions under distress, enabling the FSC to restructure multiple failing financial institutions, notably between 1998 and 2002. Its practical effectiveness led the government to extend the PCA regulation to corporate restructuring of nonbank financial institutions. Because the PCA program needed a standard for capital soundness, the FSC imposed capital regulations, similar to the BIS regulation for banks, on all regulated financial institutions. The imposition of capital regulations on all financial institutions has become a hallmark of Korea's prudential regulations.

The AFC induced an enduring transformation of the banking sector. The government had been adopting a series of policies to liberalize the financial market before the AFC, but their scope was limited. The International Monetary Fund bailout package of 1997 mandated broader financial market opening (IMF 1997), and in 1998, Korea First Bank became the first bank to be sold to foreign investors. Given the failure of many banks during the AFC, policy makers adjusted their priorities to emphasize financial sector stability over competitive efficiency and took actions to reduce the number of commercial banks. The FSC promoted restructuring schemes that involved mergers and acquisitions to reduce the number of banks and adopted a relatively restrictive stance on new entrants.

The number of banks decreased from 25 in 1997 to 14 in 2005 (figure 3.11). The five largest commercial banks were merged or sold, against the principles of "banks do not fail" and "too big to fail." The announcement of the sale of two big banks to foreign investors in 1998, with the relaxation of strict ownership regulation for domestic banks, signaled a strong political commitment to financial sector reforms. The government expected that foreign bank acquisitions would introduce international standards in the financial sector, such as on corporate loan appraisal and risk management. Foreign ownership of commercial banks was also expected to improve bank independence from the government and large corporations and enhance transparency. Korea's banking industry became concentrated, as reflected in the substantial increase of the concentration ratio of the market share of the five largest banks, from 47.6 percent in 1998 to 72.2 percent in 2002. The ratio has since remained relatively stable.[15] The commercial banks' share of total assets of financial institutions declined from 60 percent in the mid-1990s to around 52 percent in recent years (figure 3.13).

Merchant bank reforms were also carried out, decreasing their number from 30 in 1997 to three in 2001. Merchant banks were established in the late 1970s to facilitate foreign fund inflows after the oil price shock. They provided high-interest, long-term loans to domestic firms and financed the loans through low-interest, short-term foreign debt. Merchant banks were often owned by the chaebols and facilitated the chaebols' access to credit. The government policy to maintain low Korean won exchange rates had facilitated merchant banks' access to foreign debt. As a result of the AFC, it was no longer possible for merchant banks to roll over their short-term foreign debt as the exchange rate increased rapidly.

The banking sector became healthier as a result of the restructuring programs. The ratio of non-performing loans to total loans declined from 8.3 percent in 1999 to 6.6 percent in 2000 and further to 1.9 percent in 2002. Recapitalization of banks to clean up their balance sheets was a major goal of the government-led restructuring during the AFC. In 1997, the average BIS capital adequacy ratio of commercial banks was 7.0 percent, failing to meet the minimum standard of 8 percent (figure 3.14). The government mobilized a total of ₩104 trillion (approximately 18 percent of GDP) to recapitalize the financial system by guaranteeing the newly issued bonds of public agencies. Approximately half of the

FIGURE 3.13 **Assets of Major Financial Institutions, Republic of Korea, 1995–2017**

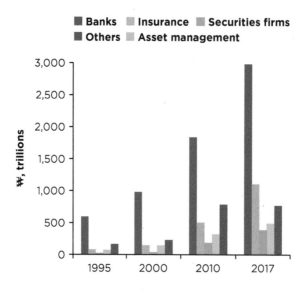

Source: Monthly Financial Statistics, Financial Supervisory Service, Government of the Republic of Korea.

FIGURE 3.14 **Bank Profitability and Soundness, Republic of Korea, 1997–2018**

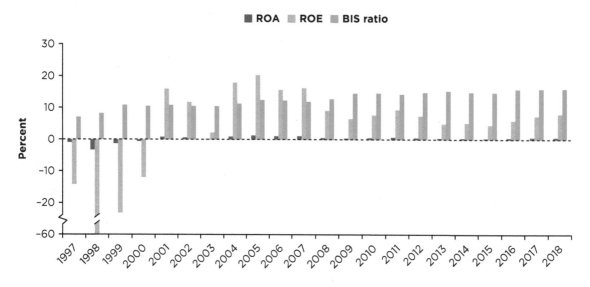

Source: Bank Management Statistics, Financial Supervisory Services, Government of the Republic of Korea.
Note: BIS ratio = Bank for International Settlements capital adequacy ratio; ROA = return on assets; ROE = return on equity.

bonds turned out to be unredeemable and were taken over by the government from 2003 to 2006. With the government-financed recapitalization program, the capital adequacy ratio increased to 10.8 percent in 1999, and subsequently stabilized at just over 10 percent until the GFC. After the GFC, the FSC set a higher standard for commercial banks, in line with the strengthened BIS regulations, raising the capital ratio of banks to around 15 percent. Along with the recapitalization of the banks, bank profitability improved in terms of the returns on assets. Mandates for outside directors, an audit committee, and compliance officers that were adopted in 2000 also helped to improve managerial capacity and transparency.

The AFC fundamentally transformed the loan portfolio of the commercial banks. During the 1990s, commercial banks were beset with low profitability and rising levels of nonperforming assets. The commercial banks targeted financial resources to priority industries and, as a result, lending to corporations accounted for 80 percent of total bank loans. The crisis brought about an abrupt end to the model. To restore capital soundness, banks were forced to reduce corporate loans, which resulted in a drastic decline in the share of corporate loans by 12 percentage points. The impact of the crisis turned out to be a permanent change of the business model of the banks in Korea, resulting in much greater emphasis on household loans and reduced emphasis on corporate loans. The share of household loans increased from less than 20 percent before the AFC to 52 percent in 2015–17 (figure 3.15).

The reduction in the share of corporate loans was mostly borne by large firms, whose borrowing from banks fell following the AFC. Increased government support for loans to SMEs, and the shift from debt to equity financing among the chaebols, led to a dramatic change in leverage ratios across large and small firms. Before the AFC, firm size was positively correlated with leverage as the largest firms had greater access to borrowing (figure 3.16). After the crisis, the relationship between size and leverage was reversed. The leverage of the largest firms decreased significantly and became the lowest in the postcrisis period. The smallest firms began increasing their leverage post-AFC, a process that gained further momentum after the GFC.

Along with the banking sector, the government carried out a major restructuring of the ITC industry from 2001 to 2003. The ITC Act underwent several amendments, including a full revision in 2004, to restructure the regulatory framework to adopt international standards for collective investment schemes. Collective investment schemes, generally known as "funds," and the asset management industry in Korea finally came to operate as modern capital market institutions, without managerial interference from the government and with a risk-bearing structure consistent with international standards. However, the guaranteed bond market has never fully recovered from the AFC, as regulations over capital soundness were strengthened since the AFC and financial institutions became cautious about reentering the guarantee business.

FIGURE 3.15 **Composition of Bank Loans, Republic of Korea, 1990–2017**

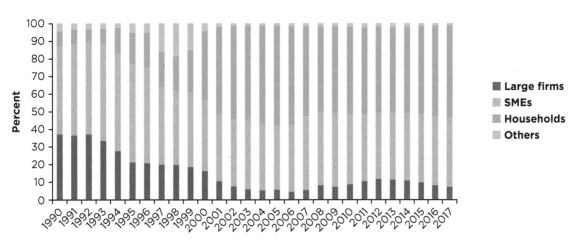

Source: Bank Management Statistics, Financial Supervisory Services, Government of the Republic of Korea.
Note: SMEs = small and medium-size enterprises.

FIGURE 3.16 **Leverage, by Firm Size: Audited Firms, Republic of Korea, 1990–2019**

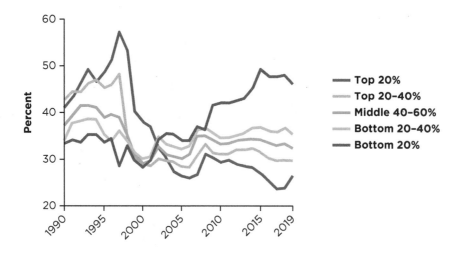

Source: FnGuide 2021.

Post-AFC, Korea's financial sector became more diversified. Although commercial banks accounted for the largest share of the financial sector, insurance companies and securities firms registered higher rates of growth (figure 3.11). The surge of the insurance sector can be attributed to Korea's demographic structure, as population aging has increased demand for long-term contractual savings products. The restructuring of the financial sector and in particular the exit of merchant banks post-AFC contributed to the surge of securities firms. Merchant banks had been the dealers and brokers in the money market, and many were owned by the chaebols. Subsequent to the significant downsizing of the merchant banks, the securities firms took over their roles in the money market.

The structural reforms of the financial sector in the aftermath of the AFC significantly strengthened Korea's financial sector stability and resilience. As a result, the country was much more successful in managing the impact of the GFC a decade later. The size of the external shock during the GFC was greater than that during the AFC. Immediately after the Lehman Brothers bankruptcy in September 2008, which triggered the GFC, panicked financial institutions rushed to secure liquidity from anywhere possible in the world, and Korea experienced an abrupt and massive capital outflow. The amount of financial capital withdrawn in October 2008 was on net US\$25.5 billion (more than 3 percent of annual GDP), which was far larger than the US\$6.4 billion outflows in December 1997, the worst month during the AFC period. The magnitude of the shock through the trade channel was also significantly larger during the GFC. Approximately 40 percent of export demand evaporated during the three-month period from September to December 2008, which was in stark contrast to the sustained export demand during the AFC period.

Despite the sizable external shocks, Korea's corporate and financial sectors remained relatively stable during the GFC. About half of the largest 30 chaebols went bankrupt and the five largest commercial banks were recapitalized with public money during the AFC. By contrast, no large conglomerates failed and no major banks needed to be rescued by the government due to the GFC. As a result, domestic demand contracted much less significantly during the GFC compared to the AFC. Private consumption contracted by 3 to 4 percent in the worst quarter during the GFC, which was far milder than the almost 14 percent decline in the first quarter of 1998. This resiliency of domestic demand was crucial for maintaining labor-intensive service sectors and hence preserving jobs, as the sharp jump in the unemployment rate during the AFC was not repeated in the GFC. During the GFC, Korea experienced a milder growth downturn than the average of OECD countries.

The economy in 2008 was equipped with far better buffers to cope with the GFC shock, compared to the AFC. First, official foreign reserves had accumulated to more than US$250 billion (over a quarter of GDP) by 2008, which was more than eight times the reserves in 1997. This helped to limit the drastic capital outflow that could have led to a domestic liquidity crunch. Second, domestic firms had undergone significant corporate and financial restructuring in the aftermath of the AFC, which significantly reduced their vulnerability to the GFC. The average debt-to-equity ratio of the manufacturing sector fell from over 400 percent in 1997 to around 100 percent in 2008 (figure 3.10), and the interest coverage ratio rose from just over 100 percent in 1997 to over 500 percent in 2008. This improvement in financial buffers greatly helped the firms weather the credit constraints and demand contraction of the GFC. Third, commercial banks had significantly improved their BIS capital adequacy ratio and return on equity (figure 3.14), building up financial buffers to withstand a significant rise in defaults.

MACROECONOMIC POLICY REFORMS

In response to the AFC, the government adopted a big-bang approach to reforming the macroeconomic framework, which included capital market liberalization and financial sector globalization. A fully floating exchange rate system was introduced in December 1997 at the onset of the AFC, along with measures for capital account liberalization. In December 1997, all regulations on the purchase of corporate bonds and government bonds by foreign investors were abolished. Subsequently, in May 1998, money markets were opened to foreign investors. The ceiling on foreign investments in equities was lifted as well. In July 1998, the government liberalized medium-term foreign borrowing, to help domestic firms attract foreign capital. In April 1999, the government abolished the restrictive "Foreign Exchange Management Act" and replaced it with the "Foreign Exchange Transaction Act," which fundamentally transformed the foreign exchange regulatory regime from a positive list system (that identified permitted foreign exchange transactions) to a negative list system (that identified restricted foreign exchange transactions), which was considered less restrictive.

After the AFC, monetary policy was reoriented from money supply to inflation targeting. A revised BOK Act was enacted swiftly after the crisis in April 1998, which established price stability as the sole objective of the BOK and transformed the BOK into an independent monetary authority by introducing a governing committee independent of the government. The revisions of the BOK Act in 1998 were preceded by an extensive deliberation and consultative process to build consensus among relevant stakeholders and a public awareness-raising campaign that drew significant media attention. Inflation has been relatively stable under this new framework and had been declining until the recent rise since 2022 in line with the global rise of inflation (figure 3.17).

After the GFC, the National Assembly revised the BOK Act and mandated monetary policy to emphasize financial sector stability in addition to price stability. Unlike price stability, which can be assessed by specific inflation targets, financial stability is less well defined and thus more subject to policy makers' discretionary interpretations. The BOK has referred to the Korea-US interest rate gap at times and household debt and housing prices at other times as indicators of financial sector risk. It is an ongoing debate among Korea's monetary policy makers to reconcile the financial sector stability goal and the price stability goal.

The AFC highlighted for Korea the importance of securing foreign currency liquidity. After the AFC, the government and the BOK accumulated significant volumes of key international currencies, financed by Foreign Exchange Equalization Bonds issued by the government and Monetary Stabilization Bonds issued by the BOK. In addition, the government established currency swaps to expand access to foreign currency during periods of abrupt capital outflows.

Freed from foreign currency liquidity concerns due to the reforms carried out in response to the AFC, Korea's monetary policy response to the GFC in 2008 was completely different from its response to the AFC. In response to the demand contraction and financial woes resulting from the GFC, the BOK swiftly lowered the policy rate to 2.00 percent, below half the pre-crisis rate of 5.25 percent (figure 3.18). This

FIGURE 3.17 **Actual Inflation and Inflation Targets, Republic of Korea, 2001–20**

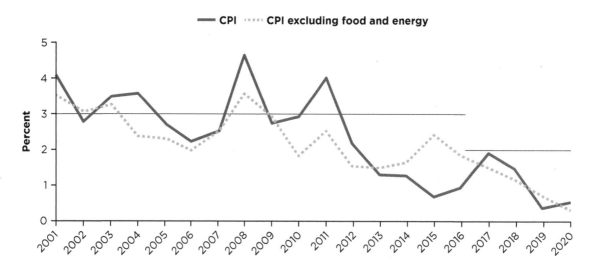

Sources: Bank of Korea; Statistics Korea.
Note: CPI = Consumer Price Index.

FIGURE 3.18 **Contrasting Monetary Policy Responses: Policy Rates around the AFC and GFC, Republic of Korea**

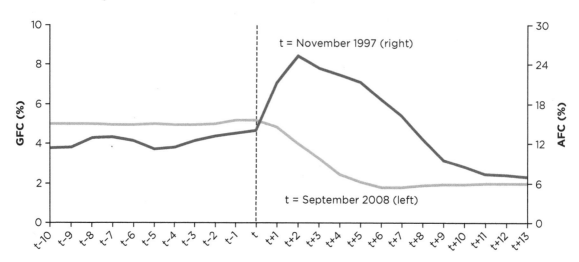

Source: Bank of Korea.
Note: The light (bold) line represents the policy rate before and after the AFC (GFC). For the AFC (GFC) lines, "t" is November 1997 (September 2008), the peak of the crisis. AFC = Asian Financial Crisis; GFC = global financial crisis.

monetary policy flexibility, made possible by the floating exchange rate system, was crucial for guarding the domestic economy from the external shock.

Compared to the focused attention on the asset side of foreign exchange, Korea had paid less attention to the liability side leading up to the GFC. Short-term foreign debts had accumulated rapidly to almost 80 percent of official foreign reserves by 2007, driven partly by forward contracts for exporters, particularly shipbuilding companies (figure 3.19). These short-term debts were recalled by global financial

FIGURE 3.19 **Foreign Reserves and External Debt, Republic of Korea, 1994–2020**

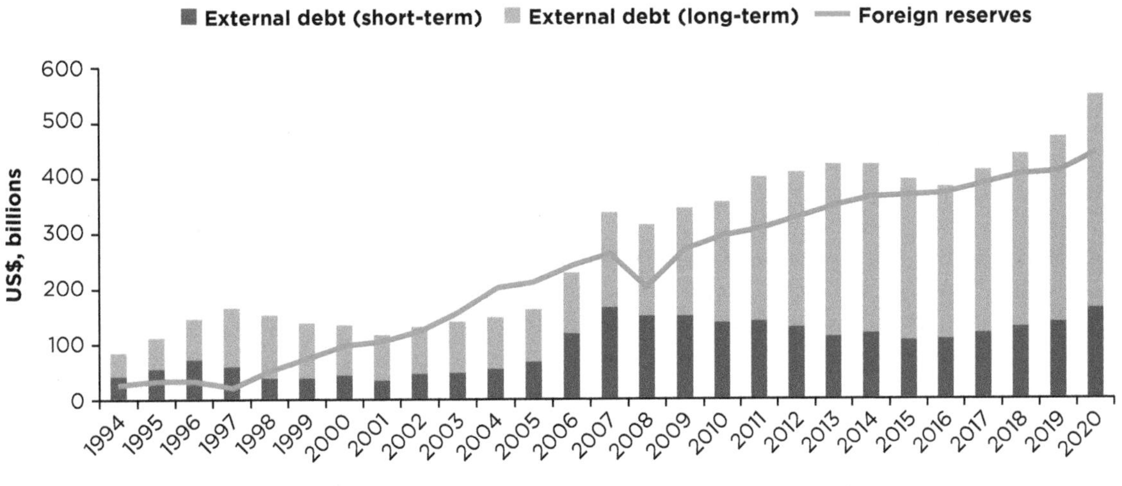

■ **External debt (short-term)** ■ **External debt (long-term)** — **Foreign reserves**

Source: Bank of Korea.

institutions when the GFC broke out, destabilizing the foreign exchange market. Learning from this experience, in 2010 the government introduced prudential policy measures to curb external short-term debt accumulation, including ceilings on foreign exchange derivatives positions of commercial banks, a macroprudential stability levy on non-deposit foreign currency liabilities, and a withholding tax on foreigners' capital gains and interest income on Korea's sovereign bonds. These measures helped to limit the accumulation of short-term debt and reduced the susceptibility of the financial sector to sudden capital outflows.

PUBLIC SECTOR REFORMS

During the AFC, the government initially aimed to maintain a balanced budget despite the anticipated recession, and this fiscal policy stance was gradually loosened only after the severe recession materialized. Learning from the AFC experience, the government announced a fiscal expansion at the onset of the GFC, to inject the necessary fiscal stimulus. A supplementary budget of ₩10 trillion (approximately 1 percent of GDP) was introduced in November 2008, and an additional supplementary budget of ₩28.4 trillion (approximately 2.8 percent of GDP) was added in March 2009. This early fiscal stimulus helped to mitigate the severity of the recession. In contrast to the massive government-financed recapitalization of the financial sector during the AFC, during the GFC strengthened fundamentals enabled the government to avoid public bailouts of the financial institutions and to pursue a more active fiscal policy.

The fiscal framework was strengthened following the AFC, in part because public finance was stretched to bail out insolvent financial institutions. The fiscal reforms included the reform of public funds, the introduction of pre-feasibility studies, and the strengthening of public-private partnership schemes.

1. Public funds used to be controlled exclusively by line ministries without scrutiny by the central budget office, and their operation produced large inefficiencies. The total number of funds was reduced from 75 in 1998 to 58 in 2002. The government also introduced the legal requirement for the periodic evaluation of the necessity of each public fund and its operational efficiency.

2. Pre-feasibility studies were introduced in 1999 on projects proposed by line ministries worth over ₩50 billion, so that low-priority projects could be systematically identified and removed. Korea Development Institute, which was in charge of conducting the studies, rejected 66 of 120 projects between 1999 and 2002.

3. To save tax money and tap into private sector resources for infrastructure investment, the administration revised the Act on Private Participation in Infrastructure in 1998 and added the minimum revenue guarantee clause, which substantially helped to boost private sector participation in public-private partnership projects in the following years. The revision of the law in 2005 abolished the minimum revenue guarantee but expanded the scope of public-private partnerships to include build-transfer-lease projects for social and residential facilities.

The Medium-Term Fiscal Management Framework was introduced in 2004 and the National Fiscal Law in 2006 to enhance the consistency of fiscal policy over time. Under this framework, the government is obliged to submit a plan to the National Assembly on the management of public debt and deficits over the medium term. Other major budgeting reforms included performance budgeting in 2003, top-down budgeting in 2004, and reforms of the fiscal information and accounting system in 2006. These reforms aimed to enhance the effectiveness, transparency, and accountability of the budget process.

To increase efficiency, employment in the public sector was reduced by 20.2 percent during 1998–2001. However, the number of public employees quickly started to rebound in 2001 and by 2019 it was 18 percent higher than it was pre-AFC.[16] In 1998, the government lowered the retirement age for civil servants from 61 to 60 years for mid- or high-ranking positions and from 58 to 57 years for others. In 2013, the retirement age was synchronized to 60 years. In response to the AFC, contributions to the Government Employees Pension Program were increased and benefits were significantly reduced; in return, the government formally accepted its obligation to fill the pension funding gap.

Important measures to strengthen transparency and ethics in the public sector were introduced post-AFC. Korea was ranked 33rd of 180 countries in the 2020 Corruption Perceptions Index by Transparency International, up from 52nd in 2016, which shows improvement in how corrupt its public sectors are perceived to be.[17] The Anti-Corruption and Civil Rights Commission was launched in 2008, through the integration of the Ombudsman of Korea, the Korea Independent Commission against Corruption, and the Administrative Appeals Commission, to enforce integrity standards of public servants and handle corruption cases. The Anti-Bribery and Graft Act, a major anti-corruption law nicknamed the Kim Young-Ran Law after its major advocate, came into effect in September 2016. An active media and freedom of speech have also significantly enhanced the transparency of government, so that government interventions could be held up to public scrutiny. Public sector transparency, self-monitoring, and public scrutiny have helped constrain government corruption and collusion and market-distorting discretionary interventions in favored firms.

Performance management in the government was strengthened and extended to local governments by a new law enacted in 2001. The law was later replaced by the Basic Law on the Government Performance Evaluation, which enabled the prime minister's office to coordinate evaluation activities across line ministries. Various ministries are involved in evaluation of government organizations, and individual ministries also have internal performance assessment units. All ministries are now evaluated annually by the Government Performance Evaluation Committee, which is co-chaired by the prime minister and an external expert who is typically recruited from academia. The performance evaluations of government ministries and agencies are publicized through news media and can influence the president's assessment of incumbent ministers.

Public agencies such as SOEs are subject to a performance management system that has been refined and expanded over the years. An SOE governance system, managed by the Ministry of Economy and Finance (MOEF), originally covered around 30 SOEs. The coverage was extended to around 300 government-affiliated organizations in 2007, and a new Committee for the Management of Public Institutions was established. This committee decides on the annual bonuses for the employees of SOEs and government-affiliated organizations, based on an annual evaluation organized by MOEF and conducted by an independent group of private sector experts. The annual bonuses can be as low as zero and as high as around US$10,000 per employee. The committee can also recommend to the government dismissal of poorly performing chief executive officers of SOEs. There have been high-performing SOEs in Korea. For example, the Incheon

International Airport was recognized as the best service airport in the world 12 years in a row in 2005–16 by the Airport Council International, and the Korea Electric Power Corporation has had among the lowest blackout rates in the world.

The public sector has remained a center of institutional and technocratic excellence throughout Korea's modern development. In the earlier decades, the state–big business coalition required a government with sufficient institutional and technocratic capacity to carry out its industrial policies while avoiding narrow interest group capture. The strong business ties facilitated coordination of industrialization, but also exposed the bureaucracy to private capture. To minimize policy capture, from as early as the 1960s, Korea initiated broad administrative reforms that aimed to strengthen meritocracy in the bureaucracy and minimize patronage, including through the introduction of a highly competitive and impartial national civil service examination. Personnel management has been improved with the introduction of an open recruiting system for senior civil servants, performance payments, and a performance evaluation system. In the 1980s, the government initiated investments, which were to continue for several decades, in digitalization of the government to improve public sector transparency, efficiency, and public service delivery (box 3.1). In 2000, the government introduced an open competitive recruitment system for 130 positions (20 percent of the total) at the Director General level. The number was increased to 390 positions by 2019, further diversifying recruitment.

BOX 3.1 The Republic of Korea's Digital Government Reforms

E-government initiatives have been a major priority for the government of the Republic of Korea, and its digital government reforms have been widely recognized. Korea was ranked first from 2010 to 2014 and among the top three countries from 2016 to 2020 in the United Nations' e-Government Development Index, a composite index that combines three dimensions of e-governance: provision of online services, telecommunications connectivity, and human capacity. In 2020, Korea was ranked second in the world in the e-Government Development Index, after Denmark (United Nations 2020). The introduction of digital government was part of a broader national strategy to use technology to shift Korea's economic paradigm from an industry-based economy to a knowledge-based economy and information society. It has contributed to improving public sector transparency, efficiency, and public service delivery.

Korea initiated investments in digital government in the 1980s, when it was still a lower-middle-income country. During the initial "foundation phase" (1980s–1995), the groundwork for e-governance was laid through the digitalization of national key databases and the building of a digital network for each government agency. Next came the "full promotion stage" (1996–2002), during which high-speed broadband networks were established across the country and 11 high-priority information technology projects were completed. The third stage of "diffusion and advance" (2003–07) saw the establishment of government-for-citizens applications and the implementation of systems to share administrative information. The fourth "integration stage" (2008–12) saw the launch of an integrated e-government platform. Finally, the fifth stage of "maturity and co-producing" (2013–17) prioritized information and communications technology (ICT) innovation for service integration at all levels of government and investment in ICT-enabled growth by collaborating with the private sector and engaging citizens.

Korea's early efforts were primarily concerned with achieving greater efficiencies within the government. They included the computerization of basic systems and processes, such as for financial and human resource management, and the creation of major databases. They also involved efforts to develop the ICT infrastructure, such as the major push toward high-speed broadband network development. Subsequent efforts have focused on ensuring the interoperability of various systems. Since 2011, for example, an integrated e-governance platform has been used by all central government departments and local governments. Under this system, all government-administered work processes, such as planning, scheduling, performance management, and decision-making, are standardized, systematized, and interlinked. All government decisions are documented and archived, resulting in greater transparency and accountability.

Continued

BOX 3.1 Continued

Support for businesses was a major priority of the digital government reforms. An important area has been public procurement. The Korea Online e-Procurement System electronically processes all procurement activities in a one-stop process in Korea. In 2009, more than 70 percent of all public procurement, totaling ₩85.7 trillion (approximately US$77 billion), was processed through the Korea Online e-Procurement System. Business Support Plus, which was completed in 2009, is a one-stop shop for accessing business-related public services. The system operates services for 15 government institutions. It handles 714 different types of business services online, such as business licensing and permitting, facility management, employment, and funding support.

Korea has also made major advances in providing e-services to citizens. The Government24 site (www.gov.kr) offers various online services, including 5,700 notifications, 2,500 application filings, and 1,034 certificate issues. Its Public Service 24 portal (Minwon 24) provides detailed information on 5,300 types of services, and 3,020 types of civil services and petitions can be requested by citizens online as of 2010. Just over 1,200 types of civil documents are also issued online. This portal provides access to a wide range of information, resources, and services directly through government agencies, such as tax services online through the National Tax Service portal. Access to public services and petitions has been made available on smartphone applications, including building registration and official assessments of land prices.

Source: Karippacheril et al. (2016).

The relatively high capacity of the public sector reflects its ability to attract and recruit highly competent staff. Historically, in Korea a career in the government has been highly sought after. The salary has been increased continuously and, as a result, it is equivalent to 86 percent of the comparable salary in the private sector (MPM 2018). The remuneration packages become even more competitive when one considers the relatively generous government pension benefits. Employment stability and prestige have also helped to attract competitive recruits. A relatively transparent and merit-based recruiting process has helped to identify and select the best recruits. Presidents of Korea have traditionally selected on average 30 percent of their ministers from career civil servants. Staff performance is closely evaluated and reflected in promotion and job assignment decisions.

Promoting Private Markets: From State-Led to Market-Led Development

DEREGULATION

Deregulation emerged as an important reform agenda as early as the late 1980s (Koh 2010). Initially, it was used as a tool to promote market competition, but the focus soon shifted to freeing businesses from red tape and thereby stimulating investments. In response to the AFC, the government carried out deregulation reforms aiming to reduce the number of regulations by 50 percent. The Regulatory Reform Committee, co-chaired by the prime minister and a private sector expert, was established under the president in 1998 to lead the deregulation drive. The Regulatory Reform Office was organized within the prime minister's office as a secretariat for the Regulatory Reform Committee, and Regulatory Impact Analysis was introduced. The number of regulations, estimated at 10,372 in 1998, fell to 7,294 in 1999. The role of KFTC, which was established in 1981 to promote domestic competition, was strengthened and expanded. For example, KFTC uncovered unfair internal transactions totaling ₩17.9 trillion by the five major chaebols and levied a fine of ₩170 billion following the AFC.

However, there were criticisms that the deregulation drive focused on quantitative targets without sufficient qualitative impact. In response, subsequent administrations explored institutional arrangements to enhance the deregulation reforms. The Regulatory Reform Planning Team with private sector experts was established and some achievements were made, but it failed to lead to far-reaching effects (M. Lee 2016). Then the National Competitiveness Reinforcement Committee was established to identify and promote priority regulatory reforms, tackle high-impact multi-ministerial regulations, and strengthen cooperation with the Korea Chamber of Commerce and Industry and the Korea Federation of SMEs. However, the total number of regulations soared to around 14,000 and there was criticism that the deregulation reforms focused only on large enterprises. Subsequent administrations proposed new targets to reduce regulations and introduced the Total Regulatory Cost System to assess and control the costs imposed by regulations, but it never advanced beyond the pilot stage. There are now concerns that business regulations are on the rise again. From May 2017 to July 2021, the number of regulatory bills proposed in the National Assembly was 3,950, three times the number in the previous four years (1,313).[18]

Overall, Korea's regulatory framework has improved, but the improvements have been outpaced by many other high-income countries. As a result of the post-AFC regulatory reforms, Korea's OECD Product Market Regulation score fell substantially, from 2.56 in 1998 to 1.95 in 2003 (figure 3.20). However, the scores of other OECD countries also declined. As a result, Korea's relative ranking improved only slightly, from the 74th percentile in 1998 to the 72nd percentile in 2003. Subsequently, Korea's ranking deteriorated further to the 92nd percentile in 2013. As of 2018, regulations were found to be particularly restrictive in retail price controls and regulation, command and control regulation, barriers in network sectors, and trade barriers. Similarly, on the "burden of government regulation" assessment of the World Economic Forum's Global Competitiveness Index, since 2007 Korea's ranking has worsened significantly compared to major advanced economies (WEF 2019) (figure 3.21).[19]

Deregulation has been actively promoted for startups. The most representative effort has been the Regulatory Sandbox program, which was introduced in Korea in 2019 through a series of regulatory sandbox acts on six sectoral and geographical themes: information and communications technology convergence, industrial convergence, financial innovation, regulation-free special zones, smart cities, and special research and development zones. Regulatory sandboxes around the world have tended to

FIGURE 3.20 **Product Market Regulation Scores of OECD Countries, 1998–2018**

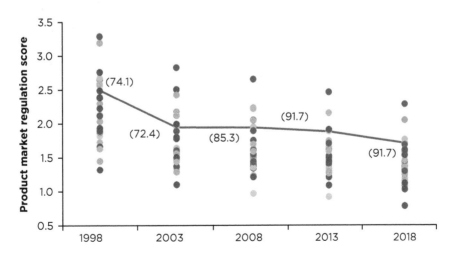

Source: OECD (https://stats.oecd.org).
Note: The dots indicate individual OECD countries and the line indicates the Republic of Korea. The numbers in parentheses are the Republic of Korea's percentile ranking. The Product Market Regulation score ranges between 0 (least restrictive) and 6 (most restrictive). OECD = Organisation for Economic Co-operation and Development.

FIGURE 3.21 **Burden of Government Regulation, Rank, Selected Countries and World Median, 2007–17**

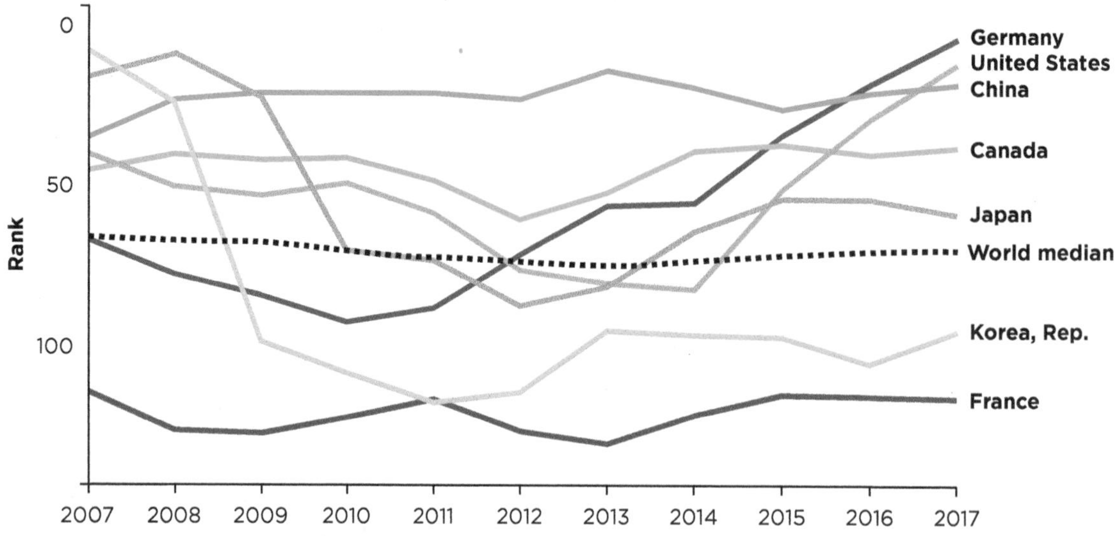

Sources: TCdata360, World Bank; calculations based on data from the World Economic Forum Global Competitiveness Index.
Note: The higher the rank is, the lower the burden of government regulation is perceived to be.

target financial technology (fintech) firms, including the United Kingdom's regulatory sandbox implemented by the Financial Conduct Authority, which was the first regulatory sandbox introduced in the world. Korea's approach is unique in that its multisector regulatory sandbox is not limited to the financial sector.

Adopting an "allow first, regulate later" approach, Korea's regulatory sandbox grants business permits temporarily and temporarily waives relevant regulations if the regulations related to new technologies or new industries are considered restrictive or are absent or ambiguous. During this period, the relevant ministries work on updating the relevant legislation and regulations. Alternatively, if there are potential safety concerns, a special exemption may be provided for firms to go through a piloting or testing process. The Office of Government Policy Coordination (OPC) assumes the overall planning and coordination of the regulatory sandbox based on the Framework Act on Administrative Regulations. Various ministries collaborate with the OPC to operate each sandbox on the basis of the relevant sandbox act for each theme. Each ministry forms a Deliberative Committee on Regulatory Exceptions, chaired by the minister for deliberation and coordination of regulatory sandbox matters. When ministries cannot resolve disagreements among key stakeholders, the OPC-supervised Regulatory Sandbox Relevant Ministries Task Force intervenes to facilitate an agreement between the opposing parties.

As of 2022, the sandbox system had been operating in Korea for fewer than three years. The legislative adjustments in response to sandbox products and services are still ongoing, so it is too early to draw conclusions about the impact of the sandbox initiative. According to the government, however, firms have been active in making use of the sandbox system (Government of the Republic of Korea 2021; OPC 2021). As of January 2021, the sandbox program has handled 410 products and services, with the highest numbers in the energy sector, the internet of things, biotechnology, and big data. As a result of the program, 31 regulations have been revised and 60 sandbox cases have been tested and approved under exemption for demonstration permits.

MARKET COMPETITION AND CHAEBOL POLICIES

Korea initiated reforms to promote market competition in the 1980s when it was still a lower-middle-income country. KFTC was launched in 1980 with the enactment of the MRFTA. In 1986, the law was revised specifically to restrain the concentration of the chaebols' economic power. Enactment of the MRFTA was a symbol of political commitment to ensuring fairness, improving economic efficiency, and promoting consumer welfare. Before the AFC, however, the "government managed" approach to competition policy was still practiced (Lim 2012) and competition policy was at times compromised to achieve industrial policy objectives, for example, by allowing anticompetitive mergers to support government-led industrial rationalization programs and by allowing cartels if they obtained prior approval.

In response to the AFC, the role of KFTC was greatly strengthened as the focus of economic policies shifted to the promotion of market competition. Post-AFC, it was necessary to strengthen KFTC and competition policy to discontinue government-supported market collusion and concentration of market power. In 1994, KFTC separated from its parent ministry to become an independent agency (KFTC 2011). In 1999, the Omnibus Cartel Repeal Act and other amendments removed legal exemptions to cartels, and the legal standard for antitrust was revised from "substantial" to "unreasonable" restraint of competition, which would be easier to substantiate. The introduction of the leniency program in 1997 for voluntary reporting of collusion and a further amendment in 2005 greatly increased the likelihood of discovering cartels.

The growing role of KFTC is reflected in the increasing number of cases of enforcement and the size of the fines (figure 3.22). The number of enforcements for three types of competition law violations—abuse of dominance, anticompetitive mergers, and cartels—increased from an annual average of 20 in 1981–95 to 125 in 1996–2000, and then to 285 in 2016–19. Total fines averaged only ₩953 million per year in 1981–95, but increased to ₩104,574 million in 1996–2000 and to ₩643,108 million in 2016–19.

KFTC and enforcement of competition policy have helped to strengthen market competition in Korea and contributed to the country's successful development (Lee et al. 2013). KFTC enforcement is now relatively active compared to other competition authorities in the world. In 2016 and 2017, KFTC won the ELITE rating in the global assessment of competition authorities conducted by the *Global Competition Review*, a leading antitrust journal in the United Kingdom. Only three countries (France, Germany, and the United States) received the ELITE rating in 2017. Between 2016 and 2019, Korea's average fines for cartels were smaller than those in Brazil and the European Union but larger than

FIGURE 3.22 Law Enforcement by the Korea Fair Trade Commission, 1981–2019

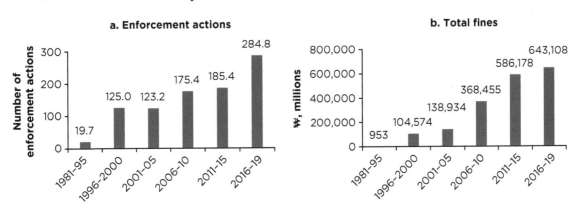

Source: Statistical Yearbook of 2019, Korea Fair Trade Commission.
Note: Panel a shows the annual average number of enforcement actions for the abuse of market dominance, merger enforcement, and cartel behaviors. Panel b shows the annual average fines for all types of violations.

those in Japan and the United States (Allen and Overy 2020). Given the size of Korea's economy, the size of the fines has been relatively large.

A unique feature of MRFTA is the policies to curb undue market concentration and the market dominance of the chaebols. In addition to concerns about monopoly power in specific markets, which are common in other countries, in Korea, "aggregate" concentration and "ownership" concentration[20] have historically been a concern due to the perceived market power and influence of the chaebols. Accordingly, MRFTA contains provisions to suppress aggregate concentration, although the intensity of regulatory enforcement has fluctuated over the decades. These provisions include restrictive policies specific to large business groups, a ceiling on the total shareholding that chaebol affiliates can hold in other companies, a prohibition on reciprocal shareholding and limits on debt guarantees among affiliated companies, and policies on holding companies.

First, MRFTA defines the standards for identifying business groups that are subject to KFTC's large business group policies, for example, the prohibition on reciprocal shareholding. As the economy has grown, the number of designated business groups and the size of their assets have also generally increased. There have been two breaks in this upward trend, in 2008 and 2016, when the standards for large business groups were modified. Currently, large business groups are defined as business groups with total assets greater than ₩10 trillion. Thirty-four business groups were designated as large business groups in 2019.

Second, until 2008, there was a ceiling on the total shareholding for a chaebol affiliate. Chaebol affiliates could not use more than 40 percent (changed to 25 percent in 1994) of their net assets to hold shares in other companies. This regulation was criticized because non-chaebol large firms that had subsidiaries and affiliated companies were also subject to this regulation, which made it difficult for large firms to expand into new markets (Ko, Cho, and Park 2006). The regulation gradually became obsolete and was abolished in 2009.

Third, MRFTA prohibits "reciprocal shareholding" (cross shareholding between two companies) if both companies belong to the same large business group. This regulation exists because owner families of the chaebols have used a high share of intragroup cross shareholdings to obtain corporate control rights without owning the majority of the shares. A variation of reciprocal shareholding is "circular" shareholding, which is a series of intercompany shareholding that constitutes a closed circle. Unlike reciprocal shareholding, circular shareholding has not been completely prohibited due to concerns that dismantling it could create a significant financial burden for some chaebol groups. Since 2014, new circular investments have been completely banned, and firms have been encouraged to reduce existing circular investments gradually.

Fourth, MRFTA originally prohibited the establishment of holding companies because they were considered to be conducive to the concentration of economic power. However, in 1999, it changed direction and allowed the establishment of holding companies but regulated their scope and behavior. This change was to encourage the chaebols that had a circular shareholding structure to become more transparent. Tax benefits were introduced to encourage the conversion to a holding company. Accordingly, the number of holding companies increased from 25 in 2005 to 193 in 2017. The numbers of subsidiaries and subsubsidiaries also increased in the same years, from 159 and 63 to 925 and 932, respectively. Recently, the minimum requirements for total assets and equity shares in subsidiary firms were increased, thus raising the minimum standards for becoming a holding company.

Fifth, MRFTA regulates internal transactions for tunneling as an unfair trade practice. Tunneling is the transfer of assets and profits out of a firm by the majority shareholders for their own benefit. In the case of the chaebols, tunneling occurs when affiliates in which the "owner" family has greater shares preferentially receive greater business opportunities from other affiliates or higher prices for goods and services provided to other affiliates. In advanced economies, these issues are generally resolved through civil disputes between shareholders in accordance with the commercial law rather than the competition law. In Korea, they have been subject to regulation by KFTC based on the MRFTA, which prohibits the provision of undue benefits to related parties. However, this prohibition has been criticized for not fitting the purpose of competition law and for unclear standards for enforcement (Yoon, Kim, and Kim 2016).

Efforts to reduce the economic dominance of large firms have been complemented by policy measures to protect SMEs, given concerns that large firms have enjoyed entrenched market power and raised barriers to entry for SMEs (Ciani et al. 2020). Such efforts were initiated in the 1970s through the third and fourth Five-Year Development Plans, which provided support to SMEs to supply parts and components to heavy and chemical industries. The SMEs benefited from the local content initiatives, but the subcontracting system has been criticized for unbalanced contract terms and concerns that it stifled SMEs' innovation (Ji et al. 2016). SMEs that subcontracted with large enterprises expanded their sales or assets but did not improve their operating profit, compared with other SMEs in 2013–14 (Chang 2020).

MRFTA and its companion statutes include provisions to protect SMEs against the abuses of large enterprises in transactions.[21] The Fair Transactions in Subcontracting Act of 1984 regulates against unfair subcontracting practices using both ex-ante and ex-post measures. The Large-Scale Retail Fair Trade Practices Act is specifically designed to curb unfair trade practices by large-scale retailers against SME manufacturers and suppliers. Finally, the Fair Franchise Transactions Act regulates trade between franchisors and franchisees. The Korea Fair Trade Mediation Agency was created in 2007 to facilitate a voluntary settlement between parties that are involved in unfair trade practices and franchise disputes.

Policies to restrict the entry of large enterprises into business sectors where SMEs are active have been in place for several decades in Korea. MRFTA prohibits barriers to entry that restrict competition, but there is strong political and social pressure to protect SMEs, and tension between the two objectives has persisted. One of the most notable entry barriers was the "Products Reserved for SMEs" regulation, which was introduced in 1979. At its peak in 1989, it restricted the entry of large enterprises in 237 product categories. However, the regulation was criticized for hindering the development of these industries and for nonconformance with the World Trade Organization. For example, restrictions in the packed soybean tofu market brought about product repositioning for large enterprises, which impaired the sales growth of both large enterprises and SMEs (Lee 2015). As a result, the regulation was gradually reduced and completely abolished in 2006.

The liberalization of the retail sector in the 1990s in the Republic of Korea illustrates the impact of firm entries on SMEs and on overall productivity. The reduction of barriers to entry in the mid-1990s led to the rapid expansion of big-box stores in the retail trade sector (Cho, Chun, and Lee 2015). Multinational retail corporations, for example, Carrefour, Tesco, and Walmart, as well as large domestic enterprises, such as Emart, opened retail stores in Korea. As a result, Korea's retail market expanded and net employment grew after the AFC, driven by the entry of large discount stores that increased from fewer than 300 in 2003 to more than 500 in 2014.

However, the number of small, independent stores declined from more than 100,000 in 2003 to about 70,000 in 2014 (Lee 2017). In response, the government-imposed restrictions on the entry and opening hours of big-box stores after 2010, and the contribution of entry and exit to productivity in the retail trade sector fell from 78 percent in 2005–10 to 56 percent in 2010–15. Similarly, studies of entry regulations in European countries show negative impacts of regulations on productivity growth and employment (see Bertrand and Kramarz (2002) for France; Schivardi and Viviano (2010) for Italy). In the United States, the entries of efficient stores and exit of inefficient stores accounted for nearly all sector-wide productivity growth of retail trade (Foster, Haltiwanger, and Krizan 2006). In response to the GFC, a move to revive entry barriers emerged as business conditions deteriorated. In 2010, the Korea Commission for Corporate Partnership was established, which introduced "products suitable for SMEs." The Commission was a private organization that managed entry regulations for large enterprises in select industries, through voluntary agreements between small and large enterprises. It set guidelines for entry and expansion regulations for 54 manufacturing businesses. The period of regulated entry is limited to up to six years, providing an opportunity for the smaller enterprises to strengthen their competitiveness during the protected period. However, evidence of such improvement is rarely found in the literature (see Lee [2015] for Korea; Martin, Nataraj, and Harrison [2017] for India), and the specified period is often extended. In 2020, the Special Act on the Designation of Types of Business Suitable for Livelihood of Micro Enterprises was enacted to reintroduce legal entry barriers. Korea's experience highlights the challenges of phasing out entry barriers given political and popular interests.

CORPORATE RESTRUCTURING AND GOVERNANCE REFORMS

An ambitious corporate restructuring program in the aftermath of the AFC complemented the comprehensive restructuring of the financial sector. The five largest chaebols were subjected to a Big Deals program, which required them to exchange business lines to streamline and prioritize their businesses. For the sixth through 64th conglomerates, firms were required to implement restructuring workout programs in return for debt reduction and rescheduling. The workout programs were led by the creditor banks but the financial supervisory authorities and the newly established Corporate Restructuring Coordination Committee oversaw and coordinated the workouts. Failure to implement successful restructuring would lead to insolvency of the firms. Altogether, 104 firms participated in the workout program. Of the 30 largest business groups in 1996, 14 went bankrupt or entered workout programs by the end of 1999, including Daewoo, one of the largest chaebols.

FDI restrictions were significantly loosened to mobilize foreign capital for the corporate restructuring. A new Foreign Investment Promotion Act (1998) streamlined investment procedures and strengthened incentives for foreign investments. Cross-border mergers and acquisitions were allowed, ceilings on foreign equity ownership in the stock market were eliminated, restrictions on foreign land ownership in the stock market were liberalized, and foreign exchange controls were liberalized. More than 30 sectors were liberalized after the AFC. Under the Foreign Exchange Transaction Act, restrictions on foreign ownership remain for 30 industrial sectors.

Corporate restructuring reforms were complemented by corporate governance reforms to promote prudent management and strengthen the transparency and accountability of corporate management. Before the AFC, corporate governance in Korea was characterized by several shortcomings, which were considered to have contributed to the AFC (Kim and Kim 2007; Nam 2004). First, there was a significant gap between the cash flow rights and control rights of the owner families of the chaebols. With complex cross holdings among affiliated firms, owner families were able to exercise significant control rights beyond their cash flow rights. In 1996, a typical controlling shareholder(s) of a chaebol had 23 percent of shares outstanding but controlled 68 percent of the votes, mainly through cross holding and circular holding of shares (Kim and Kim 2007). Second, the complex governance structure of the chaebols allowed them to rely on internal capital markets for financing through affiliated firms. As a result, the chaebols avoided having to disclose information for external financing and therefore lacked transparency. Third, there were few mechanisms to constrain the influence of the owner families. Minority shareholder rights were weak. Few Korean firms had outside directors (Kim, Kim, and Park 2021). The media was largely incapable of serving as a watchdog, as the chaebols were deeply involved in the ownership and revenue structures of the major news outlets.

After the AFC, the government implemented reform measures to improve corporate governance (Nam 2004). In 1998, the Securities and Exchange Act and the Commercial Codes were amended to relax requirements on exercising minority shareholder rights. It became easier for minority shareholders to file derivative suits, inspect accounting records, make a motion to dismiss certain directors, and file shareholder proposals (Nam 2004). Minority shareholders were more easily able to propose candidates for outside directors, and directors became more aware of their legal responsibilities in board meetings.

In 1999, the Securities and Exchange Act was amended to impose more stringent information disclosure requirements. As a result, public firms on KOSDAQ, the stock market mainly for technology businesses, had to publish financial reports more frequently and became subject to increased penalties for violation of information disclosure requirements. A subsequent amendment to the Monopoly Regulation and Fair Trade Act required large, chaebol-affiliated firms to disclose information on large-scale transactions with certain firms and obtain approval from their board of directors.

In 2000, the Securities and Exchange Act was amended to strengthen the role of outside directors. Large public firms were required to appoint at least half of their board members from outside and form a mandatory audit committee of which at least two-thirds of the members must be outside directors. Only a few firms had outside directors before the reforms, but most listed firms had outside directors five years after the crisis (Nam 2004).

As a result of the various reforms, there has been significant improvement in the quality of corporate governance according to the Korea Corporate Governance Index, which measures shareholder rights, board structure, board procedure, disclosure, and ownership parity (Black, Jang, and Kim 2005). The emergence of newly privatized, large non-chaebol firms also contributed to the increase in the Governance Index (Kim and Kim 2007). In response to the AFC, the government had decided to privatize or expedite the privatization of large SOEs, including KT, KT&G, POSCO, and state-owned banks, such as Kookmin, Shinhan, and Hana (Kim and Kim 2007). These firms were run by professional managers, and most of their shares were held by foreign investors. Therefore, they avoided the major governance issues of the chaebols and were subject to stringent international accounting standards as they were listed on foreign stock exchanges.

Korea's Growing Focus on SME and Entrepreneurship Development

Korea's chaebol-dominated industrial structure enabled the country to take advantage of economies of scale and opportunities for substantial cross subsidization, but it did not foster a dynamic group of SMEs and startups that could complement the large firms in contributing to Korea's economic growth (OECD 2009). Korea's rapid growth led by the chaebols was made possible by the significant accumulation of technological learning and managerial capabilities. However, such knowledge and learning were kept within a closed network of large firms (Oh 2010). Networking among the government research institutes, private R&D centers, and universities and with international firms and foreign R&D institutes remained relatively underdeveloped, which constrained technology diffusion across the national innovation system (Hwang et al. 2002). Since the 1990s, policies have evolved, reflecting a growing focus on SMEs and entrepreneurship development, in an effort to address some of these shortcomings. Greater attention to equitable growth and job creation also increased interest in supporting SMEs to broaden the sources and beneficiaries of growth, including firms from regions outside major cities, woman-owned businesses, microenterprises, businesses in traditional markets, and startups.

GOVERNMENT SUPPORT FOR MSMEs

Many of the policy instruments of the 1990s that provided access to finance for R&D (grants, loans, and tax incentives) and worked through the demand side of innovation (such as public procurement) were expanded in the 2000s. Government support for access to commercial borrowing from the banking system was reoriented to SMEs. As a result, SMEs accounted for about 90 percent of all corporate loans in the mid-2000s. SMEs' leverage increased substantially, and many required debt restructuring following the GFC.

Changes in the policy mix led to the expansion and diversification of the types of policy instruments targeting firms. Support was increased for firms with high growth potential (for example, technology-intensive firms, startups, and medium-size enterprises) and in different stages of growth (for example, proof-of-concept, scale-up, or restructuring), and firm type (innovative, middle-market, and small enterprises) (Jang 2009). After the dot-com bubble burst in 2000, resulting in the poor performance of venture capital (VC) firms, the government established Korea Venture Investment Corporation (KVIC) in 2005 as a fund-of-funds to support co-investment of public and private entities. Public procurement for innovation was expanded through the New Technology Purchasing Assurance Program, which was launched in 2003. Under this program, public institutions and large corporations commissioned SMEs to develop new technologies that were purchased to stimulate innovation (Kim 2007).[22] The promotion of startups ("venture firms") became a central government agenda after the AFC. Table 3.2 lists major policies that aimed to improve the startup business environment, in particular by expanding access to financing for startups.

The drive to promote technology diffusion for SMEs was initiated in the 1980s. The government began to build an extensive network of public and nonprofit technical support programs to provide technology extension services to SMEs. They included government research institutes, industry-specific R&D institutes, standards associations, and the Korea Productivity Center,[23] which delivered training and advice on quality control, value engineering, factory automation, and distribution systems (Kim 1997). Technology extension services provided support for the introduction, adoption, and utilization of innovative technologies (Lee et al. 2014). Startup support infrastructure, such as innovation centers, incubation centers, and regional centers, was also introduced during this period (Hwang et al. 2002). These technology and knowledge diffusion policy instruments were enabled by the growing market penetration of computers and cell phones, and the growth of the internet and related IT industries. The government also established clusters and networking measures targeted at firms, domestic and foreign R&D institutes, government research institutes, science and technology parks, incubators, and research centers at universities. They included the establishment of international joint R&D centers and an exchange program for researchers and engineers (Hwang et al. 2002).

Vouchers for innovation were also used for non-R&D-based innovation. In 2005, the SME Consulting Service Program introduced innovation vouchers for SMEs to receive business advisory consulting services. The program also implemented training programs, a code of ethics for consultants, and a consultancy evaluation system to build an industry of consultants who could support SMEs (Kim 2007). Policy makers helped with specialized diffusion agents, such as consultant engineering firms, capital goods producers, and researchers.

Other important MSME support policies include (a) assistance in finding and maintaining quality personnel, for example, through incentives to retain core employees, customized university education for students who are to be employed by SMEs, and support to connect job seekers with SMEs; (b) support for SME sales, through public procurement (box 3.2), export-related services, SME exclusive sales outlets,

TABLE 3.2 Major Policy Actions and Events to Support Startups, Republic of Korea

Administration	Policy actions and events
The 1980s through the early 2000s	• 1986: Support for Small and Medium Enterprise Establishment Act, Financial Assistance to New Technology Businesses Act • 1996: The Small and Medium Business Administration established; the Korean Securities Dealers Automated Quotations opened • 1997: Act on Special Measures for the Promotion of Venture Businesses • 2002: The venture firm registration system redesigned
Roh Mu-hyun (2003–08)	• 2003: Enhancing transparency of venture capital • 2004: Measures to promote venture firms • 2005: Rolling out a fund-of-funds • 2006: Measures to promote venture capital (for example, on private fund-of-funds) • 2007: Promoting new-technology spinoffs from universities and research institutions; renewing the Act on Special Measures for the Promotion of Venture Businesses
Lee Myung-bak (2008–13)	• 2008: Measures to promote technology startups • 2011: Measures to promote startups by youths
Park Geun-hye (2013–17)	• 2013: Streamlining startup and venture capital promotion programs; starting the Tech Incubator Program for Startups
Moon Jae-In (2017–22)	• 2017: Measures to further develop the innovation startup ecosystem • 2018: Measures to promote scaling-up

Source: Korea Development Institute 2021.

BOX 3.2 Public Procurement and SME Growth and Innovation in the Republic of Korea

In the Republic of Korea, public procurement has been used to promote the growth of small and medium-size enterprises (SMEs) by encouraging or requiring a level of purchases from SMEs and providing loans to SMEs that supply the government. Starting in the 2000s, the government added new public procurement policy instruments to promote technological innovation among SMEs, targeting the commercialization of research and development (R&D) products, creating new markets, and rewarding innovation through certification. New programs included designating product standards and certifications of product and service innovation, and requiring public organizations to purchase certified R&D products and pre-commercial R&D products.

Overall, the policy instruments have been successful in supporting the participation of SMEs in public procurement. SMEs accounted for 77 percent of the ₩135 trillion public procurement market in 2019 (Statistics Korea 2020b). Impact evaluations of public procurement for supporting SMEs and innovation in the 2010s indicate that public procurement policies have had positive impacts on SMEs. For SMEs that were certified to supply the "Excellent Product Market" between 2011 and 2016, their non–public sector sales increased more rapidly the higher the share of public sector sales in total sales (Lee and Jung 2018). Participation in public procurement programs led to a positive effect on product innovation among venture firms and inno-biz firms[a] (Choi et al. 2014). However, when other firms that were not designated as venture or inno-biz firms are included, public procurement programs had a negative effect on product innovations (Choi et al. 2014). The review of procurement policies by the government-led Task Force on Contract System Innovations in 2020 observed that procurement processes that did not consider the high-risk nature of R&D products and the risk aversion of procurement agencies meant that the potentially most innovative R&D projects were not being supported (Government of the Republic of Korea 2020a).

Source: Frias et al. (2021).

a. Through its certification scheme, the Korean government designates SMEs with high technological innovation capabilities as "venture firms" and "inno-biz firms." Although the specific certification criteria change over time, in general, SMEs need to score high in relevant rating systems and undergo onsite assessments to be certified as venture firms or inno-biz firms. Certified SMEs enjoy several benefits, such as tax incentives and R&D support, as well as positive recognition.

---

a dedicated TV shopping channel, and an e-commerce platform for SMEs; (c) consulting support, for example, through the "bizinfo" website and the "1357 call center"; and (d) combined support policies to provide a comprehensive menu of services, for example, the World Class 300 project.

As a result of the reorientation of the government's support policies and programs to MSMEs, MSMEs now receive 58 percent of government support for business innovation and hence are the largest beneficiary of public innovation support (Frias et al. 2021). Compared to the Ministry of Trade, Industry and Energy (MOTIE), Ministry of Science and ICT (MSIT), and MOEF, MSS programs provide a greater share of support for younger and smaller firms with high growth potential (figure 3.23). For example, 82 percent of the MSS's resources for innovation support goes to firms that have not been formally established, whereas the shares for MSIT, MOTIE, and MOEF are 42, 15, and 5 percent, respectively.

As the government's business innovation support policy expanded and became more diverse and complex, there was a need for improved coordination and efficiency in strategic policy making, design, implementation, and evaluation across ministries, implementing agencies, and regional government units (Lee 2017). The president-chaired council (under various names and configurations) continued to oversee the strategy, budget allocation, and evaluation of national R&D projects. Administrative rules to facilitate coordination provided detailed, technical guidelines and were generally respected and followed even though they were not legally binding (Chung 2016). Interagency coordination at the level of policy design and implementation became legally mandated. The Small and Medium Business Administration was elevated to the MSS, along with the establishment of the SME Policy Deliberative Council to coordinate the MSME policies of the central government. The full impact of these efforts remains to be seen.

Knowledge management systems were established to help manage the expanded SME support programs. The Small Business Integrated Management System manages all SME support programs to improve program coordination.[24] K-Startup is a portal that provides information on government support

FIGURE 3.23 **Targeting of Beneficiaries for Innovation Support, by Ministry, Republic of Korea, 2018**

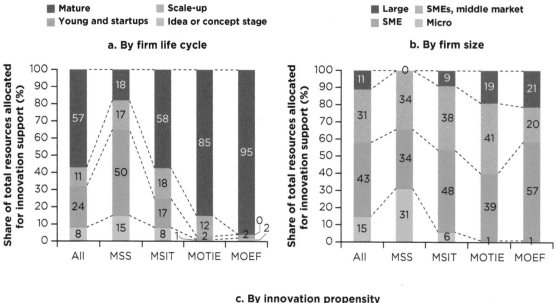

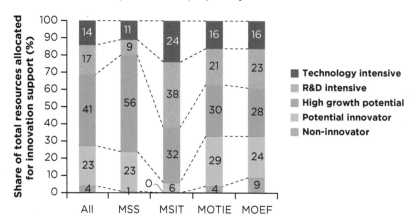

Sources: Frias et al. 2021, based on data from MOEF 2017; ministry budget and planning documents.
Note: MOEF = Ministry of Economy and Finance; MOTIE = Ministry of Trade, Industry, and Energy; MSIT = Ministry of Science and ICT;
MSS = Ministry of SMEs and Startups; R&D = research and development; SMEs = small and medium-size enterprises.

for entrepreneurs, and Business Support Plus is a one-stop shop for accessing business-related public services from 15 government institutions. The National Science and Technology Information Service (NTIS) is a portal that consolidates and provides information on national R&D programs, projects, human resources, research equipment, facilities, and outcomes. Ministries and agencies are required to utilize NTIS when designing, implementing, and evaluating R&D projects, to minimize redundancy, increase the utilization of research equipment and facilities, and ultimately increase overall R&D investment efficiency (NTIS 2020).

These national-level coordination and knowledge management efforts aimed to enhance the complementarity among policy instruments in Korea's complex innovation policy mix and maximize their impact on innovation performance (Frias et al. 2021). As an example, SMEs are certified for having developed innovative products by participating in an R&D support program and are then eligible to be sellers and participants in public procurement for innovation programs. These certifications serve as a stamp of credibility and allow innovative SMEs to access and leverage other types of support and services across their growth life cycle.

The extensive public support programs have helped SMEs to cope with financial difficulties, but a large and complex government support program inevitably raises the potential for inefficient allocation of resources. There have been concerns about insufficient public support for startups and younger SMEs compared to older SMEs, SMEs becoming complacent and too dependent on public support, and project performance evaluation and inspections that have been insufficient, allowing poorly performing companies to continue to access government support (Baek 2017; FSC 2008). Some have argued that government interventions reduced the incentives for financial institutions to improve their capacity for credit evaluation of SMEs, thus impeding the development of a private market for SME financing and prompting more government intervention (Jones and Kim 2014).

There have also been concerns about the duplication of support programs. In 2012, 51.7 percent of firms that received support from the Small and Medium Business Corporation, a government agency that was later renamed the Korea SMEs and Startups Agency, also received guarantees or loans from other policy finance institutions in the same year (Yoon 2012). From 2011 to 2013, 22 companies received financing from the central government's startup support fund at least 65 times each, and 299 companies received financing at least four times (Baek 2017).

Firm support policies are most effective when focused on promoting firm growth and productivity and when the support is not differentiated by firm size (Medvedev et al. 2021). The proliferation of SME support programs in Korea could incentivize SMEs to remain small to stay eligible for public support, thereby foregoing the efficiency gains and economies of scale associated with growth. Firms that received public funding for SMEs in 2009 had an estimated 4.92 percent lower productivity in 2011 than they would have had if they had no public funding, but their survival probability increased by 5.32 percentage points (Chang, Yang, and Woo 2013, 2014). This highlights the need to shift the emphasis of SME policies from survival to productivity. Tax incentives, tax credits, and exemptions for SMEs should be phased out when they no longer contribute to improving the performance of the firms. Many tax incentives for SMEs have sunset rules, but few of them are discontinued. The Special Tax Reduction for SMEs, the largest tax incentive for SMEs, was introduced in 1992 with a specified end date for the availability of the tax incentives, to stabilize the management of manufacturing SMEs, but it has been extended repeatedly and still existed in 2022.

PROMOTION OF ENTREPRENEURSHIP

The development of Korea's entrepreneurial ecosystem goes back to the late 1990s when the first generation of venture firms emerged (Sohn 2006). In response to the AFC, the Act on Special Measures for the Promotion of Venture Businesses was enacted in 1997 and policy support for entrepreneurial businesses was expanded. As a result, the country experienced its first venture boom that produced technology startups that have grown to become some of the largest companies in Korea. They include internet platform companies Naver and Kakao, which were established in 1999 and 2014, respectively, and bio-pharmaceutical company Celltrion, which was established in 2002. These are now among the 15 largest companies in Korea, by market capitalization, as of February 2023.

Naver, Kakao and Celltrion were essentially the earliest unicorns that have successfully gone public.[25] As of early 2022, Korea was ranked 10th in the world in the number of unicorn companies (18 unicorns) compared to the United States (489 unicorns), China (171), and India (53) (MSS 2022). Most of the unicorns in Korea are business-to-customers service startups in e-commerce, games, cosmetics, and wholesale and retail businesses. This reflects Korea's highly developed ICT-based e-commerce industry and the computer games and beauty products industries. Government policy support has targeted the creation of unicorns, including through grants for international expansion, a special credit guarantee provided by the Korea Technology Finance Corporation, and government-arranged networking opportunities with investors.

Korea's entrepreneurial environment is ranked ninth of 44 countries, according to the Global Entrepreneurship Monitor's National Entrepreneurship Context Index.[26] This is higher than the rankings of Germany, the United Kingdom, and the United States. When it comes to individual entrepreneurial framework conditions, Korea compares particularly well on government support and policies, entrepreneurial education and training, and internal market dynamics, but it compares relatively poorly on R&D transfers and cultural and social norms (GEM 2020) (figure 3.24). Korea's capital city, Seoul, has made meaningful progress in growing its entrepreneurial ecosystem in recent years, but its startup ecosystem lags that of many other cities in high-income economies, ranking 20th of 40 global startup ecosystems (Startup Genome 2020).

Korea has both the highest rate of new businesses and the highest rate of deaths of businesses among comparators (table 3.3). The number of newly registered businesses increased from about 1.2 million in 2016 to about 1.5 million in 2020. Among these firms, the number of newly registered technology-based businesses was 190,674 in 2016 and 228,949 in 2020 (KOSIS 2021). The rapid growth in recent years, especially of businesses in technology-based industries, indicates increasingly active early-stage entrepreneurial activity in Korea. In addition, Korea's total early-stage entrepreneurship activity[27] rate increased from 6.7 percent in 2016 to nearly 15 percent in 2019 (Korea Entrepreneurship Foundation 2019), significantly higher than the total early-stage entrepreneurship activity rates of China (8.7 percent); Taiwan, China (8.4 percent); and Japan (5.4 percent). However, in Korea, the one-year and two-year survival rates were 64 and 53 percent, respectively, which were lower than those in all comparators (table 3.3). The relatively high death rate suggests that startups face significant challenges to scaling up and growing.

The volume of capital flowing into startups has decreased rapidly since the second half of 2022 when VC investors became more cautious, in line with global VC investment trends. For instance, in the second half of 2022, investment in startups in Korea was ₩3.8 trillion (about US$3 billion),

FIGURE 3.24 **Entrepreneurial Framework Conditions, Selected Countries**

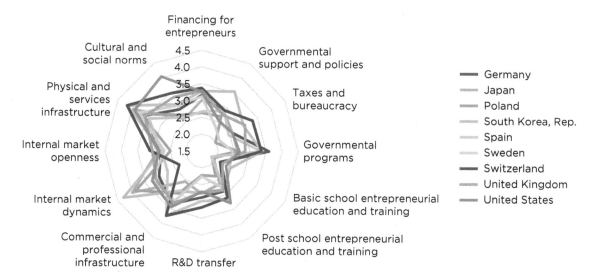

Source: Calculations based on data from Global Entrepreneurship Monitor 2020.
Note: Scores are based on expert ratings of the entrepreneurial framework conditions. For more information on the National Expert Survey conducted for the Global Entrepreneurship Monitor reports, see Global Entrepreneurship Research Association (2021). The scores range from 1 = very inadequate insufficient status, to 5 = very adequate sufficient status. R&D = research and development.

TABLE 3.3 **Birth and Death Rates of Businesses in Selected Countries, 2018 (percent)**

	Korea, Rep.	Germany	Czechia	Spain	Switzerland[a]	Sweden	Poland	Türkiye[a]
Birth rate	14.7	8.0	9.5	9.7	6.8	6.3	13.3	14.1
Death rate	11.1	8.9	8.2	8.0	6.9	5.5	11.2	12.1
Business churn (birth rate + death rate)	25.8	16.9	17.6	17.7	13.7	11.9	24.5	26.2
1-year survival rate	63.7	74.9	84.6	75.6	82.0	96.8	74.6	80.2
2-year survival rate	52.8	60.1	71.5	64.2	69.6	86.8	58.2	64.8

Sources: Calculations based on data from Statistics Korea 2020a; Eurostat 2021.
Note: The birth (death) rate of a given reference period (usually one calendar year) is the number of births (deaths) as a percentage of the population of active enterprises, as defined by Eurostat and OECD (2007).
a. Data for 2017 were used due to limited data availability.

which was a sharp decline from the ₩7.2 trillion (about US$5.7 billion) in the first half of the year (Startup Alliance 2023a, 2023b). This declining trend is aligned with the recent global slowdown in VC investment. In 2022, global venture funding totaled US$445 billion, marking a 35 percent decline year-over-year from US$681 billion in 2021 (Crunchbase 2023).

The size of Korea's VC market has grown over the past decade to one of the largest in the world. In 2021, the amount of VC investments in Korea was equivalent to 0.26 percent of GDP, the third highest among OECD countries after the United States and Canada (OECD 2021). Korea's VC investments increased from 0.05 percent of GDP in 2010 to 0.26 percent in 2021, making one of the highest jumps among OECD countries (figure 3.25). The number of VC funds increased from 101 in 2013 to 231 in 2022. Over the past several years, the concentration of VC investments in a small number of industries has intensified. The biotechnology, distribution, and IT services industries together accounted for 23.8 percent of the total amount of VC investment in 2010 and over 70 percent in 2022 (Born2Global Centre 2020; KVCA 2023).

To support technology startups and the VC market, the government established public funds and significantly expanded the promotion of technology value assessments and technology-related financing. In 2005, the government established its first fund-of-funds venture fund, the Korea Venture Investment Corporation, to catalyze and mobilize private financing and promote the expansion of the VC market. As a public organization under the Ministry of SMEs and Startups (MSS), KVIC is mandated by the Venture Investment Promotion Act. The director for the Venture Investment Division of MSS sits on KVIC's board, and the division supervises the operation of KVIC.

From 2017 to 2021, on average, the fund-of-funds accounted for about 20 percent of the total amount of new VC funds raised in Korea (KVCA 2022), indicating that public funds play a significant role in facilitating VC investments. The share of government-financed fund-of-funds in newly formed venture funds has remained relatively stable at around 20 percent over the past two decades, making the government the single largest contributor (Kwak 2019). In Brander, Du, and Hellmann's (2015) study of 25 major economies between 2000 and 2008, Korea had the highest ratio of firms with government-sponsored VC funding, with over 60 percent of firms that were financed by VC having government-sponsored VC support. The KVIC fund of funds has mobilized private co-investment in VC funds that is five times KVIC's funding, suggesting that the fund-of-funds has had a significant "crowding-in" impact (Kwak 2019).

Most domestic VC firms continue to receive financing from the government's fund-of-funds. Korea's unicorns have been the exceptions, by successfully attracting not only domestic funding, but also overseas funding (Kim, Lee, and Lee 2020). There are increasing calls for the role of the government to be reduced given the expansion of the private VC market (Asan Nanum Foundation 2021; K. H. Lee 2019; STEPI 2018).

FIGURE 3.25 **Venture Capital Investment, Selected Countries, 2010–21**

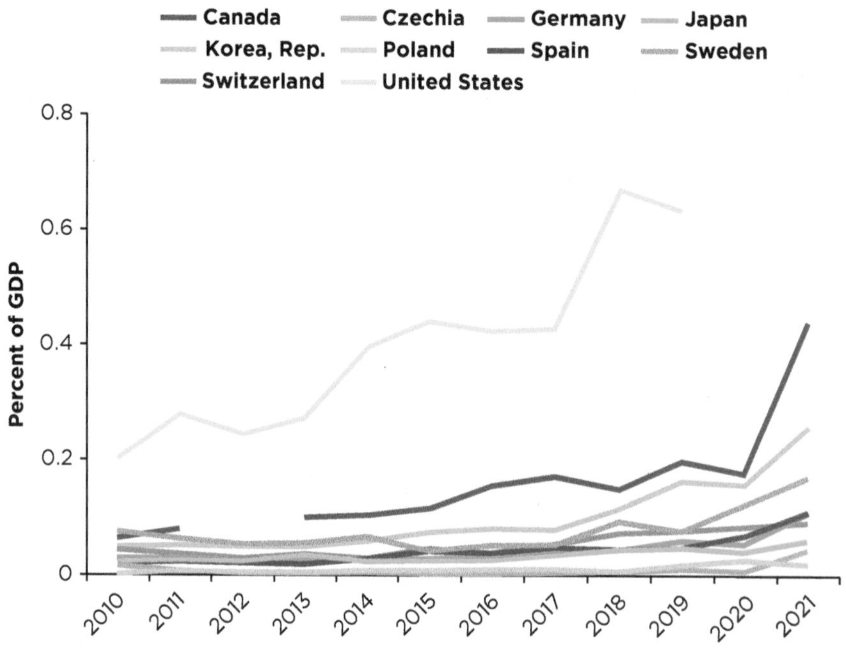

Source: Science, Technology and Innovation Scoreboard, Organisation for Economic Co-operation and Development (https://www.oecd.org/sti/scoreboard.htm).
Note: GDP = gross domestic product.

There are concerns that private fund managers can become complacent in mobilizing additional private financing after securing the government contribution (Kwak 2019).

Korea's angel investing and crowdfunding markets have also experienced significant growth. Angel investment increased from ₩959 billion (about US$65 million) invested in 251 firms in 2014, to ₩5,538 billion (about US$495 million) invested in 1,061 firms in 2018. The government supported the rapid growth of angel investments through tax benefits and support programs for startup accelerators. An amendment to the tax law in 2018, which allowed angel investors to claim tax deductions for their angel investments, is credited with having fueled the growth of angel investments (Born2Global Centre 2020; STEPI 2021).[28] As a result, the number of accelerators increased from 53 in 2017, to 133 in 2018, to 214 in 2019 (KIET 2020).

To complement the main Korea Stock Exchange, the Korean Securities Dealers Automated Quotations (KOSDAQ) and Korea New Exchange (KONEX) were established to facilitate capital flows to small and medium-size enterprises and startups. All three markets are managed by the semipublic Korea Exchange (KRX). KOSDAQ was established in 1996 to focus on technology firms, modeled on the US NASDAQ. In the early 2000s, the bursting of the IT bubble in the United States led to a similar contraction of KOSDAQ, but it has since recovered and expanded along with the expansion of the digital economy. As of September 2022, 1,578 firms were listed on KOSDAQ with a market capitalization of ₩318.5 trillion (approximately US$223 billion). Listing requirements are more lenient at KOSDAQ. Firms could qualify for further relaxed special listing conditions if the competitiveness of their technology were verified by public research and evaluation institutes. Conditions for listing at KOSDAQ have been steadily tightened since its establishment to strengthen investor protection as the market has been tumultuous, with several incidents involving KOSDAQ-listed firms that led to their delisting. As a result, it has also become increasingly difficult for smaller firms to meet the entry requirements, with the average time before listing at KOSDAQ increasing from 9.3 years in 2004 to 13.3 years in 2011.

Consequently, KONEX was established in 2013 with even less stringent requirements for listing. Most notably, unlike the Korea Stock Exchange and KOSDAQ, KONEX does not have financial requirements or requirements on the proportion of stocks owned by minority shareholders. Instead, a nominated advisor at a securities company validates the firm prior to the listing and supports the writing of firm status reports in place of quarterly and biannual reports. As of September 2022, 126 firms were listed on KONEX, with a market capitalization of ₩4.2 trillion (US$2.95 billion). Firms can transfer from the smaller to larger stock exchanges. KRX supports the transfer of stock listing from KONEX to KOSDAQ if firms satisfy one of the four requirements on marketability (revenue and operating profit threshold), profitability (profit from continuing operations and return on equity), growth potential (increase rate and size of revenue), and market capital.

Merger and acquisition activities have been on a steady rise in recent years in Korea, in both the number of deals and the size of deals. The number of merger and acquisition deals among startups increased from 22 in 2016 to 126 in 2022 (Platum 2020; Startup Alliance 2023a, 2023b). Korea's mergers and acquisitions market is expected to continue to expand as a result of the legal recognition of corporate VC firms in 2020 (Asan Nanum Foundation 2021; Sohn 2018). The reform aimed to boost investments in startups by allowing large conglomerates to own and operate corporate VC firms (Government of the Republic of Korea 2020b). However, several restrictions on the scope, financing, and investment destination of the funds were imposed to maintain the historical separation between banking and commerce. Approximately 40 business groups already had corporate VC units outside their holding firms or in the form of overseas affiliates before the legal recognition in 2020 (KOSBI 2020).

Conclusions and Implications for Developing Countries

The AFC in 1997 had devastating impacts on output, jobs, and a large segment of the population. It also provided an opportunity to overhaul the relationship between the state and the private sector. Reforms in four areas—the corporate, financial, and public sectors and the labor market—successfully instituted a modern system of financial regulation, more transparent corporate governance, more efficient public sector management practices, a clearer legal basis for some of the existing labor market practices, and most of all, stronger market discipline. The principle of "too big to fail" was undermined by the bankruptcies of some of the largest chaebols. Aided by the quick recovery of exports, Korea overcame the crisis and resumed its economic growth.

State involvement in the market has undergone significant changes during the past decades in Korea, due to the restructuring of the financial system and the introduction of modern prudential regulation and streamlined financial supervision. Financial institutions are now far stronger and more diversified than previously. In macroeconomic management, greater independence of the monetary authority, active management of external risks, and prudent fiscal policy enabled flexible responses to the GFC. In the public sector, large-scale privatization after the AFC and governance reforms in the 2000s helped to improve the efficiency and transparency of SOEs (Park and Park 2011). Finally, a multitude of programs were introduced for the working poor, the elderly, pre-school children, college students, and other vulnerable groups, accompanied by growth in public spending.

Reviewing Korea's experience to date, observers in other developing countries may want to examine closely the role of the government in their own economies. Korea's experience demonstrates the difficulties in achieving long-term and sustained reductions in the regulatory burden, as political pressure to adopt regulations tends to increase as the complexity of the economy and various social needs increase. Korea's history demonstrates the dangers to the financial system and the economy of subsidizing large firms in a way that encourages risk taking, as well as how a sound financial system and appropriate macroeconomic policies can limit the impact of an economic shock of the magnitude of the GFC. Korea's record in maintaining macroeconomic stability highlights the value of inflation targeting as a means of monetary control. Korea's experience also provides a nuanced view of the impact of capital market liberalization on stability. Dismantling of capital market controls contributed to vulnerability to the AFC in the absence of complementary financial and corporate sector reforms, but the economy was more resilient to the GFC once those reforms were addressed post-AFC.

After the AFC, Korea reoriented its enterprise support policies to promote new growth industries by establishing a market-oriented, competitive order and promoting diverse and active policies focusing on MSMEs. This laid the groundwork for Korea to continue its growth and widened the potential sources and beneficiaries of growth. Korea's current innovation policy is a continuation as much as it is a departure from its past. The country has pursued a consistent and overarching objective of developing private sector capabilities throughout the history of its modern economic development. At the same time, the Korea has regularly revised and revisited its policies as its innovation and technological capabilities evolved, to respond to changing challenges. The significant focus on SME competitiveness, entrepreneurship, and technological leadership through R&D and patenting in the 2000s was a reflection of this evolution in response to the AFC. Throughout the evolution, there is no denying that the chaebols have been and remain major drivers of economic growth, but MSMEs and new entrants have increasingly been the major targets of policy support, with the objective of fostering their competitiveness and market competition.

There are three major attributes of Korea's policy support to enterprises and entrepreneurship. First, government policy support pivoted toward establishing the foundation for new growth industries by prioritizing high-technology R&D and startup promotion. Second, post-AFC, successive administrations have attempted to promote market competition and curb the economic dominance of the chaebols, including by regulating perceived unfair trade practices in transactions between large enterprises and SMEs, and by limiting the entry of large enterprises into specific markets. KFTC's role in promoting market competition expanded after the AFC. Third, the government's policies to support MSMEs have expanded and become diverse and large in scale. Support measures include R&D support programs, financing schemes, tax benefits, and regulatory reforms to improve the business environment. These measures have helped to expand MSMEs and, in particular their access to finance, but they have also been subject to criticisms about their impact on improving firm performance and the redundancy and inefficiency of the support.

The legal framework for market competition, which has become a driving force for industrial development, and the role of KFTC were strengthened following the AFC. The size of the fines and number of enforcements of violations of the competition law have increased substantially. KFTC is now viewed as one of the top competition authorities globally. A distinct mission of KFTC has been to protect SMEs against abuses by large enterprises in transactions. The competition authority has also attempted to curb the economic influence of the chaebols, but it remains unclear whether this has been successful. Competition policy will become even more relevant for tackling the new challenges posed by the digital economy. New market dynamics related to the platform economy, data governance, and mergers and acquisitions will require new and updated tools to ensure healthy competition and market inclusion. Korea's experience in promoting market competition and SMEs indicates that ensuring a competitive and dynamic market could be one of the most significant challenges in countries that achieve economic growth based on concentrated market power.

Korea's experience also demonstrates that governments can play a major role in fostering the development of a dynamic entrepreneurial ecosystem. Korea has made impressive progress in growing its entrepreneurial ecosystem over the past decade, which is evidenced by the high rate of technology startups, growth of the VC and angel markets, and initial public offerings. This progress benefited from concentrated public interventions that leveraged a diverse set of direct and indirect support instruments that targeted both the demand and supply sides of the entrepreneurial ecosystem. Nevertheless, some challenges persist, such as the high death rate of startups and a lack of sector diversification in VC investments.

Given the already high level of government support for entrepreneurship, the priority will be to leverage greater private sector resources.

Relatedly, Korea's experience underscores the importance of ensuring ease of entry and exit for aggregate productivity improvement, particularly in the service sector. New services technologies are often introduced by entering firms, so facilitating entry and supporting an efficient reallocation of resources from unprofitable firms are essential for productivity growth. Regulatory constraints on the entry of big-box stores and chain supermarkets led to a substantial decline in the contribution of entry to the productivity of the retail trade sector during 2010–15 compared to 2005–10.

Korea made concentrated and sustained efforts to transition to a digital, knowledge-based economy. Decades of investments in digitalizing the government are reflected in the country's top ranking in the United Nations e-Government Development Index. Digitalization has contributed to improving public sector transparency, efficiency, and public service delivery. The adoption of digital technologies by firms in Korea is accelerating. Nevertheless, there are growing concerns that digital transformation might be widening the gap between large enterprises and SMEs. This is consistent with evidence from other OECD countries as well. The digital gap between small and larger Korean firms persists, especially in more advanced digital technologies, such as cloud computing and big data. In the context of developing economies, where most firms are micro and small enterprises, Korea's experience demonstrates that access to digital technologies does not necessarily translate into adoption. The low adoption of productivity-improving digital technologies by micro and small enterprises could be related to not only the lack of financing, but also the lack of complementary assets that enable the efficient use of digital technologies. These intangible assets include managerial capabilities, complementary R&D, and human and organizational capacity. Thus, approaches to supporting digital adoption in developing economies should consider complementary enabling factors to improve firm productivity and competitiveness.

Korea has consistently prioritized enterprise support throughout its modern history. Post-AFC, it adjusted and recalibrated its enterprise support policy mix to focus on MSMEs and entrepreneurship development. Korea's MSME support policies are diverse and have substantial budgets, reflecting the policy recognition that SMEs are the foundation for job creation. The government's continuous efforts, policy experimentation, and commitment to the MSME agenda could provide a good policy learning reference for developing countries. Nevertheless, it is important to recognize that as the portfolio of policy instruments expands, so do the inefficiencies and coordination costs as well as risks of market distortion. From the standpoint of developing economies that have limited resources, it is important to ensure the functionality, selectivity, and effectiveness of existing policy instruments and provide justification for the introduction of new instruments.

SME targeting policies can suffer from high failure rates, and only a small share of SMEs grow to become large firms (Ciani et al. 2020), consistent with Korea's experience. In response, some governments target their enterprise support policies to "small and growing businesses" or "gazelles" that have the potential to grow fast in a short period of time (Grover, Medvedev, and Olafsen 2019).[29] In Korea, large firms that started as SMEs have grown by strengthening their technological capabilities through substantial and sustained investments in technological upgrading, supported by public research institutes that assimilated and disseminated advanced foreign technologies to local firms. The strengthened capabilities also enabled the participation of SMEs in global value chains (Lee et al. 2021; J. D. Lee 2016). Starting from the 1990s, Korea's public support schemes became more focused on helping firms to develop new technologies as opposed to adopting existing foreign technologies, and on promoting new venture firms. Learning from Korea's experience, developing countries can initially focus on strengthening the capability of small firms to learn, access, and assimilate existing knowledge (firm capability, upgrading policies), before transitioning to an emphasis on supporting the development of new technologies and innovations.

Korea has leveraged a diverse array of policies and mechanisms to generate, acquire, and disseminate knowledge, adjusting the policy mix according to the changing technological capabilities of firms and the evolving national innovation system. The SME policy mix encompasses the full spectrum of support instruments, including those that are less commonly used by peers, such as credit guarantees and public procurement for innovation. Korea's experience with its large and comprehensive SME support policies and programs highlights the importance of coordination among the policy instruments to ensure complementarity and reduce overlaps. Despite some inefficiencies and duplications, the complementarity among policy instruments has helped to enhance their impact (Frias et al. 2021). The centralization of information and data on SME support policies, in particular through NTIS, has contributed to policy coordination and increased access for prospective participants. Korea's experience suggests that developing economies can benefit significantly from strengthening coordination among government support programs, by clearly defining their policy goals and clarifying policy ownership, complemented by a clear mission and coordinated leadership by higher level agencies.

Notes

1. The data are for 2020 and are available at the Korean Statistical Information Service website: https://kosis.kr/statHtml/statHtml.do?orgId=101&tblId=DT_2KAA906_OECD.
2. Microenterprises are defined as firms with fewer than 10 employees, and SMEs as firms with 10 to 299 employees.
3. The upper limit of the number of employees used to designate an SME varies across countries. The OECD notes that the most frequent upper limit used is 250 employees, as in the European Union.
4. https://kostat.go.kr/portal/korea/kor_nw/1/9/4/index.board?bmode=read&bSeq=&aSeq=386619&pageNo=1&rowNum=10&navCount=10&currPg=&searchInfo=&sTarget=title&sTxt=.
5. The Survey of Business Activities, which is administered by Statistics Korea, categorizes Fourth Industrial Revolution technologies into (a) internet of things, (b) cloud, (c) big data, (d) mobile, (e) artificial intelligence, (f) block chain, (g) 3D printing, (h) robotics, and (i) augmented reality and virtual reality.
6. The chapter uses the taxonomy of digital technology proposed in Hallward-Driemeier et al. (2020): transactional technologies (e-commerce platforms), informational technologies (artificial intelligence, big data analytics, and cloud computing), and operational technologies (smart robots, 3D printing, and the internet of things).
7. https://stats.oecd.org/Index.aspx?DataSetCode=ICT_BUS.
8. The survey has been implemented in several countries, including Bangladesh, Brazil, Burkina Faso, Ghana, India, Kenya, Malawi, Poland, Senegal, and Vietnam. The survey was recently conducted in Korea in collaboration with the Science and Technology Policy Institute. The results are captured in a World Bank report (Cirera, Comin, and Cruz 2022).
9. The increasing importance of these organizations is discussed in *World Development Report 2017*, using data from Varieties of Democracy (World Bank 2017).
10. They were Pohang Steel and Iron Corporation, Korea Heavy Industries and Construction Company, Korea General Chemistry Corporation, Korea Technology Banking Corporation, National Textbook Corporation, Korea Telecom Corporation, Korea Tobacco and Ginseng Corporation, and Daehan Oil Pipeline Corporation. Privatization of these SOEs not only provided the government sales revenue of ₩24.3 trillion plus US$10.7 billion in foreign currency, but also raised their stock market values substantially.
11. They were Korea Electric Power Corporation, Korea Gas Corporation, Korea District Heating Corporation, and Korea Railroad.
12. The government designated 96 government activities for outsourcing in 1998. They were subsequently expanded to 1,750 activities by 2017.
13. Calculations are based on data from Bank of Korea (2018).
14. For a detailed description of the ITC crisis, see Shin and Park (2001).
15. Calculation is based on loans of all commercial banks, which include "city banks" and "local banks."
16. The source is e-National Indicators (https://www.index.go.kr).
17. https://www.transparency.org/.

18. Based on the information provided by "Better Regulation Portal" (www.better.go.kr) and reported by *Financial News*, July 21, 2021 (https://www.fnnews.com/news/202107211834153668) (in Korean).

19. The survey question: "In your country, how burdensome is it for businesses to comply with governmental administrative requirements (e.g., permits, regulations, reporting)?" [1 = extremely burdensome; 7 = not burdensome at all]. The survey was introduced in 2007.

20. Aggregate concentration measures the relative position of the chaebols in the overall economy, reflecting economic-political power exercised based on their importance in the economy. Ownership concentration measures the extent to which shares of stock exchange listed companies are widely or narrowly held. This concept describes the control of the chaebols' corporate assets by individual families.

21. Typically, transactional disputes between the parties are not handled by competition law in most advanced countries. However, in developing countries in which there is significant imbalance of economic power and underdeveloped legal and institutional frameworks, it could be argued that the competition authority could enforce transactional disputes as a second-best solution, to promote SMEs.

22. As of 2006, the New Technology Purchasing Assurance Program had 120 projects involving 45 government agencies and public institutions, such as the Korean Electric Power Corporation and the Korea Railroad Corporation, and large firms (Kim 2007).

23. The Korea Productivity Center started as a nonprofit organization in 1957 and was reestablished as a public entity by law in 1986 to promote industrial activities.

24. The Small Business Integrated Management System's website is www.sims.go.kr.

25. "Unicorns" are privately held startups with a market valuation of more than US$1 billion before they are listed on the stock market.

26. https://www.gemconsortium.org/news/global-entrepreneurship-monitor-releases-ranking-of-countries-for-conditions-to-start-a-business.

27. The total early-stage entrepreneurship activity rate is the percentage of individuals aged 18–64 who are either nascent entrepreneurs or owner-managers of a new business (less than 42 months). It measures a country's level of early-stage entrepreneurial activity.

28. Tax incentives targeting angel investors for the purposes of boosting innovation and creating fast-growing SMEs are used in other countries as well, such as Sweden and Türkiye (OECD 2020).

29. Grover, Medvedev, and Olafsen (2019) summarize effective growth entrepreneurship support policies as improving allocative efficiency, encouraging business-to-business spillovers, and strengthening firm capabilities. Korea's experience has demonstrated the effectiveness of this model (Amsden and Chu 2003).

References

Academy of Korean Studies. 2010. "Liberalization of Public Enterprises." *Encyclopedia of Korean Culture*. http://encykorea.aks.ac.kr/Contents/Item/E0067766.

Allen & Overy. 2020. "Global Cartel Enforcement Report 2020." Allen & Overy, London. https://www.allenovery.com/en-gb/global/news-and-insights/global-cartel-enforcement-control.

Amsden, A. H., and W.-W. Chu. 2003. *Beyond Late Development*. Cambridge, MA: MIT Press.

Asan Nanum Foundation. 2021. "International Comparisons for Increasing the Competitiveness of the Korean Entrepreneurial Ecosystem." Asan Nanum Foundation, Seoul, Republic of Korea.

Baek, H. 2017. "Establishment of an Efficient SME Support Policy System." *KOSBI SME Focus* 17–08. Seoul, Korea: Korea Small Business Institute. (Korean).

Bank of Korea. 2018. *Financial System in Korea*. Seoul, Korea: Bank of Korea.

Bertrand, M., and F. Kramarz. 2002. "Does Entry Regulation Hinder Job Creation? Evidence from the French Retail Industry." *Quarterly Journal of Economics* 117 (4): 1369–1413.

Bianchini, M., and I. Kwon. 2021. "Enhancing SMEs' Resilience through Digitalisation: The Case of Korea." OECD SME and Entrepreneurship Papers. OECD, Paris.

Black, B., H. Jang, and W. Kim. 2005. "Does Corporate Governance Predict Firms' Market Values? Evidence from Korea." Working Paper No. 86/2005, ECGI Working Paper Series in Finance. European Corporate Governance Institute, Brussels, Belgium.

Born2Global Centre. 2020. "Korea Startup Index 2019." Born2Global Centre, Pangyo, Kyonggi-do, Korea.

Brander, J. A., Q. Du, and T. Hellmann. 2015. "The Effects of Government-Sponsored Venture Capital: International Evidence." *Review of Finance* 19 (2): 571–618.

Campante, F., R. Durante, and F. Sobbrio. 2013. "Politics 2.0: The Multifaceted Effect of Broadband Internet on Political Participation." HKS Working Paper No. RWP13-014. https://papers.ssrn.com/sol3/papers.cfm?abstract_id=2326705.

Chang, W. 2020. "Does Subcontracting Pay for SMEs? Case of Korea." KIPF Working Paper, Korea Institute of Public Finance, Sejong City, Korea.

Chang, W. H., Y. H. Yang, and S. Woo. 2013. "Study on the Enhancement of the Small and Medium-Sized Enterprises (SMEs) Policy in Korea (I)." Research Monograph, Korea Development Institute, Sejong City, Korea. https://doi .org/10.22740/kdi.rm.2013.08.

Chang, W. H., Y. H. Yang, and S. Woo. 2014. "Study on the Enhancement of the Small and Medium-Sized Enterprises (SMEs) Policy in Korea (II)." Research Monograph, Korea Development Institute, Sejong City, Korea. https://doi .org/10.22740/kdi.rm.2014.10.

Cho, J., H. Chun, H. Kim, and Y. Lee. 2017. "Job Creation and Destruction: New Evidence on the Role of Small versus Young Firms in Korea." *Japanese Economic Review* 68 (2): 173–87.

Cho, J., H. Chun, and Y. Lee. 2015. "How Does the Entry of Large Discount Stores Increase Retail Employment? Evidence from Korea." *Journal of Comparative Economics* 43 (3): 559–74.

Cho, Y. J., and J. K. Kim. 1997. *Credit Policies and Industrialization of Korea.* Sejong City, Korea: Korea Development Institute.

Choi J., K. H. Lee, J. Y. Seo, S. Kim, S. Lee, and B. G. Kim. 2014. "Improvement Strategies of Public Procurement Market Policy for Fostering Technology Based Innovative SMEs." Science and Technology Policy Institute, Sejong City, Korea.

Chung, S. 2016. "Improving Evaluation System for Encouraging Collaboration among Government Departments." Korea Institute of Public Administration, Seoul.

Chung, S., and S. Aum. 2021. "Organizing for Digitalization at the Firm Level." SSRN: https://ssrn.com/abstract =3976386 or http://dx.doi.org/10.2139/ssrn.3976386.

Chung, S., and M. Kim. 2021. "How Smart Is a 'Smart Factory'? Drivers and Effects of Factory Smartization." SSRN: https://ssrn.com/abstract=3934026 or http://dx.doi.org/10.2139/ssrn.3934026.

Ciani, A., M. C. Hyland, N. Karalashvili, J. L. Keller, A. Ragoussis, and T. T. Tran. 2020. *Making It Big: Why Developing Countries Need More Large Firms.* Washington, DC: World Bank.

Cirera, X, D. Comin, and M. Cruz. 2022. *Bridging the Technological Divide: Technology Adoption by Firms in Developing Countries.* The World Bank Productivity Project. Washington, DC: World Bank. https:// openknowledge.worldbank.org/handle/10986/37527.

Cirera, X., D. Comin, M. Cruz, and K. M. Lee. 2020. "Technology within and across Firms." Policy Research Working Paper 9476. World Bank, Washington, DC. https://openknowledge.worldbank.org/handle/10986/34795.

Coppedge, M., J. Gerring, S. I. Lindberg, J. Teorell, D. Altman, M. Bernhard, M. S. Fish, et al. 2015. "Varieties of Democracy: Codebook v4." Gothenburg, Sweden: Varieties of Democracy (V-Dem) Project, V-Dem Institute, University of Gothenburg; Notre Dame, IN: Helen Kellogg Institute for International Studies, University of Notre Dame.

Crunchbase. 2023. "Global Funding Slide in 2022 Sets Stage for Another Tough Year." January 5 (accessed February 9, 2023) https://news.crunchbase.com/venture/global-vc-funding-slide-q4-2022/.

Dixit, A. K. 2004. *Lawlessness and Economics: Alternative Modes of Governance*. Princeton University Press. http://www.jstor.org/stable/j.ctt7t9hw.

Doner, R. F., and B. R. Schneider. 2016. "The Middle-Income Trap: More Politics Than Economics." *World Politics* 68 (4): 608–44. http://www.jstor.org/stable/26347364.

Eurostat. 2021. "Business Demography." Eurostat, Luxembourg. https://ec.europa.eu/eurostat/web/structural -business-statistics/business-demography?p_p_id=NavTreeportletprod_WAR_NavTreeportletprod _INSTANCE_48fubot8Z80W&p_p_lifecycle=0&p_p_state=normal&p_p_mode=view.

Eurostat and OECD. 2007. *Eurostat–OECD Manual on Business Demography Statistics*. Paris: European Communities. https://ec.europa.eu/eurostat/web/products-manuals-and-guidelines/-/ks-ra-07-010.

FnGuide. 2021. "Financial Affairs." Data Guide. Seoul, Korea: FnGuide. https://dataguide.fnguide.com/eng.

Foster, L., J. Haltiwanger, and C. J. Krizan. 2006. "Market Selection, Reallocation, and Restructuring in the U.S. Retail Trade Sector in the 1990s." *Review of Economics and Statistics* 88 (4): 748–58.

Freund, C., and M. D. Pierola. 2015. "Export Superstars." *Review of Economics and Statistics* 97 (5): 1023–32.

Freund, C., and M. D. Pierola. 2020. "The Origins and Dynamics of Export Superstars." *World Bank Economic Review* 34 (1): 28–47.

Frias, J., H. Lee, M. A. Lee, and R. Balbontin. 2021. "The Korean Innovation Policy Mix: Lessons from Building Technological and Innovation Capabilities and Implications for Developing Countries." World Bank, Washington, DC.

FSC (Financial Services Commission). 2008. "Market-Friendly SME Finance Support Plans (unofficial translation)." Press release, June 11, 2008. (Korean).

GEM (Global Entrepreneurship Monitor). 2020. "Entrepreneurial Framework Conditions." GEM, London. https://www.gemconsortium.org/data/key-nes.

Global Entrepreneurship Research Association. 2021. "Global Entrepreneurship Monitor 2020/2021: Global Report." Global Entrepreneurship Monitor, London. https://www.gemconsortium.org/report/gem-20202021-global-report.

Government of the Republic of Korea. 2020a. "Three Innovative Measures for Public Procurement System for Achieving Innovative Growth and Fair Economy." Published jointly by line ministries, October 27. Government of the Republic of Korea, Seoul. https://eiec.kdi.re.kr/policy/materialView.do?num=206326. (Korean).

Government of the Republic of Korea. 2020b. Proposal for Limiting CVC Holding for General Holding Companies." Government of the Republic of Korea, Seoul. https://www.ftc.go.kr/www/selectReportUserView .do?key=10&rpttype=1&report_data_no=8642. (Korean).

Government of the Republic of Korea. 2021. "Two Years of Implementing Regulatory Sandboxes: Exemplars." Government of the Republic of Korea, Seoul. https://www.opm.go.kr/flexer/view.do?ftype=pdf&attachNo=104945.

Grover Goswami, A., D. Medvedev, and E. Olafsen. 2019. *High-Growth Firms: Facts, Fiction, and Policy Options for Emerging Economies*. Washington, DC: World Bank. https://openknowledge.worldbank.org /handle/10986/30800.

Haggard, S., W. Lim, and E. Kim. 2003. *Economic Crisis and Corporate Restructuring in Korea*. Cambridge University Press.

Hallward-Driemeier, M., G. Nayyar, W. Fengler, A. Aridi, and I. Gill. 2020. *Europe 4.0: Addressing the Digital Dilemma*. Washington, DC: World Bank.

Han, J. 2020. "Motives for Self-Employment by Life Stages." In *Study on Self-Employment and Policy Suggestions*, edited by J. Lee. Sejong City, Korea: Korea: Development Institute. https://www.kdi.re.kr/kdi_eng/pub/17140 /Study_on_Self-Employment_and_Policy_Suggestions.

Hwang, Y., Y. Bae, J. Park, H. Cho, Y. Chang, and N. S. Vornortas. 2002. "Techno-Economic Paradigm Shift and Evolution of STI Policy in Korea and the United States." Research Report 2002-12. Science and Technology Policy Institute, Seoul, Korea.

IFR (International Federation of Robotics). 2020. "Welcome to the IFR Press Conference." September 24. Frankfurt, IFR. https://ifr.org/downloads/press2018/Presentation_WR_2020.pdf.

IMF (International Monetary Fund). 1997. IMF Stand-By Arrangement. December 5. International Monetary Fund, Washington, DC. https://www.imf.org/external/np/oth/korea.htm.

Jang, J.-H. 2009. "Review of Consistency of SME Policy: Application of Disparity Theory on the Institutional Discourse." *Korean Public Management Review* 23 (2): 191–214.

Ji, M., J. Shin, M. Kang, Y. Park, and J. Park. 2016. "A Study on SME Innovation in Subcontracting." Research Paper 2016-824, Korea Institute for Industrial Economics & Trade, Sejong City, Korea.

Jones, R. S., and M. Kim. 2014. "Promoting the Financing of SMEs and Start-ups in Korea." OECD Economics Department Working Papers No. 1162, OECD Publishing, Paris. http://dx.doi.org/10.1787/5jxx054bdlvh-en.

Karippacheril, T. G., S. Kim, R. P. Beschel, Jr., and C. Choi, eds. 2016. *Bringing Government into the 21st Century: The Korean Digital Governance Experience.* Directions in Development–Public Sector Governance. Washington, DC: World Bank. https://openknowledge.worldbank.org/handle/10986/24579.

KFTC (Korea Fair Trade Commission). 2011. *Trace of Market Economy Development: Korea Fair Trade Commission, History of 30 Years.* Sejong City, Korea: KFTC.

KIET (Korea Institute for Industrial Economics & Trade). 2020. "Catalyzing Angel Investments in Start-ups." Issue Paper 2020-08, KIET, Sejong City, Korea.

Kim, E. H., and W. Kim. 2007. "Corporate Governance in Korea: A Decade after the Financial Crisis." Law and Economics Research Paper No. 123, University of Texas School of Law, Austin, TX. https://doi.org/10.2139/ssrn.1084066.

Kim, I., Y. Kim, and Y. Park. 2016. *The Expansion of Global Value Chains and Industrial Policy Implications in Korea.* Sejong City, Korea: Korea Institute for Industrial Economics & Trade. (Korean).

Kim, J.-Y. 2007. "SME Innovation Policies in Korea." In *The Policy Environment for the Development of SMEs*, 129–50. Singapore: Pacific Economic Cooperation Council.

Kim, L. 1997. *Imitation to Innovation: The Dynamics of Korea's Technological Learning.* Cambridge, MA: Harvard Business School Press.

Kim, S. W., Y. J. Lee, and J. W. Lee. 2020. *Innovative Startup and Entrepreneurship Ecosystem Monitoring (Year 6), Volume 2: In-Depth Study on the Performance Improvement of Innovative Start-up Ecosystem in Korea.* Sejong City, Korea: Science & Technology Policy Institute.

Kim, W., W. Kim, and K. S. Park. 2021. "A Survey of Research on the Corporate Governance of Korean Firms." ECGI Working Paper Series in Finance Working Paper No. 804/2021, European Corporate Governance Institute, Brussels, Belgium.

Ko, D., H. Cho, and M. Park. 2006. "The Relationship between Restriction on Total Amount of Share Holding of Other Company and Corporate Investment." Korea Institute for Industrial Economics & Trade, Sejong City, Korea. (Korean).

Koh, Y. 2010. "The Growth of Korean Economy and the Role of Government." In *The Korean Economy: Six Decades of Growth and Development*, edited by I. Sakong and Y. Koh, 7–82. Sejong City, Korea: Korea Development Institute.

Korea Development Institute. 2021. "Preparing the Three-year Plan to Support Business Startups (2021-2013)." Commissioned Report for the Korea Institute of Startup & Entrepreneurship Development (in Korean), p. 89. Korea Development Institute, Sejong City, Korea.

Korea Entrepreneurship Foundation. 2019. "Global Entrepreneurship Monitor (GEM) 2019 Korea." Korea Entrepreneurship Foundation, Seoul, Republic of Korea. https://www.gemconsortium.org/economy-profiles /south-korea-2/policy.

KOSBI (Korea Small Business Institute). 2020. "A Study on the Introduction of Corporate Venture Capital." Seoul, Korea, KOSBI. https://www.kosbi.re.kr/kosbiWar/front/functionDisplay?menuFrontNo=2&menuFrontURL=fr ont/basicResearchDetail?dataSequence=J210422K05.

KOSIS (Korean Statistical Information Service). 2021. "Status of New Businesses: Number of New Businesses by Industry"]. KOSIS, Daejeon, Korea. https://kosis.kr/statisticsList/statisticsListIndex. do?menuId=M_01_01&vwcd=MT_ZTITLE&parmTabId=M_01_01&outLink=Y&parentId=J2.1;J2_21.2;#cont ent-group.

KVCA (Korean Venture Capital Association). 2022. "Statistics and Trends of Domestic Venture Capital Investments: First Quarter of 2022." KVCA, Seoul, Korea. http://webzine.kvca.or.kr/202205/?idx=11.

KVCA (Korean Venture Capital Association). 2023. "2022 Venture Capital Brief." KVCA, Seoul, Korea. https://www .kvca.or.kr/Program/board/listbody.html?a_gb=board&a_cd=15&a_item=0&sm=4_1&page=1&po_no=6211.

Kwak, G. 2019. "Effects of the Fund-of-Funds on the Domestic Venture Capital Industry." *Korea Venture Investment Corporation Market Watch*, vol. 10. https://www.kvic.or.kr/marketWatch/marketWatch1_1.

Lee, C. 2019. "Expansion of Productivity Gaps between Firms: Trends and Implications." *KOSTAT Statistics Plus*, vol. 6 (Summer). http://kostat.go.kr/sri/srikor/srikor_pbl/8/1/index.board.

Lee, H., S. H. Kim, Y. J. Kim, W. S. Jung, H. J. Yun, S. W. Kang, T. Y. Hwang, and J. S. Hong. 2013. "Korea's Developmental Experiences in Operating Competition Policies for Lasting Economic Development." 2013 Modularization of Korea's Development Experience. KDI School of Public Policy and Management, Sejong City, Republic of Korea.

Lee, J. 2015. "The Economic Effects of Designating Suitable Businesses for SMEs: The Case of the Korean Tofu Market." Policy Study 2015-1, Korea Development Institute, Sejong City, Korea.

Lee, J. 2017. "The Economic Effects of Expanding Private Brand of Large Retail Chains." KDI Policy Research Series 2017-02, Korea Development Institute, Sejong City, Korea. https://www.kdi.re.kr/research/subjects_view .jsp?pub_no=15203. (Korean).

Lee, J. 2020. "Effects of Small Business Support Projects: Evidence from Korea." *KDI Journal of Economic Policy* 42 (1): 1–30.

Lee, J., J. Han, J. Kim, Y. Oh, M. Kim, and J. Bae. 2020. "Study on Self-Employment and Policy Suggestions." KDI Research Paper 2020-06, Korea Development Institute, Sejong City, Korea. https://www.kdi.re.kr/research /subjects_view.jsp?pub_no=17140.

Lee, J. D. 2016. "Middle Innovation Trap: Transition Failure from Implementation Capability to Concept Design Capability as a Source of the Middle Income Trap." Paper for HSE International Research Conference on Foresight and STI Policy. Higher School of Economics, National Research University, Moscow, Russian Federation.

Lee, J. D., K. Lee, D. Meissner, S. Radosevic, and N. Vonortas, eds. 2021. *The Challenges of Technology and Economic Catch-up in Emerging Economies*. Oxford, UK: Oxford University Press.

Lee, K. H. 2019. "Enhancing the Role of Risk Capital in Promoting Innovative Start-ups." National Assembly Research Service, Seoul, Republic of Korea.

Lee, M. 2016. "Analysis of the Effects of Government Regulation Reform on National Industries with Regulation Reform Index." Korean Economic Forum 9, 2. Seoul, Korea: The Korean Economic Association. http://www.kea .ne.kr/publication/kef/article/read?page=3&perPageNum=10&searchType=&keyword=&sortType=&sortOrder =&id=2137.

Lee, M., and T. Jung. 2018. "The Effects of Public Procurement on the Growth of Small and Medium Enterprises." *Asia Pacific Journal of Small Business* 40 (4): 33–50.

Lee, W., B. Kim, J. Jung, and S. Lee. 2014. "A Study on the Korean Government's Support Measures for Private Firms' Science, Technology, and Innovation Promotion." Science and Technology Policy Institute, Sejong City, Republic of Korea.

Lim, W. 2012. "Chaebol and Industrial Policy in Korea." *Asian Economic Policy Review* 7 (1): 69–86. https://ssrn.com /abstract=2073143 or http://dx.doi.org/10.1111/j.1748-3131.2012.01218.x.

Martin, L. A., S. Nataraj, and A. Harrison. 2017. "In with the Big, Out with the Small: Removing Small-Scale Reservations in India." *American Economic Review* 107 (2): 354–86.

Medvedev, D., R. Aliyev, N. Ramin, M. Bruhn, P. G. Correa, R. J. Garcia Ayala, J. P. W. Hill, S. Farazi, J. E. Lopez Cordova, C. Piza, A. Sakhonchik, and M. Seja. 2021. *Strengthening World Bank SME-Support Interventions: Operational Guidance Document.* Washington, DC: World Bank Group.

MOEF (Ministry of Economy and Finance). 2017. "2018 Tax Expenditure Budget Report 2017." MOEF, Sejong City, Republic of Korea.

MPM (Ministry of Personnel Management). 2018. "Level of Government Employees' Salaries Relative to the Private Sector." MPM, Sejong City, Republic of Korea.

MSIT (Ministry of Science and ICT) and NIA (National Information Society Agency). 2020. *Yearbook of Information Society Statistics.*

MSIT (Ministry of Science and ICT) and NIA (National Information Society Agency). 2021. *History of Korean Information and Communication Network Development.* https://www.korea.kr/archive/expDocView.do?docId =39683.

MSS (Ministry of SMEs and Startups). 2022. "Korea Reaches 18 Unicorns amid Its Second Venture Boom." Press release. MSS, Sejong City, Republic of Korea. https://www.mss.go.kr/site/smba/ex/bbs/View.do?cbIdx=86&bcId x=1031900&parentSeq=1031900.

Nam, I. C. 2004. "Corporate Governance in the Republic of Korea and Its Implications for Firm Performance." ADB Institute Discussion Paper No. 10, Asian Development Bank, Tokyo, Japan.

NTIS (National Science and Technology Information Service). 2020. "Information Partners." NTIS, Daejeon, Republic of Korea (accessed February 23, 2020), https://www.ntis.go.kr/en/GpInformationPartners.do.

OECD (Organisation for Economic Co-operation and Development). 2009. *OECD Reviews of Innovation Policy: Korea 2009.* Paris: OECD.

OECD (Organisation for Economic Co-operation and Development). 2020. *Financing SMEs and Entrepreneurs 2020: An OECD Scoreboard.* Paris: OECD Publishing. https://doi.org/10.1787/061fe03d-en.

OECD (Organisation for Economic Co-operation and Development). 2021. "Science, Technology and Innovation Scoreboard." OECD, Paris. https://www.oecd.org/sti/scoreboard.htm.

OECD (Organisation for Economic Co-operation and Development). 2022a. "Self-Employed with Employees." Indicator. OECD, Paris (accessed May 21, 2022), https://doi.org/10.1787/b7bf59b6-en.

OECD (Organisation for Economic Co-operation and Development). 2022b. "Self-Employed without Employees." Indicator. OECD, Paris (accessed September 7, 2022), doi:10.1787/5d5d0d63-en.

Oh, D. 2010. "Dynamic History of Korean Science & Technology." Korea Institute of Science and Technology Evaluation and Planning, Seoul, Republic of Korea.

OPC (Office of Government Policy Coordination). 2021. "Master Plan for Overhauling Regulations." OPC, Sejong City, Republic of Korea. https://policy.nl.go.kr/search/searchDetail.do?rec_key=SH2_PLC20210263659.

Park, J., and S. Park. 2011. "Evaluation of Privatization of State-Owned Enterprises and Suggestions." Korea Institute of Public Finance, Sejong City, Republic of Korea. https://www.kipf.re.kr/cmm/fms/FileDown.do?atchFileId=FIL E_000000000011972&fileSn=0.

Platum. 2020. "2019 Report on Domestic Start-up Investment Trends." Platum, Seoul, Republic of Korea. https:// www.slideshare.net/platum_kr/2019-platum. (Korean).

Pollack, A. 1997. "Crisis in South Korea: The Bailout; Package of Loans Worth $55 Billion Is Set for Korea." *New York Times*, December 4. https://www.nytimes.com/1997/12/04/business/crisis-south-korea-bailout-package-loans-worth-55-billion-set-for-korea.html.

Schivardi, F., and E. Viviano. 2010. "Entry Barriers in Retail Trade." *Economic Journal* 121 (551): 145–70.

Shin, I. 2006. "Evolution of Korean Financial Regulations." In *Regulatory Reforms in the Age of Financial Consolidation*, edited by J. C. Lee and J. K. Kim. Sejong City, Republic of Korea: Korea Development Institute.

Shin, I., and H. Park. 2001. "Historical Perspective on Korea's Bond Market: 1980–2000." Working Paper 2001-02, Korea Development Institute, Sejong City, Republic of Korea.

Sohn, D. 2006. "The Advancement and Evolution of the Venture Ecosystem of Korea." Science and Technology Policy Institute, Sejong City, Republic of Korea. https://nkis.re.kr:4445/subject_view1.do?otpId=STEPI00011541&otpSeq=0&popup=P#none.

Sohn, S. J. 2018. "A Review on Function of CVC." *Journal of SME Finance* (Winter).

Song, Y. 2020. "Trade Liberalization and Manufacturing Productivity Changes in Korea during the Past Three Decades." Korea Development Institute, Sejong City, Republic of Korea.

Startup Alliance. 2023a. "Report on Startup Investments in 2022." Startup Alliance, Seoul, Republic of Korea (accessed February 9, 2023), https://infogram.com/2022-1hmr6g7rnv0zz6n?live.

Startup Alliance. 2023b. "Summary of Startup Investment Trends of 2022." Startup Alliance, Seoul, Republic of Korea. https://brunch.co.kr/@startupalliance/369.

Startup Genome. 2020. "The Global Startup Ecosystem Report: The New Normal for the Global Startup Economy and the Impact of COVID-19." Startup Genome. https://startupgenome.com/report/gser2020.

Statistics Korea. 2020a. "2019 Administrative Statistics on Enterprise Births and Deaths." Statistics Korea, Daejeon, Republic of Korea. http://kostat.go.kr/portal/korea/kor_nw/1/9/6/index.board?bmode=read&bSeq=&aSeq=386537&pageNo=1&rowNum=10&navCount=10&currPg=&searchInfo=&sTarget=title&sTxt=.

Statistics Korea. 2020b. "Statistics on Public Procurement." Statistics Korea, Daejeon, Republic of Korea. https://kosis.kr/statisticsList/kosis.kr.

Statistics Korea. 2022. "2021 Trade by Enterprise Characteristics." Statistics Korea, Daejeon, Republic of Korea. https://kostat.go.kr/portal/korea/kor_nw/1/9/8/index.board?bmode=read&bSeq=&aSeq=418419&pageNo=1&rowNum=10&navCount=10&currPg=&searchInfo=&sTarget=title&sTxt=.

STEPI (Science and Technology Policy Institute). 2018. "The Role of Technology Financing and Its Efficiency Model for Korea." STEPI, Sejong City, Republic of Korea.

STEPI (Science and Technology Policy Institute). 2021. "Korean Start-up Ecosystem Dashboard." STEPI, Sejong City, Republic of Korea. https://www.stepi.re.kr/site/stepiko/report/View.do?reIdx=36&cateCont=A0204.

United Nations. 2020. *UN E-government Survey 2020*. New York: United Nations. https://publicadministration.un.org/egovkb/en-us/Reports/UN-E-Government-Survey-2020.

WEF (World Economic Forum). 2019. *Global Competitiveness Report 2019*. Geneva: World Economic Forum. https://www3.weforum.org/docs/WEF_TheGlobalCompetitivenessReport2019.pdf.

World Bank. 2017. *World Development Report 2017: Governance and the Law*. Washington, DC: World Bank. https://openknowledge.worldbank.org/handle/10986/25880.

World Bank and V-Dem (Varieties of Democracy). 2016. Measuring Elite Power and Interactions Survey (database). World Bank, Washington, DC.

Yoon, S. 2012. "Evaluation of SME Lending Support Programs." National Assembly Budget Office, Seoul, Republic of Korea. (Korean).

Yoon, S., J Kim, and Y. Kim. 2016. "Regulation on Tunneling According to the Monopoly Regulation and Fair Trade Act: Focusing on Prohibition of Exploitation for Private Gains." *Business, Finance & Law* 78, 78. ISSN 1598-9887. (Korean).

CHAPTER 4

Leveraging Global Integration and International Trade

Introduction

The Republic of Korea is well known for its successes with manufacturing exports. It has also been broadly recognized in the literature that successful developments in Korea's exports prior to the 1990s were largely attributed to the government's export promotion policies (Connolly and Yi 2015; Krueger 1997; Nam 1995; Westphal 1978, 1990).[1] A rich literature describes Korea's reliance on government-led trade and industrial policies to promote manufacturing exports from the 1960s to the 1980s, which was a key factor supporting Korea's sustained economic growth.

However, few studies systematically review the more open trade and foreign investment policies since the 1990s, when the government undertook a unilateral liberalization of import tariff rates, entered into multiple free trade agreements, and strengthened trade facilitation. The country also increased its overseas direct investments (ODIs) to expand its manufacturing base in foreign countries. These policies have helped Korea to become deeply integrated into global value chains (GVCs), outsource business activities and functions, and incentivize domestic firms to focus on more innovative and higher value-added activities. They helped Korea transition from a producer of light manufacturing products to a major global supplier of capital- and technology-intensive manufactured goods. The modernization of Korea's manufacturing sector was a key driver of the country's enhanced international competitiveness and economic growth.

In contrast to the more rapid and proactive trade liberalization, Korea's financial liberalization process has been slower and more nuanced. A critical shortage of foreign safe assets left Korea vulnerable to the Asian Financial Crisis (AFC). In response, the government has accumulated a significant volume of foreign reserves. Korea's global financial integration was relatively more rapid in the early 2010s, after the significant accumulation of international reserves.

Korea's global integration provides notable policy lessons. First, trade openness and active participation in GVCs are essential for enhancing the competitiveness of an economy, particularly the manufacturing sector. Second, financial liberalization can be strategically implemented with calibrated countercyclical

This chapter was prepared by Ekaterine T. Vashakmadze, Jongrim Ha, Daisuke Fukuzawa, and Juncheng Zhou (World Bank); Woo Jin Choi (University of Seoul); Sunghoon Chung (Korea Development Institute); and Ju Hyun Pyun (Korea University). Ruth Banomyong (Dean, Thammasat Business School, Thammasat University) contributed on trade facilitation.

macroeconomic policies to achieve stable and resilient economic growth. Third, developing countries should be technologically ready for the ongoing wave of digital globalization of goods, services, and labor markets so that they can fully exploit the new opportunities, as Korea did through integration into GVCs.

This chapter provides a comprehensive review of Korea's integration process into the world trade and production systems over the past three decades, focusing on government policies that facilitated this integration. The chapter provides an integrated analysis of Korea's trade and financial liberalization and explains its benefits for economic growth and resilience to external shocks. The chapter starts by examining trade liberalization episodes in Korea. After a brief review of the historical background that links the experiences before and after the 1990s, the chapter describes the country's overall trade performance since the 1990s and presents key characteristics of Korea's international trade. These characteristics are further investigated through the lens of GVCs, which are arguably the most important feature of globalization in this era. The chapter then analyzes Korea's financial integration. It discusses how increased precautionary savings contributed to a favorable environment for economic stability and growth in the real sectors. The chapter examines the evolution of Korea's vulnerability to global macroeconomic shocks. The empirical analysis demonstrates Korea's experience in insulating the domestic economy from increased global shocks following the liberalization processes. The last section examines remaining policy challenges in Korea and draws key policy implications for developing countries.

Trade Liberalization in the GVC Era

HISTORICAL BACKGROUND

In its earlier development stages, from the 1960s to the 1980s, exporting manufactured products was Korea's key policy choice for economic growth, considering the country's small domestic market, lack of natural resources, and unsuccessful import substitution industrialization. Government intervention played a central role in incentivizing firms to participate in the global market. Export promotion became a main pillar in the series of Five-Year Economic Development Plans. Thirty-eight separate export promotion schemes, with provisions affecting tariffs, domestic taxes, subsidies, credit rationing, and licensing, were implemented by the end of the 1970s (Hong 1979).

The literature highlights two trade policies (Westphal 1990; Connolly and Yi 2015). The first is the tariff exemption on imported intermediate and capital goods that were used to produce goods for export, and the second is the gradual reduction of general tariff rates, initiated in the 1980s. These policies reflected the government's intention to gain price competitiveness by combining Korea's lower cost domestic labor with foreign intermediate and capital goods and, at the same time, to protect domestic infant industries from foreign competition.

Although the trade policies in the 1960s and 1970s are generally considered to have helped Korea's economy to take off, there was increasing criticism in the 1980s that the assembly and processing industries expanded too much by overprotecting finished products and under-protecting raw and production materials. The concern is empirically supported in the literature (Aw, Chung, and Roberts 2003; Don, Gunasekera, and Tyers 1990; Kim 2000; Lee 1996). The literature indicates that the distortion driven by trade protection in selective industries contributed to resource misallocation and reduced these industries' productivity (Lee 1996).

In the meantime, the global trade environment had changed substantially and pushed Korea's trade policies to be more harmonized with the global trend. Two rounds of the General Agreement on Tariffs and Trade (GATT), the Kennedy Round (1964–67) and the Tokyo Round (1973–79), resulted in substantial tariff reductions on industrial products and new rules for anti-dumping duties recognized by GATT Article VI.[2] As a GATT member since 1967, Korea was directly affected by the agreements. Political pressure from advanced countries to open markets became greater since the mid-1980s when the Plaza Accord took effect and the current account balance became a surplus in Korea. In particular, Article 301 of the US Trade Act led to trade negotiations with the United States to open Korea's domestic markets to foreign investments, including the tobacco and insurance markets. Finally, the fall of communism at the end of the 1980s provided substantial momentum for global economic integration.

In the 1990s, three interlinked events promoted the next round of global integration: (a) the establishment of the World Trade Organization (WTO), (b) widespread adoption of information and communications technology (ICT), and (c) China's global integration.

First, the Uruguay Round (1986–94) concluded with the agreement on establishing the WTO, a new trade system to replace the "provisional" GATT system. The WTO established rules on services trade, intellectual property protection, and trade-related investments that were not covered by the GATT. Furthermore, various exceptions to the trade rules, such as for multilateral textile agreements, voluntary export restraints, and agricultural products, were abolished or restricted. Launched in 1995, the new multilateral trading system provided an international institutional framework for expedited globalization.

Second, the world in the 1990s experienced a rapid diffusion of ICT.[3] ICT revolutionized the global production system, allowing manufacturing to be optimized by locating different stages of the production process across different countries. Since ICT can deliver production know-how and managerial skills across countries, the location of production was no longer restricted to a single country. Firms in developed countries began to relocate their production facilities to foreign countries (figure 4.1, panel a) and offshore tasks to third parties based on comparative advantage, forming global production networks.

Finally, the 1990s saw the integration of China into the global market. After the open door policy in 1979, foreign direct investment (FDI) flows into China had increased, but they accelerated in the 1990s (figure 4.1. panel b). In 1994, for instance, more than 13 percent of foreign investments worldwide was absorbed in China. Its export share also steadily increased. China's rise as a global manufacturing hub was the result of increased demand by developed countries for production sites with lower cost labor and materials and China's policy incentives to attract foreign investment and promote exports.

These three factors jointly promoted a new form of global production system by distributing production processes internationally, described as the "the second unbundling" of globalization (Baldwin 2016). The first big wave of globalization came with the separation of production and consumption, and the

FIGURE 4.1 **Global FDI Trend and China's Integration, 1970–2020**

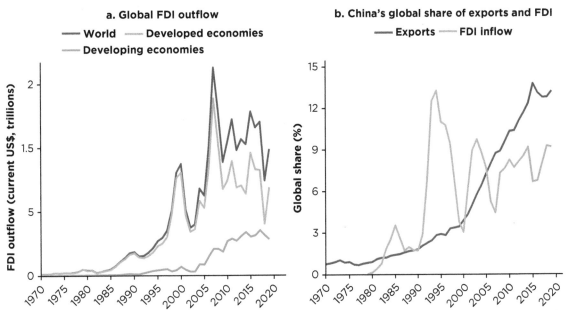

Source: United Nations Conference on Trade and Development Data Center.
Note: FDI = foreign direct investment.

second wave resulted from the unbundling of production across countries, forming the GVCs. The ratio of global value added to exports declined by 8.5 percentage points from 1990 to 2008, which is about three times as large as the decline over 1970–89 (Johnson and Noguera 2017). The decline in the ratio indicates a rise in multi-stage production (GVC) activities across countries.

Given the historical background and the changing global environment, Korea's trade policy reoriented to liberalizing the domestic market and reducing government intervention. A major tariff rate reduction scheme was implemented from 1984 to 1988 and from 1989 to 1994 (table 4.1). The scheme announced in advance the future schedule of general tariff reductions over the next five years, which aimed to provide domestic firms time to prepare for potential import competition. The simple average tariff rates of all products in table 4.1, panel a, were 23.7 percent in 1983 prior to the reduction scheme but fell to 7.9 percent in 1994 when the scheme finished, similar to the levels in major advanced countries. The tariff reductions mainly targeted manufactured final goods. Previously, Korea's tariff system had imposed differential tariff rates depending on the processing stage, with the highest rates on final goods. The tariff reduction scheme abolished the differential tariff system and imposed a uniform tariff rate of 8 percent on most manufactured goods. By 1994, this rate was applied to more than 60 percent of all imported products.

The median tariff rate of 8 percent has been maintained from 1994 until now, with 1 to 2 and 3 percent for noncompetitive raw materials and competitive raw materials, respectively; 5 to 8 percent for primary simple processing products; 8 percent for other manufactured products; and 20 to 50 percent for agricultural products. Although there have been incremental tax rate adjustments since the mid-1990s, including tariffs on textiles, there have been no fundamental changes in the general tariff rates in Korea over the past 30 years. The major overhaul of the tariff system for trade liberalization was completed in the mid-1990s when Korea was still an upper-middle-income economy.

TRADE PERFORMANCE SINCE THE 1990s

Liberalization policies at home and the conducive global environment in the 1990s and 2000s helped Korea to take full advantage of the extraordinary growth in international and regional trade. The export

TABLE 4.1 **Reduction of General Tariff Rates, Republic of Korea (average tariffs, percent)**

Products	1983	1984	1988	1989	1994	2000
a. Simple average tariff rates						
All	23.7	21.9	18.1	12.7	7.9	8.6
Agricultural products	31.4	20.6	25.2	20.6	16.6	18.6
Industrial products Raw materials	11.9	10.6	9.5	3.9	2.8	2.5
Intermediate goods	21.5	18.7	17.7	11.7	7.0	6.8
Final goods	26.4	24.7	18.9	13.3	7.1	7.0
b. Detailed tariff rates on industrial products						
Median of all industrial products	20	20	20	15	8	8
Raw materials Noncompetitive	5–30	5–10	5	1–2	1–2	0–2
Competitive		10	10	5	3	1–3
Intermediate goods (primarily processed)	20–50	20–30	10–20	10	8	5–8
Final goods General	40–80	40–50	20–30	15	8	8
Textiles						10–16

Source: Ministry of Finance and Economy, Press Releases (1994 and 1997).

share in gross domestic product (GDP) in Korea rose from 11.4 percent in 1970 to 34.8 percent in the late 1980s, after which the share fell for a few years (figure 4.2, panel a). The share has resurged since the mid-1990s at a rapid pace, rising from 24.6 percent in 1995 to 53.3 percent in 2011, an increase of nearly 30 percentage points. A similar pattern is also observed in imports. The increase in trade openness, measured by the sum of export and import shares in GDP, from 1995 to 2011 was one of the largest among major countries, and far exceeded the world average growth (figure 4.2, panel b). As a result, in 2012, Korea became the fourth Asian economy to enter the top 10 global exporters and importers list, after China, Japan, and Singapore. In 2020, trade came close to 80 percent of Korea's GDP.

The total share of the top five exporters to Korea was close to 60 percent in the 1990s but fell to less than 50 percent over the past decade, indicating that Korea's imports have gradually diversified (figure 4.3, panel a). Korea's top five export destinations accounted for about 50 percent of total exports in all three decades (figure 4.3, panel b). However, there have been significant changes in the composition within the five countries. The reliance on Japan and the United States has declined, and China's share has increased substantially to about 20 percent in imports and 25 percent in exports as of 2019. Rapid export growth to Vietnam is also a notable phenomenon in recent years. The composition changes suggest the important roles of China and Southeast Asian economies—referred to as Factory Asia—in the growth of Korea's trade.

The product compositions of imports and exports, according to the Broad Economic Categories, have exhibited different patterns (figure 4.3, panels c and d). First, the high share of raw material imports throughout the sample period sharply contrasts with the minimal export share of the same goods, which indicates that Korea has a significant comparative disadvantage in raw material exports. Second, most of the imported products prior to the 1990s were intermediate (parts and components and semifinished) and capital goods, in part due to the government's trade policies, but their shares declined steadily as the

FIGURE 4.2 **Trade Performance, by Country, 1970–2019**

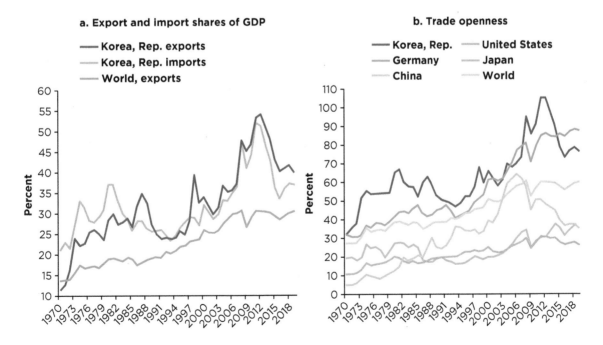

Source: World Development Indicators, World Bank, 2020 (https://databank.worldbank.org/source/world-development-indicators).
Note: Trade values include both goods and services. GDP = gross domestic product.

FIGURE 4.3 Compositional Changes in Korean Merchandise Trade

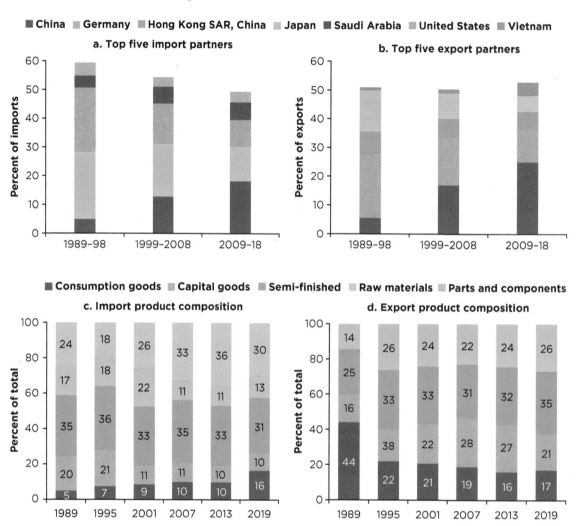

Source: Calculations based on data from World Integrated Trade Solution, World Bank.
Note: The product classification in panels c and d is based on the Broad Economic Classification.

market was liberalized. By contrast, the import share of consumption goods increased by more than 10 percentage points over the past 30 years. The opposite is true in exports. Korea used to export manufactured final goods through its processing industries (44 percent in 1989), but subsequently became one of the major exporters of intermediate and capital goods.

Korea experienced significant structural changes in merchandise exports (figure 4.4). First, the foreign content of exports (panel a) declined up to 1995 and has since been increasing, showing a V-shaped trend.[4] Second, Korea's export products began to become sophisticated in the mid-1990s (panel b) and, as a result, high-technology products became the largest share of total exports. These two structural changes coincided with the rapid increase of the export share in GDP (figure 4.2), rising share of China as a trading partner and expansion of exports of intermediate and capital goods (figure 4.3), and the global trend of FDI acceleration and China's integration into GVCs (figure 4.1).

Korea's large firms have been at the forefront of its trade expansion. As of 2015, the share of Korea's large firms in total exports was close to 80 percent, one of the highest across countries (figure 4.5).

FIGURE 4.4 **Structural Changes in Merchandise Exports, Republic of Korea, 1980–2010**

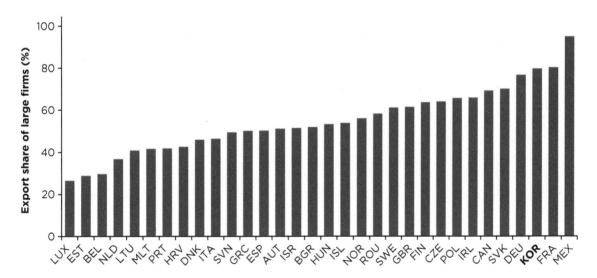

Sources: For panel a, calculation using input-output tables from the Bank of Korea (for available years); for panel b, Observatory of Economic Complexity V3.0 (https://legacy.oec.world/en/rankings/country/eci/).

FIGURE 4.5 **Export Share of Large Firms across Countries, 2015**

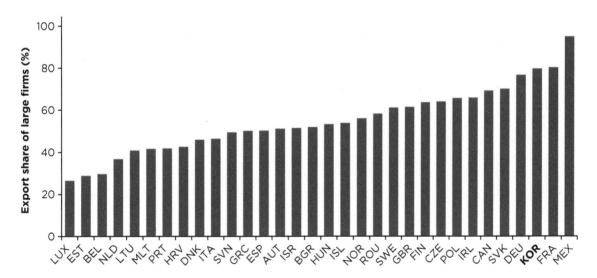

Source: Trade by Enterprise Characteristics database, Organisation for Economic Co-operation and Development.
Note: The export shares are based on 2015 values. Large firms are defined as those with 250 or more regular employees. For a list of country codes, go to https://www.iso.org/obp/ui/#search.

Trade liberalization can exacerbate the gap between large and smaller firms (Melitz 2003). Korea faces the challenge of reducing the performance gap between large firms and small and medium-size firms.

Compared to its strong manufacturing competitiveness, the underperformance of services is often pointed out as one of the major challenges to economic growth in Korea. Figure 4.6 shows the trend in services trade in Korea (panels a and b) and the performance of services exports compared to merchandise exports (panels c and d).

FIGURE 4.6 Services Trade and Relative Performance of Exports of Services, Republic of Korea and across Countries, 1980–2019

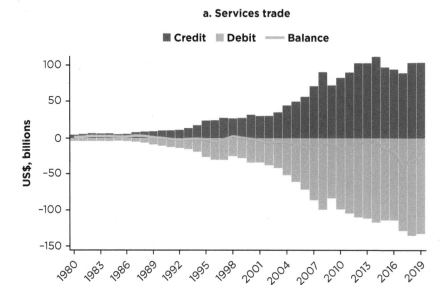

a. Services trade

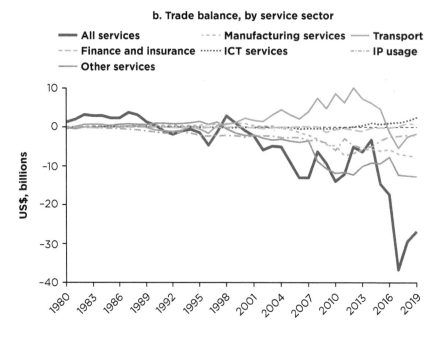

b. Trade balance, by service sector

Continued

FIGURE 4.6 Continued

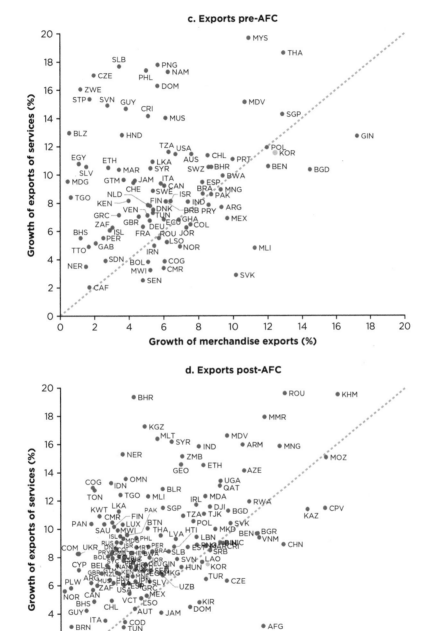

Sources: For panels a and b, Bank of Korea; for panels c and d, calculations based on data from World Integrated Trade Solution, World Bank.
Note: AFC = Asian Financial Crisis; ICT = information and communications technology; IP intellectual property. For a list of country codes, go to https://www.iso.org/obp/ui/#search.

Trade in services has increased significantly since the 1990s along with merchandise trade, reflecting both the new trade rules set by the WTO and the rise of ICT-driven service activities. Although Korea was a net exporter of services prior to the 1990s, the volume of services trade was low. As the volume of services trade expanded, Korea became a net importer. Figure 4.6, panel b presents the trade balance by major service sectors. Most of the sectors have had a trade deficit, but the deficit is particularly significant in manufacturing services and other business sectors. Korea's services exports rose by an average of 11.5 percent in the pre-AFC period and by 7.5 percent in the post-AFC period, slightly lower than its merchandise exports growth rate. In contrast, services export growth has been higher than merchandise export growth in most countries, especially in the post-AFC period (figure 4.6, panels c and d). The faster growth in services exports was also typical in advanced countries as they transformed into services-based economies. In comparison, Korea has relied on foreign services while focusing on manufacturing activities.

Korea's service sector has underperformed compared to its manufacturing sector. The service sector has also been more protected compared to the manufacturing sector. Although some sectors of the services trade are less restricted compared to other Organisation for Economic Co-operation and Development (OECD) countries (figure 4.7), business-related sectors such as accounting and legal services are more restricted. The weak international competitiveness of the service sector in Korea constrains its long-term growth as the service sector accounts for about 70 percent of economic activity, and global services trade has been rising rapidly.

Along with the acceleration of the expansion of international trade, Korea's FDI, both inward and outward, started to take off in the mid-1990s. Prior to 1990, the stock of outward FDI was close to zero, and the stock of inward FDI was around 0.2 percent of the global FDI stock (figure 4.8, panel a). Korea's FDI began to increase in both directions in 1994. Although Korea's share of the global FDI stock was still small compared to the country's export and import shares, capital movements into and out of Korea were more active than in other countries. The extensive margin of outward FDI (the number of newly established foreign affiliates of Korea's firms) began to increase in the mid-1990s, mainly driven by investments in China for manufacturing facilities (figure 4.8, panel b). In 1994, about three-quarters of the total number of new foreign affiliates were established in China, of which more than 80 percent were in manufacturing. Although outward FDI was diversified to other countries in the 2000s, manufacturing affiliates in China still accounted for most of Korea's ODIs until the global financial crisis (GFC).

FIGURE 4.7 **Services Trade Restrictiveness Index, by Sector, Republic of Korea and OECD**

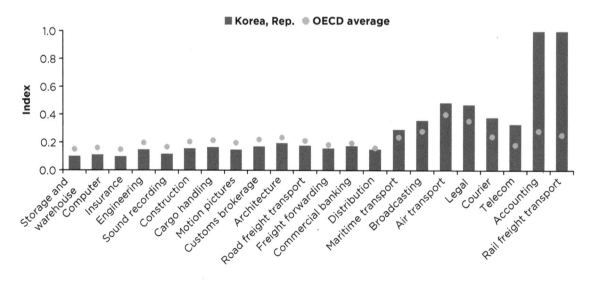

Source: OECD Services Trade Restrictiveness Index database 2021.
Note: Index values are based on 2021. In the index, 1 is the most restrictive and 0 is the least restrictive. Sectors are ordered by how far the Republic of Korea's score is from the OECD average. OECD = Organisation for Economic Co-operation and Development.

FIGURE 4.8 Foreign Direct Investments, Republic of Korea, China, and Other Countries, 1982–2018

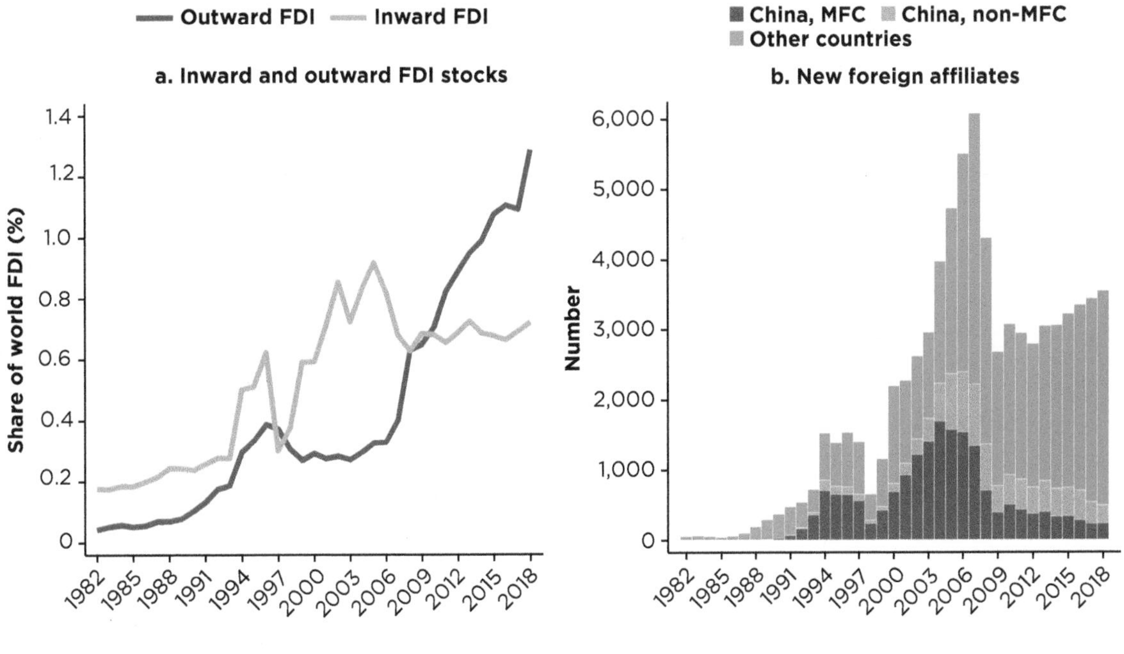

Sources: Panel a: UNCTAD Data Center; panel b: Korea Export-Import Bank.
Note: FDI = foreign direct investment; MFC = manufacturing.

Relatively low FDI inflows compared to the rapidly rising outflows remains a challenge for Korea's economy. In the earlier decades of Korea's modern development, the government preferred licensing and imported equipment over FDI to absorb foreign technologies. Companies used debt rather than equity financing, to retain corporate control. Korea started to liberalize FDI in the 1980s, when it converted a positive list of industries in which FDI was allowed to a negative list of industries that restricted or prohibited FDI. The negative list is generally considered a more transparent and predictable approach to FDI restrictions. FDI reforms accelerated after the AFC, including the removal of restrictions on cross-border mergers and acquisitions and land ownership. Spurred also by the depreciation of the won, FDI sharply increased, especially in the financial sector.

Despite the liberalization of inflows and policies to attract foreign investments, inward FDI has remained relatively modest. The accumulated stock was only 12.4 percent of GDP in 2018, the second lowest among OECD member countries. Korea's share of the global inward FDI stock, at around 0.5 percent, is significantly less than its GDP share, which was about 1.9 percent in 2020, according to the latest available data from the OECD and the World Development Indicators. Although the stagnation of global FDI in the 2010s may have disproportionately affected some countries (figure 4.9), more fundamental problems could be discouraging foreigners from investing in Korea.

KOREA'S PARTICIPATION IN GLOBAL VALUE CHAINS[5]

The most important feature of globalization in the 1990s and 2000s was the GVC revolution. The sustained growth of Korea's trade in the world market and its compositional changes can be largely explained by the GVC-related production activities. This subsection analyzes Korea's trade performance through the lens of GVCs from 1995 through 2011, a period of rapid trade growth (figure 4.2).

Figure 4.10, panel a, compares the shares of Korea's gross exports and value-added exports in the world market. Value-added exports measure domestic value added that is ultimately absorbed in foreign countries (Johnson and Noguera 2012). In other words, it is the GDP accounted for by foreign final

FIGURE 4.9 **Inward FDI Stock across Countries, 2018**

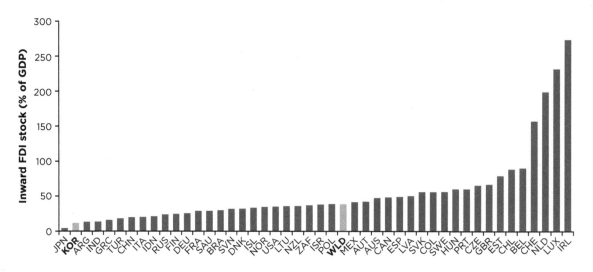

Source: Organisation for Economic Co-operation and Development International Direct Investment database.
Note: Values are based on 2018. FDI = foreign direct investment; WLD = world average. For a list of country codes, go to https://www.iso.org/obp/ui/#search.

FIGURE 4.10 **Global Shares of Gross and Value-Added Exports and Imports, Republic of Korea, 1995–2011**

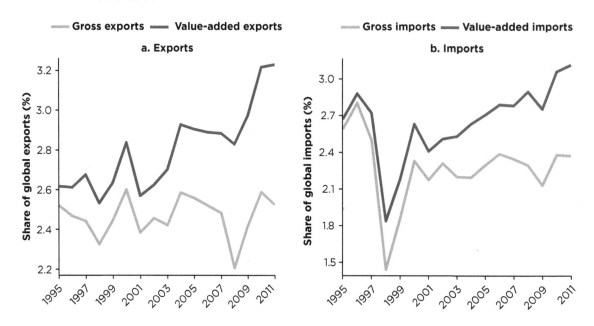

Source: Trade-in-Value-Added 2016 indicators, Organisation for Economic Co-operation and Development.

demand. Korea's share of the world's gross exports rose from 2.6 percent in 1995 to over 3.2 percent in 2011, when Korea became the seventh largest exporter in the world. However, Korea's share of global value-added exports remained between 2.4 and 2.6 percent throughout the period. A similar pattern appears in imports, as shown in figure 4.10, panel b. Korea's gross import share has increased since the AFC, but the country's value-added import share remains stable at around 2.3 percent.

The gap between the global (gross) export share and the GDP share has widened since the 2000s due to the spread of GVCs across countries. Products repeatedly cross borders, carrying the values created in all previous stages. This amplifies the accumulated values of gross exports but not necessarily the value added embedded in them. The gap between the two shares can be summarized by the ratio of value-added exports to gross exports (VAX). The VAX ratio at the country level roughly measures how much of one dollar of exports is linked with the domestic value-added, showing an inverse relationship with the foreign content of exports, as shown in figure 4.11.

Among all the countries in the sample, the VAX ratio in Korea fell the most, from 77.2 percent in 1995 to 57.6 percent in 2011 (figure 4.11). This implies that the contribution to domestic value added from a unit value of exports to GDP fell by nearly 20 percentage points. The top 10 countries with the largest declines in the VAX ratio are Korea, Hungary, Türkiye, Poland, India, Thailand, Vietnam, the Slovak Republic, Czechia, and Taiwan, China (from largest to smallest). Except India, all these countries have been part of the regional GVCs of East Asia and Eastern Europe. Among the top 10 countries, Korea is the largest economy after India. Countries such as Hungary and Czechia are only about one-fifth of Korea in terms of GDP, and Poland and Taiwan, China are around half. Considering that countries with large domestic markets tend to have high VAX ratios, the large decline of Korea's VAX ratio is significant, reflecting Korea's expanded participation in GVCs. It underlies Korea's relatively higher trade growth compared to GDP, although this phenomenon is not unusual from the conventional development perspective (Eichengreen, Perkins, and Shin 2012).

The sharp rise in Korea's participation in GVCs from the mid-1990s until the early 2010s was associated with compositional changes within and across industries in Korea. The changes are analyzed following the method of Timmer et al. (2013, 2014), in which the value-added and employment contributions to a final product—GVC income and GVC employment, respectively—can be decomposed into source countries and industries. Figure 4.12 shows the analytical framework for GVC income. If there are M countries and N industries, then $M \times N$ global value chains would form a square matrix. Each column represents a value chain for the corresponding product, and each row indicates a participant in the value chain. For example, the total final product of country 1 and industry 1 in column 1 comprises the value added contributed by all countries and industries in each row. The sum of all the value added in a column

FIGURE 4.11 **VAX Ratios, Selected Economies, 1995 and 2011**

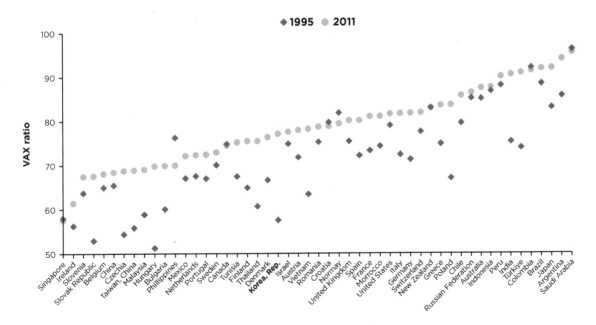

Source: Trade-in-Value-Added 2016 indicators, Organisation for Economic Co-operation and Development.
Note: VAX = ratio of value-added exports to gross exports.

FIGURE 4.12 Accounting Framework for Global Value Chains

			Final products of a global value chain, identified by country and industry of completion							Value added
			Country 1			...	Country M			
			Industry 1	...	Industry N	...	Industry 1	...	Industry N	
Value added from country industries participating in global value chains	Country 1	Industry 1								
		...								
		Industry N								
	...	...								
	Country M	Industry 1								
		...								
		Industry N								
Total final output value										**World GDP**

Source: Timmer et al. 2014, figure 1.
Note: GDP = gross domestic product.

thus equals the total final output value. The sum of all the value added in a row is the total value added or GDP of the corresponding country-industry earned from participating in all GVCs.

The GVC incomes for 2,108 GVCs (= 62 countries × 43 industries) for each year were estimated using the OECD Inter-Country Input-Output tables from 1995 to 2011. The matrix was aggregated into Korea and the rest of the world, and two industries, manufacturing (MFC) and nonmanufacturing (NMFC). The simplified GVC income matrix is shown in table 4.2. Panels a and b show the matrixes for 1995 and 2011, respectively. Panel c calculates the level difference between the two years in each cell, and panel d presents the corresponding growth rates of GVC income over the years. In all the panels, the first row and column are shaded to indicate the value added relevant to Korea's manufacturing. All values are expressed in billions of constant 1995 US dollars.

In 1995, Korea's manufacturing final output amounted to US$181.2 billion, and it increased by US$94.2 billion (52 percent) to US$275.4 billion in 2011. Thus, the value of exports of manufacturing final goods increased by 3.25 percent per year. Of the US$94.2 billion, US$23.6 billion was contributed by Korea (MFC + NMFC in Korea), and $70.7 billion by foreign countries. Although both contributions increased, the increase in the foreign contribution was much greater. In terms of the growth rate, real GVC income increased by 17.4 percent in Korea and by 154.4 percent in foreign countries. Moreover, further decomposition reveals that the contribution of Korea's nonmanufacturing declined by close to 10 percent, implying a substantial change in the composition of the GVC income structure.

Two effects can potentially explain this phenomenon. First, the growth of final output may in part be driven by increased offshoring (productivity effect). Second, offshoring necessarily induces the substitution of domestic tasks for foreign tasks (substitution effect). The two effects may not conflict with each other at the firm level, but theoretically they conflict at the aggregate level. Whereas improved productivity helps to increase domestic GDP through final output growth, offshoring reduces the domestic gains from producing and selling per unit of output. Indeed, there has been significant concern about hollowing out of domestic manufacturing due to offshoring of manufacturing.

In Korea, tasks that were previously carried out by the domestic nonmanufacturing industry—which mainly included the supply of raw materials and business services—in manufacturing GVCs have been significantly replaced by the foreign nonmanufacturing industry. Figure 4.13, panel a, shows the compositional change in Korea's GVC income over time. In each column, the four colors represent the income

TABLE 4.2 **GVC Income, Republic of Korea and Rest of the World, 1995 and 2011**

a. 1995 (US$, billions, 1995 prices)						b. 2011 (US$, billions, 1995 prices)					
		KOR		ROW		GDP		KOR		ROW		GDP
		MFC	NMFC	MFC	NMFC			MFC	NMFC	MFC	NMFC	
K O R	MFC	80.3	24.7	15.0	19.1	139.1	K O R	MFC	109.1	41.3	46.3	52.3	249.0
	NMFC	55.0	272.9	16.3	24.6	368.8		NMFC	49.8	398.2	36.4	54.0	538.4
R O W	MFC	18.0	12.7				R O W	MFC	35.3	27.8			
	NMFC	27.8	24.9					NMFC	81.2	82.2			
Total		181.2	335.2				Total		275.4	549.6			

c. Difference between 2011 and 1995 (US$, billions, 1995 prices)							d. Change from 1995 to 2011 (%)					
		KOR		ROW		GDP			KOR		ROW		GDP
		MFC	NMFC	MFC	NMFC				MFC	NMFC	MFC	NMFC	
K O R	MFC	28.8	16.6	31.2	33.2	109.8	K O R	MFC	35.8	67.4	207.6	174.2	78.9
	NMFC	−5.2	125.3	20.2	29.4	169.6		NMFC	−9.5	45.9	123.7	119.1	46.0
R O W	MFC	17.3	15.1				R O W	MFC	95.8	118.3			
	NMFC	53.4	57.4					NMFC	191.6	230.6			
Total		94.2	214.4				Total		52.0	63.9			

Source: Calculations based on data from Inter-Country Input-Output Tables, Organisation for Economic Co-operation and Development.
Note: Data on ROW are omitted to concentrate on Korean industry. Values may not add to total/GDP due to rounding. GDP = gross domestic product; GVC = global value chain; KOR = Korea; MFC = manufacturing; NMFC = nonmanufacturing; ROW = rest of the world.

shares of each participant in Korea's manufacturing GVCs. The share of domestic nonmanufacturing fell rapidly, from more than 30 percent in 2005 to 18.1 percent in 2011. The share of foreign nonmanufacturing rose by roughly the same degree. The substitution effect was large enough to outweigh the productivity effect, resulting in negative growth of the contribution of value added to Korea's nonmanufacturing (table 4.2, panel c). Korea's manufacturing share also fell by about 5 percentage points (figure 4.13, panel a), but the substitution effect was smaller than the productivity effect. Thus, there was not such a hollowing out within manufacturing, at least in value-added terms.

The analysis of foreign industries' contribution to Korea's manufacturing final output quantitatively captures their active involvement in backward production sharing. In the same manner, Korea's manufacturers' forward participation in GVCs can be analyzed by looking at the first row in the simplified GVC income matrix. In table 4.2, panels a to d, the first rows show how much income the manufacturing industry earned each year through involvement in the other three GVCs (as well as its own) and how much income changed over time. Figure 4.13, panel b, calculates the income shares from participation in each GVC.

Korea's manufacturing's contribution to value added in its own final output in 1995 was US$80.3 billion, which accounts for more than half of its total income (or GDP). Combined with its contribution to Korea's nonmanufacturing outputs, US$24.7 billion, three-quarters of the income comes from domestic industries. In 2011, however, the corresponding income share fell substantially due to the increased participation in foreign GVCs. The income earned from participating in foreign manufacturing and nonmanufacturing GVCs nearly tripled over this period (increases of 207.6 and 174.2 percent, respectively). Thereby, in 2011, 40 percent of the value added of Korea's manufacturing was accounted for by its contribution to foreign GVCs. As a result, the annual GDP growth rate was 4.93 percent in constant 1995 prices.

FIGURE 4.13 Value-Added Composition of Manufacturing and Nonmanufacturing GVCs, Republic of Korea and Rest of the World, 1995–2011

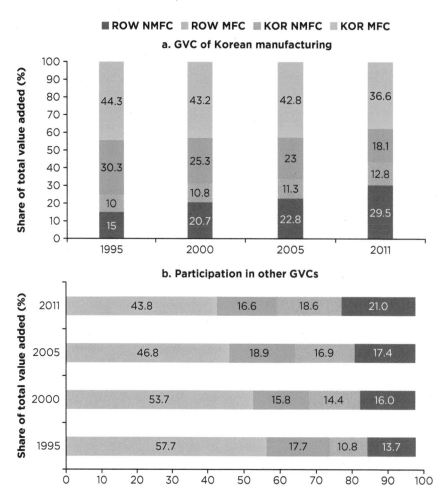

Source: Calculations based on data from Inter-Country Input-Output Tables, Organisation for Economic Co-operation and Development.
Note: GVC = global value chain; KOR = Republic of Korea; MFC = manufacturing; NMFC = nonmanufacturing; ROW = rest of the world.

In sum, Korea's manufacturing has been significantly globalized through backward and forward participation in GVCs. As a final producer, its reliance on the contribution of foreign companies' output rose from 25.4 percent in 1995 to 42.3 percent in 2011. As an intermediate supplier, Korean manufacturing firms' value-added contribution to foreign industries in total income increased from 24.5 percent in 1995 to 39.6 percent in 2011. Hence, involvement in the global production system in both directions increased by a similar degree.

The changes in the structure of GVC income have been accompanied by a reallocation of workers involved in value chain activities. GVC employment was estimated to analyze the adjustment in employment (table 4.3). Total employment in Korea's manufacturing GVC fell from 8.8 million in 1995 to 8.4 million in 2011, due to a decline in the number of domestic workers involved in the value chain. Although the number of foreign workers in the GVC increased by about 1.5 million, it fell short of covering the reduction of 1.9 million domestic workers. The share of foreign workers in Korea's manufacturing GVC already exceeded 30 percent in 1995 (figure 4.14, panel a). Given that the share of foreign value added was 24.5 percent in 1995, foreign workers contributed lower value added on average

TABLE 4.3 GVC Employment, Republic of Korea and Rest of the World, 1995 and 2011

a. 1995 (millions)						
		KOR		ROW		
		MFC	NMFC	MFC	NMFC	Total
K O R	MFC	3.1	0.8	0.5	0.6	5.0
	NMFC	2.9	11.1	0.8	1.0	15.8
R O W	MFC	0.8	0.6			
	NMFC	2.2	1.9			
Total		8.8	14.4			

b. 2011 (millions)						
		KOR		ROW		
		MFC	NMFC	MFC	NMFC	Total
K O R	MFC	2.0	0.7	0.7	0.8	4.2
	NMFC	2.0	15.3	1.4	1.9	20.7
R O W	MFC	1.2	0.9			
	NMFC	3.3	3.4			
Total		8.4	20.3			

Source: Calculations based on data from Inter-Country Input-Output Tables, Organisation for Economic Co-operation and Development.
Note: Data on ROW are omitted to concentrate on Korean industry. GVC = global value chain; KOR = Korea; MFC = manufacturing; NMFC = nonmanufacturing; ROW= rest of the world.

FIGURE 4.14 Employment Composition of Manufacturing and Nonmanufacturing GVCs, Republic of Korea and Rest of the World, 1995–2011

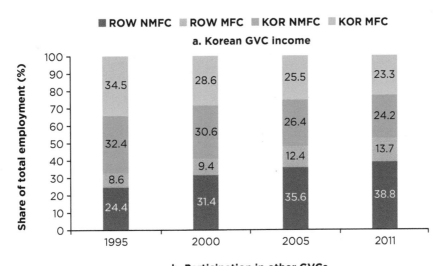

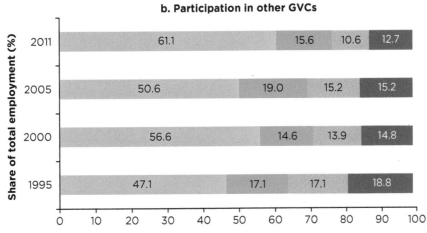

Source: Calculations based on data from Inter-Country Input-Output Tables, Organisation for Economic Co-operation and Development.
Note: GVC = global value chain; KOR = Republic of Korea; MFC = manufacturing; NMFC = nonmanufacturing; ROW = rest of the world.

to the final outputs compared to domestic workers. This would be consistent with lower labor costs, the main offshoring motive. The share of foreign workers increased gradually to 52.5 percent in 2011. Thus, the substitution of foreign tasks for domestic tasks—the hollowing-out phenomenon—has been more pronounced in terms of employment than value added.

Some of Korea's manufacturing workers were reallocated to tasks that contributed to foreign GVCs as intermediate suppliers. The share of Korea's manufacturing workers involved in creating value added embedded in foreign final outputs increased from 23.3 percent in 1995 to 35.9 percent in 2011 (figure 4.14, panel b). The number of domestic workers involved in foreign manufacturing GVCs increased by 0.3 million from 1995 to 2011 (compare the rows in table 4.3, panels a and b). Despite the significant change in the share, which is comparable to the change in the income share, the increment is much smaller than the loss of 1.1 million jobs in the manufacturing GVC. Consequently, the total number of manufacturing workers in Korea fell by approximately 0.8 million during the period. Five million additional jobs were created in Korea's nonmanufacturing industries, driving a structural change in the economy, from manufacturing to nonmanufacturing industries.

TRADE LIBERALIZATION, GVC PARTICIPATION, AND SECTORAL COMPETITIVENESS

GVC participation in Korea has contributed to its international competitiveness. The argument that the task of offshoring of Korea's manufacturing can enhance the productivity of the final goods (productivity effect) is widely supported by the literature. The seminal paper by Grossman and Rossi-Hansberg (2008) provides an offshoring model where the productivity of unskilled domestic workers is augmented by foreign workers who perform the same task. This enhanced productivity effect is consistent with the findings in the empirical literature (Amiti and Wei 2009; Choi and Hahn 2013; Goldberg et al. 2010; Halpern, Koren, and Szeidl 2015; Ottaviano, Peri, and Wright 2013).

Increased backward participation in GVCs is particularly important for explaining improved labor productivity in manufacturing (Constantinescu, Mattoo, and Ruta 2019). The impact of forward participation on productivity can be explained by the tendency of highly productive firms to enter export markets (Melitz 2003) and the learning effect of exporting firms to become highly productive (De Loecker 2013). The learning-by-exporting effect is significantly present among Korea's exporters (Hahn 2012).

Across countries, the change in the VAX ratio is correlated with trade and economic performance (figure 4.15). The VAX ratio fell the most in Korea, which is located on the left in all the panels. A decline in the VAX ratio is associated with: (a) a rise in the export share of capital goods, including transportation equipment, as GVCs tend to be active in capital-intensive industries (figure 4.15, panel a); (b) an increase in the Economic Complexity Index developed by the Atlas of Economic Complexity, as GVCs necessarily involve several vertical production stages, which tend to occur when the products are complex and thus require high technologies to produce (panel b); and (c) higher per capita GDP growth and aggregate TFP growth (panels c and d, respectively).

The average labor productivity of Korea's manufacturing final output rose from US$20,500 in 1995 to US$32,600 in 2011 (table 4.4, calculated by dividing GVC income from table 4.2 by GVC employment from table 4.3). All participants in the value chain exhibited higher value-added per worker in 2011, but the most significant improvement occurred in domestic manufacturing. As an intermediate supplier, the average productivity of Korea's manufacturing more than doubled, from US$27,800 in 1995 to US$59,600 in 2011 (table 4.4). However, the level and growth rate of productivity in each manufacturing GVC differ because the productivities and contributions to the GVCs of the 16 subsectors within manufacturing differ. Table 4.4 shows the weighted average of the productivities of the 16 subsectors, weighted according to the value-added contribution to GVCs. Higher manufacturing productivity in one cell means that more productive subsectors tend to contribute more to that GVC. The highest manufacturing productivity in 1995 was in Korea's nonmanufacturing GVC (31.6). By contrast, in 2011, the highest value was in the foreign nonmanufacturing GVC (66.7), followed by the foreign manufacturing GVC. This result implies that

FIGURE 4.15 Change in the VAX Ratio and Economic Performance, Selected Economies, 1995–2011

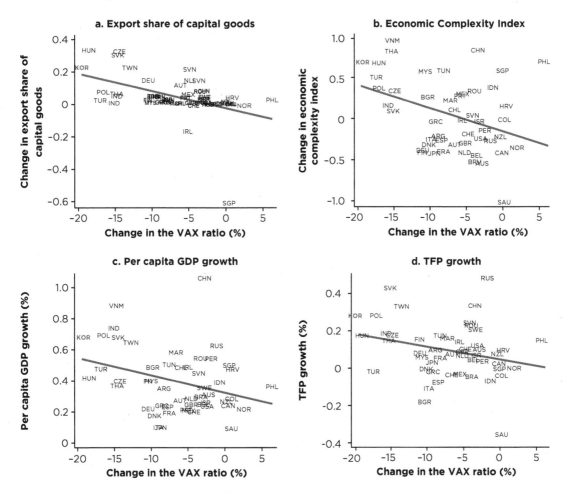

Sources: Calculations based on data from Penn World Table v10.0; Inter-Country Input-Output Tables, Organisation for Economic Co-operation and Development; Atlas of Economic Complexity.
Note: GDP = gross domestic product; TFP = total factor productivity; VAX = ratio of value-added exports to gross exports. For a list of country codes, go to https://www.iso.org/obp/ui/#search.

TABLE 4.4 Labor Productivity, Republic of Korea and Rest of the World, 1995 and 2011

		a. 1995 (US$, thousands, 1995)							b. 2011 (US$, thousands, 1995)				
		KOR		ROW					KOR		ROW		
		MFC	NMFC	MFC	NMFC	Avg.			MFC	NMFC	MFC	NMFC	Avg.
K O R	MFC	26.3	31.6	28.4	30.1	27.8	K O R	MFC	55.5	57.9	64.8	66.7	59.6
	NMFC	19.2	24.5	21.3	23.8	23.4		NMFC	24.3	26.0	27.0	27.7	26.1
R O W	MFC	23.8	21.0				R O W	MFC	30.5	29.4			
	NMFC	12.9	13.3					NMFC	24.8	24.4			
Average		20.5	23.3				Average		32.6	27.0			

Source: Calculations based on data from Inter-Country Input-Output Tables, Organisation for Economic Co-operation and Development.
Note: Data on ROW are omitted to concentrate on Korean industry. KOR = Korea; MFC = manufacturing; NMFC = nonmanufacturing; ROW = rest of the world.

highly productive industries in Korea's manufacturing sector are more involved in forward participation in foreign GVCs.

Another commonly used measure of international competitiveness at the industry level is the revealed comparative advantage (RCA) suggested by Balassa (1965). The RCA is calculated as follows:

$$RCA_{ci} = \frac{GX_{ci} / \sum_i GX_{ci}}{\sum_c GX_{ci} / \sum_c \sum_i GX_{ci}} \tag{4.1}$$

where GX_{ci} is the gross exports in industry i and country c. If industry i's export share in country c is greater than the corresponding share in the world, the country is regarded as having a comparative advantage in industry i. However, as gross exports include the value-added contributed by other industries and countries in all previous production stages, the RCA can misrepresent the true competitiveness of an industry. For example, many electronic products, such as the iPhone, are assembled and exported from China to countries all over the world. Although China is involved in a low value-added activity (assembly in this example), the amount of gross exports is largely due to the price of the iPhone, and so is the RCA index. Therefore, the RCA index measured by gross exports is likely to overestimate the true competitiveness of the Chinese electrical and electronic products industry. Another important problem when using gross exports is that it is hard to measure the competitiveness of services that are inherently linked to the exported goods.

Using value-added exports in the RCA calculation, instead of gross exports, can circumvent these problems. It can be used for evaluating the competitiveness of domestic activities in the international market. In the China example above, as only the value of the assembly process is factored into value-added exports, the value-added RCA would correctly measure China's share in its exports of electronic products. Moreover, because the value of the service provision to manufacturing is accounted for in the RCA calculation with value-added exports, it is possible to make a meaningful comparison of the service competitiveness among countries. The value-added RCA (VRCA) is calculated simply by replacing gross exports with value-added exports in equation (4.1).

A considerable gap between VRCA and RCA is found in three major industries in Korea (figure 4.16). In 2011, the petroleum and chemical industry enjoyed a comparative advantage according to the RCA index, but the VRCA index shows that the value added from its production activity in Korea was not competitively high. The other leading industries—electric and electronic products and transportation equipment—had a comparative advantage according to both the RCA and VRCA indexes, but the VRCA is higher and even diverging from the RCA. Indeed, these two industries are exactly the ones in which GVCs are most active and are regarded as the most innovative industries.

By contrast, there are no meaningful differences between the RCA and VRCA indexes in the nine service industries shown in figure 4.16, panels l to t (industries including utilities and construction). One interpretation is that service sectors are not active enough to participate in value chains other than direct exports. In addition, the fact that they are all found to have a comparative disadvantage as of 2011 in terms of VRCA reveals the overall weak competitiveness of Korea's services in the international market.[6]

Another important implication of the patterns of RCA and VRCA in figure 4.16 is the structural change within the manufacturing sector. In 1995, the textiles and footwear industry had the highest comparative advantage according to both indexes, but they both fell over the next 10 years to less than one. By contrast, Korea gradually achieved a comparative advantage in capital-intensive and high-technology industries such as machinery, electrical equipment, and transportation equipment. This is consistent with the sharp increase in Korea's share of global capital goods exports from 1995 to 2011 (figure 4.15).

TRADE AND INVESTMENT PROMOTION

Korea has taken a gradual approach to trade and foreign investment liberalization, except during the AFC, when domestic markets were opened to foreign investments at an accelerated pace to mobilize urgently

FIGURE 4.16 Revealed Comparative Advantage, by Industry, Republic of Korea, 1995–2011

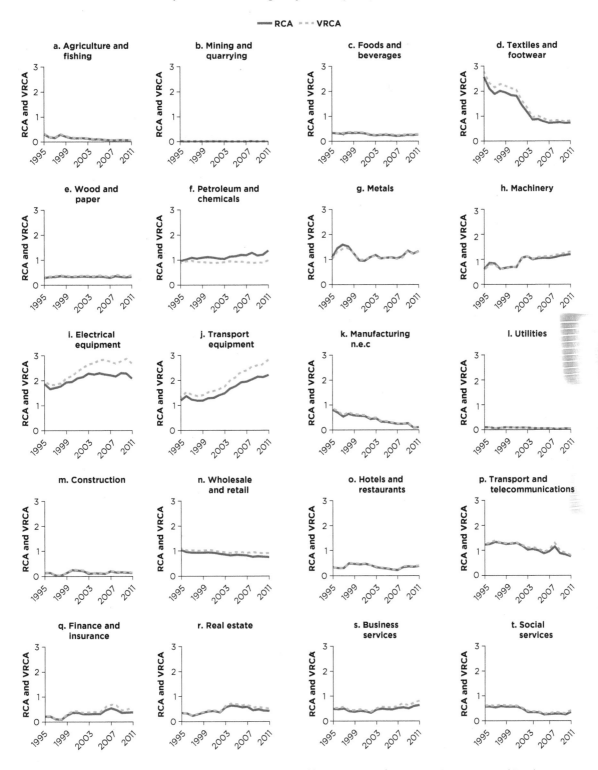

Source: Calculations based on data from Inter-Country Input-Output Tables, Organisation for Economic Co-operation and Development.
Note: n.e.c. = not elsewhere classified; RCA = revealed comparative advantage; VRCA = value-added revealed comparative advantage.

needed foreign capital. This subsection briefly introduces some of the main characteristics of Korea's trade and investment policies since the 1990s, focusing on: (a) bilateral free trade agreements (FTAs), (b) autonomous tariff rate quotas, (c) trade finance by export credit agencies (ECAs), (d) export promotion agencies (EPAs), and (e) trade facilitation reforms, including e-customs and e-trade.

Since 1994 when the general tariff rates were lowered to 8 percent for most imported goods, Korea has pursued tariff reductions mainly through bilateral FTAs to facilitate trade with partner countries and regional trade agreements to promote GVC-related trade (Johnson and Noguera 2017). Starting with Chile in 2004, 17 FTAs with more than 50 major countries have been made effective as of January 2021 (table 4.5). FTAs with the Association of Southeast Asian Nations (2007), the European Union (2011), the United States (2012), and China (2015) are regarded as the mega-FTAs. Box 4.1 describes the preparation and implementation process of the Korea-US FTA as an illustration of how Korea built public support for market opening through FTAs despite opposition by domestic incumbents in the protected markets impacted by the FTAs. The FTAs have helped to open domestic markets that had been protected, such as the agricultural market, which was one of the more protected markets in Korea.

Korea has also utilized autonomous tariff quotas (ATQs) to respond flexibly and quickly to domestic and foreign shocks. The ATQ system designates products every year for which tariff rates can be adjusted flexibly. Changing the legal tariff rate requires a revision of the law, which is a slow process. ATQs provide the government discretion to change the tariff rate temporarily within a certain range of the legal tariff rate if certain requirements are met.

The purpose of ATQs is clearly stated in the law. They can be activated: (a) if it is necessary to promote the import of certain goods for their smooth supply or to strengthen the competitiveness of the industry, (b) if it is necessary to stabilize the domestic price of goods whose import price has soared, or (c) if the tariff rates between similar goods are significantly different and need to be aligned. The first ATQs date back to 1991, and since then autonomous tariff rate changes have been applied to about 80 to 100 products every year (79 products in 2019). More than two-thirds of the applied products are raw materials.

TABLE 4.5 Chronology of Korean Free Trade Agreements

Partner	First effective since	Partner	First effective since
Chile	2004.04	Australia	2014.12
Singapore	2006.03	Canada	2015.01
EFTA[a]	2006.09	China	2015.12
ASEAN[b]	2007.06	New Zealand	2015.12
India	2010.01	Vietnam	2015.12
European Union[c]	2011.07	Colombia	2016.07
Peru	2011.08	Central America[d]	2019.10
United States	2012.03	United Kingdom	2021.01
Türkiye	2013.05	RCEP[e]	2022.01

Source: World Bank.
Note: The effectiveness dates refer to year.month (for example, 2004.04 is April 2004).
a. EFTA (European Free Trade Association, four countries): Switzerland, Norway, Iceland, and Liechtenstein.
b. ASEAN (Association of Southeast Asian Nations, 10 countries): Brunei, Cambodia, Indonesia, the Lao People's Democratic Republic, Malaysia, Myanmar, Philippines, Singapore, Thailand, and Vietnam.
c. European Union (27 countries): Austria, Belgium, Bulgaria, Croatia, Czechia, Cyprus, Denmark, Estonia, Finland, France, Germany, Greece, Hungary, Ireland, Italy, Latvia, Lithuania, Luxembourg, Malta, the Netherlands, Poland, Portugal, Romania, Slovak Republic, Slovenia, Spain, and Sweden.
d. Central America (5 countries): Panama, Costa Rica, Honduras, El Salvador, and Nicaragua.
e. RCEP (Regional Comprehensive Economic Partnership Agreement): the Republic of Korea, ASEAN (10), Australia, China, Japan, and New Zealand.

BOX 4.1 Republic of Korea-US Free Trade Agreement

Although trade liberalization improves overall economic welfare, there can be both winners and losers; therefore, the resistance of the potential losers makes implementation of liberalization policies challenging. This was the case for the Republic of Korea-US free trade agreement (FTA), as there was significant resistance on the part of import-competing industries. Agricultural workers were concerned that the tariff reductions and the resulting rise in imported agricultural products would significantly disrupt the domestic market. Public hearings in the early preparation stage were often canceled due to opposition from farmers and civic groups. Such resistance delayed the National Assembly's passage of the FTA ratification bill by about four years (see table B4.2.1).

TABLE B4.2.1 Timeline of the Republic of Korea-US FTA

Timeline	Description
February–April 2005	First three working-level consultation meetings were held
April 2005–February 2006	Preparation through internal government meetings, expert research, seminars, consultations, public hearings, polls, and others
February 2006	Declaration of the start of official negotiations
June 2006–March 2007	First eight official negotiations held
April 2007	Negotiations concluded
June 2007	Signed the FTA
September 2007	Submitted a bill for ratification of the FTA to the National Assembly
February 2011	Signed the agreement document for additional negotiations
November 2011	FTA ratification bill passed by the National Assembly
February 2012	Agreement on effective date of the FTA
March 2012	Korea-US FTA went into effect

Source: World Bank.

The government prepared for negotiations through extensive internal discussions, expert studies, seminars, consultations, public hearings, and opinion polls. It established supplementary policy measures for actively utilizing the FTA and minimizing negative effects on the domestic market. It prepared a comprehensive plan to strengthen industrial competitiveness, expand income sources in rural households, and provide direct support to domestic stakeholders adversely impacted by the FTA. In the agriculture and fishing industry, which was expected to suffer from the highest competitive pressure, a total financial support plan of ₩21.1 trillion was implemented over 10 years, from 2008 to 2017. The initial plan was modified twice to reflect rapid changes in the market environment before the final measures were executed. The revised measures ultimately covered more potential losers from the FTA, for example, by easing the eligibility for direct damage support and trade adjustment assistance. The budget for supporting the agriculture sector was eventually expanded to ₩24.1 trillion. These government policy measures helped the government to reach an agreement on the Korea-US FTA despite the significant domestic opposition, by helping to alleviate the concerns in import-competing industries.

FIGURE 4.17 **Effectively Applied Weighted Tariff Rates, Republic of Korea, 1989–2019**

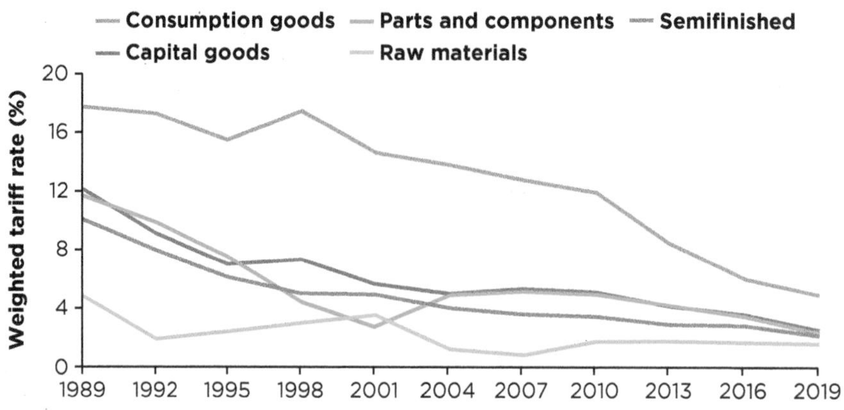

Source: Calculations based on data from the Korea Trade Statistics Promotion Institute.
Note: Tariff rates are weighted by the product import shares.

Both the FTA tariff rates and ATQs have contributed to the reduction of tariff rates in Korea (figure 4.17). Except for consumption goods, tariff rates were reduced significantly from 1989 to 1995. Hence, although the government controls import prices for selected products through ATQs, its influence on the market has fallen since the mid-1990s. In 2019, the weighted tariff rate was under 5 percent on consumption goods and 3 percent on other goods.

The provision of trade finance has also been an important policy instrument in Korea for promoting international trade. The importance of trade finance in promoting trade is emphasized in the literature (Manova 2008, 2013). Korea's ECAs have played an important role in the export finance market (figure 4.18). ECAs are a larger source of export finance in Asian countries than in Europe and North America. The volume of export finance from ECAs in Korea is larger than in Japan. In Europe and the United States, the private sector supplies most of the credit, but in Korea public ECAs have been dominant over the past five decades.

The dominance of ECAs in the market can be considered problematic from the viewpoint of efficient resource allocation. The quantities and prices of credit, such as credit limits, interest rates, and insurance premiums, supplied by Korea's public ECAs are largely controlled by the government, constraining private sector competition. However, trade finance through public ECAs can be advantageous in certain cases. First, when the private financial market is underdeveloped, as was the case in Korea in the earlier decades of its development and is the case in many developing countries today, ECAs can effectively supply credit to exporters. Second, ECAs can act as a safety net during economic turmoil. During the GFC, private financial institutions reduced their supply of credit, which contributed to the credit shortage in the economy, leading to a major collapse in trade (Amiti and Weinstein 2011; Chor and Manova 2012). In contrast, the ECAs in Korea expanded their credit supply, which helped to mitigate the credit shortage faced by exporters. More recently, ECAs helped to mitigate the economic and trade impacts of the COVID-19 pandemic (Demir and Javorcik 2020).

In Korea, EPAs were actively used to support exporting firms and help develop new export markets. The traditional role of an EPA is to provide exporters information on foreign markets and match the exporters with foreign buyers. Information frictions result from the cost of searching for trading partners and assessing their trustworthiness, as well as other unknown risks related to completing transactions. The trade literature finds that information frictions can be as large as half of all trade costs and possibly even greater for smaller firms (Allen 2014). Hence, reducing such frictions can boost trade (Steinwender 2018).

FIGURE 4.18 **Trade Finance by Public Export Credit Agencies, Germany, Japan, Republic of Korea, and United States, 2014**

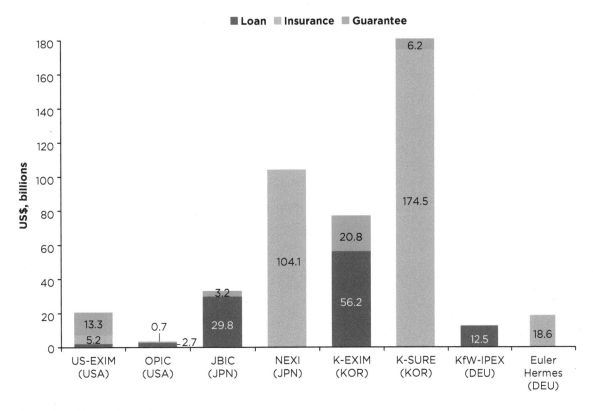

Source: Annual Reports from each agency.
Note: All values are as of 2014. JBIC = Japan Bank for International Cooperation; K-EXIM = Export-Import Bank of Korea; KfW-IPEX = KfW IPEX-Bank; K-SURE = Korea Trade Insurance Corporation; NEXI = Nippon Export and Investment Insurance; OPIC = Overseas Private Investment Corporation; US-EXIM = Export-Import Bank of the United States.

The Korea Trade-Investment Promotion Agency, the national export promotion agency, was established in 1962. Its main functions are similar to those of EPAs in other countries (table 4.6). However, the role of the Korea Trade-Investment Promotion Agency and other similar government agencies has evolved in accordance with the changing economic environment in Korea and the global economy. Many of the programs provided by Korea's EPAs are now more targeted, customized, packaged, and demand driven. For example, firms can receive customized assistance based on diagnostic assessments. They can be matched with a retired trade expert who can provide assistance ranging from tacit know-how on trade practices to implementation of export contracts. Firms can voluntarily select a service menu using an "export voucher" consisting of government and private sector support. These contingent support programs are not limited to manufacturing exporters, but also have been increasingly available to service providers with further customization.

As with the ECAs, some observers are concerned that EPA export and investment promotion programs could impair efficiency. Research typically finds that EPAs can be effective when trade costs or information frictions are high (Lederman, Olarreaga, and Payton 2010; Volpe Martincus and Carballo 2008). There may be diminishing returns to scale in resources devoted to export promotion (Lederman, Olarreaga, and Payton 2010, 264). More targeted, customized, and packaged support by Korea's EPAs could be expected to be at least as effective as the types of support that prior studies have assessed.

TABLE 4.6 **Main Activities of Korean Export Promotion Agencies (as of 2020)**

Activity	Description
1. Support (potential) exporting firms	• Support for participations in trade fair, trade mission, and business trip • Customized support for capacity building, according to level of export experience (start-up/domestic firm/infant exporter/gazelles/world-class) • Export voucher • Business-to-business e-market promotion
2. Create new opportunities and discover new business areas	• Help overseas expansion of leading firms in several service industries (e.g., health care, culture (Hallyu), contents, education, franchise) • Facilitate business partnership during president's overseas tour and official summit
3. Provide market information	• Foreign market research • Organize meetings and consulting service for foreign customers
4. Foreign investment attraction	• Operating portal (Invest Korea) for investment attraction • Packaged assistance of investors • Addressing difficulties of overseas companies

Source: Modified from the official website of the Korea Trade-Investment Promotion Agency, accessed February 25, 2021. (https://www.kotra.or.kr/foreign/kotra/KHENKT030M.html).

TRADE FACILITATION REFORMS

Korea has emphasized the strengthening of trade facilitation and reforms of customs clearance since the late 1980s. The government implemented several key trade facilitation reforms, which became increasingly important as the substantial increase in the trade volume threatened to increase transaction inefficiencies. Table 4.7 provides a timeline of key trade facilitation reforms. Korea moved its import clearance system from a permit system to a self-declaration system in 1996, and the Korea Customs Services moved toward post-entry investigation for cargo clearance. Korea then introduced an "on-dock" immediate delivery system in 1998, which allowed importers to unload and release imported goods simultaneously at the time of entry. These measures provided the necessary infrastructure for the development of e-customs and e-trade in the 2000s.

Korea gradually introduced and expanded the scope of electronic documents for comprehensive coverage of major export- and import-related tasks. The government needed a reliable private sector counterpart; therefore, it partnered with the Korea International Trade Association, a private organization composed of traders, which often acts as an intermediary between traders and the government. Working together, the Korea Trade Network (KTNET) was established to build and operate e-trade infrastructure and services.

In the 2000s, the need for internet-based services became critical with the rapid development of information technology and widespread use of the internet. In 2003, Korea began building an internet-based "single window" for submission of documents. Currently, almost all trade transactions are carried out entirely via this national "single window." In 2007, the uTradeHub was launched, which provides real-time information on the status of cargo and paperwork and allows submission of electronic paperwork in real time. The system links government agencies with traders and other trade-related organizations and private agencies. The goal is not to limit submissions of electronic paperwork to the government, but to cover all trade-related transactions. Under the e-Trade Facilitation Act, the Ministry of Knowledge Economy designated KTNET as the e-trade service provider for operating the uTradeHub services and systems.

Korea Customs Services estimates that the new system has significantly contributed to reducing the time and costs involved in the distribution of imported and exported goods. Samsung Electronics estimates that it reduced its ordering time from 10 to 2 days and saved US$800 million by using the trade automation system (Jeong 2005). Currently, KTNET links around 97,000 customers and trade-related

TABLE 4.7 **Timeline of Key Trade Facilitation Reforms, Republic of Korea, 1989–2010**

Year	Reform
	Introduction stage
1989	The Basic Plan for Foreign Trade Process Automation was prepared.
1991	The Act on Promotion of Trade Business Automation was enacted. KTNET was established by the Korea International Trade Association.
	Growth stage
1994	EDI service for export/import approval, letter of credit, and export declaration was launched.
1996	EDI service for import declaration, and the Export/Import Manifest Consolidation System was launched.
1997	EDI service for export/import freight and tariff duty refunds was launched.
2000	Certificate of Origin and notary of Commercial Invoice and Internet-based EDI service was launched.
	Take-off stage
2001	Internet Management System of Logistics was developed.
2003	National e-Trade Committee, chaired by the prime minister, was established; the Plan for e-Trade Facilitation was prepared.
2005	The e-Trade Facilitation Act was amended and the project for the internet-based national paperless trading system was launched.
2007	uTradeHub was opened.
	Upgrade stage
2008	Ministry of Justice designated KTNET as Electronic Bill of Lading (e-B/L) Title Registry. Purchase confirmation service was launched.
2010	Electronic negotiation (financial settlement) system was built and a pilot project with Hyundai Motor Corporation was completed.

Source: UNESCAP 2010.
Note: EDI = Electronic Data Interchange; KTNET = Korea Trade Network.

organizations, including trading companies, banks, customs brokers, shipping companies, insurance firms, forwarders, and bonded storage warehouses. KTNET has digitalized about 614 types of export and import documents in the government-to-business and business-to-business sectors and processes an annual average of 370 million cases of paperless documents.[7] Korea was ranked first in the 2021 Global Survey on Digital and Sustainable Trade Facilitation, with a score of 94.6 percent, reflecting its comprehensive use of digital technologies for trade facilitation.

Financial Integration and Economic Consequences

This section analyzes Korea's global financial integration and its effect on economic outcomes.[8] It first analyzes the history of financial account liberalization in Korea. Korea's opening of the financial account has been relatively slow, especially from the 1990s to the 2000s, compared to advanced economies and Korea's more rapid integration into global trade. The relatively slow financial liberalization has resulted in a relatively slower pace of financial integration into the global economy. External savings have grown rapidly, and current account surpluses have been sustained for more than a couple of decades. Since the AFC, Korea has accumulated significant external wealth as safe assets, in the form of international reserves. Those precautionary savings continued to increase until the GFC, to reduce the likelihood and severity of a financial crisis. Precautionary savings now account for a significant fraction of the national wealth.

Accumulated reserves and active decumulation at the peak of capital reversal during the GFC provided a buffer to prevent deeper turmoil. Accumulation of foreign reserves can contribute to reducing the probability of crisis (Gourinchas and Obstfeld 2012), but running large current account surpluses to accumulate foreign reserves could provoke an adverse reaction from trading partners. Since the GFC, reserve accumulation has slowed, reserves have remained around 25 percent of GDP, and the financial account has been rapidly liberalized.

FINANCIAL ACCOUNT LIBERALIZATION

Korea has participated in the global trend toward greater financial openness since 1990. Figure 4.19 shows an index of financial account management for a sample of countries including Korea, based on Chinn and Ito (2006), which introduces a de jure measure of financial openness using the International Monetary Fund's Annual Report on Exchange Arrangement and Exchange Restrictions database. The index codifies four categories of restrictions on the current account and the financial account. Each circle in the figure represents the relative number of countries. Since the number of countries in the sample varies each year, the sizes of the circles are normalized so that all the bubbles add up to unity for a given year. Higher values indicate a less liberalized financial account. The median level (0.5) can be used as a threshold to divide all the economies into financially open versus financially closed groups. The financial openness measures are dispersed. More countries have shifted toward greater financial openness (moved downward) over time. Although not all economies have shared the same intensity of globalization, relatively rapid changes have been made since 2015. Until then, the speed of opening up was heterogeneous. Many advanced economies have maintained an open financial account throughout the time period.

Contrary to Korea's rapid liberalization of trade in goods and services, the pace of its financial openness was relatively slow until 2007 (figure 4.21). For instance, the level of financial closedness was above 0.5 (the median level of restrictiveness) until 2007. This indicates that Korea's policy framework for external financial transactions was more restrictive than that of half the world's countries until 2007. Korea maintained a pegged exchange rate system and a relatively closed capital account until the AFC.

FIGURE 4.19 Financial Closedness: World versus the Republic of Korea, 1990–2018

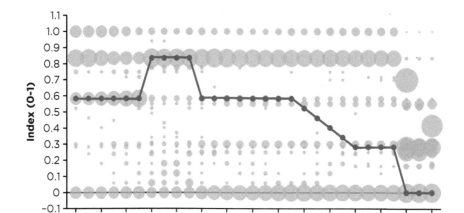

Source: Calculation based on the updated data of Chinn and Ito (2006).
Note: Each circle reflects the relative number of countries in the index each year. For each year, the sample includes 148 to 182 countries. The dark blue line shows the level of the index of Korean financial closedness.

When it joined the OECD in 1996, Korea was reluctant to liberalize its capital account due to concern that foreign capital inflows would increase significantly because of the interest rate differentials between home and abroad. The government therefore planned to delay capital account liberalization until the interest rates converged (Kim and Yang 2010).

Many capital account restrictions began to be loosened after the AFC. Measures taken after the AFC included the easing and discontinuation of restrictions on foreign investments in the bond, equity, and real estate markets, and an increase in the ceiling for foreign ownership of firms. Requirements of prior government authorization of financial transactions were eliminated (transactions still had to be reported) in 2004 for securities and in 2005 for derivatives, increasing external capital inflows. As a result, the index of financial closedness began to fall in 2007, reaching a new, lower level by 2012.

Figure 4.20 compares the index based on Chinn and Ito (2006) with two other indexes constructed from monthly financial closedness indexes, based on Fernandez et al. (2016). Slightly different patterns emerge due to the different ways of recording the changes in financial sector restrictions. In both the Chinn and Ito financial closedness index and the monthly indexes, the pace of liberalization was faster in 2005–06.[9] Both indexes indicate that the report-based financial transactions had a significant impact on financial account restrictions in the 2000s.

The pattern of capital account liberalization after the GFC has differed from that of the previous periods. Various measures of financial closedness capture the restrictions and, thus, show different trends. The Chinn and Ito index shows further progress on liberalization with the elimination of the repatriation and surrender requirements for exports. By contrast, Fernandez et al. (2016) capture new restrictions imposed by the government beginning in 2010, known as the triple exchange stability measures. A leverage cap on banks' foreign exchange derivative positions and a levy on foreign exchange funding were intended to prevent excessive buildup of short-term external liabilities and currency exposure risks by banks. Consequently, Fernandez et al.'s (2016) indexes show a slight increase in restrictiveness after 2015 (figure 4.20).

A large literature on the relationship between financial liberalization and macroeconomic outcomes has shown a variety of conflicting results, and the evidence remains relatively inconclusive

FIGURE 4.20 **Financial Closedness Indexes: Aggregate Level, Republic of Korea, 1990–2018**

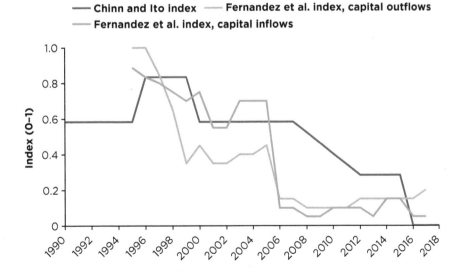

Sources: Calculations based on the updated data of Chinn and Ito 2006; Fernandez et al. 2016.
Note: The Fernandez et al. Index was converted to a monthly basis.

(Kose et al. 2009). Unlike widespread support for trade liberalization, the view on financial account management lacks consensus. It is an old idea that volatile capital flows can generate economic instability. More recent research has focused on externalities associated with foreign capital flows and the role that capital controls can play in buffering against the transmission of exogenous shocks (Kim and Pyun 2018; Korinek and Mendoza 2014; Ostry et al. 2011).

ACCUMULATION OF INTERNATIONAL RESERVES

A shortage of foreign currency assets was viewed as a major cause of the AFC. In response, the government has accumulated a significant volume of reserves since the AFC. Right after the crisis, around 5 percent of annual GDP was used to purchase international safe assets. The level of reserves reached around 25 percent of GDP by the GFC (figure 4.21, panel b). The magnitude was surprisingly large given that the assets consisted of a single kind of safe, liquid asset (US Treasury Bills or notes). Reserves also greatly exceeded short-term external liabilities, almost quadruple in 2004 (figure 4.21, panel b). Aggregate capital outflows closely followed reserve accumulation until 2011. With a relatively managed capital account during this period, capital flows were mostly driven by the reserve flows.

Massive holdings of reserves helped to moderate the impact of the GFC. Foreign bank flows (other flows by nonresidents in the balance of payments) reversed sharply in late 2008. Outflows reached US$19.1 billion in October and US$11.9 billion in November 2008 (figure 4.22). Without sufficient reserves and timely interventions by the Bank of Korea, the significant volume of outflows would have devastated the external sector. Reserve flows almost topped US$20 billion in October and reached US$10.9 billion in November 2008. These reserve flows compensated for the capital outflows and prevented them from sharply increasing volatility in the domestic economy.

The rapid accumulation of reserves halted after 2011, when reserve levels reached 25 percent of GDP. Since then, the overall increase in external assets has been mainly driven by the private sector.

FIGURE 4.21 Financial Market Openness in the Republic of Korea

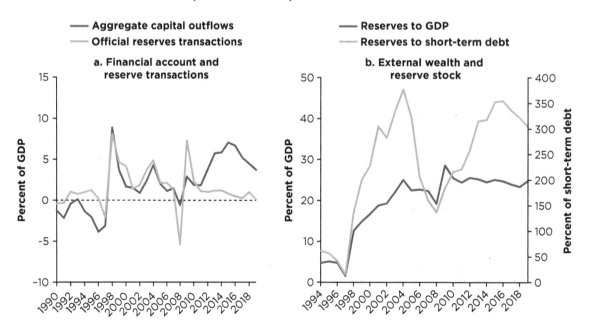

Source: Calculations based on data (balance of payments and other) from the Bank of Korea.
Note: GDP = gross domestic product.

FIGURE 4.22 **Capital Flows during the Global Financial Crisis, Republic of Korea**

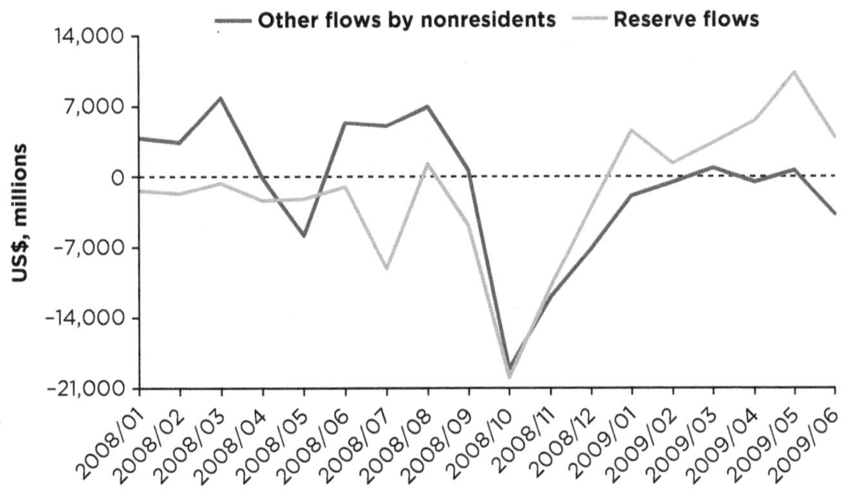

Source: Calculation based on data (balance of payments and other) from the Bank of Korea.
Note: Values are the averages for each year/month during the crisis.

Since 2012, aggregate capital outflows normalized by GDP have decoupled from reserve accumulation. Reserve accumulation has been subdued, while aggregate outflows have taken off (figure 4.21, panel a). The discrepancy between the two trends has been filled by domestic investors who have searched for yields and tried to accumulate risky assets.

Countries have increased holdings of foreign reserves to reduce the likelihood of a crisis. Research suggests that foreign reserves can help to reduce the probability of a crisis (Gourinchas and Obstfeld 2012; Frankel and Saravelos 2012). Recent literature also suggests that precautionary stockpiling of reserves could favor manufacturing exports by limiting real exchange rate appreciation and encouraging real-location of resources to the tradable sector (Benigno and Fornaro 2012; Choi and Pyun 2019; Guzman, Ocampo, and Stiglitz 2018; Korinek and Servén 2016).

Reserve accumulation achieved through a sustained current account surplus can provoke adverse reactions from trading partners (box 4.2). However, Korea has not increased its reserve accumulation for almost a decade. Improved institutional features along with improved policy reactions have substituted for precautionary measures such as capital controls and reserve accumulation.

Trade and Financial Integration and Macroeconomic Stability

Korea's participation in global trade and financial markets has contributed to economic growth through a variety of channels. Equally important is the question of the impact of the openness to trade and finance on macroeconomic volatility. The resilience of growth has become increasingly important against the backdrop of the economic slowdown and heightened political and policy uncertainty since the GFC and the COVID-19 global recession. Vulnerability to global macroeconomic shocks is a critical issue, especially for emerging markets which are integrated into the global economy but, unlike most high-income countries, lack well-established policies and institutions to cope with shocks.

Classical theories often predict that economic and financial integration could increase output volatility. Openness to international trade leads to higher output volatility if trade openness is associated with increased interindustry specialization across countries and if industry-specific shocks are

BOX 4.2 Reserve Accumulation and Global Imbalances

Reserve accumulation may be one of the most important phenomena in global economics in the last couple of decades. East Asian countries, including China and Japan, oil exporters, and other emerging economies, have significantly accumulated international reserves (figure B4.3.1). Several advanced economies have also piled up reserves, but only after the global financial crisis (GFC). Reserve accumulation by these groups of countries has broadly matched their overall current account imbalances. A significant fraction of widening

FIGURE B4.3.1 **International Reserves and Global Imbalances, Selected Countries and Regions, 1990–2014**

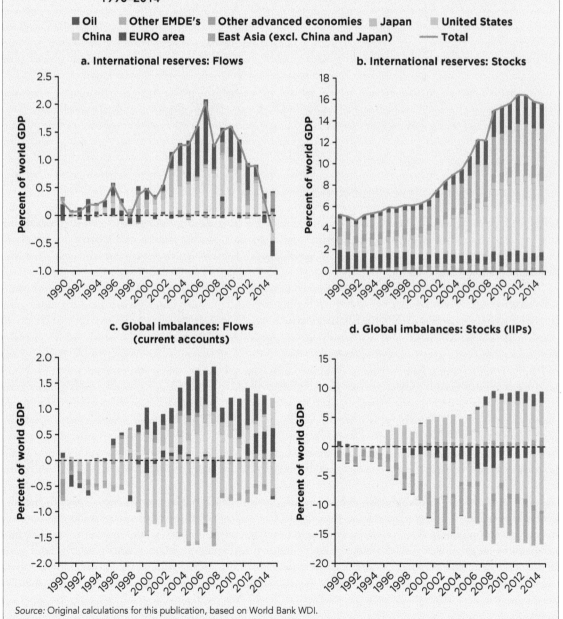

Source: Original calculations for this publication, based on World Bank WDI.

Continued

global imbalances is driven by countries with massive reserve accumulations. In figure B4.3.1, panels c and d show the trend of the global imbalances from 1990 to 2015, for flows (current account) and stocks (international investment positions), respectively. The United States was the major supplier of capital during that period (figure B4.3.1, panel c). Oil exporters and the East Asian countries, along with China and Japan, have had sustained current account surpluses and large increases in reserves. The global imbalance has not widened since the GFC, a period also marked by subdued accumulation of reserves. Overall, global imbalances and reserve accumulations have been driven by the same group of countries.

Source: Calculations based on data from World Development Indicators, World Bank (https://databank.worldbank.org /source/world-development-indicators).
Note: EMDEs = emerging markets and developing economies; GDP = gross domestic product; IIP = international investment position.

important drivers of business cycles (di Giovanni and Levchenko 2009; Krugman 1993; Rodrik 1998). However, the empricial results have so far been inconclusive. There is empirical evidence that suggests that trade openness can instead decrease macroeconomic volatility (Caselli et al 2020; Haddad, Lim, and Saborowski 2010; Strotmann, Döpke, and Buch 2006). Other research indicates that financial liberalization, if mismanaged, can be a source of banking and currency crises (Stiglitz 2002) and thus could increase output fluctuations.

The literature seeks to reconcile the mixed results, especially on the trade side, by arguing that the relationship could be heterogeneous depending on countries' structural characteristics. Whether output volatility increases or decreases with specialization depends on the intrinsic volatility of the sectors in which the economy specializes (Kose, Prasad, and Terrones 2003).[10] Other studies consider the importance of monetary and fiscal policies in the process of the transmission of trade and financial shocks (Buch, Döpke, and Pierdzioch 2002; Ko 2008; Sutherland 1996).[11]

ROLE OF GLOBAL TRADE SHOCKS IN KOREA'S BUSINESS CYCLE FLUCTUATIONS

Has integration into global markets affected economic fluctuations in Korea? Has it left the country more vulnerable to external shocks? To answer these questions, an econometric analysis is carried out to explore the transmission of global shocks to domestic macroeconomic variables (box 4.3 describes the modeling approach).

The structural vector autoregression (SVAR) analysis suggests that Korea's economy has been increasingly exposed to global trade shocks over time. Before the AFC, the contributions of global shocks to domestic macro variables were minor (below 10 percent) and not statistically significant. In contrast, during 1996–2020, an unexpected one standard deviation decline in global trade volume led to around a 1 percentage point drop in Korea's output, and the effects persisted until around half a year after the shock (figure 4.23, panel a). The same type of shock was associated with around a 2 percentage point decline in Korea's exports, which lasted for a year (panel b). Forecast error variance decompositions of macroeconomic variables suggest that the global trade shocks explained around a third and a fifth, respectively, of total variations in exports and GDP growth in Korea (panel c). The effects on private investments were also significant on impact but were short-lived. That said, domestic shocks still played a more important role than global shocks.

Historical decomposition of Korea's economic growth suggests that during the global economic recessions in 2008–09 and 2020, the impact of (positive) macroeconomic shocks counterbalanced the large negative impact of global shocks, such as the collapse of global trade. After the outbreak of the GFC, for instance, the global shocks in total accounted for up to 5 percentage points of the decline in

BOX 4.3 Empirical Analysis of the Impact of Global Trade Shocks on Macroeconomic Fluctuations

To investigate the transmission of global shocks to domestic macroeconomic fluctuations in a wide range of countries, an open-economy structural vector autoregression (SVAR) model is estimated on a country-by-country basis for 23 advanced economies and 23 emerging markets.[a] The model consists of three global variables—real trade volume, real output growth, and the Chicago Board Options Exchange's volatility index—and five domestic variables—exports, output, investment, nominal exchange rates, and interest rates.

In its structural form, the SVAR model is represented by:

$$B_0 Z_t = \alpha + \sum_{i=1}^{L} B_i Z_{t-i} + \varepsilon_t$$

where Z_t consists of global and domestic endogenous variables. The vector ε_t consists of a shock to the global trade volume (global trade shock) and other types of structural macroeconomic and financial shocks corresponding to the other variables.

Impulse responses of the endogenous variables are estimated following different types of global and domestic structural shocks.[b] Since the main focus of this exercise is on the identification of the impact of global trade shocks, the identification is achieved by using Cholesky decomposition of residuals with the global trade volume being ordered first. Thus, it is assumed that a structural shock in global trade simultaneously impacts other global and domestic variables within a period (quarter) while not vice versa. Based on the estimated impulse response functions, as is standard in the SVAR literature, forecast error variance decompositions of the endogenous variables are estimated. In addition, case studies of the contributions of global shocks to domestic macroeconomic variables are performed focusing on three periods: the Asian Financial Crisis in 1997–98, the global financial crisis in 2008–09, and the COVID-19 pandemic in 2020.

The Bayesian method is used in estimating the model. The procedure searches for 1,000 successful draws of at least 2,000 iterations with 1,000 burn-ins. The median of the 1,000 successful draws and the 90th percentile confidence intervals for each forecasting horizon are presented as the results. In the Bayesian estimation, the Minnesota priors proposed by Litterman (1986) are used where the variance-covariance matrix of residuals is estimated by ordinary least squares.[c]

To obtain the stationarity of the data, quarterly growth rates of endogenous variables (seasonally adjusted) except interest rates (10-year government bond yields) are employed. The baseline sample period is 1996–2020, reflecting the data availability as well as the trend of economic globalization as reported in the previous sections. The pre–Asian Financial Crisis period (1970–95), which coincides with the pre-globalization period, is also tested for Korea to explore any changes in the estimation results over time. The database includes a balanced set of 46 countries, including 23 emerging markets. The cross-country data were obtained from multiple sources, including Haver Analytics, the International Monetary Fund, the World Bank, and country-specific sources.

a. Country classification is based on the World Economic Outlook reports of the International Monetary Fund.
b. Although the recursive identification scheme enables identification of multiple global and domestic shocks, the focus here is on the impact of global *trade* shocks on domestic macroeconomic variables. Other results are available upon request.
c. Although some studies assume a block exogeneity between global and domestic variables, the analysis here did not impose such a restriction, considering that the sample includes some large economies.

Korea's GDP growth (figure 4.23, panel d).[12] However, Korea's GDP growth declined by only 1 percentage point during the period. The greater-than-expected economic growth suggests that other factors, which may include domestic industrial activity and macroeconomic policies, contributed to the resilience of Korea's economic growth. Similarly, the global trade collapse after the outbreak of the COVID-19 pandemic was accompanied by only a moderate decline in Korea's growth.

The impact of global trade shocks on Korea's growth appears to have been smaller than the average impact in other countries. Using country-specific SVAR models, the impacts of global trade shocks explain a similar magnitude of export decline in Korea as in other countries (not shown), but the

FIGURE 4.23 Impact of Global Real Trade Shocks on the Macroeconomy, Republic of Korea

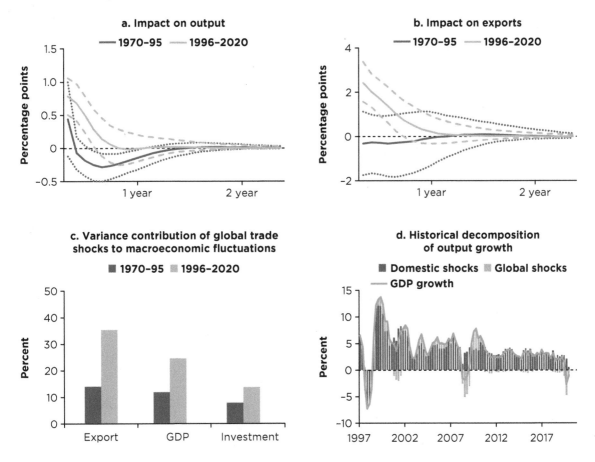

Source: Calcuations based on structural vector autoregression model.
Note: Panels a and b show the impulse response of Korean variables to a one standard deviation positive global trade shock. The solid lines are the median Bayesian draws; the broken lines indicate 90th percentile confidence invervals. GDP = gross domestic product.

impacts on Korea's output growth were around one-half of the impacts of other countries' growth, and the impacts were much less persistent in Korea (figure 4.24, panel a).[13] Forecast error variance decompositions lead to a similar conclusion. Although during 1996–2020, the global shocks explained around 60 and 30 percent, respectively, of total variations in output and investment growth in the median country across 45 countries, the shocks explained only around 20 and 10 percent, respectively, for Korea (figure 4.24, panel b).

Compared with other countries with a similar level of income and similar degree of economic and financial openness (for example, Finland and Singapore), the contribution of external shocks to domestic macroeconomic fluctuations was much more muted in Korea. Historical decomposition of the variables suggests that around the GFC and after the COVID-19 pandemic, the negative impacts of global trade collapse were much more moderate in Korea than in other economies.

These findings are consistent with findings in the literature. For instance, using a set of SVAR models that estimate the effects of cross-border spillovers of output collapse in large economies, World Bank (2016) finds that the impacts of income shocks in the Group of Seven economies were statistically insignificant in Korea, in contrast to the cases of most other countries in Asia (figure 4.25, panel a). Moreover, Korea was one of few countries where the impacts of output decline in China were insignificant, despite the two countries' strong economic interconnectedness (figure 4.25, panel b).

FIGURE 4.24 Impact of Global Real Trade Shocks on the Republic of Korea and Other Countries

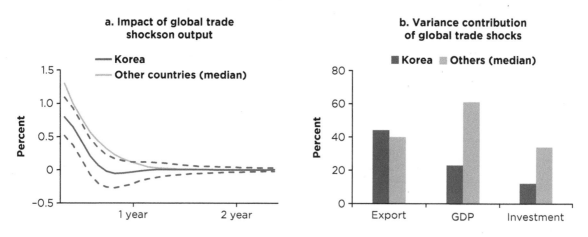

Source: Calcuations based on structural vector autoregression models for 46 countries.
Note: Panel a shows the impulse response of output growth to a one standard deviation increase in global trade volume. The solid lines indicate the median Bayesian draws; the broken lines indicate 90th percentile confidence inveravls. See box 4.3 for a description of the analysis. GDP = gross domestic product.

FIGURE 4.25 Impact of Global Output Decline on Economic Growth in Asian Economies

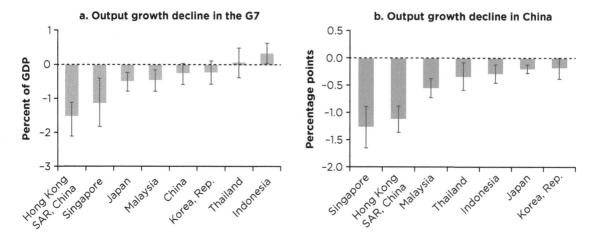

Source: World Bank 2016.
Note: The values show the impulse response of output growth following a one standard deviation decline in output in the G7 (panel a) or China (panel b). G7 = Group of Seven.

The empirical results collectively suggest that Korea's economic fluctuations have been less vulnerable to global shocks compared with other advanced economies and emerging markets and developing economies, in particular around the occurrence of large global shocks. This result is somewhat unexpected given Korea's increasing economic integration into global markets over the recent decades, as indicated in the previous sections. The question is then how Korea has achieved such a resilient economic performance. There could have been a variety of factors, including developments in financial markets, industrial policies, and macroeconomic and structural policies, which helped to enhance the resilience of the domestic economy.

Korea has successfully transitioned to high value-added industries in the process of economic integration into global markets. The share of the ICT sector in real GDP has increased fivefold (and threefold in exports) since 1995. The transition to ICT sectors, which are less sensitive to fluctuations in both external and domestic demand, contributed to reducing macroeconomic volatility.[14] Through interindustry productivity spillovers, the developments in the ICT sector boosted labor and total factor productivity in other sectors in Korea and enhanced economic resilience (Bertschek et al. 2019; Jung, Na, and Yoon 2013). Other domestic policies contributed to strengthening Korea's manufacturing export competitiveness by keeping production costs relatively low. For instance, Korea was able to limit its vulnerability to shocks by avoiding excessive currency appreciation and amassing a large volume of foreign assets that could serve as a buffer in the face of external shocks.

Countercyclical macroeconomic policies also contributed to stabilizing the domestic economy. Korea has maintained fiscal sustainability by consistently running a budget surplus. Government debt in Korea has remained around 30 percent of GDP, which is around one-half the magnitude of the average for advanced economies and emerging markets and developing economies (figure 4.26, panel a). The financial guarantee and public investment programs that were part of the countercyclical fiscal policy

FIGURE 4.26 Role of Fiscal and Monetary Policies, Republic of Korea and Country Groups

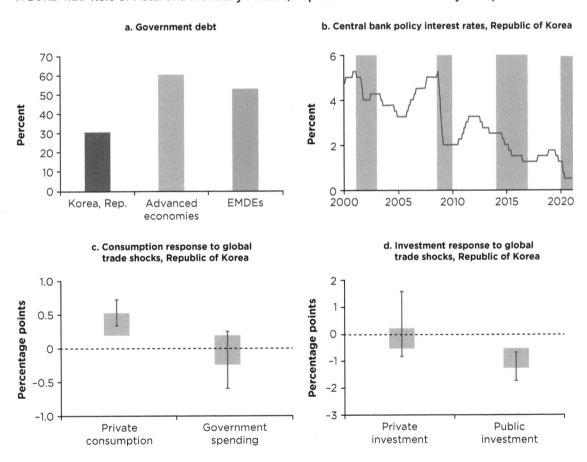

Sources: Calculations based on data from Bank of Korea; Kose et al 2020.
Note: In panel a, values are percent of gross domestic product, based on the average over the past decade. In panel b, the blue columns indicate periods of global recessions and economic slowdowns. In panels c and d, values show the impulse response following a one standard deviation increase in global trade volume. In panels c and d, the light blue bars indicate median draws; the dark blue lines indicate 90 percent confidence intervals. EMDEs = emerging markets and developing economies.

response to crises also contributed to maintaining macroeconomic stability (Eskesen 2009; Lee, Rhee, and Sung 2006).[15]

Since adopting inflation targeting in 1998, Korea has sustained low inflation of 2 to 3 percent, which is within the inflation target band except during a few periods when severe external commodity price shocks (including food and energy prices) temporarily led to fluctuations in headline consumer prices. Strong central bank independence in Korea has contributed to anchoring inflation expectations, which has supported the use of monetary policies to boost (or cool down) domestic economic output in a timely manner (Dincer and Eichengreen 2014; Ha, Kose, and Ohnsorge 2019).[16] These robust policy frameworks have enabled the authorities to respond flexibly to adverse macroeconomic shocks (Han and Hur 2020; Kim 2014) (figure 4.26, panel b).[17]

Public consumption and investment in Korea were significantly and negatively associated with global trade shocks, as opposed to the procyclical reactions of private consumption and investment (figure 4.26, panels c and d, based on the SVAR model explained in box 4.3). These countercyclical policies appear to have helped to enhance the stability of the economy as Korea continued to integrate into the global economy.

Conclusion and Policy Implications for Developing Countries

This chapter provides an overview of Korea's experience with integration into the global economy since the 1990s. In the goods and services markets, the country successfully leveraged the opportunities created by GVCs. The government's focus on promoting exports, the overhaul of the import tariff system with unilateral liberalization and a series of bilateral free FTAs, along with external developments—the WTO system, ICT development, and the rise of China—created a conducive environment for Korea's active participation in GVCs. Expanded backward and forward participation in GVCs helped to improve firm productivity, especially in the manufacturing sector.

Korea's trade facilitation reforms were built on transparency in trade regulations and successful digitalization of customs. The single-window system facilitated cross-border trade. Korea strengthened its trade facilitation infrastructure and bilateral cooperation to achieve prompt customs clearance with its major trading partners. Korea Customs Services also reduced the number of customs investigations, foreign exchange inspections, and origin verifications during the COVID-19 pandemic and released "Emergency Guidelines for Origin Verification in Response to COVID-19" on the simplified procedures for FTA claims.

Korea has been successful not only in achieving economic growth, but also in stabilizing the economy as it integrated into the global economy. Although Korea became more exposed to external trade and financial shocks as it became more globally integrated, its macroeconomic outcomes have been stable and resilient. Capital controls and foreign reserves alone cannot explain this result. Export specialization in the ICT-related sectors and countercyclical fiscal and monetary policies also contributed to this economic performance. In financial markets, concerns about the potential for capital flight were heightened after the devastation of AFC. This prompted Korea to accumulate significant foreign reserves and slow the pace of financial liberalization until the early 2010s.

Several policy implications can be drawn from Korea's experience. First, the literature consistently shows that trade openness and participation in GVCs are critical for enhancing the productivity of the tradable sectors. This general conclusion is well exemplified by Korea. Therefore, it is critical to facilitate and promote trade and foreign investment. This chapter outlined Korea's major trade promotion and facilitation policies, which would need to be adapted and customized to a country's specific circumstances.

Second, liberalization of trade and foreign investment would need to be complemented by domestic policies. The literature typically emphasizes lowering entry-exit barriers, encouraging more flexible labor markets, and building more efficient infrastructure (Harrison and Rodríguez-Clare 2010). Efficient reallocation of production factors within and across firms as well as industries is essential (Melitz 2003).

Domestic constraints to the efficient reallocation of resources would undermine the full gains from trade liberalization and GVC participation.

Third, developing countries must prepare for the next path-breaking wave of globalization, the so-called third unbundling (Baldwin 2016).[18] In the third unbundling, the development of digital technology means that labor services are not necessarily conducted in a specific location or carried out by laborers. The COVID-19 pandemic has accelerated this trend by inducing firms to allow their employees to work remotely and to prepare an adequate system for the new work environment. Thanks to robotics and artificial intelligence innovations, production and transaction tasks are increasingly being automated, and firms are automating routine work and creating new tasks. The question is which countries can leverage the next revolution, just as Korea successfully exploited GVCs? Developing countries would need to be technologically ready to benefit from automation technologies and participate in the globalized labor market.

Finally, financial liberalization can be strategically implemented with properly designed and calibrated countercyclical macroeconomic policies. Policy makers must carefully examine their international financial environment and formulate policies, such as accumulating adequate levels of reserves, to ensure that global financial integration supports macroeconomic stability.

Notes

1. See Rodríguez and Rodrik (2000) for an alternative explanation for trade policies.
2. The weighted Most Favored Nation tariff rates of industrial countries for industrial products (except petroleum) fell by 38 percent after the Kennedy Round and by 33 percent after the Tokyo Round (WTO 2007).
3. Since the mid-1990s, the intensive use of ICT promoted productivity growth in the United States over the next 10 years (Bloom, Sadun, and Van Reenen 2012; van Ark, O'Mahony, and Timmer 2008).
4. The foreign content of exports is equivalent to the vertical specialization suggested by Hummels, Ishii, and Yi (2001).
5. The content of this section is largely based on Chung (2016), with revisions.
6. Because the standard RCA indexes for services may not correctly reflect the competitiveness of Korean services, they are not interpreted here.
7. https://www.ktnet.com/mobile/viewStaticHtmlPage.do?viewName=mobile_kre/mcomp_prof_en&tab _id=HA5&menu_id=HB5C4.
8. Capital account and financial account are used interchangeably throughout this section.
9. Chinn and Ito's (2006) measure takes the lag of the implementation of the restrictions, and their different ways of recording protocol measure the pace of liberalization differently.
10. Limited diversification of exports and imports makes some economies particularly susceptible to sudden fluctuations in terms of trade and foreign trade shocks. Senhandji (1998) shows the important role played by foreign demand shocks. Caselli et al. (2020) find that openness can reduce a country's exposure to domestic shocks, and it allows countries to diversify their sources of demand and supply, leading to potentially lower overall volatility.
11. Using a two-country general equilibrium model, Ko (2008) finds that economies with high ICT development or a high degree of financial integration exhibit lower output fluctuations in the face of fiscal policy shocks.
12. Global shocks include global trade shocks, other global output shocks, and global financial shocks as reflected in the fluctuations in global trade volume, global output growth, and Chicago Board Options Exchange's (CBOE) Volatility Index (VIX), respectively.
13. The difference seems to be statistically significant for many countries; the confidence bands for the estimated impacts on the other countries did not include the confidence bands for Korea.
14. The strides in the ICT industry are mainly attributable to the large investments in research and development, which have been even greater than those in the United States and Japan, two of the global leaders in innovation (Santacreu and Zhu 2018).

15. Hong (2010) suggests that Korea's fiscal stimulus in 2009, which was unusually large compared with typical fiscal responses during economic downturns, contributed to the economy's fast recovery.

16. According to the central bank transparency index by Dincer and Eichengreen (2014), transparency in Korea (index = 9.5) is much higher than the average of other countries in the Asia region or other regions.

17. Consistent with the overall findings in this section, using a time-varying SVAR model, Han and Hur (2020) find that although the volatility of exogenous shocks hitting the Korean economy declined precipitously after the GFC, monetary policy remained effective in boosting output throughout the period.

18. The first unbundling is the separation of production and consumption, driven by the reduced transportation cost. The second unbundling, also known as the GVC revolution, is the separation of production itself across countries.

References

Allen, T. 2014. "Information Frictions in Trade." *Econometrica* 82 (6): 2041–83.

Amiti, M., and S.-J. Wei. 2009. "Service Offshoring and Productivity: Evidence from the US." *World Economy* 32 (2): 203–20.

Amiti, M., and D. E. Weinstein. 2011. "Exports and Financial Shocks." *Quarterly Journal of Economics* 126 (4): 1841–77.

Aw, B. Y., S. Chung, and M. J. Roberts. 2003. "Productivity, Output, and Failure: A Comparison of Taiwanese and Korean Manufacturers." *Economic Journal* 113 (491): F485–F510.

Balassa, B. 1965. "Trade Liberalisation and 'Revealed' Comparative Advantage." *The Manchester School* 33 (2): 99–123.

Baldwin, R. 2016. *The Great Convergence: Information Technology and the New Globalization*. Cambridge, MA: Harvard University Press.

Benigno, G., and D. Fornaro. 2012. "Reserve Accumulation, Growth and Financial Crises." CEP Discussion Papers dp1161, Centre for Economic Performance, London School of Economics.

Bertschek, I., M. Polder, and P. Schulte. 2019. "ICT and Resilience in Times of Crisis: Evidence from Cross-Country Micro Moments Data." *Economics of Innovation and New Technology* 28 (8): 759–74.

Bloom, N., R. Sadun, and J. Van Reenen. 2012. "Americans Do IT Better: US Multinationals and the Productivity Miracle." *American Economic Review* 102 (1): 167–201.

Buch, C. M., J. Döpke, and C. Pierdzioch. 2002. "Financial Openness and Business Cycle Volatility," Kiel Working Paper No. 1121, Kiel Institute for the World Economy, Kiel, Germany.

Caselli, F., M. Koren, M. Lisicky, and S. Tenreyro. 2020. "Diversification through Trade." *Quarterly Journal of Economics* 135 (1): 449–502.

Chinn, M. D., and H. Ito. 2006. "What Matters for Financial Development? Capital Controls, Institutions, and Interactions." *Journal of Development Economics* 81 (1): 163–92.

Choi, W. J., and J. H. Pyun. 2019. "Catching Up by Deglobalization: Capital Account Policy and Economic Growth." https://ssrn.com/abstract=3516385 or http://dx.doi.org/10.2139/ssrn.3516385.

Choi, Y.-S., and C. H. Hahn. 2013. "Effects of Imported Intermediate Varieties on Plant Total Factor Productivity and Product Switching: Evidence from Korean Manufacturing." *Asian Economic Journal* 27 (2): 125–43.

Chor, D., and K. Manova. 2012. "Off the Cliff and Back? Credit Conditions and International Trade during the Global Financial Crisis." *Journal of International Economics* 87 (1): 117–33.

Chung, S. 2016. "Korea's Participation in Global Value Chains: Measures and Implications." *KDI Journal of Economic Policy* 38 (4): 45–76.

Connolly, M., and K.-M. Yi. 2015. "How Much of South Korea's Growth Miracle Can Be Explained by Trade Policy?" *American Economic Journal: Macroeconomics* 7 (4): 188–221.

Constantinescu, C., A. Mattoo, and M. Ruta. 2019. "Does Vertical Specialisation Increase Productivity?" *World Economy* 42 (8): 2385–2402.

De Loecker, J. 2013. "Detecting Learning by Exporting." *American Economic Journal: Microeconomics* 5 (3): 1–21.

Demir, B., and B. Javorcik. 2020. "Trade Finance Matters: Evidence from the COVID-19 Crisis." *Oxford Review of Economic Policy* 36 (Supplement_1): S397–S408.

di Giovanni, J., and A. Levchenko. 2009. "Trade Openness and Volatility." *Review of Economics and Statistics* 91 (3): 558–85.

Dincer, N. N., and B. Eichengreen. 2014. "Central Bank Transparency and Independence: Updates and New Measures." *International Journal of Central Banking* 10 (1): 189–259.

Don, H., B. H. Gunasekera, and R. Tyers. 1990. "Imperfect Competition and Returns to Scale in a Newly Industrialising Economy: A General Equilibrium Analysis of Korean Trade Policy." *Journal of Development Economics* 34 (1): 223–47.

Eichengreen, B., D. H. Perkins, and K. Shin. 2012. *From Miracle to Maturity: The Growth of the Korean Economy.* Cambridge, MA: Harvard University Press.

Eskesen, L. L. 2009. "Countering the Cycle: The Effectiveness of Fiscal Policy in Korea." IMF Working Paper No. 09/249, International Monetary Fund, Washington, DC. https://ssrn.com/abstract=1512253.

Fernandez, A., M. Kelin, A. Rebucci, M. Schindler, and M. Uribe. 2016. "Capital Control Measures: A New Dataset." *IMF Economic Review* 64 (3): 548–74.

Frankel, J., and G. Saravelos. 2012. "Can Leading Indicators Assess Country Vulnerability? Evidence from the 2008–09 Global Financial Crisis." *Journal of International Economics* 87 (2): 216–31.

Goldberg, P. K., A. K. Khandelwal, N. Pavcnik, and P. Topalova. 2010. "Imported Intermediate Inputs and Domestic Product Growth: Evidence from India." *Quarterly Journal of Economics* 125 (4): 1727–67.

Gourinchas, P. O., and M. Obstfeld. 2012. "Stories of the Twentieth Century for the Twenty-First." *American Economic Journal: Macroeconomic* 4 (1): 226–65.

Grossman, G. M., and E. Rossi-Hansberg. 2008. "Trading Tasks: A Simple Theory of Offshoring." *American Economic Review* 98 (5): 1978–97.

Guzman, M., J. A. Ocampo, and J. E. Stiglitz. 2018. "Real Exchange Rate Policies for Economic Development." *World Development* 110: 51–62.

Ha, J., M. A. Kose, and F. Ohnsorge, 2019. *Inflation in Emerging and Developing Economies.* Washington, DC: World Bank.

Haddad, M., J. Lim, and C. Saborowski. 2010. "Trade Openness Reduces Growth Volatility When Countries Are Well Diversified." Working Paper S5222, World Bank, Washington, DC.

Hahn, C. H. 2012. "Learning-by-Exporting, Introduction of New Products, and Product Rationalization: Evidence from Korean Manufacturing." *B.E. Journal of Economic Analysis & Policy* 12 (1).

Halpern, L., M. Koren, and A. Szeidl. 2015. "Imported Inputs and Productivity." *American Economic Review* 105 (12): 3660–3703.

Han, J., and J. Hur. 2020. "Macroeconomic Effects of Monetary Policy in Korea: A Time-Varying Coefficient VAR Approach." *Economic Modelling* 89 (C): 142–52.

Harrison, A., and A. Rodríguez-Clare. 2010. "Trade, Foreign Investment, and Industrial Policy for Developing Countries." In *Handbook of Development Economics,* edited by D. Rodrik and M. Rosenzweig, 4039–4214. Elsevier.

Hong, K. 2010. *Fiscal Policy Issues in Korea after the Current Crisis.* Tokyo, Japan: Asian Development Bank Institute.

Hong, W. 1979. *Trade, Distortions and Employment Growth in Korea: Studies in the Modernization of the Republic of Korea.* Research Monograph, Korea Development Institute, Sejong City, Republic of Korea.

Hummels, D., J. Ishii, and K.-M. Yi. 2001. "The Nature and Growth of Vertical Specialization in World Trade." *Journal of International Economics* 54 (1): 75–96.

Jeong, Y. S. 2005. "The Present and Future of Korea's E-Trade (Paperless Trading)." Presentation given at the Capacity-Building Workshop on Trade Facilitation Implementation for Asia and the Pacific Region, March 18, Kuala Lumpur, Malaysia.

Johnson, R. C., and G. Noguera. 2012. "Accounting for Intermediates: Production Sharing and Trade in Value Added." *Journal of International Economics* 86 (2): 224–36.

Johnson, R. C., and G. Noguera. 2017. "A Portrait of Trade in Value-Added over Four Decades." *Review of Economics and Statistics* 99 (5): 896–911.

Jung, H., K. Na, and C. Yoon. 2013. "The Role of ICT in Korea's Economic Growth: Productivity Changes across Industries Since the 1990s." *Telecommunications Policy* 37 (4): 292–310.

Kim, E. 2000. "Trade Liberalization and Productivity Growth in Korean Manufacturing Industries: Price Protection, Market Power, and Scale Efficiency." *Journal of Development Economics* 62 (1): 55–83.

Kim, K., and J. H. Pyun. 2018. "Exchange Rate Regimes and the International Transmission of Business Cycles: Capital Account Openness Matters." *Journal of International Money and Finance* 87: 44–61.

Kim, S., and D. Y. Yang. 2010. "Managing Capital Flows: The Case of the Republic of Korea." In *Managing Capital Flows*, edited by M. Kawai and M. B. Lamberte, chapter 11. Edward Elgar Publishing.

Kim, T. 2014. "Effectiveness of Monetary Policy in Korea Due to Time Varying Monetary Policy Stance." *KDI Journal of Economic Policy* 36 (3): 1–23.

Ko, K. W. 2008. "Financial Integration, Information and Communication Technology, and Macroeconomic Volatility: Evidence from Ten Asian Economies." *Research in International Business and Finance* 22 (2): 124–44.

Korinek, A., and E. G. Mendoza. 2014. "From Sudden Stops to Fisherian Deflation: Quantitative Theory and Policy." *Annual Review of Economics* 6: 299–332.

Korinek, A., and L. Servén. 2016. "Undervaluation through Foreign Reserve Accumulation: Static Losses, Dynamic Gains." *Journal of International Money and Finance* 64: 104–36.

Kose, M. A., E. Prasad, K. Rogoff, and S.J. Wei. 2009. "Financial Globalization: A Reappraisal." *IMF Staff Papers* 56 (1): 8–62.

Kose, A., E. Prasad, and M. Terrones. 2003. "Financial Integration and Macroeconomic Volatility." *IMF Staff Papers* 50 (SI): 119–42.

Kose, M. A., N. Sugawara, and M. E. Terrones. 2020. "Global Recessions." Policy Research Working Paper 9172, World Bank, Washington, DC.

Krueger. A. O. 1997. "Trade Policy and Economic Development: How We Learn." *American Economic Review* 87 (1): 1–22.

Krugman, P. R. 1993. "The Narrow and Broad Arguments for Free Trade." *American Economic Review* 83 (2): 362–66.

Lederman, D., M. Olarreaga., and L. Payton. 2010. "Export Promotion Agencies: Do They Work?" *Journal of Development Economics* 91 (2): 257–65.

Lee, J.-W. 1996. "Government Interventions and Productivity Growth." *Journal of Economic Growth* 1 (3): 391–414.

Lee, Y., C. Rhee, and T. Sung. 2006. "Fiscal Policy in Korea: Before and after the Financial Crisis." *International Tax and Public Finance* 13: 509–31.

Litterman, R. B. 1986. "Forecasting with Bayesian Vector Autoregressions—Five Years of Experience." *Journal of Business & Economic Statistics* 4 (1): 25–38.

Manova, K. 2008. "Credit Constraints, Equity Market Liberalizations and International Trade." *Journal of International Economics* 76 (1): 33–47.

Manova, K. 2013. "Credit Constraints, Heterogeneous Firms, and International Trade." *Review of Economic Studies* 80 (2): 711–44.

Melitz, M. J. 2003. "The Impact of Trade on Intra-Industry Reallocations and Aggregate Industry Productivity." *Econometrica* 71 (6): 1695–1725.

Nam, C. H. 1995. "The Role of Trade and Exchange Rate Policy in Korea's Growth." In *Growth Theories in Light of the East Asian Experience*, edited by T. Ito and A. O. Krueger, 153–79. Chicago: University of Chicago Press.

Ostry, J. D., A. R. Ghosh, M. Chamon, and M. S. Qureshi. 2011. "Capital Controls: When and Why?" *IMF Economic Review* 59 (3): 562–80.

Ottaviano, G. I. P., G. Peri, and G. C. Wright. 2013. "Immigration, Offshoring, and American Jobs." *American Economic Review* 103 (5): 1925–59.

Rodríguez, F., and D. Rodrik. 2000. "Trade Policy and Economic Growth: A Skeptic's Guide to the Cross-National Evidence." *NBER Macroeconomics Annual* 15: 261–325.

Rodrik, D. 1998. "Why Do More Open Economies Have Bigger Governments?" *Journal of Political Economy* 106 (5): 997–1032.

Santacreu, A. M., and H. Zhu. 2018. "How Did South Korea's Economy Develop So Quickly?" *St. Louis Fed On the Economy*, Federal Reserve Bank of St. Louis, St. Louis, MO.

Senhandji, A. S. 1998. "Dynamics of the Trade Balance and the Terms of Trade in LDCs: The S-curve." *Journal of International Economics* 46 (1): 105–31.

Steinwender, C. 2018. "Real Effects of Information Frictions: When the States and the Kingdom Became United." *American Economic Review* 108 (3): 657–96.

Stiglitz, J. E. 2002. *Globalization and Its Discontents*. New York: W.W. Norton.

Strotmann, H., J. Döpke, and C. Buch. 2006. "Does Trade Openness Increase Firm-Level Volatility?" Discussion Paper Series 1: Economic Studies 2006, 40, Deutsche Bundesbank, Frankfurt, Germany.

Sutherland, A. 1996. "Financial Market Integration and Macroeconomic Volatility." *Scandinavian Journal of Economics* 98 (4): 521–39.

Timmer, M. P., A. A. Erumban, B. Los, R. Stehrer, and G. J. de Vries. 2014. "Slicing Up Global Value Chains." *Journal of Economic Perspectives* 28 (2): 99–118.

Timmer, M. P., B. Los, R. Stehrer, and G. J. de Vries. 2013. "Fragmentation, Incomes and Jobs: An Analysis of European Competitiveness." *Economic Policy* 28 (76): 613–61.

UNESCAP (United Nations Economic and Social Commission for Asia and the Pacific). 2010. "Case of Korea's National Paperless Trade Platform—uTradeHub." UNESCAP, Bangkok, Thailand.

van Ark, B., M. O'Mahony, and M. P. Timmer. 2008. "The Productivity Gap between Europe and the United States: Trends and Causes." *Journal of Economic Perspectives* 22 (1): 25–44.

Volpe Martincus, C., and J. Carballo. 2008. "Is Export Promotion Effective in Developing Countries? Firm-Level Evidence on the Intensive and the Extensive Margins of Exports." *Journal of International Economics* 76 (1): 89–106.

Westphal, L. E. 1978. "The Republic of Korea's Experience with Export-led Industrial Development." *World Development* 6 (3): 347–82.

Westphal, L. E. 1990. Industrial Policy in an Export-propelled Economy: Lessons from South Korea's Experience. *Journal of Economic Perspectives* 4 (3): 41–59.

World Bank. 2016. *Global Economic Prospects: Spillovers amid Weak Growth*. January. Washington, DC: World Bank.

WTO (World Trade Organization). 2007. *World Trade Report 2007: Six Decades of Multilateral Trade Cooperation: What Have We Learnt?* Geneva: World Trade Organization.

CHAPTER 5

Promoting Innovation and Technology

Introduction

The contribution of technological progress and knowledge accumulation to economic growth in developing countries has been widely examined and documented (Aghion and Howitt 2008; Romer 1987, 1990). Prior to the Asian Financial Crisis (AFC), technological catching up enabled the Republic of Korea to achieve rapid growth. By the 1990s, Korea's industry was approaching the technological frontier and the country began to move from technological imitation to innovation to sustain industrial competitiveness (Kim 1997). In response, the government and the major chaebols (family-owned conglomerates) began deepening the country's capacity in science, technology, and innovation (STI) to foster the creation of new, frontier innovations and expand the foundation for industrial innovation and future growth engines.

Korea caught up to the high-income economies by acquiring international competitiveness in major industrial sectors, including semiconductors, displays, mobile phones, steel, petrochemicals, shipbuilding, and automobiles. By the 1990s, Korea began to recognize the limitations of the "catch-up" strategy, as a large gap remained with the technologically advanced countries, which were developing new digital technology, biotechnology, and nanotechnology. Korea also became increasingly concerned about China and other emerging economies, which, armed with low-cost labor and government subsidies, moved quickly to close the gap with Korea. The AFC at the end of the 1990s laid bare the structural weaknesses of Korea's industries. In response, Korea further strengthened its core industrial capacity and aimed to transform the structure of the economy through the development and application of new frontier technologies.

The government's investments post-AFC have been broadly effective in spurring science and technology (S&T)–based innovations. The S&T plans since the 2000s have aimed to improve capacity and funding for research and development (R&D), develop an R&D workforce, increase funding for basic science, and support small and medium-size enterprises (SMEs) and technology entrepreneurs (startups) to invest in and commercialize R&D. These policies have resulted in increased R&D intensity, a rise in patents and publications, and expansion of high-technology exports, all of which have contributed to Korea's shift from a technological follower to a technological leader in products such as semiconductors. The renewed focus on entrepreneurship and the spread of globalization and rapid expansion of exports post-AFC also boosted innovation and technology in Korea, which were increasingly led by the private sector.

This chapter was prepared by Marcin Piatkowski (World Bank), Shahid Yusuf (Growth Dialogue), and ChiUng Song and Ji Hyun Kim (Science and Technology Policy Institute).

This chapter discusses the industrial and technology policies that have enabled Korea to become a global innovation powerhouse and shares the lessons learned from this experience with other countries. The chapter addresses the following questions:

- How did Korea transition from technological imitation to a knowledge- and innovation-based economy?

- How did Korea increase and maintain its high R&D investment rates?

- How much have the investments in R&D contributed to gross domestic product (GDP) growth?

- How does Korea's STI system compare with that of international peers?

- What are the key lessons from Korea's experience for developing and middle-income countries?

The next section documents Korea's position as one of the global innovation leaders, as reflected in multiple international innovation rankings and numerous input and output indicators. The following section describes Korea's national innovation system and examines Korea's overall R&D performance. The chapter then analyzes the development of Korea's STI system over the past decades, including policies to promote R&D investment, the role of the government and public institutions in supporting R&D, the government's shift from promoting imitation to original innovation, and Korea's STI performance compared with global peers. The chapter then highlights Korea's current challenges in ensuring that R&D investments improve productivity. The final section draws lessons from Korea's experience for developing countries. Those lessons consider how the global economic environment has evolved since Korea was a developing country and the challenges confronting countries today.

Korea's Innovation Leadership

Korea is widely considered to be one of the most innovative economies in the world. Korea is known for its innovative and internationally competitive companies, such as Samsung, Hyundai, and LG. It is also highly ranked in multiple global innovation rankings (OECD and World Bank Institute 2000). The European innovation Scoreboard 2020,[1] which compares more than 40 leading economies around the world on 27 indicators, including investment in R&D, business innovation, and the quality of human capital, ranks Korea at the global top and one-third higher than the European Union average (figure 5.1). Since 2012, Korea has extended its lead over the rest of the sample (figure 5.2), with only China improving its innovation outcomes faster than Korea. According to the Scoreboard, Korea's lead is greatest in the number of patent and design applications, but it lags in exports of high technology, knowledge-intensive products, and services.

The Bloomberg Innovation Index 2020, a ranking of the world's 50 most innovative countries,[2] placed Korea in the second position, just behind Germany. It was ahead of Germany, however, in R&D intensity, manufacturing value added, and researcher concentration. The World Competitiveness Ranking has consistently placed Korea in the global top 20s during the past decade. Korea's innovation capacity is reflected in science and technology infrastructure competitiveness, which was ranked even higher (third and 13th places, respectively) (IMD 2019). The World Economic Forum's *Global Competitiveness Report 2019* included Korea among the 10 leading countries in five pillars: macroeconomic stability (first), information and communications technology (ICT) adoption (first), innovation capability (sixth), infrastructure (sixth), and health (eighth). With respect to competitiveness, Korea was ranked fifth in East Asia, a region with many competitive countries, and 13th in the world (WEF 2019).

Korea was ranked 10th in the Global Innovation Index 2020[3] and achieved the top place in human capital and research. Korea is at the forefront or among the top three countries in the world in terms of tertiary enrollment, expenditure on R&D, and number of full-time-equivalent researchers. According to the same ranking, Korea was also among the top countries globally in the efficiency of transforming

FIGURE 5.1 **European Innovation Scoreboard, 2020**

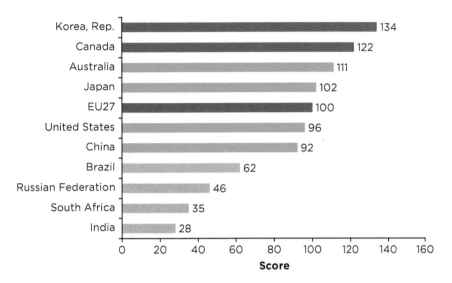

Source: European Commission, https://ec.europa.eu/commission/presscorner/detail/en/QANDA_20_1150 (accessed July 29, 2021).

FIGURE 5.2 **Change in Global Performance since 2012**

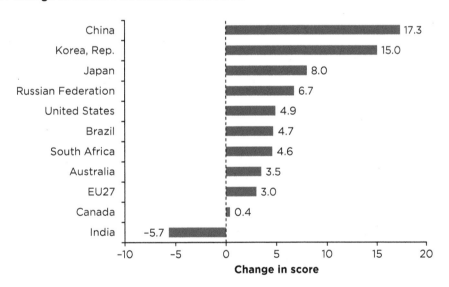

Source: European Commission, https://ec.europa.eu/commission/presscorner/detail/en/QANDA_20_1150 (accessed July 29, 2021).

innovation inputs—infrastructure, institutions, R&D, research, and human capital quality—into innovation outputs, such as the quality of knowledge, technology, and creative outputs of the economy (figure 5.3).[4]

Sustained focus on science and R&D has helped Korea to become one of the most science-intensive countries in the world. Compared with seven countries with a relatively similar level of GDP per capita, Korea has the third highest share of Science Citation Index papers, after Germany and Japan. Korea's share of Science Citation Index papers increased from 3.1 percent in 2011 to almost 3.5 percent in 2019.[5] Korea's top five publication areas included Materials Science (fourth), Engineering (fifth), Chemistry (eighth), Computer Science (eighth), and Pharmacology and Toxicology (eighth). The number of institutions that contributed papers almost doubled, from 1,807 in 2009 to 3,437 in 2019 (So et al. 2020).

Korea is also among the top patenting countries in the world. At the beginning of the 1990s, Korea filed eight times fewer patent applications to the US Patents and Trademarks Office than Germany; 10 years later, the ratio was less than two times (Nature 2020a). The number of Patent Cooperation Treaty patents in Korea has almost doubled since 2010.[6] In 2019, Korea was ranked fourth in the world in the number of Patent Cooperation Treaty applications (figure 5.4) and first compared to the size of its GDP. Samsung and LG were among the top 10 global companies in the number of Patent Cooperation Treaty applications, ranked third and tenth, respectively.

Patent applications in various technical fields related to the Industrial Revolution 4.0, such as artificial intelligence and autonomous driving, also increased over the past decade. In the field of digital health care, the number of applications more than doubled in the past 10 years due to the development of diagnostic technology using artificial intelligence and ICT technologies. Technology applications in the field of biometric medical devices have increased the most. The field of intelligent robots has the largest number of applications in component technology, but applications in the field of robot intelligence have also increased (KIPO 2020, 36).

Korea's strong performance in Science Citation Index papers and patents is a robust indicator of the country's scientific capacity. According to a recent World Intellectual Property Organization report,

FIGURE 5.3 Innovation Inputs versus Outcomes for the Republic of Korea and Selected Countries

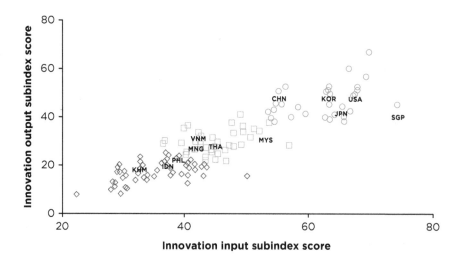

Source: World Bank 2021.
Note: The figure shows a scatter plot using Global Innovation Index data on innovation inputs and outputs. The relationship is positive and linear. Most of the countries on the right of the graph, except China, are high-income countries, whereas the countries on the left side of the graph are low- and middle-income countries. For a list of country codes, go to https://www.iso.org/obp/ui/#search.

FIGURE 5.4 Top 10 Countries in Patent Cooperation Treaty Applications, 2019

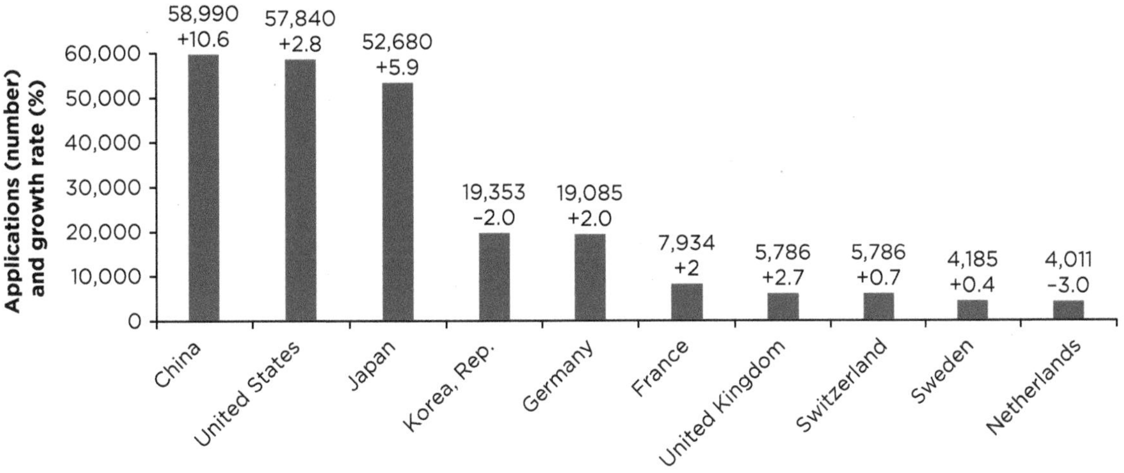

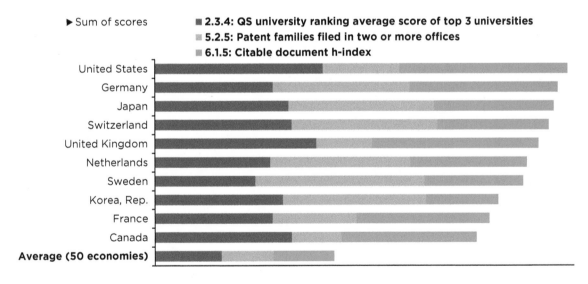

Source: WIPO 2020.

FIGURE 5.5 Metrics for the Quality of Innovation: Top 10 High-Income Economies, 2019

► Sum of scores
■ 2.3.4: QS university ranking average score of top 3 universities
■ 5.2.5: Patent families filed in two or more offices
■ 6.1.5: Citable document h-index

United States
Germany
Japan
Switzerland
United Kingdom
Netherlands
Sweden
Korea, Rep.
France
Canada
Average (50 economies)

Source: WIPO 2019.
Note: The QS university ranking is an annual publication of university rankings by Quacquarelli Symonds. The h-index is an author-level metric that measures both the productivity and citation impact of the publications, initially used for an individual scientist or scholar. The x-axis is the sum of the scores for the three indicators. See WIPO (2019, 26) for detailed definitions.

Korea ranked eighth in a comparison of the innovation quality among 10 high-income countries (figure 5.5). In particular, the quality of Korea's universities was found to be higher than those in Sweden, France, and Germany. Patent performance was remarkably high. However, the h-Index, which evaluates the quality of the papers, was relatively low, indicating that the performance of Korea's university and research institutes was somewhat at odds with the apparent high quality of the patents and universities.

National Innovation System and R&D in Korea

HIGH LEVELS OF R&D INVESTMENTS

In the 1990s, Korea's R&D investment as a share of GDP was around 2 percent, which was below the shares in the United States, Japan, and the Organisation for Economic Co-operation and Development (OECD) average. Since 2013, however, Korea's R&D investment has exceeded 4 percent of GDP and reached 4.8 percent of GDP in 2020. Korea's R&D investment is now much higher than the OECD and European Union averages of 2.8 and 2.0 percent of GDP, respectively. Only Israel has achieved a higher rate of R&D spending than Korea, and R&D spending in innovation-leading European countries, such as Switzerland and Sweden, has remained around 3.0 to 3.5 percent of GDP (figure 5.6).

The increase in R&D spending was mostly driven by the steep increase in the share of business R&D, which in 2020 was more than three times higher than government's R&D spending (figure 5.7). Private sector spending on R&D, mostly led by the chaebols, increased from 0.3 percent of GDP in 1980, to 1.6 percent by the AFC, and to 3.6 percent of GDP in 2018, about twice the OECD average. The number of corporate R&D centers skyrocketed from 46 in 1981 to 1,718 in 1990, 1,840 in 1999, and 42,155 in 2020, and their role shifted from helping to absorb foreign technology to developing new products and services.

Korea's government provided substantial fiscal and nonfiscal incentives to stimulate R&D in the private sector. In 2019, Korea's direct and indirect support for business R&D was the fifth largest among OECD countries (figure 5.8). Korea led all other OECD countries in government support for private sector R&D via fiscal incentives, which amounted to 0.3 percent of GDP and 46 percent of government support for business enterprise research and development (BERD). To promote potential new sources of growth, selected industries were provided additional tax deductions for developing and acquiring new technologies, and universities received greater support for technology R&D and related research capacity building.

Large firms account for the bulk of private sector R&D. Conglomerates such as Samsung and Hyundai have become renowned global competitors in high-technology fields through investments in R&D. However, although large enterprises accounted for the largest share of total R&D spending, their share

FIGURE 5.6 **R&D Investment in Israel, the Republic of Korea, Sweden, and Switzerland, 1996–2020**

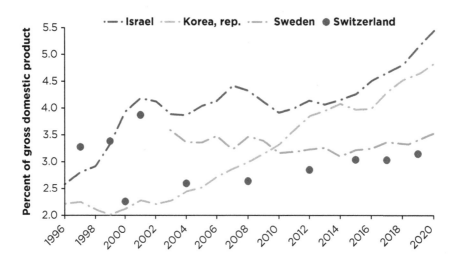

Source: World Development Indicators, World Bank 2020.

FIGURE 5.7 Sources of Research and Development Spending: Private and Public Sectors, 2015–20

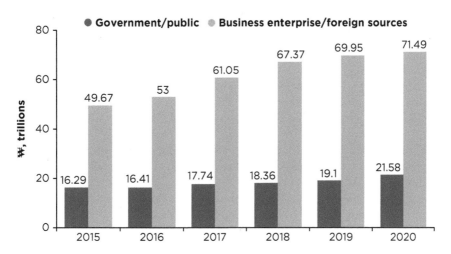

Source: Statista 2022 (https://www.statista.com/statistics/1326562/south-korea-randd-spending-by-source-of-funds/).

FIGURE 5.8 Direct Government Funding and Government Tax Support for Business R&D, 2006 and 2020

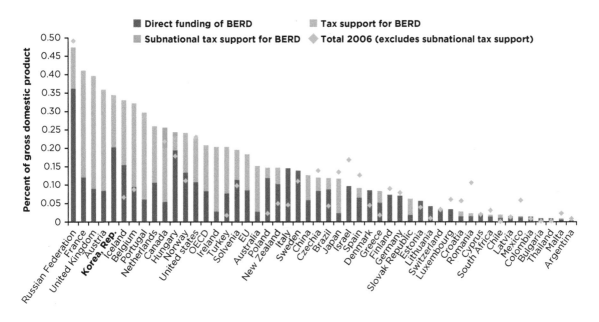

Source: R&D Tax Incentive Database, Organisation for Economic Co-operation and Development, April 2023.
Note: BERD = business enterprise research and development; R&D = research and development. For a list of country codes, go to https://www.iso.org/obp/ui/#search.

declined from 88.6 percent in 1995 to 62 percent in 2019 (figure 5.9). Mid-size companies, small firms, and venture firms were responsible for the remainder, with each representing a little more than 10 percent of the total. The rise of venture firms as significant investors in R&D has been a major success in Korea. In 2018, venture companies (new technology-based firms) accounted for 11.5 percent of the total business R&D and about half of SMEs' R&D, although venture companies make up only 1 percent of the total number of SMEs (KISTEP 2018).

A small number of chaebols accounted for a significant share of total R&D spending. According to the 2021 Industrial R&D Investment Scoreboard, five chaebol companies—Samsung, LG Electronics, SK Hynix, Hyundai Motor Company, and Kia—invested more than US$1 billion each in R&D in 2020. Samsung alone spent almost US$16 billion on R&D and was ranked the fourth most R&D-intensive company in the world, behind Alphabet, Huawei, and Microsoft.[7] This contrasts with the majority of developing countries, which typically have low domestic business R&D as multinational companies carry out most of the business R&D.

Almost 90 percent of BERD is concentrated in the manufacturing sector, driven by the massive R&D investments of the large manufacturing conglomerates (*Financial Times* 2017). Large firms accounted for 81 percent of manufacturing R&D but only 39 percent of nonmanufacturing R&D. Communication equipment (28.1 percent of total R&D spending), automobiles (12.3 percent), and home appliances (8.8 percent) represented more than half of R&D spending within manufacturing in 2018.[8] The top five enterprises accounted for 54 percent of manufacturing R&D spending, with nearly all of it in the electronics industry (figure 5.10). The R&D concentration in the electronics industry reflects the industrial structure of the economy. Korea has the highest value-added share of the ICT sector to GDP among OECD countries,[9] mainly due to the large ICT manufacturing sector. The share of R&D in services,

FIGURE 5.9 R&D Expenditures, by Firm Size, 1995–2019

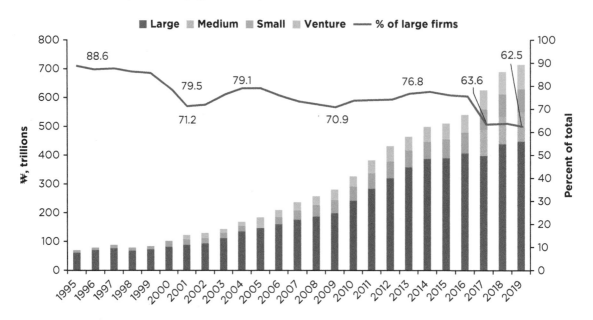

Source: Data from Korea Institute for Advancement of Technology; NTIS Stats, National Science and Technology Information Service, https://www.ntis.go.kr/rndsts/ (accessed December 23, 2020).
Note: The unit of R&D expenditures is 100 million KRW, which is around US$93,000. The R&D expenditures of medium-size companies from 2002 to 2016 were not collected and were newly added after 2017. Large firms are those with restricted mutual investment of ₩10 trillion or more; medium-size companies are those with 1,000 or more regular workers. R&D = research and development.

FIGURE 5.10 Concentration of Enterprise R&D, 2018 (percent of total)

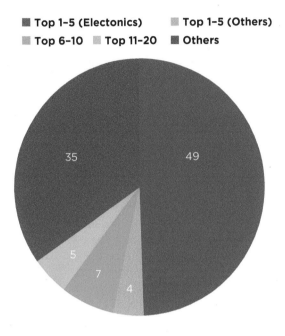

■ Top 1–5 (Electonics) ▨ Top 1–5 (Others)
▨ Top 6–10 ▨ Top 11–20 ■ Others

Source: KISTEP 2018.
Note: R&D = research and development.

TABLE 5.1 Evolution of R&D Expenditure, by Firm Size, 1997–2006

	R&D expenditure (₩, billions) (% of sales)				Number of researchers (doctoral level)			
	1997	2000	2003	2006	1997	2000	2003	2006
SMEs	1,090.2	2,106.4	3,425.4	5,105.1	17,703	36,494	52,332	74,875
	(2.82)	(3.14)	(3.57)	(2.10)	(474)	(1,543)	(2,291)	(6,573)
Large firms	7,755.1	8,148.2	11,084.2	16,021.7	56,990	57,839	71,698	99,029
	(2.07)	(1.81)	(2.05)	(222)	(3,613)	(3,878)	(5,562)	(15,814)

Sources: Frias and Lee 2021; Keenan 2012.
Note: R&D = research and development; SMEs = small and medium-size enterprises.

such as printing, publishing, and professional S&T activities, in total R&D spending has been stable and remained small at only 5.4 percent of total spending in 2018.[10]

Investment in R&D by SMEs expanded following the AFC. Between 1997 and 2006, the number of SMEs increased by about 30 percent (Statistics Korea 2020), but R&D expenditure by SMEs grew almost fivefold (table 5.1). R&D expenditure by SMEs also increased at a faster rate than that of large firms, going from 1.2 percent of total private sector R&D expenditure in 1997 to 2.4 percent in 2006 (Statistics Korea 2020). The number of researchers increased more than fourfold to almost 75,000 people, who worked across thousands of SME research facilities (table 5.1). R&D spending among SMEs focused on ICT (21.6 percent of total), biotechnology and health care (13.5 percent), and material and nanotechnology (10.7 percent).

Evolution of Korea's STI Policy

EVOLUTION OF THE S&T LEGAL FRAMEWORK, POLICIES, AND INFRASTRUCTURE

Korea's rapid economic growth has been driven by the successful integration of advanced technology into manufacturing, initially through the absorption of foreign technology before sufficient domestic capacity was built to start producing innovations at the technology frontier. During the 1960s and 1970s, Korea aggressively imported foreign technologies and implemented all-out efforts to learn and assimilate such transferred technologies (Choi 2010). Private enterprises did not have a sufficient level of in-house STI capabilities in the early stages of economic development and thus could not fully internalize these technological capabilities.

Korea's reliance on technology transfers progressively diminished during the 1980s and 1990s, as the country transitioned from absorbing and implementing technology from other sources to building the domestic capability to develop homegrown, cutting-edge technologies. In the 1990s, Korea increasingly faced intensifying competitive pressure from late-movers, in particular China, pushing the country to accelerate the transition from a strategy of catching up to a strategy of global leadership in S&T. These efforts enabled Korea to transition from light industries in the 1960s and heavy and chemical industries in the 1970s and 1980s to high-technology industries in the 1990s and beyond (Choi 2010).

Korea laid the foundation for its S&T legislative framework and infrastructure from the earliest years of its modern development, indicating the high priority placed on the development of S&T capabilities. The Science and Technology Promotion Act (1967), enacted when Korea was still a low-income economy, provided the initial legislative framework for national S&T policies, covering national R&D planning and programs, expansion of S&T investments and human resource capacity building, and foreign technology importation and cooperation. The legal framework for R&D has gradually expanded to include acts covering the promotion of S&T in specific fields, such as the environment, transport, and agriculture.

From the 1960s to the 1980s, targeted industrial policy supported imports of technology embodied in capital equipment and acquired through licensing, reverse engineering, overseas tours, and training. To support the private sector, the government began to establish the country's basic S&T infrastructure. The government established new ministries and institutions, including a new Ministry of Science and Technology (MOST); the Korea Advanced Institute of Science, a leading S&T university; a range of government research institutes (GRIs), including the multidisciplinary Korea Institute of Science and Technology; and the Daedeok Science Town, a technology hub that is home to numerous GRIs and private research institutes. Research outposts were established in technology hotspots abroad.[11] Education and the development of industrial skills were also a high priority, to supply the researchers and support the drive to diversify and upgrade industry.

The GRIs that were established in the 1960s and 1970s were responsible for a significant share of the country's research in the early decades of its development. This stands in contrast with the experience of many OECD countries where research, in particular basic research, is carried out by universities, and with the experience of developing countries, which typically attempt to build research capacity in leading public universities (Lim 2008). Many of the GRIs were mission oriented and played an instrumental role in developing industrial technology. The Electronics and Telecommunication Research Institute was responsible for development of the Time Division eXchange electronic switching system in the 1980s and the Code Division Multiple Access mobile communication system in the 1990s, which became the foundation of Korea's telecommunications equipment industry. The Korea Institute of Electronics Technology developed the Dynamic Random Access Memory semiconductor technology in the 1980s, which was transferred to Samsung Electronics, to help start the semiconductors industry.

In the 1990s, MOST (currently the Ministry of Science and ICT) and the Ministry of Knowledge Economy began reorienting research toward high-tech industries such as memory chips and processors (Nature 2020a). The Five-Year S&T Principal Plan and the National R&D Program managed by MOST launched funds to support research on, for example, space vehicles and satellites and bio-science. Fifty-seven research centers received grants to finance research, which would enhance Korea's industrial competitiveness. This was bolstered by the Creative Research Initiative in 1997, the National Technology Roadmap and the 21st Century Frontier R&D Program in 1999, the Biotech 2000 Plan, and the Nanotechnology Development Plan in 2001. These have been superseded by the Creative Material Development Program.

The new, large-scale R&D projects of the 1990s had clear goals with strategic orientation from govern-ment ministries. For instance, the G7 Project introduced in the early 1990s sought to transform Korea into one of the world's top seven technology powerhouses. The project was markedly different from the Specific R&D Program and the Industry-based R&D Program of the 1980s, as it focused on supporting frontier technology development rather than technology absorption, and the choice of research priorities was led by private sector experts and opened to international research collaboration (table 5.2).

The two representative programs of the 1980s were implemented using a bottom-up method in which a government-funded research institution led each research project. The G7 Project of the 1990s imple-mented a top-down, government-led planning method. Earlier, government R&D projects in Korea were designed and planned by researchers from GRIs. Implementing R&D using a top-down style in the G7 Project was a departure because it was more mission oriented (MOST 2017). Strong public-private collaboration led to several technological breakthroughs, such as the Time Division eXchange–Code Division Multiple Access technology, which helped to lay the foundation for the success of the Korean mobile telecommunications industry (Chung et al. 1998). Korea's S&T policy focused on enhancing the

TABLE 5.2 **Comparison of Large-Scale R&D Projects Conducted by Korean Government, 1980s and 1990s**

	R&D program	Industry-based R&D program	G7 Project (advanced technology development program)
Period	1982–91 (mid- to long-term perspective)	1987–97 (short-term perspective)	1992–2002 (mid- to long-term perspective)
Leading entity	Ministry of Science and Technology	Ministry of Commerce, Industry and Energy	Joint project between eight ministries
Method of execution	Bottom-up (changed from a top-down approach, starting in the 1990s)	Bottom-up	Top-down
Policy goal	Replicate the technologies developed by high-income countries	Replicate the technologies developed by high-income countries	Develop into the world's top technology powerhouse
Scope of research	Technology application	Technology application and development	Vertical integration of technology and product development
Planning independence	None	None	Planning independence
Subject planning	Led by GRI	Led by GRI	Led by private experts
Evaluation method	Evaluated by subprojects	Evaluated by subprojects	Evaluated by subprojects and project phases
Globalization	None	None	Allocate 10% of research funds to international cooperation research

Source: Cho et al. 2013, 12.
Note: GRI = government research Institute; R&D = research and development.

country's capacity for developing innovative products, particularly in the field of consumer electronics and semiconductors (box 5.1 discusses how cooperation between the private sector and government led to the development of Korea's semiconductor industry).

As Korea has advanced closer to the global frontiers in STI since the 2000s, government policies have evolved away from assimilation policies toward frontier innovation policies. Korea's S&T policy focused on enhancing the country's capacity for developing innovative products, particularly in the field of consumer electronics and semiconductors. The government and industry-academia-research institutes worked together to advance the country's technology innovation system, develop promising technologies of the future, and strategically pursue national R&D projects (Yoo 2019). The government took various actions to strengthen S&T capacity, such as fostering and utilizing creative S&T human resources, promoting basic research, strengthening the regional capacity for innovation, and improving the capacity for innovation among SMEs and ventures firms.

BOX 5.1 Korea's Semiconductor Industry

Lee Byung-Chul, the founder of Samsung, decided in 1969 that Samsung would make its mark in consumer and industrial electronics. To achieve this goal, the company needed to master Large Scale Integration and later Very Large Scale Integration (VLSI) technology (Mathews and Cho 2000). The first step was an alliance with NEC and Sanyo to acquire expertise. This provided Samsung a foothold but was not enough for it to enter the production of Dynamic Random Access Memory (DRAM). Fearing competition from Samsung, Japanese and US firms were reluctant to license the technology.

The government introduced several initiatives to complement the industry's efforts. It enacted the Electronics Industry Promotion Law (1969) and the Basic Plan for Electronics Industry Promotion (1969–76), which included support for semiconductor product development, export promotion, and fundraising. A government research institute (GRI), the Korea Institute of Electronics Technology, was established in 1976, to intensify domestic semiconductor research and development (R&D). It developed the DRAM semiconductor technology in the 1980s and transferred it to Samsung Electronics. The government issued the Long-Term Plan for the Promotion of the Semiconductor Industry (1981), Details of the Plan for Fostering the Semiconductor Industry (1982–86), and the Semiconductor Industry Comprehensive Development Plan (1985), which supported the semiconductor industry through tariff reduction, preferred interest rates, R&D subsidies, and the provision of adequate water supply and electricity (Cho, Kim, and Rhee 1998). In the 1980s, the government invested US$400 million in the semiconductor industry and established a public-private research consortium for 4M DRAM development (1986 and 1989), composed of Samsung, Hyundai, and Goldstar in the private sector; the Electronics and Telecommunications Research Institute, a GRI; and academia.

Samsung leveraged the government support by licensing the 64K DRAM technology from a US company, Micron, recruiting semiconductor engineers from US firms by offering high salaries, and procuring equipment for fabricating DRAMs from multiple suppliers. Foreign firms, such as AT&T and Nortel, were persuaded to share technology to gain entry into the Republic of Korea's telecommunications market (Choi 1996). Korea's manufacturers had built capacity in chip assembly, packaging, and testing in the mid-1970s. By the mid-1980s, the chaebols (family-owned conglomerates) were manufacturing and exporting VLSI circuits, having accumulated expertise in the assembly and fabrication processes by importing foreign technology. They trained a corps of engineers, invested massively in production facilities, and invested in both public and private research institutes (Gereffi and Wyman 1990). Although the market for DRAMs softened in the mid-1980s, Korea's semiconductor industry continued to press ahead with the next generation 256K DRAM and was ready to grab market share once the market rebounded. Encouraged by Samsung's success, Goldstar and Hyundai expanded their investments in semiconductors after entering the market in 1981. Between 1983 and 1987, Samsung, Goldstar, and Hyundai invested US$1.9 billion in fabrication plants and by 1987 were exporting US$2 billion worth of VLSI circuits.

Continued

BOX 5.1 Continued

By the latter half of the 1980s, the leading chaebols had pulled abreast of their foreign competitors in the memory chip business and were pushing the technology frontier (Lee 2013; Mathews and Cho 2000). By the 1990s, Korean firms dominated the world's DRAM market and became technology leaders, developing the world's first 64M DRAM in 1992, the first 256M DRAM in 1994, and the first 1GB DRAM in 1996. To maintain the competitive edge in this knowledge-intensive industry, the IC Design Education Center was established in 1995 to train semiconductor experts, as a joint effort of major companies, the government, and academia. As of 2019, Korea's global semiconductor market share was 18.4 percent, the second largest after the United States, and its semiconductor exports amounted to US$93.9 billion (figure B5.1.1).

FIGURE B5.1.1 Outlook for the Republic of Korea's Semiconductor Industry, 1997–2019

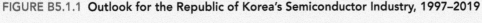

Source: Calculations based on data from the Korea Semiconductor Industry Association.

A rethinking of the STI strategy over the decades has reflected the slowing of Korea's growth and mounting competitive pressure from China (Kang 1998; Seong et al. 2005). With the center of gravity of Korea's research shifting from the public to the private sector, since the 2000s, the government has focused on strengthening linkages between GRIs and industry.

The government worked closely with the corporate sector to build innovation centers, for example, the Pangyo Techno Valley in Gyeonggi province near Seoul and, with less success, in other parts of the country (Dayton 2020).[12] With the major conglomerates focused on applied research and product development, the government began paying more attention to basic and fundamental research that could eventually underpin disruptive innovation (Zastrow 2020a). This was the start of the Big Science programs, in particular the "577 Program," which aimed to take Korea to the technological frontier in seven major fields. The founding of the Institute for Basic Science (a network of multiple centers) in 2011 was one outcome (Zastrow 2020b). Increased collaboration with international scientific agencies was a second, although it has had a slow start (OECD 2017).

In the post-AFC period, the role of the GRIs has been relatively reduced in response to increased private sector R&D. However, the GRIs continue to play a prominent role in basic and applied technologies supported by the government's investment in R&D. Under the National Science and Technology Research Council, today there are 11 GRIs on fundamental research and 14 GRIs on applied research, in diverse fields such ICT, aerospace and aviation, nuclear power, marine engineering, energy, natural resources, and information and data processing technology. Corporate research institutes and GRIs, which facilitate technology transfer, undertake spending that is greater than university R&D spending, making it a unique system among OECD countries.

Starting in 2003, every five years, the government has published a Science and Technology Master Plan, the nation's most important action plan on STI development. The objectives of the Master Plans have evolved over the years. In 2010, the government enacted a "Long-Term Vision for Science and Technology Development and a Future Vision for S&T: Towards 2040," which aimed to shift the locus of the "national innovation system from government to the private sector, enhancing the efficiency of R&D investments, upgrading R&D to world standards, and harvest the opportunities presented by new technologies" (Ministry of Education, Science and Technology 2008, 2010). Other Basic Plans followed in 2013 and 2018, and the Future Vision was updated in 2017 (UNESCO 2020). For instance, the current Master Plan (2018–22) aims to expand national STI capacity, enhance the S&T ecosystem, and help to create new industries.[13]

In parallel with the increasing reliance on private sector R&D spending, the specific industries targeted by technology support policies have evolved over the past several presidential administrations (table 5.3). Some notable changes include the emphasis on green growth technologies under the Lee administration, which reflected the administration's overall policy priorities on green growth and environmental sustainability, and the subsequent administrations' increased focus on Fourth Industrial Revolution technologies, such as big data and the internet of things. Although the selection of the priority technologies may have changed over different administrations, what remains consistent is that each administration aimed to target support to selected specific technologies. This reflected an evolution of the previous industrial policies, which targeted support to industries to support the development of technologies.

Much like Japan, but unlike many other successful economies in Europe and recently China, Korea's technological development was not based on inflows of foreign direct investment, which have played a relatively minor role. Instead, Korea heavily invested in R&D to adopt imported technologies and meet the challenge of implementing increasingly sophisticated technologies in the process of industrial development (Kim 1999). Korea's investments built the firm-specific, tacit, often uncodified, and difficult to imitate knowledge that was necessary to adopt, modify, and implement technologies (Lall 1992; Westphal 1990). Such knowledge helped Korea to transition from implementation capability to design capability (Lee 2016).

Implementation and design capabilities can be measured using proxy indicators, and their relationship with economic growth was tested over 1996–2016 (Lee, Baek, and Yeon 2021). The relationship between technological capabilities and income levels is nonlinear, reflecting the challenges of transitioning from implementation to design capability. Korea has successfully transitioned to design capability. In contrast, developing countries that have failed to transition to high income have gradually increased their implementation capability but have not sufficiently improved their design capability over the past 20 years, constraining their ability to transition to a high-income economy (figure 5.11).

Korea also avoided succumbing to the middle-income trap by "leapfrogging" to the technology frontier (Lee 2013, 2019; Lee and Lim 2001; Lee, Lim, and Song 2005; Mu and Lee 2005). Two examples of technological leapfrogging are POSCO outperforming the Japanese incumbent Nippon in the steel sector and Samsung surpassing Nokia in the transition from fixed telephony to mobile telephony and smartphones (Lee 2021). Countries have used various leapfrogging strategies, by adopting the latest technologies, leveraging global value chains to import foreign technology, and specializing in short-cycle technology-based sectors, such as the information technology (IT) industry, which facilitates rapid technology upgrading (Lee 2021).

DEVELOPMENT OF KOREA'S ICT INFRASTRUCTURE

Korea's success in establishing a world-class telecommunications industry was a critical contribution to the country's technological progress. Korea carried out major investments in its ICT infrastructure when it was a middle-income economy. As a result, the ICT Development Index of the International

TABLE 5.3 Changes in Policy for the Development and Promotion of Innovative Growth Drivers

Administration	Kim (1998–2003)	Roh (2003–08)	Lee (2008–13)	Park (2013–17)	Moon (2017–22)
Policy theme	Future Prominent New Technologies (6T)	Growth Engine for Next Generation	New Growth Engine for 3 Sectors	Future Growth Engine	Innovation Growth Engine for 4 Sectors
Priority technologies	• Information technology • Biotechnology • Nanotechnology • Environment technology • Culture technology • Space technology	• Intelligent robots • Intelligent home networks • Future mobility • Digital contents/ SW solutions • New generation semiconductors • New generation batteries • Digital TV/ broadcasting • Biomed • New generation mobile communications (especially display)	*Sector 1: Green Growth Industry* • Renewable energy (especially low-carbon energy) • Applying LED • Advanced water treatment • Green transportation systems • High-tech green cities *Sector 2: Advanced Convergence Industry* • Broadcasting and communication convergence projects • IT convergence systems • Robotics convergence • New material nanoconvergence • Biomed *Sector 3: Other* • Health care • Virtual reality • Intelligent robots	• Intelligent robots • Wearable smart applications • Smart bio production systems • Virtual training systems • Smart mobility • Marine plants • 5G mobile communications • Unmanned aerial vehicles • Wellness care • New renewable hybrids • Disaster management systems • HVDC systems • Micro power generation systems • Fusion material • Intelligent semiconductors • Internet of things • Big data • Advanced material processing systems	*Sector 1: Big Data* • New generation mobile communications • Artificial intelligence *Sector 2: Autonomous Vehicles* • Drones *Sector 3: Health Care* • Virtual reality • Intelligent robots *Sector 4: Intelligent Semiconductors* • New materials • New meds • Renewable energy

Source: Ahn 2019, 38.
Note: HVDC = high voltage direct current; IT = information technology; LED = light emitting diode; SW = software.

Telecommunication Union ranked Korea first in the world in ICT infrastructure in 2016 and second in 2017.[14] Effective broadband networks facilitate the growth of technology startups; provide a platform that other sectors can leverage to develop new business models and services, such as distance education and telemedicine; and enable the development of digital content, all of which can help to promote new drivers of growth. Access to broadband also supports the expansion of domestic and international knowledge networks, thereby promoting dissemination, research, innovation, and growth (Czernich et al. 2011).

In the 1970s, Korea's decision to champion the IT industry was far from consensual. Policy makers agreed on the importance of the ICT sector due to its spillovers, but they were undecided on the country's prospects in the technologically advanced and fast-moving sector. The Economic Planning Board, at the time the top economic planning and coordination agency, was unconvinced that Korea could become a major player in this knowledge- and capital-intensive sector and was opposed to making significant budget allocations to promote it. However, the president's office believed in the potential of the IT sector

FIGURE 5.11 **Development Patterns of Concept Design Capability and Implementation Capability, 1995–2015**

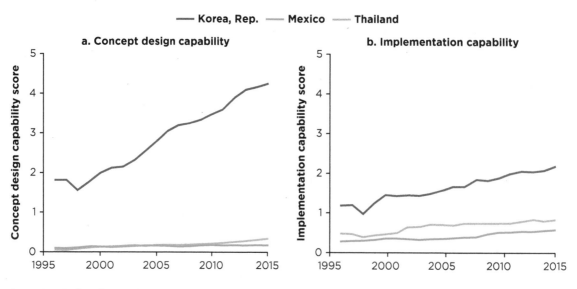

Source: Lee, Baek, and Yeon 2021.

TABLE 5.4 **Broadband Investment Program, 1995–2014 (US$, millions and percent)**

Investment	Information infrastructure, 1995–2005	Broadband convergence network, 2005–14	Total, 1995–2014
Government	806 (2.4%)	981 (38.0%)	1,787 (5.1%)
Private	31,721 (97.5%)	1,599 (62.0%)	33,320 (94.9%)
Total (US$ millions)	32,527	2,580	35,107

Sources: World Bank 2016; Kim, Kelly, and Raja 2010; World Bank and Korea Development Institute 2015.

and promoted it in the 1980s (Lim 2012). The government prioritized support for high-technology ICT industries such as semiconductors, computers, and electronic switching systems, as part of the National Basic Information System (1987–91) program. It established government-funded research institutes, launched large-scale technology development projects through industry-university collaboration, and adopted policies to strengthen the R&D capacity of the universities.

Central to the government's plans to promote the ICT industries was the establishment of the national ICT infrastructure. The government implemented a phased plan. The first phase was the Korea Information Infrastructure Program from 1995 to 2005 to invest in the national ICT infrastructure. The second phase was the Broadband Convergence Network program from 2005 to 2014 (table 5.4) to expand the ICT infrastructure. Investments in ICT infrastructure were a public-private partnership that combined government catalytic funding and policy direction with a much larger volume of private financing and project implementation and management capacity. Private investments dominated in the initial phase, which focused on building the backbone network and ICT infrastructure in the larger cities. The share of government investments increased from 2.4 percent in the first phase to 38 percent in the second phase when the network was extended to rural areas where there was less commercial interest. The government also eased regulations to encourage private sector participation in the communications market,

FIGURE 5.12 **Fixed Broadband Subscriptions of Speed Tier over 100 Mbps, 2019**

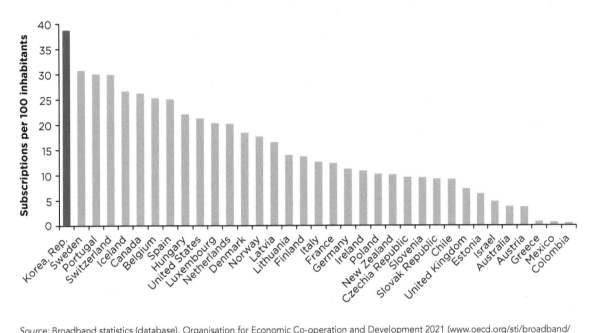

Source: Broadband statistics (database), Organisation for Economic Co-operation and Development 2021 (www.oecd.org/sti/broadband/broadband-statistics).
Note: Mbps = megabits per second.

allowing free competition to set lower prices, expand public computer education, and diversify high-speed internet products (MSIT and NIA 2021).

As the broadband network expanded, so did internet usage. In 2019, the number of fixed broadband subscriptions per person was the largest among OECD countries, with almost 40 subscriptions per 100 inhabitants (figure 5.12). Korea was also one of the first countries to roll out the 5G network, which offers a faster mobile connection that can compete with fixed lines in terms of connection speed (OECD 2021).

To mobilize financing for investments in the ICT sector and the national R&D development plans, in 1993 the government established the Information and Communications Promotion Fund through contributions from communications service providers. The fund provided ₩7.37 trillion between 1993 and 2001 for investments in the broadband networks, informatization, IT industry support, and research development (MSIT and NIA 2021). In 2021, the size of the fund amounted to ₩1.7 trillion.[15] Today, the ICT sector is central to Korea's economy. The sector accounted for 11.7 percent of GDP in 2020, one of the highest shares among OECD countries (figure 5.13).

PROMOTION OF BASIC RESEARCH

Until the mid-1990s, the government and the business sector prioritized applied and developmental research to promote manufacturing exports. Following the AFC, the government shifted gears, recognizing that future economic performance would require more upstream basic research capabilities. Public spending on basic research by government and private research institutes was incentivized by government grants and other measures. The chaebols were encouraged to engage more actively in upstream research in areas where they already enjoyed a comparative advantage, such as automobiles, mobile phones, semiconductors, and telecommunications equipment. Major universities were encouraged to undertake more fundamental research and expand collaboration with the business sector (Lee 2014).

FIGURE 5.13 **ICT Sector Value Added, 2020**

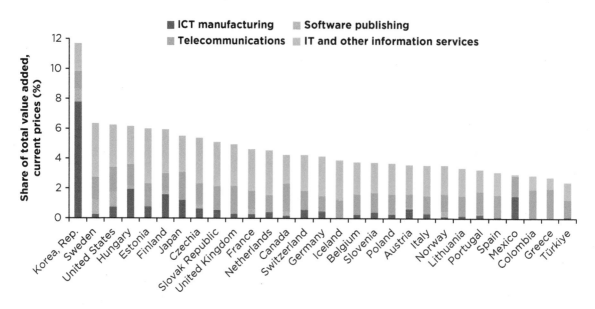

Source: STAN structural indicators (iSTAN), 2022 edition, Organisation for Economic Co-operation and Development (https://stats.oecd.org/Index.aspx?DataSetCode=STANI4_2020#).
Note: ICT = information and communications technology; IT = information technology.

In 2002, the government launched several support projects, including the medical research center project and basic science laboratory project to support creative research in basic science. From 2003, the administration has appointed and supported national core research centers to encourage joint research in frontier S&T fields that require strategic promotion at the national level.

In 2005, the "Comprehensive Plan for the Promotion of Basic Research (2006–10)" was formulated based on the Basic Research Promotion and Technology Development Support Act, and the Basic Scientific Research Promotion Association was established under the National Science and Technology Council. In addition, the government increased R&D investments in basic research, and basic research's share of the R&D budget was increased from 19.4 percent in 2003 to 25.4 percent in 2008 and about 33 percent in 2012 (MOST 2017). The budget for individual researchers' basic research was increased significantly to promote creative basic research, and the share of research funds for individual science and engineering professors and small-scale research projects rose. These policy efforts aimed to complement the government's traditional emphasis on large-scale research tasks by establishing a secure foundation for basic research conducted by individual researchers. From 2008, the government has also launched projects to develop world-leading research-centered universities and research institutes (MOST 2017).

In 2012, the government formulated the "Third Comprehensive Plan for the Promotion of Basic Research (2013-2017)" to enhance the quality of basic research and its utilization in the economy and society (National Science and Technology Council 2013). The plan aimed to increase the share of basic sciences in the government's R&D budget to 40 percent by 2017. The increased budget was used to expand research opportunities to new and mid-career researchers. In particular, the government established a project to fund research for new researchers no older than 39 years so that they could begin their research at an earlier phase in their career. "My Life's First Research Project" selected 1,000 new researchers and subsidized their research. The government also pursued Small Grants for Exploratory Research and X-Project initiatives to provide support for innovative research in novel fields. In 2014, the government formulated the "Master Plan to Construct the Institute for Basic Science." Research platforms for the Institute for Basic Science were established, and 28 research platforms were founded by 2017. As of 2016, 204 world-renowned scientists were working at the Institute for Basic Science (MOST 2017).

Between 2017 and 2022, the budget for the National Research Foundation, which is the main government agency for basic research, doubled to US$2 billion.[16] However, development R&D has continued to dominate basic research in BERD (Arora, Belenzon, and Patacconi 2015) (figure 5.14). Korea's share of

FIGURE 5.14 Distribution of R&D Expenditures, by Research Stage: GERD and BERD, 2002–19

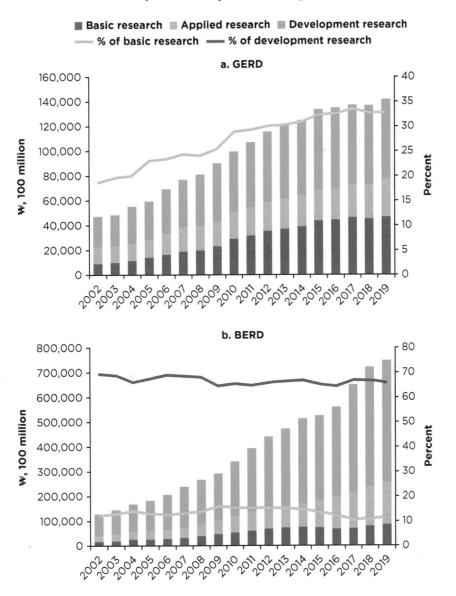

Source: Industrial Statistics Analysis System (https://istans.or.kr/wh/whAbout.do?chn=1) (accessed: February 1, 2021).
Note: The units for R&D expenditures are ₩, 100 million, around US$93,000. BERD = business enterprise research and development; GERD = gross expenditure on research and development; R&D = research and development.

basic research, at around 12 percent of total R&D spending, is comparable to that of Japan and lower than in the United States (17.6 percent) and the OECD average (17 percent), but it is much higher than that of China (5 percent) (Medvedev, Piatkowski, and Yusuf 2019).

REORIENTING SUPPORT FOR RESEARCH FROM LARGE BUSINESS GROUPS TO INNOVATIVE SMES AND ENTREPRENEURSHIP

Prior to the AFC, few policies focused on supporting SMEs' R&D investments. With the establishment of the Small and Medium Business Administration in 1996 and the introduction of the Korea Small Business Innovation Research program in 1998, direct and indirect support for SMEs' R&D began in earnest. The program, modeled after the US Small Business Innovation Research program, required the government and public agencies to allocate a minimum share of their R&D budget to SMEs. As a result, public financing for research conducted by SMEs has steadily increased, from 13 percent of total government spending on R&D in 2002 to 22 percent in 2019 (MSS 2021), especially through the Korea Small Business Innovation Research program.

The Act on Special Measures for the Promotion of Venture Business (1997) represented the government's increasing attention to strengthening the technological competitiveness of SMEs, in particular venture firms (technology startups). Since 2001, the government has pursued the Development and Fostering of SMEs through Technology and Innovation (also called INNO-BIZ) policy. Under this policy, innovative SMEs were granted priority in winning government support if they participated in technology support projects of the Small and Medium Business Administration. Support to SMEs integrated financial, marketing, human resources, and information support. The government also eased regulations on entrepreneurship and expanded relevant infrastructure, such as incubation centers, to support technology startups (see chapter 3).

After the mid-2000s, collaboration between large conglomerates and SMEs was emphasized. Large conglomerates have carried out significant investments in R&D and innovation that strengthened their international competitiveness, but R&D investments and productivity growth among SMEs remained subdued. In response, the Third Science and Technology Master Plan (2013–17) increased government investments in R&D by SMEs and adopted an SME support quota system operated through government-funded research institutes. Support for SMEs was further increased under the Third Five-Year Plan for Innovation of SMEs (2014–18).

The government formulated the "Plan to Create an Open Cooperative Ecosystem by Government-funded Research Institutes" in 2013 and the "Plan to Make Government-funded Research Institutes into SME and MME [mid-market enterprises] R&D Outposts" in 2014. They introduced the mandatory allocation of 5 to 15 percent of the major project costs of government-funded research institutes to support the technology, human resources, and equipment of SMEs and doubling of the number of subsidized workers at SMEs from 1,500 in 2013 to 3,000 in 2017 (NSTC 2014). The government also facilitated the technology startups spun off from GRIs. With active government support for technology startups, the number of spin-off companies increased significantly, from 46 in 2013 to 339 in 2015 (MOST 2017). Finally, the government supported the development of startups through innovation hubs such as the Pangyo Techno Valley (box 5.2).

The government has leveraged different types of policy instruments and implementing organizations to target SMEs and innovative entrepreneurship. As an example, the National Research Foundation, the principal government R&D funding agency, is tasked with bringing the productivity of the SME sector closer to that of the leading firms by accelerating the diffusion of digital technology and encouraging startup activities in frontier areas such as biotechnology. On the regulatory side, the government has been actively utilizing regulatory sandboxes that permit experimentation and prototyping, by temporarily relaxing regulatory restrictions (see chapter 3).

BOX 5.2 Pangyo Techno Valley

Starting in the late 1990s, the establishment of a regional innovation system through the formation of industrial clusters became a central element of the Republic of Korea's industrial policy (Yun and Lee 2004). Since then, five research and development (R&D)–focused innovation clusters, 19 technology parks, and six technology valleys have been created by central and local governments across the country, nurturing local industries, developing networks with regional innovative institutions, and fostering knowledge-oriented talent.

Pangyo Techno Valley (PTV) is considered one of the most successful cluster initiatives in Korea (Choi, Lee, and Shin 2018). PTV was established as an innovation cluster centered on high-technology industries by Gyeonggi province, which borders Seoul, the capital city. As of the end of 2021, PTV has been the home of nearly 2,000 resident companies, with revenue of almost ₩110 trillion, 25,000 researchers, and 65,000 employees.[a] The majority of the companies specialize in information technology (IT) (65.9 percent), cultural technology[b] (13.1 percent), and biotechnology (13.0 percent). Leading companies include MIDAS IT, AhnLab, POSCO ICT, Nexon (internet gaming), NHN (internet platform), Kakao (the largest mobile messaging app in Korea), SK Chemical (chemical and life sciences), CHA Hospital (biotechnology), and Institut Pasteur Korea (biotechnology). PTV support infrastructure includes the Gyeonggi Center for Creative Economy and Innovation, a startup accelerator that provides "one-stop" advisory services, including on legal, patenting, global certification, regulatory sandbox, and financing matters.

The success of PTV has been due to several factors. First, Gyeonggi province provided strategic investments, land, tax concessions, and administrative support. The province supplied land at cost, less than half the price of land in Seoul's business district. PTV is designated as a Venture Business Development and Promotion Zone. As such, various tax benefits are provided, including property tax reduction and exemptions from the acquisition and registration tax, development charge, and traffic inducing charge.

Second, PTV strategically focused on IT companies and related R&D institutions and knowledge-based industries. PTV positioned itself as an innovation cluster by limiting its tenant businesses to those that focus on new technologies, convergence technologies, and new growth engines related to IT and high-technology R&D businesses (Lee, Im, and Han 2017). Pangyo strengthened its position as Korea's IT hub by attracting not just technology startups, but also medium-size and large IT companies, such as NCSOFT, NHN, and Kakao. To promote cooperation between large and medium-size enterprises and startups, PTV promotes networking, technical cooperation, and strategic alliances, such as by organizing business matching and demo days.

Third, the location of PTV provides a geographical advantage, given its proximity to Seoul and its manufacturing and service industries and talent from its universities (Lee, Im, and Han 2017). This is critical because innovation clusters need access to talent, high-technology manufacturing, and knowledge-based services to thrive. As of the end of 2019, employees in their 20s and 30s accounted for 64 percent of all employees, and 23,249 researchers accounted for 36 percent of total employees in PTV. There are 674 corporate R&D centers in PTV.

Fourth, PTV has reinvested its income in R&D spending. Gyeonggi province holds a PTV special account and has invested at least ₩20 billion since 2012. The budget was drawn up to construct the PTV infrastructure until 2015, then to support PTV R&D activities. Forty-four percent of PTV's tenant businesses operate R&D centers in PTV and have reinvested their profits in R&D (Chung, Im, and Chung 2017). High R&D spending helped to attract R&D talent and innovative enterprises and facilitated the government's policy support.

Following the success of PTV, Gyeonggi province and the central government are expanding PTV by developing the Pangyo Second Techno Valley (PTV2), which will target startups focused on Fourth Industrial Revolution technologies, such as artificial intelligence, 5G, big data, and autonomous vehicles. PTV2 is expected to be completed in 2024. There are also plans for a Pangyo Third Techno Valley.

a. https://www.24-7pressrelease.com/press-release/486103/pangyo-technovalley-92-of-pangyo-technovalley-companies-are-in-high-tech-industry-with-109-tril-won-in-revenue.

b. Cultural technology refers to K-Pop and other cultural (media and entertainment) businesses.

Source: Chung, Im, and Chung 2017.

Current STI Policies

The current Korean STI system is vast and complex, with more than 20 government agencies involved in allocating the R&D budget. The STI support policy is regulated by 300 R&D management regulations, more than 60 research support systems, and more than 400 innovation support instruments. The agencies charged with managing STI are also responsible for managing the large number of GRIs (Frias and Lee 2021).

By 2018, support for business innovation in Korea relied on a large number of policy instruments, including direct support instruments such as loans (under the Ministry of SMEs and Startups), grants (under the Ministry of Trade, Industry, and Energy and the Ministry of Science and ICT), technical assistance, procurement preferences, and indirect support such as tax incentives (provided by the Ministry of Economy and Finance) and credit guarantees (Frias and Lee 2021) (table 5.5 describes the main instruments). Box 5.3 provides an example of the use of incentives to promote the online gaming industry. In 2018, direct financial support (loans, grants, and other financial support) accounted for 52 percent total spending, indirect support instruments represented 37 percent, and the remaining spending included technology extension services, technology transfer offices, and technology parks (figure 5.15).

Budgetary expenditures on innovation by the five leading innovation-related ministries mainly focused on enhancing access to finance and promoting business R&D and R&D-based innovation, although policy

TABLE 5.5 **Selected Innovation Policy Instruments, 2019**

Instrument	Implementation
R&D tax incentives	Tax credit for expenditure on R&D is a tax credit provided to firms on their business income tax or corporate income tax for eligible expenditure on research and human capital development. The tax incentive helps to address market failures in the form of lack of appropriability of investments in R&D and coordination failures. In the Republic of Korea, 20 to 30 percent (30 percent for SMEs) of total R&D expenditure on New Growth Engine and Original technology or general research areas are eligible for the tax credit. All domestic firms are eligible. In 2017, the total tax credit (tax incentives) was estimated to be ₩2.1 billion.
Loans for innovation	Loans are direct financial instruments, typically targeting SMEs and startups, and are directly supplied by the government or via intermediaries to address financial market imperfections that prevent commercial banks from properly funding innovation projects. The Policy Fund Program implemented by the Korea SMEs and Startups Agency provides long-term and lower interest loans to SMEs that create jobs, expand markets, or invest in facilities and firms in the areas of innovative growth. The maximum limit for a loan is ₩6 billion. For exceptional cases, the limit is up to ₩10 billion.
Credit guarantees for innovation	Credit guarantee schemes mitigate lenders' risks by covering a portion of their potential losses when firms default on loans, thus inducing banks to lend to innovation projects that otherwise would lack sufficient collateral. KOTEC extends credit guarantees to firms with viable technology but that have limited access to credit due to lack of collateral. The viability of the technology is assessed through a technology assessment. In 2021, about ₩350 billion was allocated for KOTEC's guarantee activities.
Early-stage equity finance	The government provides capital that is used by financial intermediaries to invest in equity in small and young innovation-intensive companies. These intermediaries can be individuals, angel investor groups, organized funds, funds tied to service providers like accelerators, or larger companies. A policy promoting early-stage equity finance often seeks to promote networking and positive spillovers from the co-location. The Korea Fund-of-Funds, established in 2005, reinvests funds from ministries to partnership funds that directly invest in SMEs and venture companies. In 2020, the size of the fund was ₩5.6 trillion.
Public procurement for innovation	Korea uses public procurement to create demand for innovations and technologies developed by SMEs, thereby encouraging investments in innovation and technology. At least 50 percent of procurement expenditures awarded by the public sector must be to SMEs, and at least 10 percent of the procurements from SMEs must be "technology products" (those with at least one of 19 government technology certifications) developed by SMEs.

Source: Frias and Lee 2021.
Note: KOTEC = Korea Technology Finance Corporation; R&D = research and development; SMEs = small and medium-size enterprises.

BOX 5.3 Case Study of the Information Technology Gaming Industry in the Republic of Korea

The Republic of Korea ranks as the fourth largest gaming market, at 6.3 percent of the global gaming industry, after the United States, China, and Japan. In 2019, Korea's gaming industry had the fifth largest revenue of ₩15 trillion (US$1.2 billion). The gaming industry exported US$6.9 billion, which was 10 times more than that of the music industry (US$640 million), and the gaming market accounted for 8.8 percent of Korea's total trade surplus (2018). Many of Korea's major gaming companies today, such as NXC and NC Soft, were established in the late 1990s to early 2000s.

The gaming industry requires high-level programming technology with interactive user-based services (Tschang 2007). A key contributing factor to the emergence of Korea's online gaming industry was the rapid broadband internet access resulting from the government's investments in information and communications technology infrastructure. As a result of the investments in the 1990s, the broadband penetration rate in Korea reached 13.8 percent of the population by 2000, compared to 3.2 percent in the United States (OECD 2002). The expansion of the broadband infrastructure helped to support the growth of the online gaming industry.

In addition, online gaming firms benefited from various entrepreneurship support policies. The government established the 1997 Law of Special Measures to Promote Venture Businesses and the Law of Promotion of Technology for SMEs. These laws contained support measures for high-technology startups, including additional tax incentives, incubator programs, and special treatment for research and development. The Game Industry Promotion Act of 2006 and the industry promotion plans of 2003 and 2008 provided targeted support to the gaming industry, including to support technology development, partnerships between government research institutes and private sector firms, and globalization of the firms. To facilitate these policy measures, new agencies to support the industry's development, such as the Korea Game Industry Agency—an investment promotion agency—and the Game Academy—a training agency for the Human Resources Development Service of Korea—were introduced.

Source: Song (2020).

FIGURE 5.15 Composition of the Policy Mix across Selected Ministries, by Instrument, 2018 (percent of total)

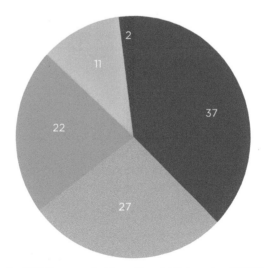

Sources: Frias and Lee 2021, based on the 2018 Government of Korea Financial Statement and 2018 Government of Korea Tax Expenditure Report.

priorities differed among the five institutions, in line with their policy mandates (figure 5.16). The Ministry of SMEs and Startups focuses on supporting access to finance, including loans for new growth industries; the Ministry of Science and ICT and the Ministry of Trade, Industry, and Energy prioritize supporting business R&D and R&D-based innovation; the Ministry of Trade, Industry, and Energy supports export promotion for cutting-edge industries; and the Ministry of Economy and Finance emphasizes supporting research excellence and management practices. The government also supports corporate R&D centers to promote the R&D activities of private companies and enhance their innovation capabilities. The number of corporate R&D centers increased from 46 in 1981 to 1,840 in 1999 and 42,155 in 2020.[17]

A World Bank report reviews 22 impact evaluation studies on the impact of the innovation policy instruments in Korea over the past decade (Frias and Lee 2021).[18] The studies focus on six key support instruments: (a) R&D grants for SMEs, (b) non-R&D innovation grants for SMEs, (c) R&D tax incentives, (d) credit guarantees for innovation, (e) fund-of-funds that support early-stage finance, and (f) public procurement for innovation. The impact evaluations that assessed the efficiency of SME R&D grant programs implemented in the 2010s by the Small and Medium Business Administration and Korea Small Business Innovation Research suggested that these R&D grant programs helped to increase the sales, assets, employment, and R&D expenditure of the grant recipients, but the impacts were not always significant (Oh and Kim 2018). Despite the increased funding, Korea's SMEs had less developed technological capabilities and lower rates of successful commercialization compared to peers in other high-income countries (Ahn 2019). There has also been significant duplication of projects (Oh and Kim 2018). The relatively low success rate of commercialization of R&D could be due to the short-term nature of Korea's R&D support policy and the insufficient volume of support (Lee 2021).

COMPARISON OF KOREA'S INNOVATION POLICY MIX AGAINST GLOBAL PEERS

Korean STI policies were compared against their global peers in high-income countries and developing countries (Frias and Lee 2021). The objective of the comparison was to highlight the features of Korea's policy mix that could serve as a useful blueprint for developing countries. The analysis studied 39 countries—32 high-income and seven middle-income countries, including Brazil, China, Peru, and South Africa. It focused on 3,514 STI policy instruments, classified as direct (financial and nonfinancial) and indirect support, based on the definitions developed by Cirera and Maloney (2017). Direct financial instruments include, inter alia, project grants for public research, grants for business R&D and innovation, and innovation vouchers. Indirect instruments include corporate tax relief for R&D and innovation, tax relief for individuals supporting R&D and innovation, and debt guarantees and risk-sharing schemes. The remaining instruments are categorized as nonfinancial mechanisms of intervention (Frias and Lee 2021).

The study concluded that Korea's innovation policy mix was comprehensive and covered all the direct and indirect innovation policy instruments in the innovation policy space for supporting R&D and non-R&D innovation activities. Korea's innovation policy mix for business innovation features more than 400 instruments, many more than the peer countries have. The innovation activities cover nearly the entire spectrum of support instruments, more than the average for the OECD countries and significantly greater than the number and types of instruments in developing countries (table 5.6).

Korea's top five innovation support programs are three types of tax incentives for R&D and non-R&D innovation and two types of innovation loans and credits.[19] They accounted for almost 40 percent of the total STI policy budget allocations. This concentration of resources is in line with peer countries. The budgetary allocation for the five major types of direct and indirect support instruments was relatively more evenly distributed than in comparator developing countries (figure 5.17).

Korea utilizes innovation support instruments, such as debt guarantees and risk-sharing schemes, technology regulation, innovation vouchers, and tax incentives to support R&D, which are relatively underutilized in most of the developing countries included in the study (Hall 2019).[20] The use of R&D matching grants in Korea is in line with other OECD countries, as the grants require more co-financing from beneficiaries than in developing countries. The same applies to grants focused on promoting

FIGURE 5.16 Innovation Support Programs, by Responsible Ministry, 2018

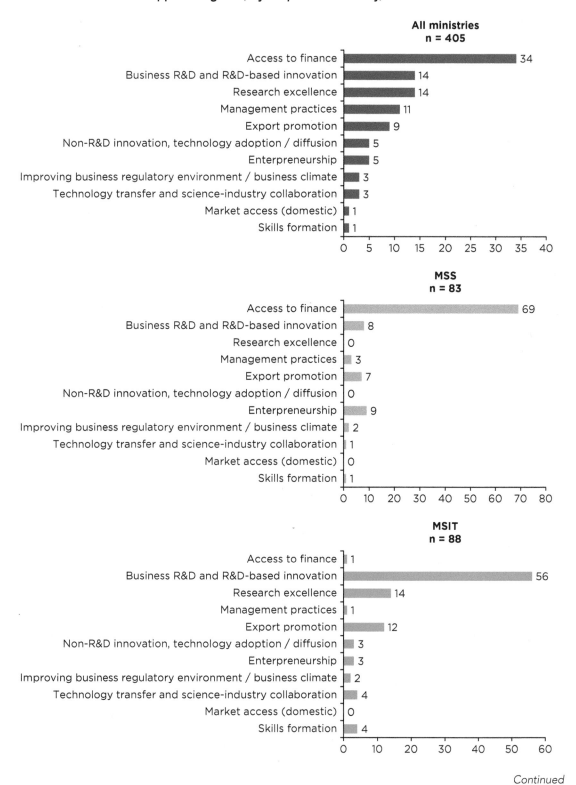

Continued

FIGURE 5.16 **Continued**

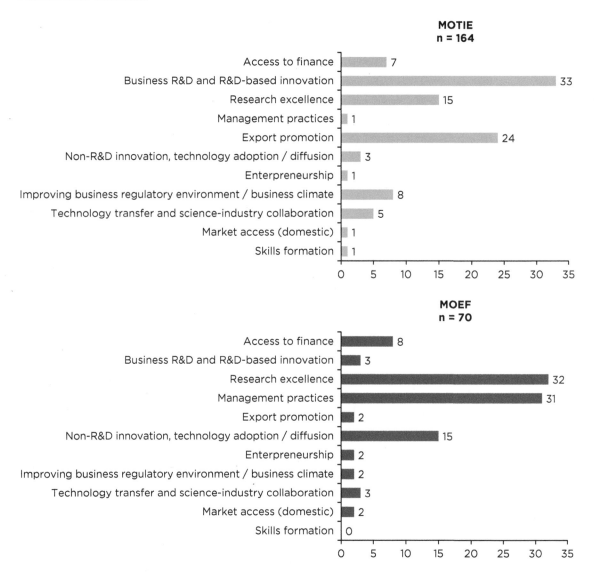

MOTIE
n = 164

Source: Frias and Lee 2021, based on the 2018 Government of Korea Financial Statement and 2018 Government of Korea Tax Expenditure Report.
Note: MOEF = Ministry of Economy and Finance; MOTIE = Ministry of Trade, Industry, and Energy; MSIT = Ministry of Science and ICT; MSS = Ministry of SMEs and Startups; R&D = research and development.

business and research collaboration. The eligibility requirements for public support in Korea are similar to those in other OECD countries, but in developing countries a lower percentage of grants require at least one form of collaboration. Korea has a particularly strong focus on promoting digital innovation programs, which represented 15 percent of the total number of programs, more than the OECD average and three times more than in developing countries (Frias and Lee 2021).

The innovation policy mix in Korea and other OECD countries has been changing more rapidly than in developing countries. Two-thirds of the innovation policy instruments in Korea were developed only after 2010, which was 10 percentage points more than in developing countries. This indicates that more

TABLE 5.6 **Innovation Support Instruments, Republic of Korea, OECD, and Developing Countries**

	Korea, Rep.	OECD countries (% of countries)	Developing countries (% of countries)
Grants for business R&D and innovation	Yes	100	100
Institutional funding for public research	Yes	100	100
Project grants for public research	Yes	100	100
Information services and access to datasets	Yes	97	100
Networking and collaborative platforms	Yes	97	100
Technology extension and business advisory services	Yes	97	100
Fellowships and postgraduate loans and scholarships	Yes	100	86
Dedicated support to research infrastructures	Yes	100	86
Corporate tax relief for R&D and innovation	Yes	81	86
Centers of excellence grants	Yes	94	71
Science and innovation challenges, prizes, and awards	Yes	77	86
Equity financing	Yes	87	71
Intellectual property regulation and incentives	Yes	90	57
Procurement programs for R&D and innovation	Yes	71	71
Loans and credits for innovation in firms	Yes	74	57
Labor mobility regulation and incentives	Yes	84	43
Tax relief for individuals supporting R&D and innovation	Yes	55	14
Innovation vouchers	Yes	52	14
Emerging technology regulation	Yes	42	0
Debt guarantees and risk sharing schemes	No	39	0

Type of instrument

Direct—Financial

Direct—Nonfinancial

Indirect

Sources: Frias and Lee 2021, based on EC/OECD STIP-Compass, 2019.
Note: R&D = research and development.

advanced countries that are closer to the technology frontier tend to experiment more and adapt more rapidly to new challenges, compared to developing countries, which have more limited capacity to experiment with new support instruments.

Innovation and Growth: Remaining Challenges

A reconsideration of Korea's STI strategy over the past decade shows that growth has slowed and competitive pressure from China has mounted (Kang 1998; Seong et al. 2005). Despite its significant investments in R&D and vast array of innovation support policies and instruments, Korea's total factor productivity (TFP) growth slowed after 2010, in line with the experience of other high-income countries (see chapter 2 for more detailed analysis of the productivity growth slowdown).

The slowdown in productivity growth reflects declining returns on high investment in R&D in Korea and global peers (figure 5.18). During 2009–18, Korea invested 4.1 percent of GDP in R&D, but TFP

FIGURE 5.17 Budget Applications for Direct and Indirect Support Instruments

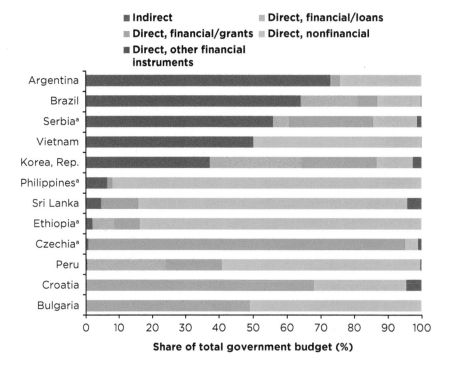

Source: World Bank, based on the META Analysis of Systematic Evaluation of Enterprise Development Policies, September 2020.
a. Instruments that focus on small and medium-size enterprises.

FIGURE 5.18 R&D Spending and TFP Growth, Selected Countries, 2009–18 Average

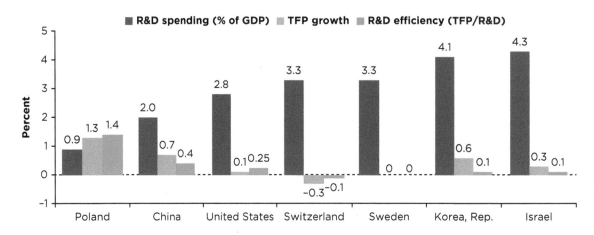

Sources: Calculations based on data from the World Development Indicators database, World Bank (for R&D spending); The Conference Board Total Economy Database (for TFP growth).
Note: Countries are sorted by average spending on R&D as a percentage of GDP. GDP = gross domestic product; R&D = research and development; TFP = total factor productivity.

growth was only 0.6 percent. Even China's rapidly growing R&D investment has not mitigated a large drop in TFP growth, from 2.8 percent in the decade before 2009 to 0.7 percent since then. R&D spending has been correlated with rapid TFP growth only in countries such as Poland, which are still relatively far from the technology frontier. In Poland, 1 percent of GDP invested in R&D during the past decade was associated with 1.3 percent growth in TFP, although other factors also contributed to the improvement in productivity.

Korea's declining returns on R&D investments may be due to a combination of factors. The country's innovation system remains relatively inward looking (Park and Lee 2020). According to the OECD, Korea has one of the lowest levels of international collaboration in science and innovation among OECD countries (figure 5.19).

Korea's productivity growth has been especially slow in tradable services. Korea devotes fewer resources to R&D in services than any other country in the OECD (figure 5.20). R&D investments have been heavily dependent on the large manufacturing firms. Larger and more effective R&D investments in the service sector, where the returns to innovation can be as high as in manufacturing (Audretsch et al. 2018), combined with other policy measures, such as deregulation, could help to spur higher productivity and promote export diversification beyond manufacturing exports.

Korea's STI system can be compared with global innovation peers such as Switzerland, Sweden, and Israel (the Global Innovation Index 2020 ranks Switzerland and Sweden in first and second place, respectively; Korea is 10th; and Israel is 13th), and developing countries such as Brazil, the Philippines, and Poland.

Compared to Korea, *Sweden* has embraced a more open innovation system and promotes universities as key drivers of STI (OECD 2016). The government of Sweden has identified a few strategic innovation areas, but it is a bottom-up decision process grounded in extensive consultations. The Ministry of Education and Science and the Ministry of Commerce and Industry play leading roles in promoting research. The former is responsible for policies and financing affecting universities and training institutions, with inputs from the Swedish Research Council. The latter manages

FIGURE 5.19 **Firms Engaged in International Collaboration for Innovation, Selected Countries**

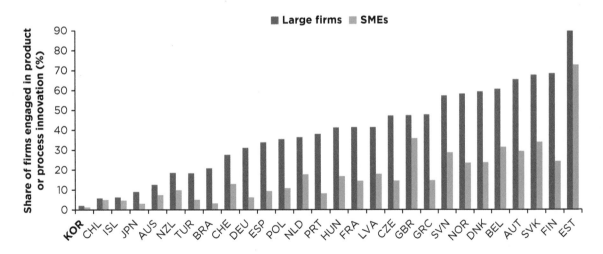

Source: OECD 2018.
Note: The data for Korea are for 2013–15; data for the other countries are for 2012–14. SMEs = small and medium-size enterprises. For a list of country codes, go to https://www.iso.org/obp/ui/#search.

FIGURE 5.20 **R&D in Services, 2015**

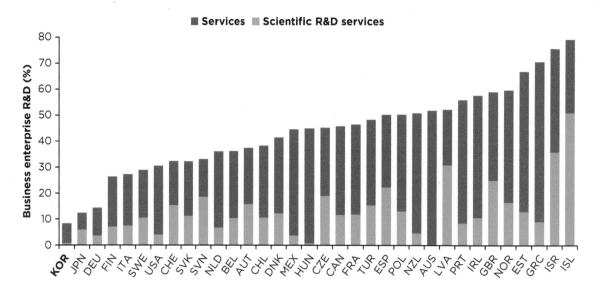

Source: OECD 2018.
Note: R&D = research and development. For a list of country codes, go to https://www.iso.org/obp/ui/#search.

Vinnova, Sweden's innovation agency, which finances research in selected areas. Funding consortia are favored over individual projects. A sister agency is responsible for competition, entrepreneurship, and regional growth. The welfare state provides a safety net for aspiring entrepreneurs, which has encouraged a vigorous startup culture, from which international companies such as Skype and Spotify have successfully emerged.

Much like Korea, Sweden promotes innovation through close collaboration among the government, research institutes, business, and academia to share the gains from innovation. The dominance of multinationals in Sweden's R&D is also comparable to that of Korea, but, unlike Korea, foreign multinational enterprises also figure prominently in research in Sweden. A larger share of researchers in Sweden are foreign, which makes for a less insulated research system than in Korea (Woolston 2020). Like Korea, Sweden is struggling with weak productivity gains despite substantial investments in research, which could be due to lack of domestic commercialization of research, duplication of research financed by a multiplicity of ministerial agencies, and poor integration of SMEs into the national innovation system.

Like Korea, *Switzerland* has prospered through investments in the education and skills required for high technology, and by developing a strong, outward oriented industrial base supported by world class infrastructure (OECD 2016). Switzerland's annual investment in R&D of 3.4 percent of GDP is high, although below that of Korea. As in Korea, the bulk of R&D is carried out by the private sector, but the participation of foreign multinational enterprises and foreign researchers is greater.

Switzerland's scientific excellence and research output has not always resulted in tangible productivity gains. One reason common to Korea, Sweden, and other high-income countries is that the fruits of research do not seem to percolate down to SMEs. Another shortcoming that Switzerland shares with Korea is that university training alone does not equip graduates with the practical and operational skills demanded by firms. Switzerland has sought to address this by creating a hybrid system that integrates vocational and academic learning (Graf 2014), similar to Korea's efforts to provide multiple educational pathways for those interested in vocational education.

Israel's emergence as a technology hotspot has also been driven by government support, in the form of investments in the defense and aerospace industries, which laid the groundwork for Israel's high-technology industries specializing in telecommunications, medical devices, cybersecurity, aviation electronics, computer software, and hardware. R&D spending over 2009–18 was 4.3 percent of GDP, the highest in the world and slightly above Korea's level. Foreign multinational enterprises play a more important role in Israel's R&D than in Korea's.

As in Korea, the Israeli government has devoted significant resources to developing high-technology startups. The Technology Incubator program initiated in the early 1990s provided funding and assistance to immigrants who launched entrepreneurial careers. Now, 25 incubators, all privatized, continue to support startups, with more than 6,000 incubated to date. The matching grants program managed by the Office of the Chief Scientist is another signature initiative. Israel's venture capital industry was launched in the mid-1990s with the highly successful Yozma program, which created 10 early-stage venture funds. However, Israel is facing the serious challenge of the declining number of startups with productivity-enhancing innovations. Much like Korea, Sweden, and Switzerland, Israel's productivity growth has declined to low levels, rising by only 0.3 percent per year from 2010 to 2018, despite the heavy investments in R&D.

Poland has achieved even more rapid GDP growth than Korea over the past 25 years, although investment in R&D amounted to only 0.9 percent of GDP during 2009–18, or less than a quarter of Korea's level. The share of the private sector was about half of total spending, much less than the more than 80 percent in Korea. In 2017, foreign direct investment was responsible for almost half of total corporate R&D spending in Poland, compared to only 8 percent in Korea. Poland has relatively few large firms and virtually none of the large firms is private, which is unlike the important role played by the chaebols in Korea.

Unlike Korea's complex system supporting innovation, Poland has only one innovation agency—the National Center for Research and Development—which is responsible for more than half of direct support to business innovation at the national level. However, it is considered to be one of the leading innovation agencies in the region, with evidence that its support provides large additionality.[21] National-level direct support is complemented by large outlays on indirect support through tax credits for R&D, although the support programs managed by the regions tend to be small, inefficient, and duplicative.

Brazil's GDP growth has averaged a little over 2 percent per year since 2000, below its regional and global peers, and TFP growth has hovered around zero since 2000. R&D spending amounted to 1.3 percent of GDP in 2019, or less than a third of Korea's level. However, Brazil's innovation system has achieved remarkable successes, including successful innovations to increase agricultural production, Petrobras's world class technology in deep sea drilling for oil, and Embraer's becoming one of the few successful manufacturers in a highly competitive segment of the aircraft industry.

These islands of excellence have flourished in the face of economic and budgetary fluctuations, thanks in part to the guidance and long-term funding provided by the innovation supporting agencies CNPq, FINEP, and BNDES. However, STI in Brazil has lacked key elements of Korea's policy framework. Brazil lacks a long-term strategy to harness innovation to boost outward oriented industrialization (the share of manufacturing plummeted from 30 percent of GDP in 1985 to 10 percent in 2019 (Luque et al. 2020)), and it has not sustained support for innovation across administrations. STI also has been hampered by bureaucratic inefficiencies and limits on research, due to a scarcity of high-level knowledge capital and the tendency for those with science, technology, engineering, and mathematics (STEM) skills to seek positions in universities and research institutes rather than private firms.

Finally, *the Philippines* has a GDP per capita that is only a fifth of Korea's level (in purchasing power parity), R&D spending was less than 0.2 percent of GDP in 2016, and the economy is dominated by relatively low value-added foreign direct investment–led manufacturing and a large service sector with low productivity. Public support for technology absorption and innovation is sparse and does little to support the private sector (World Bank 2021). The STI system suffers from a weak rationale for the choice of support instruments, lack of a strong conceptual framework to inform the design and implementation of policy interventions, and absence of monitoring and evaluation mechanisms to track the impact of public policies.

However, the Philippines has developed a thriving business process outsourcing sector. Total services exports in 2018 amounted to US$34.2 billion, of which nearly US$6 billion were exports of computer and information services. Moreover, the country's GDP growth between 2010 and 2019 averaged a little over 6 percent. This suggests that relatively basic factors, such as access to the internet, basic human capital, and the ability to speak English, may be sufficient for a country to initiate exports of digital services.

Conclusion and Policy Implications for Developing Countries

Identifying the lessons learned from Korea's STI strategy must necessarily be selective because Korea's STI capabilities were developed through manufacturing industrialization, which is a development path that is not necessarily available to all developing countries. Korea's economy remains rooted in manufacturing, which represents almost 25 percent of GDP, compared to the OECD average of about 15 percent of GDP and even less in most developing countries. For example, manufacturing's share of GDP in Sub-Saharan Africa is less than 10 percent. The share of manufacturing in many developing countries has stagnated or is on a declining trend. Automation may drag the share down further (World Bank 2021), and the prospects for services-based growth are still relatively uncertain (Nayyar, Hallward-Driemeier, and Davies 2021).

Furthermore, the developmental, trade, and technological opportunities for developing economies may be different going forward from those available to Korea in the last quarter of the twentieth century. That said, it is possible that a handful of countries could create an industrial base as broad and sophisticated as Korea's, as have several countries in Eastern Europe, such as Czechia and Poland. While noting the caveats, there are 10 key lessons from Korea's developmental experience that could be relevant for developing countries.

First, strong government leadership is key. Robust, enduring, and development oriented leadership has been a central feature of Korea's STI and associated industrial policies. Government leadership translated into sustained support for rapid technological advancement in targeted, promising sectors through financing, fiscal incentives, the early creation of GRIs, and public procurement. In the early decades of Korea's modern development, technology policy focused on adopting foreign technology and coordinating with industrial policies. Technology policy was also supported by the government's foresight to start investing in and promoting STI at an early stage, allowing for the long gestation period, and sustaining the investments in STI and complementary human capital development over the decades.

Second, the national STI system should be built in the early stages of development. Few other governments have been as single minded and focused on creating an innovation system from the ground up by first establishing a base of GRIs and expanding tertiary-level institutions. This approach produced a highly educated and skilled workforce to drive R&D and high-technology manufacturing industries. Korea then incentivized the private sector to expand its R&D effort, tailored for export competitiveness. This effort was supported by conducting and financing STI and gradually building linkages with universities to expand their roles vis-à-vis GRIs. Consistent top-level support for innovation is a key message on what it takes to become a top-tier innovative economy. The important lesson is to get a head start in prioritizing investments in building the national STI system and be persistent in maintaining this prioritization throughout the stages of development.

Third, innovation policy support needs to be in line with a country's stage of development. Korea simultaneously concentrated on getting the developmental basics right—infrastructure, human capital, and macroeconomic stability—and absorbing and diffusing technology from abroad in light- and medium-technology manufacturing. At a much later stage, it concentrated on investing in frontier innovation. Korea's example suggests that although more developed economies can effectively target reaching the global technology frontier in selected, fast-moving technology areas, innovation policy in developing countries needs to focus on technology absorption. This approach was broadly aligned with the concept of a "capabilities escalator" developed by Cirera and Maloney (2017), which argues that the mix of innovation policies should be designed with reference to a country's current capabilities and distance from the technological frontier. As the technology gap narrows and the government's administrative capacity matures, it can introduce policy instruments of increasing complexity.

Fourth, building STI capabilities must be a public-private partnership. The principal objective of research through the 1990s was to absorb and disseminate industrial technology to accelerate diversification into targeted industries. GRIs established the research base and as private companies grew and their revenues expanded, they complemented and over time largely supplanted the GRIs and customized the research to suit their own purposes. In other words, a state-guided industrial strategy necessitated the creation of supporting research infrastructure, with the state initially playing the lead role and laying the foundation for scientific and technology research. Large private firms quickly built on those foundations. The state's role was catalytic, but industrial success rested on the early and effective participation of the private sector, which needed research inputs to grow and diversify its exports. Much of the research conducted during the first three decades of Korea's industrialization was applied, downstream research taking advantage of existing technologies to improve productive efficiency, which led to incremental innovation and development of new products and services. This approach yielded substantial dividends for Korea and is suited to the needs and capabilities of most low- and middle-income countries seeking to build an industrial base.

Fifth, the size and quality of research and innovation are largely a function of the quality of human capital. The success of Korea's industrial and technology policies rested on the parallel accumulation of workforce skills. The education and training systems were built rapidly from the ground up, starting with primary education and extending to vocational and tertiary institutions. The quality of primary and secondary education was critical, and there was a focus on STEM education. It was achieved through teacher selection and motivation, long school days, low dropout rates, and high expenditures on facilities, textbooks, and extra tutoring (see chapter 6). Korea was already spending a substantial share of GDP on education in the 1960s and increased it further in the following decades, reaching a higher rate of investment than many global peers. As a result, the educational outputs quickly caught up to the level of a country with double the income per capita. The government supported repatriation programs and ample job opportunities in public and corporate research institutes and GRIs, which helped to convince foreign-trained Korean scientific talent to return to Korea. The lessons learned for the less developed countries is that improvements in human capital, including higher enrollment in STEM, a focus on vocational skills, and absorption of scientific talent from the diaspora, can facilitate absorption of technologies from abroad and maximize their impact.

Sixth, a thriving private sector, with a critical mass of large firms, helps to leverage investment in R&D. Korea was successful because it created globally competitive large companies. Korea's large firms worked with GRIs, universities, and the entire National Innovation System, to assimilate knowledge and innovate. The large firms shouldered two-thirds or more of the research expenditure, conducted most of the downstream research, and invested in basic research as well. Increasingly, startups account for a relatively large share of R&D. However, the large firms still carry out the bulk of Korea's total R&D because they have the resources and the incentives to invest and engage in R&D on a large scale to maintain international competitiveness in export markets, and because they focus on manufacturing, which tends to exhibit higher levels of R&D than services.

Seventh, innovation policy should nurture an environment conducive to the emergence of high-growth, entrepreneurial firms. Korea supported the growth of large firms, but in recent decades it has reoriented its support for innovation from the large to smaller firms. Korea aimed to support smaller and entrepreneurial firms by expanding access to finance, lowering barriers to market entry, and strengthening competition policies to ensure a level playing field between the large and smaller firms. In particular, Korea has experienced successes in promoting technology startups (chapter six). Support for SMEs can bear fruit if it focuses on identifying and nurturing high-growth, entrepreneurial firms, by bringing innovations to the market, driving exports in new market niches, and creating new high-value-added jobs (Grover, Medvedev, and Olafsen 2019). Such high-growth firms can be an important policy priority in developing countries, where there are few large firms, and can expand opportunities for the emergence of "gazelles."

Eighth, public innovation support systems need to be efficient and calibrated to the needs and capacity of the country. Despite its success in driving innovation outcomes, Korea's innovation system seems to be quite complex, and it is not clear which policy initiatives have had the biggest impacts on research productivity and innovation. Korea has continued to experiment with its innovation policies, recognizing the need to continue to evolve and explore new drivers of growth. It strengthened its monitoring and evaluations systems to assess the results of its experimentation, although the impacts of innovation policies have often been challenging to measure. Overall, the government has aimed to enhance the accountability, transparency, and efficiency of its innovation policies.

Innovation systems could take various forms across countries. Although Korea has taken a comprehensive approach to its National Innovation System that led to a proliferation of institutions, agencies, and policies, comparator countries such as Israel, Poland, Sweden, and Switzerland opted for a more streamlined institutional framework, with only a few flagship institutions, light regulatory control over the business sector, and a small group of GRIs. The comparison of Korea and its global peers suggests that there is no "one size fits all" and that various innovation policy mixes can be productive, depending on a particular country's specific circumstances, endowment, and government capacity. Developing countries with limited government capacity could opt for a relatively lean innovation system that would focus on a few flagship support instruments, which are then closely monitored and evaluated for impact and are supportive of building the innovation capacity of the private sector.

Ninth, there are high returns to R&D investment at an early stage of development, but complementary investments in skills, infrastructure, and access to finance are needed. Korea and Israel have been the global leaders in innovation spending, with R&D investment verging on 5 percent of GDP. Yet, this large investment has failed to stem the recent decline in productivity growth. High investment in basic research in Sweden and Switzerland also has not been associated with productivity growth. It is not clear what would need to change to alter these trends. However, developing countries invest in R&D at only a fraction of the spending in high-income countries. Evidence suggests that returns to R&D investment in developing countries can be large, but they are not uniform and tend to be shaped like an inverted U, increasing up to the income level of Argentina, Brazil, and Türkiye but falling thereafter due to inadequate complementarity capacities in skills, infrastructure, and access to finance (Cirera and Maloney 2017). Increased investment in R&D should thus be coupled with higher spending on complementary capacities to leverage technology absorption and accelerate convergence.

Finally, tenth, developing countries can learn from Korea's experience in harnessing digital technologies to kick-start innovation. Korea prioritized building world class ICT infrastructure to provide easy, affordable access to high-speed broadband internet connections, supporting computer and IT literacy, and promoting the diffusion of digital technologies in the private sector. Korea's exports of online services are on the rise, several unicorns offering innovative services have emerged, and digital technologies have been diffused in manufacturing and services. Governments in low- and middle-income countries could learn from Korea by prioritizing the expansion of ICT infrastructure to encourage the adoption of technologies and promote technology literacy. Countries that do not take advantage of digital technologies will find that the gap with the high-income economies will continue to widen.

Notes

1. https://ec.europa.eu/commission/presscorner/detail/en/QANDA_20_1150.
2. https://www.bloomberg.com/news/articles/2020-01-18/germany-breaks-korea-s-six-year-streak-as-most-innovative-nation.

3. Global Innovation Index, https://www.globalinnovationindex.org/Home (accessed July 29, 2021).

4. The Global Innovation Index 2020 ranking also shows a ranking of high-tech clusters: Seoul was ranked in third place, after Tokyo-Yokohama and Shenzhen-Hong Kong SAR, China-Guangzhou, owing to a higher number of publications and patent applications. A second Korean innovation cluster, Daejeon City, was ranked seventh for science and technology intensity, just behind Boston-Cambridge and ahead of Seattle.

5. National Science and Technology Information Service database, https://www.ntis.go.kr/rndsts/selectStatsDivIdctVo.do (accessed March 31, 2021).

6. NTIS Stats, National Science and Technology Information Service, https://www.ntis.go.kr/rndsts/ (accessed December 23, 2020). WIPO defines the Patent Cooperation Treaty (PCT) as "an international treaty with more than 145 contracting states. The treaty makes it possible to seek patent protection for an invention simultaneously in many countries by filing a single 'international' patent application, instead of filing separate national or regional applications." https://www.wipo.int/pct/en/faqs/faqs.html (accessed April 25, 2023).

7. "2021 R&D ranking of the world top 2,500 companies," https://iri.jrc.ec.europa.eu/scoreboard/2021-eu-industrial-rd-investment-scoreboard (accessed March 15, 2022).

8. Industrial Statistics Analysis System, https://istans.or.kr/wh/whAbout.do?chn=1 (accessed February 1, 2021).

9. OECD's Structural Analysis (STAN) industry database, which is a tool for analyzing industrial performance, https://stats.oecd.org/Index.aspx?DataSetCode=STANI4_2020.

10. Research in printing, for example, can help to conserve the use of solvents, toner cartridges, ink, and minimize waste of paper and packaging material. Printing firms can reduce waste through process innovations. Computer-to-plate technology has enabled printers to dispense with films and smelly chemicals and to use email attachments to distribute documents. In addition, there have been large advances in the automation of printing using robotics, sensors, and radio-frequency identification trackers (*Publishers Weekly* 2022).

11. Korea's STI strategy from the 1960s through the 1980s is described by Wheeler (1990).

12. https://www.natureindex.com/news-blog/how-south-korea-made-itself-a-global-innovation-leader-research-science.

13. The Master Plan for 2018–22 is available at https://stip.oecd.org/stip/interactive-dashboards/policy-initiatives/2021%2Fdata%2FpolicyInitiatives%2F24489.

14. https://www.itu.int/hub/2020/05/how-the-republic-of-korea-became-a-world-ict-leader/: ICT Development Index 2017: https://www.itu.int/net4/ITU-D/idi/2017/index.html (accessed April 2, 2023).

15. Korea Communications Agency, https://www.kca.kr/contentsView.do?pageId=www149.

16. https://www.nature.com/articles/d41586-020-01464-9#:~:text=Under%20President%20Moon%2C%20who%20was,won%20(US%242%20billion).

17. Korea Industrial Technology Association, https://www.koita.or.kr/certificate/graph.aspx.

18. The review covered a total of 132 impact evaluations, but most of the evaluations used methodologies that were not rigorous enough to provide statistically significant results.

19. Tax deduction for research and human capital development, tax deduction for SMEs, Credit for Investment in Productivity Enhancing Infrastructure, SMTMSF Line of Credit for Small Traders and Enterprises, and the Startup Fund.

20. Hall (2019), for instance, shows that tax credits for R&D and super deductions can be effective.

21. A recent rigorous econometric impact evaluation study by Bruhn and McKenzie (2017) shows that one of the National Center for Research and Development's flagship support programs for consortia of firms and research entities provided large levels of additionality, which led to more science-industry collaboration and increased patenting.

References

Aghion, P. A., and P. W. Howitt 2008. *The Economics of Growth*. Cambridge, MA: MIT Press.

Ahn, S. 2019. "How Will the Government Design the SME R&D Strategy?" KISTEP Issue Paper 2019-16 (Vol. 274). KISTEP, Chungcheongbuk-do, Republic of Korea. https://www.kistep.re.kr/board.es?mid=a10306010000&bid=0031&act=view&list_no=35405. (Korean).

Arora, A., S. Belenzon, and A. Patacconi. 2015. "Killing the Golden Goose: The Decline of Science in Corporate R&D." NBER Working Paper 20902, National Bureau for Economic Research, Cambridge, MA. https://www.nber.org/papers/w20902.

Audretsch, D., M. Hafenstein, A. Kritikos, and A. Schiersch. 2018. "Firm Size and Innovation in the Service Sector." DIW Berlin Discussion Paper, IZA DP No. 12035, December.

Bruhn, M., and D. McKenzie. 2017. "Can Grants to Consortia Spur Innovation and Science-Industry Collaboration? Regression-Discontinuity Evidence from Poland." Policy Research Working Paper No. 7934. World Bank, Washington, DC.

Cho, D. S., D. J. Kim, and D. K. Rhee. 1998. "Latecomer Strategies: Evidence from the Semiconductor Industry in Japan and Korea." *Organization Science* 9 (4): 489–505.

Cho, H. H. et al. 2013. "Analysis of the Values of the G7 Program in Terms of Korean R&D History and Comprehensive Performance Analysis." National Research Foundation of Korea, Science & Technology Policy Institute, Daejeon, Republic of Korea.

Choi, Y. 1996. *Dynamic Techno-management Capability: The Case of Samsung Semiconductor Sector in Korea*. Aldershot, England: Avebury.

Choi, Y. 2010. "Korean Innovation Model, Revisited." *STI Policy Review* 1 (1): 93–109.

Choi, J. N., Y. S. Lee, and G. W. Shin (eds.). 2018. *Strategic, Policy and Social Innovation for a Post-industrial Korea: Beyond the Miracle*. New York: Routledge.

Chung, G., J. Im, and S. Chung. 2017. "A Study on the Success Factors of Innovation Cluster: A Case of the Pangyo Techno Valley in South Korea." *Journal of Korea Technology Innovation Society* 20 (4): 970–88.

Chung, K.-H., J. Hong, S. Seo, and K. Kim. 1998. "Recommendations from the Commercialization of Government-Sponsored Telecommunications R&D with Multiple Development Cycles in Korea." *IEEE Transactions on Engineering Management* 45 (4): 331–37.

Cirera, X., and W. Maloney. 2017. *The Innovation Paradox*. Washington, DC: World Bank. https://openknowledge.worldbank.org/handle/10986/28341.

Czernich, N., O. Falck, T. Kretschmer, and L. Woessmann. 2011. "Broadband Infrastructure and Economic Growth." *Economic Journal* 121 (552): 505–32. https://onlinelibrary.wiley.com/doi/abs/10.1111/j.1468-0297.2011.02420.x.

Dayton, L. 2020. "How South Korea Made Itself a Global Innovation Leader." *Nature* 581: S54–S56. https://doi.org/10.1038/d41586-020-01466-7.

Financial Times. 2017. "Korea Struggles to Make Its R&D Work." *Financial Times*, November 23. https://www.ft.com/content/99450bd8-ba71-11e7-bff8-f9946607a6ba.

Frias, J., and H. Lee. 2021. "The Korean Innovation Policy Mix: What Can Practitioners in Developing Countries Learn from Korean Innovation Policy and Its Role in Promoting Innovation and Technological Learning?" World Bank, Washington, DC. Unpublished manuscript.

Gereffi, G., and D. L. Wyman, eds. 1990. *Manufacturing Miracles*. Princeton, NJ: Princeton University Press.

Graf, L. 2014. "The Swiss Apprenticeship System: Its Institutional Specificities and Strengths in International Perspective." American-German Institute, St. Paul, MN.

Grover, A., D. Medvedev, and E. Olafsen. 2019. *High-Growth Firms: Facts, Fiction, and Policy Options for Emerging Economies*. Washington, DC: World Bank.

Hall, B. H. 2019. "Tax Policy for Innovation." NBER Working Paper No. 25773, National Bureau of Economic Research, Cambridge, MA. https://www.nber.org/papers/w25773.

IMD (International Institute for Management Development). 2019. "World Competitiveness Ranking 2019." Lausanne, Switzerland: International Institute for Management Development.

Kang, C.-H. 1998. "Korean Science and Technology." *Science*, August 7. https://science.sciencemag.org/content/281/5378/781.

Keenan, M. 2012. "Moving to the Innovation Frontier: Lessons from the OECD Review of Korean Innovation Policy." In *Korean Science and Technology in an International Perspective*, edited by J. Mahlich and W. Pascha, 15–40. New York: Springer.

Kim, L. 1997. *Imitation to Innovation*. Cambridge, MA: Harvard Business Review Press.

Kim, L. 1999. "Building Technological Capability for Industrialization: Analytical Frameworks and Korea's Experience." *Industrial and Corporate Change* 8 (1): 111–36.

Kim, Y., T. Kelly, and S. Raja. 2010. *Building Broadband: Strategies and Policies for the Developing World*. Washington, DC: World Bank. https://doi.org/10.1596/978-0-8213-8419-0.

KIPO (Korean Intellectual Property Office). 2020. "Statistics Collection on Technology Patents Related to the Fourth Industrial Revolution." KIPO, Daejeon, Republic of Korea. (Korean).

KISTEP (Korea Institute of S&T Evaluation and Planning). 2018. "Survey of Research and Development in Korea." KISTEP, Chungcheongbuk-do, Republic of Korea.

Lall, S. 1992. "Technological Capabilities and Industrialization." *World Development* 20 (2): 165–86. https://doi.org/10.1016/0305-750X(92)90097-F.

Lee, B. 2021. *Analysis of Research Outputs Utilization System of National R&D Program*. Seoul, Korea: National Assembly Budget Office. (Korean).

Lee, J. D. 2016. "Middle Innovation Trap: Transition Failure from Implementation Capability to Concept Design Capability as a Source of the Middle Income Trap." Paper prepared for the HSE International Research Conference, "Foresight and STI Policy," National Research University, Higher School of Economics, Moscow.

Lee, J. D., C. Baek, and J. Yeon. 2021. "Middle Innovation Trap: Capability Transition Failure and Stalled Economic Growth." In *The Challenges of Technology and Economic Catch-up in Emerging Economies*, edited by J. D. Lee, K. Lee, D. Meissner, S. Radosevic, and N. Vonortas, 100–22. Oxford, UK: Oxford University Press. https://doi.org/10.1093/oso/9780192896049.001.0001.

Lee, K. 2013. *Schumpeterian Analysis of Economic Catch-up: Knowledge, Path-creation, and the Middle-income Trap*. Cambridge, UK: Cambridge University Press.

Lee, K. 2021. "Economics of Technological Leapfrogging." In *The Challenges of Technology and Economic Catch-up in Emerging Economies*, edited by J. D. Lee, K. Lee, D. Meissner, S. Radosevic, and N. Vonortas, 123–59. Oxford, UK: Oxford University Press. https://doi.org/10.1093/oso/9780192896049.001.0001.

Lee, K., B. Im, and J. Han. 2017. "The National Innovation System (NIS) for the Catch-up and Post-Catch-up Stages in South Korea." In *The Korean Government and Public Policies in a Development Nexus*, vol. 2, edited by J. Choi, H.-J. Kwon, and M. G. Koo, 69–82. Springer.

Lee, K., and C. Lim. 2001. "Technological Regimes, Catching-up and Leapfrogging: Findings from the Korean Industries." *Research Policy* 30 (3): 459–83.

Lee, K., C. Lim, and W. Song. 2005. "Emerging Digital Technology as a Window of Opportunity and Technological Leapfrogging." *International Journal of Technology Management* 29 (1–2): 40–63.

Lee, K.-R. 2014. "University-Industry R&D Collaboration in Korea's National Innovation System." *Science, Technology, and Society* 19 (1): 1–25. https://journals.sagepub.com/doi/abs/10.1177/0971721813514262.

Lim, C. 2008. "Towards Knowledge Generation with Bipolarized NSI: Korea." In *Small Country Innovation Systems: Globalization, Change and Policy in Asia and Europe*, edited by C. Edquist and L. Hommen. Edward Elgar Publishing.

Lim, W. 2012. "Chaebol and Industrial Policy in Korea." *Asian Economic Policy Review* 7: 69–86.

Luque, C. A., S. D. Silber, and F. V. Luna. 2020. Reagindo à crise: não faz sentido diferenciar problemas de liquidez de problemas de solvência. Valor Econômico. Opinião. São Paulo: Faculdade de Economia, Administração, Contabilidade e Atuária, Universidade de São Paulo. https://valor.globo.com/opiniao/coluna/reagindo-a-crise.ghtml. (Portuguese).

Mathews, J. A., and D.-S. Cho. 2000. *Tiger Technology: The Creation of a Semiconductor Industry in East Asia*. Cambridge, UK: Cambridge University Press.

Medvedev, D., M. Piatkowski, and S. Yusuf. 2019. *Promoting Innovation in China: Lessons from International Good Practice*. FCI Policy Insight Series. Washington, DC: World Bank.

Ministry of Education, Science and Technology. 2008. *The Second Science and Technology Master Plan*. Seoul, Republic of Korea: Ministry of Education, Science and Technology.

Ministry of Education, Science and Technology. 2010. *2040 Future Vision for Science and Technology*. Seoul, Republic of Korea: Ministry of Education, Science and Technology.

MOST (Republic of Korea, Ministry of Science and Technology). 2017. *The 50-Year History of Science and Technology*. Gwacheon, Republic of Korea: MOST.

MSIT and NIA (Republic of Korea, Ministry of Science and IT and National Information Society Agency). 2021. *History of Korean Information and Communication Network Development*. Sejong City: MSIT and NIA. https://www.korea.kr/archive/expDocView.do?docId=39683.

Mu, Q., and K. Lee. 2005. "Knowledge Diffusion, Market Segmentation and Technological Catch-Up: The Case of the Telecommunication Industry in China." *Research Policy* 34 (6): 759–83.

National Science and Technology Council. 2013. *Third Comprehensive Plan for the Promotion of Basic Research (2013–2017)*. Seoul, Republic of Korea: National Science and Technology Council. (Korean).

National Science and Technology Council. 2014. *Plan to Make Government-funded Research Institutes into SME and MME R&D Outposts*. Seoul, Republic of Korea: National Science and Technology Council. (Korean).

Nayyar, G., M. Hallward-Driemeier, and E. Davies. 2021. *At Your Service? The Promise of Services-Led Development*. Washington, DC: World Bank.

OECD (Organisation for Economic Co-operation and Development). 2002. *Measuring the Information Economy*. Paris: OECD Publishing.

OECD (Organisation for Economic Co-operation and Development). 2016. https://read.oecd-ilibrary.org/science-and-technology/oecd-reviews-of-innovation-policy-sweden-2016_9789264250000-en#page22.

OECD (Organisation for Economic Co-operation and Development). 2017. https://www.oecd.org/korea/sti-scoreboard-2017-korea.pdf.

OECD (Organisation for Economic Co-operation and Development). 2018. *2018 OECD Economic Survey of Korea: Achieving a New Paradigm for Inclusive Growth*. Paris: OECD. https://read.oecd-ilibrary.org/economics/oecd-economic-surveys-korea-2018_eco_surveys-kor-2018-en#page137.

OECD (Organisation for Economic Co-operation and Development) and World Bank Institute. 2000. *Korea and the Knowledge-based Economy*. Paris: OECD Publishing. https://openknowledge.worldbank.org/handle/10986/13845.

OECD (Organisation for Economic Co-operation and Development). 2021. Broadband statistics database. https://www.oecd.org/sti/broadband/broadband-statistics/.

Oh, S., and S. Kim. 2018. "The Achievements and Direction of R&D Support for Small and Medium-sized Enterprises." *STEPI Insight* 224: 1–26. Sejong City, Republic of Korea: STEPI. https://www.stepi.re.kr/site/stepiko/report/View.do?reIdx=226&cateCont=A0501. (Korean).

Park, E., and A. Lee. 2020. "Neighbors with Different Innovation Patterns: The Implications of Industrial and FDI Policy for the Openness of Local Knowledge Production." *Transnational Corporations* 27 (1): 3–33.

Publishers Weekly. 2022. "Press P for Printing and for Progress." *Publishers Weekly*, April 19. https://www.publishers weekly.com/pw/by-topic/industry-news/manufacturing/article/88989-press-p-for-printing-and-for-progress .html.

Romer, P. 1987. "Growth Based on Increasing Returns Due to Specialization." *American Economic Review* 77 (2): 55–62.

Romer, P. 1990. "Endogenous Technological Change." *Journal of Political Economy*, October: S71–S102.

Seong, S., S. W. Popper, and K. Zheng. 2005. *Strategic Choices in S&T: Korea in the Era of a Rising China*. Santa Monica, CA: Rand Corporation. https://www.rand.org/content/dam/rand/pubs/monographs/2005/RAND _MG320.pdf.

So, M. H., et al. 2020. "Analysis of the Research Achievements in the Science & Technology Fields." Korea Institute of S&T Evaluation and Planning, Chungcheongbuk-do, Republic of Korea. https://www.kistep.re.kr/c3/sub2_5 .jsp?brdType=R&bbIdx=14268. (Korean).

Song, J.-W. 2020. "New Wine in Old Bottles? Korean State Actors' Policy Engagement with the Online Gaming Industry." *Competition & Change* 25 (1): 97–123.

Statistics Korea. 2020. *Survey on SMEs*. https://kosis.kr/index/index.do.

Tschang, F. T. 2007. "Balancing the Tensions between Rationalization and Creativity in the Video Games Industry." *Organization Science* 18 (6): 989–1005.

UNESCO (United Nations Educational, Scientific and Cultural Organization). 2020. *UNESCO Science Report*. Paris: UNESCO.

WEF (World Economic Forum). 2019. *The Global Competitiveness Report 2019*. Geneva: WEF.

Westphal, L. 1990. "Industrial Policy in an Export-Propelled Economy: Lessons from South Korea's Experience." *Journal of Economic Perspectives* 4 (3): 41–59.

Wheeler, J. W. 1990. "Comparative Development Strategies of South Korea and Taiwan as Reflected in Their Respective International Trade Policies." *Michigan Journal of International Law* 11 (2): 472–508.

Woolston, C. 2020. "South Korean Institutions Lure Global Talent." *Nature* 581, S66–S67. https://doi.org/10.1038 /d41586-020-01467-6.

World Bank. 2016. *World Development Report 2016: Digital Dividends*. Washington, DC: World Bank.

World Bank. 2021. *The Innovation Imperative for Developing East Asia*. Washington, DC: World Bank.

WIPO (World Intellectual Property Organization). 2019. *Global Innovation Index 2019*. Geneva: WIPO. https:// www.wipo.int/edocs/pubdocs/en/wipo_pub_gii_2019.pdf.

WIPO (World Intellectual Property Organization). 2020. *PCT Yearly Review 2020*. Executive Summary. Geneva: WIPO. https://www.wipo.int/edocs/pubdocs/en/wipo_pub_901_2020_exec_summary.pdf.

Yoo, S. Y. 2019. "Rules in Disarray, Orientation Imposed: Establishment of the Framework Act on Science and Technology, 1998-2015." *Journal of Science & Technology Studies* 19 (2): 41–83.

Yun, Y., and J. Lee. 2004. "Promoting Regional Industries and Building Up Regional Innovation Systems." *Korea Development Institute Research Monograph* (2004-13). Seoul, Republic of Korea: Korea Development Institute.

Zastrow, M. 2020a. "Boosting South Korea's Basic Research." *Nature* 581, S50–S52. https://doi.org/10.1038 /d41586-020-01464-9.

Zastrow, M. 2020b. "South Korea's Institute for Basic Science Faces Review." *Nature* 581: S53. https://doi.org/10.1038 /d41586-020-01465-8.

Investing in Human Capital and Strengthening the Labor Market

Introduction

Increasing incomes and reducing poverty in developing countries has required shifting workers from the low-productivity agriculture sector to the higher productivity manufacturing and service sectors (Paik 2020, 36). To achieve the investment required for this transformation, a country needs to be able to supply a large number of high-quality workers who have the set of knowledge and skills demanded in the manufacturing and service sectors. In a developing country, a sluggish labor market can become both the cause and the consequence of economic backwardness. Slow growth constrains job creation, and a lack of skills constrains growth.

This underlines the importance of education and skills development systems that can provide quality education and training opportunities for all. However, education systems in developing countries face several critical problems, including low enrollment rates in secondary and tertiary education, low levels of knowledge and skills of graduates due to the poor quality of education, and lack of continuing education and training opportunities. These problems substantially hinder the implementation of national economic development plans. In addition, developing countries have an urgent need to redesign and strengthen their education and skills development systems to prepare for the Fourth Industrial Revolution.

Although the challenges faced by individual countries require distinctive solutions, it is possible to draw lessons from the Republic of Korea for developing countries. Korea's successful investments in human capital development laid the foundation for the country's rapid and sustained growth into a high-income economy. Korea today has among the highest levels of human capital development in the world. Even in the East Asia and the Pacific region, which is home to countries that have relatively successfully invested in human capital and upgraded the skills of their workforces, up to 60 percent of the students are in poorly performing school systems, and most have learning outcomes that are below proficiency or unknown (World Bank 2018).

Korea's experience shows that investments in education and training can support rapid development and the rising demand for labor. Korea also prioritized strengthening the labor market infrastructure

This chapter was prepared by Soonhwa Yi, Aija Maarit Rinkinen, Hayeon Kim, and Ryo Sun Jang (World Bank); Yong-seong Kim (KOREATECH); and Sung Joon Paik (KDI School of Public Policy and Management). Kangyeon Lee (World Bank) provided review comments.

so that the labor market functions smoothly in support of economic development. This includes government promotion of individual human capital investments and assistance with job searches and job matching. Over time, policies and interventions were increasingly reoriented to support market mechanisms.

This chapter first discusses human capital development in Korea, through formal education and technical and vocational training. It then describes developments in Korea's labor market, including the impact of population aging, labor market duality, youth and female labor market participation, labor market programs, and administrative reforms. The overall goal is to highlight key strategies and policies that Korea has adopted to make education, skills development, and the labor market supportive of national economic development. The final section considers key lessons for developing countries.

Human Capital Development in Korea

Since the 1950s when it was poor country, Korea has prioritized human capital development. Sustained investments have made Korea one of the top countries in the world in human capital development. The World Bank Human Capital Index ranks Korea fourth of 173 countries (World Bank 2020). In Korea, the cognitive skills of students at age 15 have been among the top ranks in reading, science, and math on the Programme for International Student Assessment (PISA) test since its inception in 2000 (table 6.1). Korea ranked fourth in higher education achievement and 11th in graduates in sciences in the World Digital Competitiveness ranking 2020 (IMD 2020). As of 2019, 70 percent of individuals ages 25–34 had tertiary education, which was higher than Canada (63 percent), the United Kingdom (52 percent), the United States (50 percent), France (48 percent), the European Union 23 average (44 percent), and the Organisation for Economic Co-operation and Development (OECD) average (45 percent) (OECD 2019a).

The appropriate balance between general and vocational education, top-down and bottom-up approaches to reforms, and the importance of qualitative versus quantitative expansion of education differs at different stages of development. Korea's experience shows that rather than seeking universal strategies and rules, the provision of education systems in terms of access and quality should evolve depending on a country's socioeconomic and technological conditions (Lee, Jeong, and Hong 2018). Since the late 1990s, as the country transitioned to a high-income economy, the government of Korea has reprioritized its human capital policy from high school to junior college and university, and from the government-controlled and supply oriented approach to a more market-based and demand oriented approach to meet the rapidly changing labor market demands.

INVESTMENTS IN EDUCATION

The Six-Year Plan for Completing Compulsory Education (1954–59) and adult literacy campaigns (1945–48 and 1954–58) laid the early groundwork for the expansion of education since the 1970s (figure 6.1). Increasing enrollment in formal education, combined with the growth of the national

TABLE 6.1 **PISA Scores and Rank, Republic of Korea, 2000–18**

Subject	Score (OECD rank)						
	2000	2003	2006	2009	2012	2015	2018
Reading	525 (6)	534 (2)	556 (1)	539 (1–2)	536 (1–2)	517 (3–8)	514 (2–7)
Math	547 (2)	542 (2)	547 (1–2)	546 (1–2)	554 (1)	524 (1–4)	526 (1–4)
Science	552 (1)	538 (3)	522 (5–9)	538 (2–4)	538 (2–4)	516 (5–8)	519 (3–5)

Source: OECD 2019c.
Note: OECD = Organisation for Economic Co-operation and Development; PISA = Programme for International Student Assessment.

FIGURE 6.1 **Changing Trends in Gross Enrollment Rates, by Level of Education, Republic of Korea, 1975–2020**

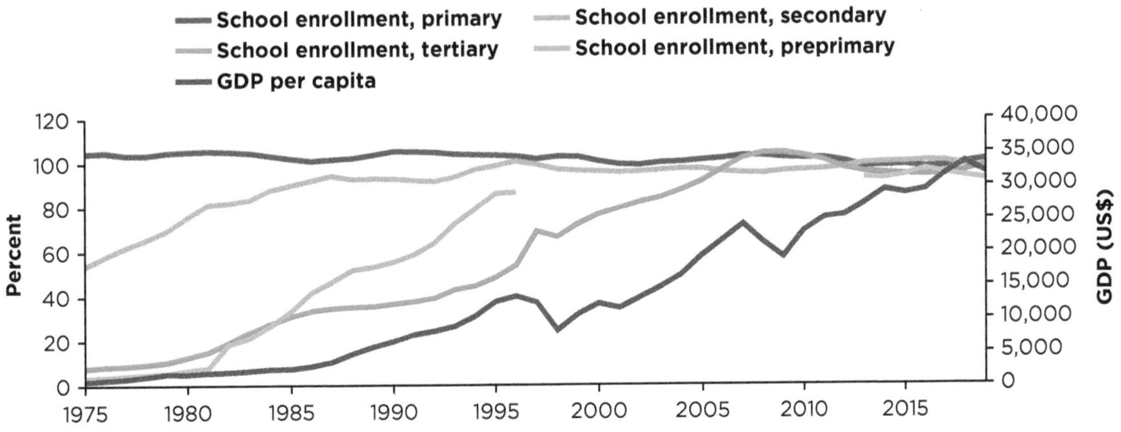

Source: World Development Indicators, World Bank (https://databank.worldbank.org/source/world-development-indicators).
Note: GDP = gross domestic product.

vocational training system since the late 1960s, played an important role in building the human capital stock required for Korea's national economic development plans (Paik 2015).

The expansion of education was made possible by the government's strong and long-term commitment to investing in education and the mobilization of the private sector's contribution to education (figure 6.2). Primary schools in Korea were all public schools (approximately 2 percent are private), but the proportions of students in private schools in secondary and higher education were quite high (figure 6.3), reflecting the significant contribution of private schools to the expansion of education. Parents paid tuition and fees for their children's education from primary to higher education, indicating that households also contributed to financing education. Increasing investments in education supported a continuing increase in the average years of schooling, from 5.4 in 1970 to 12.1 in 2015.[1]

In Korea, a national curriculum and textbooks, high quality teachers with university education, and parents' prioritization of their children's education made it possible for students to receive high-quality education. Since the 1960s, Korea has succeeded in recruiting high-quality teachers by providing a relatively high salary, guaranteeing job security with the retirement age of 65 (now 62), and providing a lifetime pension after retirement. The average salary of lower secondary teachers with 15 years of experience and the most prevalent qualification in Korea was estimated to be US$56,648 in 2015, which was higher than the OECD average of US$48,562 (OECD 2020). The qualification requirement for primary school teachers was increased from two-year junior college to four-year university education, and secondary school teachers require a four-year university education.

Investments in higher education have earned significant returns, thus creating the demand for higher education and expanding the market for private schools. In the 1980s, the wage premiums for junior college (two or three years) were 10 to 20 percent compared to a high school education, and the premiums for four-year college or higher levels of education were greater than 40 percent (figure 6.4). These premiums appear to reflect the increasing demand for skills due to Korea's expanding industrialization. In the 2000s, the premiums on tertiary education started to rise again, driven by the expanding high-technology industries and deeper integration into the global production network (Koh 2019). However, there are concerns that the rapid expansion of higher education has resulted in deteriorating college premiums among lower tier universities and a large and widening gap between the top and bottom tier universities (Lee, Jeong, and Hong 2018).

An important key to Korea's success in education has been close and systematic linkages between national economic development planning and human capital policies (table 6.2). National education

FIGURE 6.2 Ratios of the Ministry of Education Budget to the Government Budget and GDP, Republic of Korea, 1963–2019

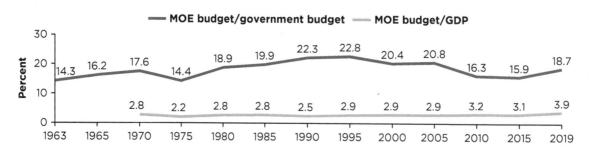

Source: Korean Educational Development Institute (https://kess.kedi.re.kr/index).
Note: GDP = gross domestic product; MOE = Ministry of Education.

FIGURE 6.3 Share of Private School Students, by Level of Education, Republic of Korea, 1965–2020

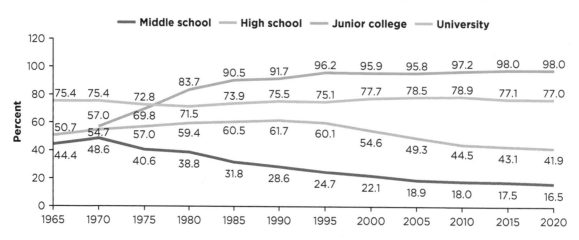

Source: Korean Educational Development Institute (https://kess.kedi.re.kr/index).

FIGURE 6.4 Wage Premium, by Level of Education, Republic of Korea, 1980–2016

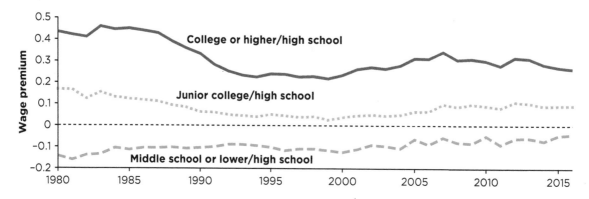

Source: Koh 2018.
Note: Values are based on estimates of Mincer-type wage equations.

TABLE 6.2 **Linkage between the Labor Force and National Economic Development Strategies**

	Major Strategies for National Econ. Dev.	**Major Strategies for Manpower Development**
1950s	**Build** SOC and industry base	**Universalize** 6-yr primary education **Decrease** Adult illiteracy
1960s	**Develop** Labor-intensive light industry with export-promotion	**Introduce** Vocational high school curriculum and junior college system and vocational training system
1970s	**Build** Self-reliant growth base **Develop** Heavy and chemical industries	**Expand** Secondary school and junior college **Introduce** Compulsory vocational training system
1980s	**Develop** Technology-intensive industry	**Expand** Higher education **Promote** Research and development
1990s	**Promote** High-tech innovation **Develop** Information industry	**Strengthen** Higher education (science and technology) **Introduce** Employment insurance system
2000s	**Promote** High-value added technology innovation	**Develop** Highly skilled human resources for new technology area **Strengthen** Industry-higher education collaboration
2010s	**Promote** Innovation-led and balanced growth	**Restructure** High school system **Expand** Industry-higher education collaboration **Cultivate** Basic sciences and high tech R&D manpower

Source: Adapted from Paik 2018, 84, table 1-15.
Note: R&D = research and development.

development plans accounted for the demand for workers and the capacity of the education system to supply workers. Thus, Korea was able to educate, train, and supply quality labor by adapting the education and training system to the changing demand for skills resulting from the structural transformation of the economy.

Coordination across the relevant ministries, external agencies, and the private sector, within an institutionalized governance framework, is essential for systematically connecting education and vocational training to national economic development plans. During the early development period (1960s to 1990s), the Economic Planning Board, the planning and coordination ministry headed by the deputy prime minister for the economy, allocated the government budget and played a leading role in coordinating economic development plans and human resources development (HRD) policies. After the 1990s, the government established the Inter-Ministerial Meeting for HRD (2001–07), presided over by the deputy prime minister for education and HRD experts, to play the coordination role. To strengthen the coordination mechanisms between the budget allocation and personnel administration, this structure was replaced by the National Human Resource Council (2007–08), chaired by the president and with representatives from related ministries, private sector representatives, and HRD experts.

Thus, Korea continued to experiment with the institutional arrangements to strengthen coordination between economic and HRD planning. Its experience highlights the importance of the chairperson of the coordinating body or the leading ministry having practical power and professional expertise to lead discussions and ensure coordination and collaboration among the ministries, agencies, and private sector. In addition, Korea clearly defined the roles and responsibilities of each participant in the coordination body and established the decision-making procedures in the relevant laws, rules, and regulations.

STRENGTHENING SCIENCE AND TECHNOLOGY EDUCATION

From the early decades of its development, Korea has prioritized science and technology (S&T) education and research and development (R&D) in higher education to strengthen its capacity for S&T research and develop a highly skilled workforce. From the 1960s to the early 2000s, the government established a series of Five-Year Science and Technology Development Plans to expand the supply of S&T workers. Since the 2000s, the government budget for R&D in higher education as a share of gross domestic product (GDP) has increased significantly and reached the level of the United States (figure 6.5).

FIGURE 6.5 **Ratio of Research and Development Budget in Higher Education to Gross Domestic Product, Selected Countries, 1997–2018**

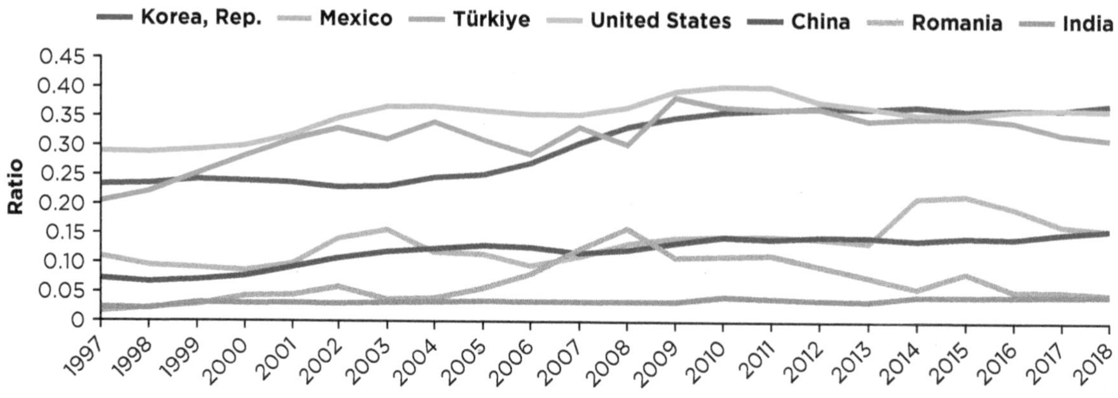

Source: Organisation for Economic Co-operation and Development (https://stats.oecd.org/).

The number of researchers in R&D in Korea increased from 2,173 per million population in 1996 to 7,980 per million in 2018, which was the second largest in the world after Denmark. However, the Korea Employment Information Service (2017) projected a shortage of 80,000 S&T workers in the fields of natural sciences, engineering, and pharmaceutical sciences over the next 10 years. The Korean government and the Presidential Committee on the 4th Industrial Revolution (2017, 77–80) estimated a shortage of 30,000 software engineers in the fields of artificial intelligence, cloud, big data, and augmented reality/virtual reality over the next five years. Hence, promoting S&T research capability remains a national priority.

In the 1960s and 1970s, two important initiatives enhanced S&T research capacity in tertiary education. In 1966, the government strengthened R&D by establishing the Korea Institute of Science and Technology (KIST). In 1973, the government established the Korea Advanced Institute of Science & Technology (KAIST) as a special purpose S&T research oriented university under the jurisdiction of the Ministry of Science, Technology and ICT.[2] KAIST was established to increase the supply of scientists with advanced qualifications in Korea.

At the time, many Korean students who went abroad to be educated in S&T fields did not return to Korea. The government invested significantly to convince top-class professors and students to return to Korea, including by upgrading the facilities and equipment for S&T education and R&D (Song 2005, 8–11). The government also provided free education to KAIST students and exempted military service duty for male students with the special act on the establishment and operation of KAIST.[3] These efforts contributed to securing the core S&T brains needed for economic development (Kim 2012, 160).

KAIST operates the Korea Science Academy as an annexed special purpose high school for gifted students. Graduates from the Korea Science Academy and other special purpose science high schools can be admitted to KAIST without going through the standard admission procedures, including the national scholastic aptitude test. This simplified admission procedure helped to recruit the most gifted high school students and allowed them to complete a bachelor's degree program within three years and continue their studies in S&T up to the doctoral level without interruption. The government expanded this policy to other science- and technology-focused, special purpose research oriented universities, such as the Gwangju Institute of Science and Technology, Daegu Gyungbuk Institute of Science and Technology, and Ulsan National Institute of Science and Technology.[4]

KAIST and these other S&T-focused universities played a significant role in supplying S&T brains and conducting high-quality research. They contributed significantly to technology transfer, the national innovation system, and the high share of science, technology, engineering, and mathematics (STEM) graduates. As a result, Korea's share of STEM tertiary graduates is significantly higher than the OECD average (figure 6.6). In 2015, 29 percent of tertiary school graduates were in the STEM fields, the third highest among OECD countries after Germany (37 percent) and Austria (30 percent). Recently, however, these research oriented universities have faced increasing competition in recruiting highly competent students with other universities that have strengthened their research capacity and with world class foreign universities (Science and Technology Policy Institute 2014).

In the 1990s, the government devoted increased attention to enhancing Korea's S&T competitiveness by increasing the supply of high-caliber researchers. The Ministry of Education introduced the Brain Korea 21 Project in 1999, which supports high-performing research oriented universities (box 6.1). But by the late 1990s, Korea experienced relatively high unemployment among graduates from S&T colleges and universities and, as a result, students were reluctant to study S&T.

In 2006, the government issued the National Basic Plans for Human Resources in Science & Technology as the first in a series of five-year plans. The Fourth Plan (2021–25) is now under implementation. The Second Basic Plan (2011–15) focused on primary and secondary education. It attributed primary and secondary school students' low academic interest in mathematics and science to the theory-based, one-way (noninteractive), and rote memory-based teaching methods. According to the PISA report in 2006, the level of Korean students' interest in science was 55th of 57 countries, despite their high scores. Students lacked opportunities to experience how math and science are utilized in real life. As a result, many competent students preferred medical science and pharmaceutics instead of S&T.[5]

Recognizing these problems, the government supported a more integrated approach to education in science, technology, engineering, arts, and mathematics (STEAM) to enhance students' academic interest in S&T, and to cultivate creative thinking and problem-solving skills through a multidisciplinary and teamwork-based approach. The Korea Foundation for the Advancement of Science & Creativity (KOFAC) has managed the implementation of STEAM education programs at the national level.

FIGURE 6.6 **Share of Tertiary Graduates in STEM Fields, Selected Countries, 2015**

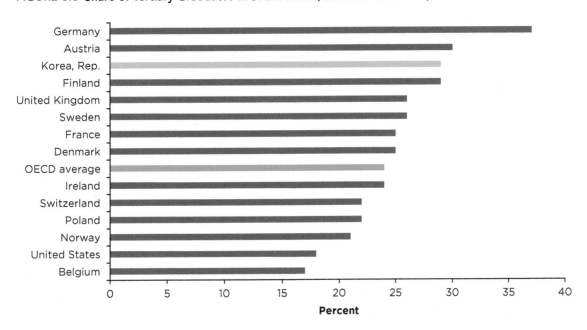

Source: OECD 2017.
Note: OECD = Organisation for Economic Co-operation and Development; STEM = science, technology, engineering, and mathematics.

BOX 6.1 Brain Korea 21

The main purpose of the Brain Korea 21 (BK21) program is to develop world class research oriented universities and educate high-caliber research workers (master's and doctoral students and post-doc researchers) in the Republic of Korea. To participate in BK21, universities form project teams in collaboration with related departments, to submit project proposals for the Ministry of Education to review and select. Since its inception, BK21 has been implemented in seven-year terms. The first stage of BK21 (1999–2006) supported 247 project teams with investment of ₩1,400 billion. The second stage of BK21 (2006–13) invested ₩2,300 billion to support 568 project teams.

The third stage of BK21, called BK21 Plus (September 2013 to August 2020) was implemented to strengthen the education and research and development capacity of high-performing graduate schools and educate future research workers. It had three components: education of researchers to enhance research competitiveness through international cooperation in convergence areas, education for practical professionals with high qualifications in selected areas, and development of top-tier graduate schools in all areas of science and provision of scholarships to graduate students. In 2019, BK21 Plus supported 525 project teams with ₩269 billion.

Overall, BK21 contributed to investments in research infrastructure, the education of an increasing number of participating graduate students and post-doc researchers, and enhanced research competitiveness measured by the increase in the number of Science Citation Index research articles with a high impact factor. Challenges have included budget constraints, the rigidity of using project budgets, and a standardized evaluation framework that has not always allowed for evaluation of the full potential of research project proposals.

The government is now implementing the fourth stage of BK21 (September 2020 to August 2027) to respond to increasing demand for greater creativity and innovation in interdisciplinary education and convergence research, and to enhance the roles of research oriented universities as knowledge creators. The fourth stage of BK21 has three components: education for future researchers to enhance research capacity in basic and core sciences, education for research workers to lead new innovative industries for national economic growth, and graduate school innovation. As of 2020, 578 project teams had participated.

Sources: https://www.korea.kr/special/policyFocusView.do?newsId=135089540&pkgId=49500110, https://bkplus.nrf.re.kr/sub01/sub111/list.do; https://www.moe.go.kr/boardCnts/view.do?boardID=294&boardSeq=32761&lev=0&searchType=null&statusYN=W&page=379&s=moe&m=050201&opType=N (accessed January 18, 2021).

KOFAC emphasized that the integrative approach of STEAM is a critical element for improving school education and developing deeper understanding of the content, process, and characteristics of science through "creative design" and "emotional learning" (Yakman and Lee 2012). To realize the objectives of STEAM education, the government set up action plans that reoriented school teaching to emphasize creative problem solving, experimentation, advanced technologies and their practical applications in real life, and the convergence of arts and humanities and S&T (Yakman and Lee 2012).[6]

In 2015, 27.1 percent of all schools provided STEAM education (Park et al. 2016). In 2016, 55 percent of primary schools, 48 percent of middle schools, and 32 percent of high schools provided STEAM programs to their students once or twice a month, according to a survey by KOFAC. STEAM programs were offered through individual teachers' initiatives or local education offices' support. The survey results indicate that STEAM policy has been well implemented (Kang 2019, 8–9). Two meta-analysis studies on the effect of STEAM programs on student learning (2018) found significant positive effects on variables like academic achievement, thinking skills, interest in STEM and STEM-related careers, information and communications technology (ICT) skills, and creative problem-solving skills (Kang et al. (2018), who analyzed 60 papers, and Shin (2018)). In addition, the STEAM programs in secondary schools have had long-term positive effects on improving the core competencies of university students whose majors were mostly science or engineering, compared with those who did not have experience with STEAM programs (Kang (2019, 17–18) analyzed 95 papers).[7]

To complement the emphasis on S&T education, Korea prioritized the use of technology in its schools and skills training through a series of national Master Plans. The first Master Plan (1996–2000) focused on establishing ICT infrastructure in all schools. The second Master Plan (2001–05) aimed to improve access to and quality of technology-based teaching by expanding access to online educational content and training teachers to enhance their digital and pedagogical skills for using technology. The third Master Plan (2006–10) focused on creating innovative and inclusive learning environments through more flexible educational services, such as digital textbooks. The fourth and fifth Master Plans (2010–18) focused on providing more flexible and personalized learning. The plans facilitated "Self-directed, Motivated, Adaptive, Resource enriched, Technology embedded (SMART)" education by innovating the entire education system and promoting student-centered learning using data and technology (KERIS 2016). Throughout the phases, the government aimed to strengthen linkages between ICT and education policies through a multi-stakeholder approach to mobilize the participation of industry, the private sector, nongovernmental organizations, and the general public (Yarrow, Yoo, and Kim, forthcoming).

The government developed and implemented an information technology (IT) investment plan to support the large and sustained financial investment required to establish the IT infrastructure, including networks, facilities, equipment, and platforms. The School Advancement Project, which established schools' local area networks and multimedia labs and provided personal computers and ICT devices for classrooms, was implemented during the first three Master Plans (Kim, Gu, and Kim 2001). As a result, the average number of students per personal computer was reduced to four in 2021, and schools were equipped with enhanced internet service and ICT teachers and staff (KERIS 2021).

Capacity building of teachers has been central to the education technology policy. The government has provided ICT training to teachers since the 1980s, focusing on ICT literacy and curriculum integration. The ICT Skills Standards for Teachers, which focus on information processing skills, are the basis for accrediting teachers' ICT skills and guiding the planning for ICT teacher training. The ICT infrastructure and associated teacher capacity helped Korea to minimize the learning loss during the COVID-19 pandemic, through the nationwide rollout of online and hybrid learning (Yarrow, Yoo, and Kim, forthcoming).

Despite the emphasis on promoting S&T education, the number of high school students who choose advanced mathematics and science in the national college scholastic ability examination has declined rapidly (155,627 in 2013, 34,585 in 2017, and 19,518 in 2020). The Fourth Basic Plan includes several action plans to enhance primary and secondary school students' mathematics and science competencies, establish artificial intelligence education standards for primary and secondary school education, induce students with mathematics and science talent into science and engineering tracks, and provide innovative science and engineering education in higher education.

PROMOTING INDUSTRY-ACADEMIA COLLABORATION

Colleges and universities contribute to national economic development by educating students according to high standards of knowledge and skills, and by generating new knowledge and innovative technologies through R&D. The government of Korea began increasing its budget for higher education in the 1980s, primarily to accommodate increasing social demand for higher education and to ensure that colleges and universities would supply the technicians, engineers, and scientists who were needed to strengthen the country's S&T capabilities and facilitate the transition to a high-income economy.

These efforts included fostering collaboration between industry and the educational institutions. However, the efforts were initially undermined by the focus on the supply-side promotion of universities, colleges, and public agencies, rather than reflecting sufficiently on the demand-side needs of industries. Furthermore, the universities and industries lacked the urgency to collaborate. Until the 1990s, universities had little difficulty in recruiting students due to the high demand for higher education, and firms had adopted existing and imported technologies that did not require research collaboration with universities.

However, university-industry collaboration became more critical as Korea approached the global technology frontier and the transition from a technology follower to a leader. Thus, in the late 1990s, the government adopted a new paradigm for university-industry collaboration in the early 2000s (table 6.3). The new paradigm emphasized demand-side oriented approaches to address industry's needs for technical workers and innovation. It also promoted comprehensive support for the universities and focused on commercializing the research and providing practical training. The government guided universities and colleges to change their academic administration system to fit the university-industry collaboration. The government urged universities and colleges to establish an Industry-Academic Cooperation Foundation to promote commercialization of technology (for example, intellectual property rights acquisition and management and financial rewards to researchers and technology contributors) and the establishment of startups (for example, help with contracting and account management) (Kim and Kim 2017).

Following the new paradigm, the Hub University/College for Industrial Collaboration (HUNIC) program was designed to encourage increased collaboration between industries and academia in engineering and to strengthen the training and supply of technical workers. Participating universities provided financial incentives to participating professors and reflected their participation in their performance appraisals; acknowledged the intellectual property rights of professor(s) who developed new technology, which in the past had belonged to the university; and hired professional accountants, lawyers, and industry-academic collaboration experts to facilitate the collaboration. Private firms that participated in the project provided incentives to their staff to participate in the joint research with academia, acknowledge co-ownership of intellectual property rights with collaborating professors, and support the development and implementation of university curricula and internship programs. Under HUNIC, the numbers of industry-academia collaboration agreements, joint research projects, patent registrations, and technology transfers increased rapidly (Yim and Jyung 2009). However, HUNIC lacked direct targets for employment, and the internship program did not function as an effective linkage to employment due to the lack of commitment of the universities, colleges, and firms involved (Choo et al. 2011).[8]

The Leaders in Industry-University Cooperation (LINC) program was launched in 2012 to build on the HUNIC program (Ministry of Education, Science, and Technology (2011). Compared to HUNIC, LINC expanded the coverage of the program beyond engineering and strengthened support for startups and firms. It aimed at educating and supplying technical workers and researchers to support the development of new, innovative technologies and the transfer of existing technologies to the private sector. In addition, LINC aimed to continue to promote industry-academia collaboration and strengthen the roles of the Industry-Academic Cooperation Foundation (Ministry of Education, Science and Technology 2012, 1–8). Under LINC, the pace of improvement in industry-academia collaboration differed across regions, indicating that policy measures need to be customized to the regional characteristics and environment (Kim, D. J. 2018). Compared to universities that were not participating in the project, professors at participating universities engaged in more technology transfers and startups (Moon and Lee 2015).

TABLE 6.3 **Paradigm Shift in University-Industry Collaboration in the Republic of Korea**

	Old ways	New ways
Approach	Supply based (from the perspectives of junior colleges, universities, and the government)	Demand oriented (from the perspectives of firms, small and medium-size industries, and industry)
Support strategy	Project-based/department-based partial support	College-based comprehensive support (college system change)
Scope	Partial participation (projects and professors)	Comprehensive (students, professors, and firms' workers)
Focus	Research and development focused	Commercialization focused/startups
Education	Theory/research based	Practical job skills training

Source: Paik 2017, 86.

Korea's experience with industry-academia collaboration policies indicates that it is critical for universities to align their programs with the interests and needs of firms. There would be demand for collaboration if universities provided education and conducted research that firms valued. The government can play an important role in promoting and coordinating this collaboration by providing financial and administrative support.

SKILLS DEVELOPMENT: TECHNICAL AND VOCATIONAL TRAINING

Restructuring Vocational High Schools

In 1991, the government initiated the restructuring of high schools to increase the share of vocational high schools (VHSs) relative to general academic high schools, to meet the manufacturing sector's demand for skilled workers. As living standards improved and the enrollment quotas of colleges and universities expanded in the 1980s, the proportion of VHS students declined from 45.0 percent in 1980 to 35.5 percent in 1990. The proportion of firms that provided vocational training to new employees with a high school diploma also declined. The training was mandatory, but a large number of firms decided to pay the levy instead of providing training.

In response, the government aimed to increase the proportion of VHS students from 35.5 percent in 1990 to 50.0 percent of total high school students by 1995 and increase the ratio of technical high school[9] students to VHS students from 24.0 percent in 1990 to 45.0 percent in 1995. The restructuring fell well short of these targets. The proportion of VHS students increased only to 42.2 percent in 1995, and the ratio of technical high school students to VHS students increased to 35.0 percent in 1995. After 1995, the VHS student ratio fell to 36.1 percent in 2000, and then to 23.8 percent in 2010. The technical high school student ratio increased to 40.0 percent in 1999, significantly below the target, and then stagnated. The government discontinued the policy in 1998.

The government had targeted the increase of VHSs in response to workforce demand projections, which anticipated a shortage of skilled workers. However, this anticipated shortage did not necessarily mean that the country needed to expand VHSs. In the 1990s, industrial automation replaced many jobs whose main responsibilities were routine and repetitive, so that the high demand for skilled technical workers did not materialize. In hindsight, the government should have emphasized short-term training programs and provided financial support to private firms to train their employees according to actual demand (Paik 2013, 14–17).

The demand for higher education was high and increasing. It was assumed that the demand for higher education could be reduced by warning of an oversupply and the potential for high unemployment among higher education graduates (Gill and Ihm 2000, 267–68). However, such concerns were not necessarily shared by parents and were insufficient to reduce the demand for higher education.

In response to the declining interest in VHS, the Ministry of Education introduced Meister high schools as a new model for VHS to train and supply high-quality technicians in new and promising industries. Meister high schools recruit high-caliber middle-school graduates from all regions of Korea through aptitude tests and in-depth interviews with industry experts. Junior college–level programs are provided, tailored to the specific skill needs of relevant industries and firms that participate in curriculum development and operation, thus ensuring a higher chance of employment. Meister high schools enter memorandums of understanding with firms (5,569 firms with 48 schools, 116 per school in 2020), and students enter employment contracts with firms that provide workplace training. Meister high schools are encouraged to recruit former chief executive officers as principals (there were 13 among 41 principals in 2015) and teachers with industry experience (there were 147 industry teachers in 37 Meister high schools in 2010–13), to strengthen industry linkages.

The employment ratio of Meister high school graduates has been higher than 90 percent, substantially higher than that of specialized VHS graduates. The employment duration rate one year after being employed is also high. Meister high school students are required to work for three years after graduation before attending a college or university. Employers' satisfaction with Meister high school graduates has been very high. Employers have indicated that Meister high school graduates have a higher level of work ethic and interpersonal skills compared with junior college graduates (Kim and Kim 2017).

In the 2000s, Korea faced multiple challenges: a shortage of skilled workers, high unemployment rates among college and university graduates, and an anticipated sharp decline in the population of young workers. The share of VHS graduates who were employed after graduation declined from 76.6 percent in 1990 to 19.2 percent in 2010, and graduates who went to colleges and universities increased from 8.3 percent in 1990 to 71.1 percent in 2010. This resulted in a shortage of skilled workers and an over-supply of college and university graduates. In addition, VHSs failed to adapt and upgrade their curricula according to the changing skills demanded in new industries, such as e-commerce, animation, and ICT, which meant that many VHS graduates lacked the job competencies required by employers. College and university graduates faced increasing unemployment as their numbers increased (Paik 2017, 84–85). Finally, the number of high school students was projected to decline sharply, from 2.1 million in 2010 to 1.4 million in 2030, due to demographic trends (Park 2011).

In response, the government restructured and downsized the VHS system in 2010. The government rearranged the three types of VHSs—Meister high schools, specialized VHSs, and comprehensive high schools[10]—into Meister high schools and specialized VHSs and planned to reduce the number of VHSs from 692 in 2010 to 400 by 2015 (50 Meister high schools and 350 specialized VHSs). To implement this policy, the government provided a financial subsidy for transforming comprehensive and specialized VHSs into general academic high schools and consolidating specialized VHSs. It also provided financial support to retrain private school teachers whose majors were mismatched with the demand for skills (Paik 2013, 17–20; Paik 2018, 87–88). The restructured high school system in Korea is presented in figure 6.7.

The number of specialized VHSs was significantly reduced (489 as of 2019),[11] although the target was not achieved. The employment rate of specialized VHS graduates declined before 2010, but subsequently increased from 19.2 percent in 2010 to 50.4 percent in 2017 (figure 6.8), indicating that the government's policy efforts to restructure and downsize VHSs and revise the curricula and programs may have had an impact. However, since 2018, the employment ratio of VHS graduates has declined.

To enhance the attractiveness of VHSs, the government emphasized employment-focused education. The government increased the number of scholarships, emphasized the provision of tailor-made

FIGURE 6.7 High School System in the Republic of Korea

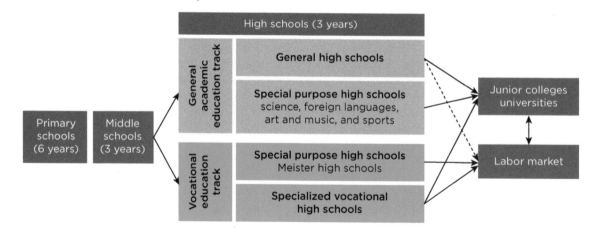

Source: Park 2011, 31.
Note: Arrows indicate graduates' pathways.

FIGURE 6.8 **Employment Rate of Specialized Vocational High School Graduates, Republic of Korea, 2007–19**

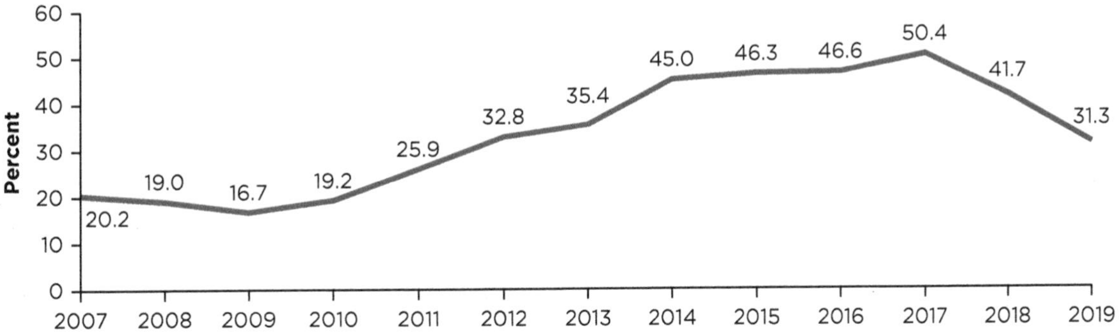

Source: KRIVET 2020, 32.

vocational education and internship programs, encouraged the hiring of teachers from industry, promoted industry linkages, and supported career guidance and job search services. To encourage firms to hire VHS graduates, the government deferred the military enlistment of male graduates to age 24[12] and provided tax incentives to firms that hired VHS graduates. The government also provided administrative support for industry initiatives to establish corporate extension of universities where employees could study,[13] encouraged universities to offer programs designed for VHS graduates who had worked for more than three years after graduation, provided financial subsidies to university and college departments that contracted with small and medium-size enterprises (SMEs) through the Employment Insurance Fund (EIF), and expanded student loans.

This campaign aimed to guarantee open pathways for students in the vocational education track. One of the main reasons why middle-school students were reluctant to enroll in VHSs was that VHS education was regarded as a one-way track that took away options for future education, which was also a key reason for VHS students' preference to enroll in a university after graduation. In response, the government promoted horizontal and vertical pathways for students in vocational education, to facilitate transfers from the vocational track to the academic track. This also requires active collaboration from employers by allowing their employees to take college courses and reflecting employees' learning results in individual performance appraisals, promotions, and wage increases.

Overall, the VHS restructuring and downsizing contributed to building a new, positive image of vocational education during the 2010s. However, VHS education in Korea still has challenges to overcome, including the need to strengthen school-industry cooperation in education and employment and to expand career development support to graduates and reduce their financial burden. Although various government initiatives, including the Meister high schools, contributed to making vocational education a more attractive option, the strong preference for academic education over vocational education remains.

Employment Insurance System and Employee Training

To complement formal vocational schools, in 1967, the government introduced nonformal vocational in-house training in the workplace. Initially, employee training by employers was on a voluntary basis. However, employers poached experienced workers from other companies instead of training their employees. In 1976, the government enacted the Basic Act for Vocational Training, which introduced compulsory training, by mandating that firms with 300 or more employees had to provide employee training. The obligation was expanded to firms with 200 or more employees in 1989 and further to firms with 150 or more employees in 1992. Firms that did not provide training to their employees were required to pay a levy, which financed the Vocational Training Promotion Fund.

The Employment Insurance System (EIS) was introduced in 1995 to support vocational training of incumbent workers and the unemployed, to help workers adapt to advances in technology and the changing industrial structure,[14] and to support the unemployed by providing financial subsidies. Employers had to pay an employment insurance fee to the EIF.[15] The EIF consists of two components, one for employment security and the Vocational Competency Development Program (VCDP), and the other for unemployment benefits.

Under the first component, the EIF provides financial support for training to employers, individual employees, and the unemployed. Firms and individuals can select vocational training institutes and programs based on their own training needs. Training providers must compete for trainees, which was intended to improve the quality of the training. Employers can obtain a refund from the EIF for providing training to their employees.

Initially, the compulsory training system focused on pre-service training, mainly for the manufacturing sector. Training was provided by public vocational training institutes and a small number of private training institutes that have been vetted by the government to be eligible for financing from the Vocational Training Promotion Fund. Over time, the VCDP shifted its focus to training for incumbent workers and training for the unemployed. It also expanded training to all sectors and expanded eligibility to all public and private training institutes, including private colleges and universities (table 6.4). The vocational training changed from a supply-based system focused on providing vocational training to a more demand-oriented focus on firms, SMEs, and industry, to account for industry's changing demand for skills. The curriculum and training approach were also revised, from theory-based to practical job skills training, and matched with the needs of local firms.

The EIS played a significant role in providing training programs and financial assistance for upskilling during the Asian Financial Crisis (AFC) (1997–98). After the AFC, the number of unemployed individuals who received training declined from 2000 to 2009, while the number of employed individuals who received training increased (figure 6.9), indicating that the VCDP was effective in training incumbent workers during the 2000s. Upskilling incumbent workers accounted for almost all the training, and training for the unemployed and new workers accounted for only a small share of the total.

As of 2019, approximately 13.9 million workers (41 percent of the total workforce) were insured by the EIS, which was an increase from 9.8 million workers in 2009, and 28.6 percent of the training was financed by the EIF. In every year from 2009 to 2019 (except 2015), more than 25 percent of the insured workers had training opportunities, indicating that the EIS has maintained its role in supporting recurrent vocational training (MOEL 2020b).

TABLE 6.4 **Paradigm Shift of Korea's Vocational Training System**

	Compulsory Training System (1977–98)	**Vocational Competency Development Program (1995–present)**
Financial source	Training Levy	Employment insurance fee
Fund used	Vocational Training Promotion Fund	Employment Insurance Fund
Operation mode	Government-controlled/supply-oriented	Demand-driven/market-oriented/incentive system
Training market	Closed	Open to private training institutes
Target industry	Manufacturing sector focused	All industries and occupations
Main training	Initial training	Continual training
Target groups	Youth without skills	Incumbent workers/unemployed

Source: Paik 2018, 92.
Note: There were three years of transition (1995–98) from the compulsory training system to the Vocational Competency Development Program.

FIGURE 6.9 Trainees, by Type of Training, Republic of Korea, 1998–2019

Sources: MOEL 2000, 2004, 2014, 2020a.

The VCDP provides financial subsidies for training in all sectors of industry. The manufacturing sector has the largest proportion of trainees, although its share has declined recently. The share of trainees in the service sectors has increased, reflecting the economy's changing industrial structure and the resulting changes in the skills demanded. Since 2019, the Ministry of Employment and Labor has aimed to redesign vocational training for incumbent workers, with a greater focus on new and advanced technologies and financial support for new technology training by SMEs (MOEL 2019).

Vocational training by SMEs has been relatively limited due to the SMEs' lack of human and financial capacity. In response, the government has introduced various programs, including the HRD Consortium Program, SME Learning Organization Program, and training programs for the chief executive officers and HRD staff of SMEs. The HRD Consortium Program, which was introduced in 2001, supports the establishment and operation of training facilities and equipment in SMEs through consortia of private firms, employers' associations, and universities. It provides training matched to the needs of regional industries based on an analysis of SME labor demand and supply, in collaboration with the Regional HRD Councils, which have representatives from local government, labor unions, government agencies, and private experts. In 2019, approximately 3.3 percent of SMEs participated (MOEL 2020b, 177–79). The SME Learning Organization Program (introduced in 2006) supports team learning, learning competition, networking, external expert training, and strengthening of the learning infrastructure in SMEs. Although a survey indicates high levels of satisfaction, the number of SMEs that participated in the program was quite small and fell from 355 in 2012 to 79 in 2019.

Overall, the VCDP contributed to providing significant training opportunities to incumbent workers. It provided financial support directly to employers and individuals and expanded training to all industry sectors. It also played an important role in providing training programs for the unemployed. These positive results were due to the design of the EIS, which combines support for vocational training programs with unemployment benefits, financial support to target groups, differential fee and reimbursement rates by firm size (a lower insurance fee rate and higher rate of refunds to SMEs), and access to a large number of training providers for better choice.

Despite the positive effects, however, several challenges remain. First, there is a significant gap between the number of trainees in large and small firms, although the gap has declined. Second, the relevance of vocational training programs to the skills demanded by firms can be further strengthened (Paik 2013, 31). Part of this is due to the local governments' lack of capacity to forecast the future demand for skills. Third, only 0.17 percent of insured workers benefited from paid leave for training opportunities in 2019 (MOEL 2020a, 44; MOEL 2020b, 165), which indicates that it remains difficult to access training without financial loss.

The Labor Market in Korea

HISTORICAL OVERVIEW

The labor market in Korea has exhibited a variety of features over various stages of Korea's economic development. These range from excess labor supply until the early 1970s, to the more recent population aging and labor market dualism, which are commonly observed in developed countries. Korea's experience in managing labor market challenges provides an example of adaptive labor market policies and offers key lessons for policy makers in developing countries.

During the 1960s and 1970s, the labor market in Korea faced issues commonly seen in low-income countries, such as unemployment and the lack of a skilled workforce. Unemployment declined steadily during the 1960s and 1970s as the economy expanded and more jobs were created. With rapid industrialization, the demand for skilled workers rose in the early 1970s, but the supply of qualified labor was still limited.

In transitioning to a middle-income country, from the mid-1970s to the mid-1980s, Korea's labor market transitioned from excess labor supply to labor shortages. To support more efficient labor allocation, the government invested in building labor market infrastructure and expanding the outreach of public employment services. The Central Job Security Office was established in 1979, and the number of regional employment service offices increased to 44 branches by 1987. To enhance the quality and effectiveness of public employment services, these offices were later connected through online networks and shared information on job seekers (figure 6.10).

FIGURE 6.10 **The Expanding Labor Market, Republic of Korea, 1970s–1987**

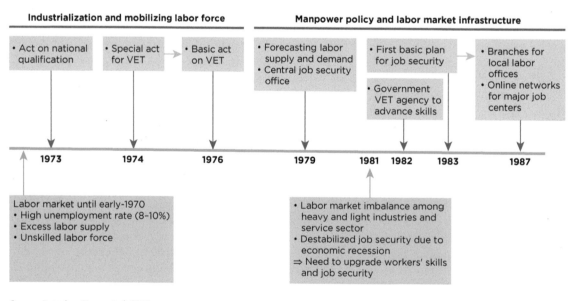

Source: Based on Keum et al. 2017.
Note: VET = vocational education and training.

In the late 1980s when Korea was still a middle-income economy, labor protection increasingly became an important issue. The labor market tightened further, and workers raised their voices for labor rights and fair treatment, which had been suppressed in the past. The government implemented a minimum wage in 1988 and passed laws to protect disadvantaged groups, such as women (1988), the disabled (1990), and the elderly (1992).

Greater openness and globalization in the 1990s increased the country's exposure to global risks. Lifelong employment, which was once taken for granted, was no longer common as firms sought greater labor flexibility to remain competitive in the global economy. The country's regional labor markets suffered sizable job losses, as firms started to relocate their production facilities abroad to take advantage of cheaper labor. There was increasing demand to expand the relatively underdeveloped social safety net and welfare system. The EIS, which was introduced in 1995, became a central policy tool for stabilizing the labor market (figure 6.11).

The AFC was a turning point for Korea's labor market development. The unemployment rate spiked from around 2–3 percent pre-AFC to about 9 percent after the AFC. The massive layoffs from the restructuring and bankruptcies of firms were unprecedented. Job losses were particularly acute among low-skilled workers, as small firms that employed a large share of low-skilled workers were hit hard by the AFC.

In response to the AFC, the government introduced several measures to address unemployment and vulnerability, including extending the coverage of employment insurance (providing unemployment benefits coupled with vocational training and job search support) to all firms in October 1998, expanding the coverage of public assistance programs (cash transfers to those in home or institutional care and in-kind transfers or subsidized loans to those in self-support programs), and later introducing the Basic Livelihood Support Program. These measures have continued to evolve and expand over time. In parallel, the government promoted labor market flexibility by clarifying the legal conditions for collective dismissals and allowing firms to hire temporary nonregular workers and outsource workers from employment agencies on temporary contracts.

FIGURE 6.11 **Balancing Labor Demand and Supply in an Expanding Labor Market, Republic of Korea, 1987–97**

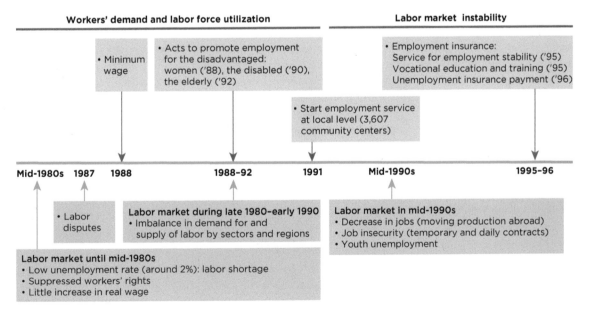

Source: Based on Keum et al. 2017.

The AFC had important implications for the framework for labor disputes. The massive layoffs during the AFC were the impetus for revising the labor laws to facilitate employment adjustment. The crisis brought great financial difficulties to domestic firms and made massive layoffs unavoidable. But the firms faced legal uncertainties concerning collective dismissals, which were allowed at the time only on a case-by-case basis by court decisions if "urgent economic needs" could be demonstrated. A legal change was made in early 1997 when these court decisions on the criteria for urgent economic needs were codified into law, and the change was scheduled to become effective only in early 1999. Toward the end of 1997, the government, businesses, and labor unions agreed to organize a tripartite committee to reach a consensus on the labor market reforms. Businesses demanded greater flexibility in hiring and firing workers. Labor unions hoped to secure several legal changes that would increase their influence. For the government, eliminating the impediments to large-scale restructuring of banks and firms was critical for crisis management.

The tripartite committee was established in mid-January 1998, and important agreements were quickly reached by the following month. The agreements included (a) immediate implementation of legal changes to facilitate collective dismissals, including by clarifying and broadening the definition of "urgent economic needs" to allow for dismissals under mergers and acquisitions; (b) introduction of a legal basis for the use of temporary work agency workers to allow for more flexible labor contracts, although under relatively stringent conditions; (c) legalization of labor associations of low-level civil servants and teachers; and (d) legalization of political activities of labor unions. The gains to each of the three stakeholders of the tripartite committee have been debated, but a precedent was set for a successful social partnership.

Unfortunately, the partnership was difficult to sustain as the Korean Confederation of Trade Unions, one of the labor representatives in the tripartite committee, received significant internal criticisms for supporting mass collective dismissals. The Korean Confederation of Trade Unions subsequently exited the tripartite committee after a change in its leadership. Since then, the tripartite committee has lost much of its representativeness and legitimacy and has produced few significant outcomes.

As the economy recovered from the AFC, the government aimed to reorient labor market policies from a passive to a more active approach. Passive labor market policies aim to increase flexibility in the labor market and mitigate the financial needs of the unemployed, such as through unemployment insurance. Active labor market policies (ALMPs) are designed to improve the employability of the unemployed and other vulnerable populations and help them to find work, for example, through upskilling and public employment services.

Post AFC, the government placed greater emphasis on ALMPs, such as job matching and counseling services and skills development programs. One-stop employment service centers were introduced to provide job matching services, vocational education and training guidance, and a job seekers' allowance to the unemployed. The Work-Net system, an online recruiting and employment portal, was built to connect job applicants with employers with vacancies and to offer information on training, career guidance, employment policies, and labor laws. The HRD-Net allowed participants in vocational education and training courses to monitor and manage their training (figure 6.12).

Korea's labor market today faces several challenges, including population aging, labor market dualism, disadvantaged groups such as youths and women, and labor market rigidity. These challenges are not unique to Korea, as many developing and developed countries face similar issues. The remainder of this section delves into these labor market issues and discusses in detail the policies and measures the government has taken to address them.

POPULATION AGING AND THE LABOR MARKET

Korea is aging rapidly. The share of elderly people (65 years and older) in the total population expanded from approximately 3 percent in the 1960s to 5 percent in the 1990s, and then doubled in recent years from 7 percent in 2000 to 14 percent in 2018. The slopes in figure 6.13 show how quickly Korea has moved from an aging society to an aged society, compared to other developed countries.

FIGURE 6.12 **Labor Market Challenges, Republic of Korea, 1997–2016**

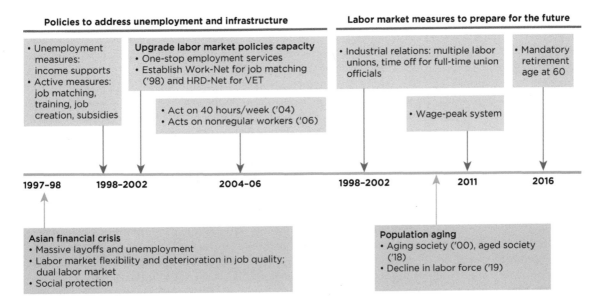

Source: Based on Keum et al. 2017.
Note: HRD = human resources development; VET = vocational education and training.

FIGURE 6.13 **Transition from an Aging Society to an Aged Society, Selected Countries, 1860–2020**

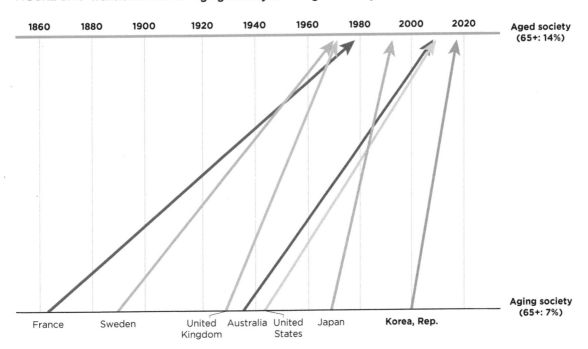

Source: Kinsella and He 2009.

Population aging in Korea is gaining momentum due to several factors. As advanced countries have experienced, Korea has seen a dramatic increase in life expectancy, from an average life expectancy of 62 years in the 1970s to 83 years today. Korea's fertility rate is the lowest in the world. It declined from 6.3 in 1960 to 1.5 in 1990 and 0.84 in 2020, far below the population replacement rate of 2.1 children per woman. The low fertility rate stems from socioeconomic factors, including delayed marriage; lack of childcare services; high costs of raising children, especially for education[16]; and inequality in access to education, according to Statistics Korea.[17] The elderly population is projected to expand sharply until 2028.

Due to population aging, the labor force is projected to shrink in the near future. However, the impact on total productivity is ambiguous. As the more educated, younger generation replaces the less educated, older generation in the future, the higher productivity of the former could partly offset the loss of labor inputs. A key concern about population aging is not the size of the labor force but the quality of older workers. Elderly workers are less able to remain productive unless they are given the opportunity to upgrade obsolete skills. Recent statistics show that the participation rates of older workers in training programs are just 9.7 percent for the employed and 12 percent for the unemployed, about half the rates of workers ages 50 or younger (MOEL 2016).

Misalignment of wages and productivity and skill deficiencies hinder the employability of older workers. A firm's decision to retain a worker depends fundamentally on the worker's labor productivity and costs. A seniority-based pay schedule, a dominant form in Korea, would make older workers unattractive by raising costs (wages) relative to productivity (Chung et al. 2011; Lazear 1979, 1981). Lack of skills is also a key barrier to the employment of older workers (Chung et al. 2011) and, as a result, older workers tend to take unskilled jobs (Kang 2016). Among employees ages 60 or older, approximately 70 percent have nonregular status, their average monthly earnings are the lowest among all age groups (Statistics Korea 2020), and they are heavily concentrated in small service firms (OECD 2021). Older workers account for a high share of self-employment,[18] and the majority of older workers are self-employed.

Having limited training opportunities, returning to a second career job at low pay and low quality, and the weak social welfare system contribute to the high poverty rate among the old-age population in Korea. Almost half of the elderly (age 65 or older) in Korea were below the relative poverty line in 2018,[19] the second highest rate among OECD countries (figure 6.14). The employment rate of the elderly (the ratio of older workers to working-age people) is expected to reach 70 percent in 2050. Hence, in Korea it will be critical to leverage the contribution of the older labor force to the economy and alleviate their poverty (Lee 2019).

Since the 2000s, the government of Korea has implemented a series of policy measures aiming to utilize the older labor force. In 2006, the government announced "The First Basic Plan" to promote employment for the elderly. It comprehensively included job matching, consulting, and career development services for the older unemployed. In the 2010s, two important steps were taken, the wage-peak system and the extension of mandatory retirement at age 60. In the "wage-peak system," the government subsidizes a part of wage cuts if employers and employees agree on the extension of retirement at a reduced wage. In 2016, the government introduced a new retirement system, which entitled employees to work until age 60 unless they voluntarily left the job or provided reasons for dismissal. The new policy was enforced in phases, in 2016 for firms with more than 300 employees and in 2017 for firms with fewer than 300 employees.

The combined effects of the wage-peak system and the extension of mandatory retirement are unclear. The percentage of workers who may have benefited from the extension of mandatory retirement—workers who retired at age 60—declined and involuntary retirement increased after 2016 when the policies came into effect (figure 6.15). From the comparison of employment in firms with and without a wage-peak system, the wage-peak system is estimated to have promoted employment among older workers (Nam 2017; Nam, Kim, and Park 2019). However, the evaluation results on the extension of mandatory retirement are mixed (Han 2020; Nam, Kim, and Park 2019). The extension of the mandatory retirement age would tend to encourage employment of an elderly worker who is below the retirement age only if it is accompanied by a wage-peak system that reduces wages to match decreased productivity.

FIGURE 6.14 **Poverty Rate among Individuals Ages 65 and Older, Selected Countries, 2018**

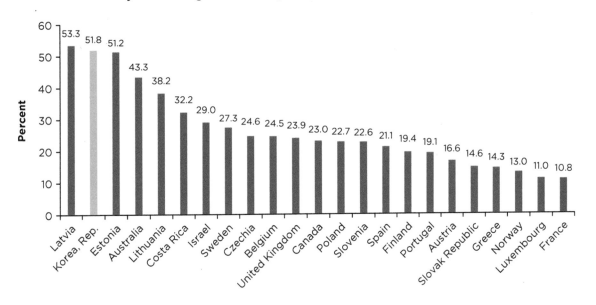

Source: Distribution Database, OECD Stat, Organisation for Economic Co-operation and Development.
Note: The poverty line is defined as 60 percent of median income.

FIGURE 6.15 **Mandatory and Involuntary Retirement, Republic of Korea, 2005–19**

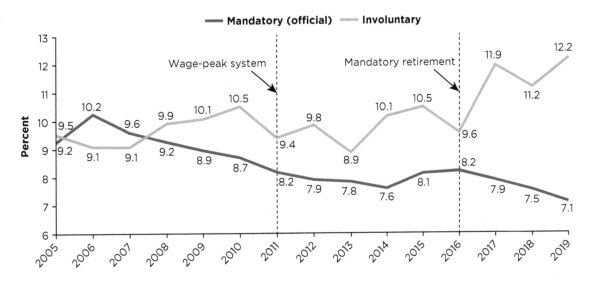

Source: Statistics Korea 2020.
Note: Involuntary retirement refers to retirement due to voluntary redundancy, advised to resign, and business downsizing. It does not include retirement due to personal reasons such as health and family care.

LABOR MARKET DUALITY

In the late 1990s, the AFC led to a rapid increase in nonregular workers given the greater need for flexible, low-cost labor (figure 6.16). The share of nonregular workers in total employment increased significantly, particularly among the youth cohort; 30 percent of young workers had nonregular employment in 2021, compared to 11 percent in 2008 (Korea Office of Government Policy Coordination 2022). Nonregular workers accounted for more than one-third of total salaried workers according to Statistics Korea, which was the highest rate among OECD countries.[20] The expansion of workers in the "gig economy," many providing delivery and transport services, is another variant of nonregular employment that poses new policy challenges, including on labor contracts, labor standards, and protection.

Nonregular workers tend to have lower job tenures, fewer working hours, and lower coverage of job-related social insurance, compared to regular workers. Nearly all regular workers are covered by employment insurance, but only 75 percent of nonregular workers are covered (2020), although the coverage has improved from 51 percent in 2006 (Statistics Korea). Nonregular workers in Korea have limited access to vocational education and training programs, contributing to the significant skill differences between regular and nonregular workers. Low participation in vocational education and training programs means that many nonregular workers have limited upskilling opportunities, which reduces their long-term labor market prospects. Finally, there is limited mobility between regular and nonregular employment in Korea (Jones and Urasawa 2012; Kim 2009; OECD 2015). In Korea, work experience as a nonregular worker does not improve the chance of subsequently finding regular employment, in contrast to most other OECD countries (figure 6.17). Hence, nonregular workers can be stuck in low-paid and insecure jobs.

The dual labor market has become a major barrier to an inclusive society. Disadvantaged groups, such as women, youths, and the elderly, are overrepresented in nonregular jobs. For example, 41.5 percent of female employment was in nonregular jobs in 2018, compared to 26.3 percent of male employment. Nonregular workers are concentrated in less productive industries (for example, services), smaller firms, and unskilled, low-paid occupations (for example, laborers). Nonregular workers generally receive lower wages than regular employees and, even among regular workers, wages vary greatly depending on the size of the firm (figure 6.18). However, the wage gap between regular and nonregular employees is surprisingly negligible, except in large firms (figure 6.19). This suggests that labor market duality is a product of employment types compounded by firm size.

FIGURE 6.16 **Unemployment Rate and Number of Nonregular Workers, Republic of Korea, 1995–2014**

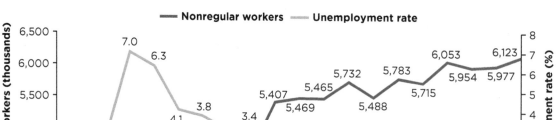

Sources: Statistics Korea, various years; KLI 2020.
Note: The numbers of nonregular workers are available after 2003. The unemployment rate is on a one-week basis.

FIGURE 6.17 **Effect of Nonregular (Temporary) Status on the Probability of Standard Employment, Selected Countries**

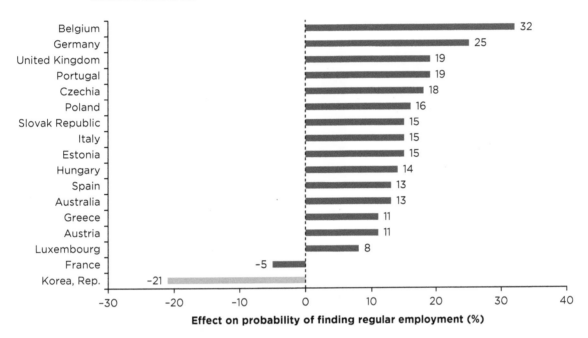

Effect on probability of finding regular employment (%)

Sources: Keum 2015, figure 4.11; OECD 2015.
Note: The probabilities are calculated as Prob(Standard at t | Temporary at t–1) – Prob(Standard at t | Unemployed at t–1).

FIGURE 6.18 **Relative Wage, by Firm Size, Republic of Korea**

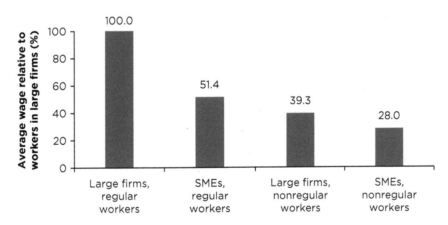

Sources: Recalculated based on Lee and Park 2016; survey on working conditions by contract type, Ministry of Employment and Labor.
Note: Large firms refer to those with more than 300 employees. The relative wage is calculated by accounting for nonregular and regular workers' characteristics. The control variables are gender, age, education, experience, occupation, and industry. SMEs = small and medium-size enterprises.

In 2006, the government enacted the "Act on the Protection of Fixed-term and Part-time Employees" and amended the "Act on the Protection of Temporary Agency Workers," to promote fair treatment of nonregular workers by prohibiting unreasonable discrimination against them and regulating repeated non-regular contracts. The acts were enforced in phases, in 2007 for large firms with 300 or more employees, a year later for firms with 100 or more employees, and finally in 2009 for firms with five or more employees.

FIGURE 6.19 **Relative Wage of Nonregular to Regular Workers, by Firm Size, Republic of Korea**

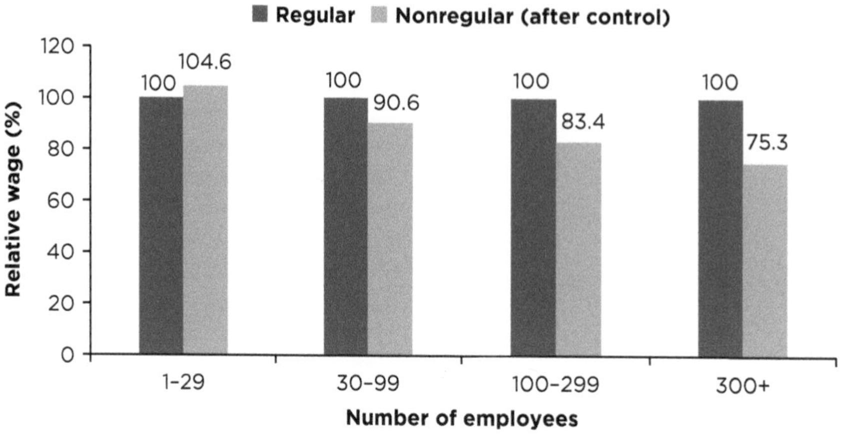

Source: Recalculated based on Lee and Park 2016; survey on working conditions by contract type, Ministry of Employment and Labor.
Note: The relative wage is calculated by accounting for nonregular and regular workers' characteristics. The control variables are gender, age, education, experience, occupation, and industry.

Despite the good intensions, several studies find that the quality of nonregular jobs deteriorated after the acts (Nam and Park 2010; Park and Park 2018; Yoo and Kang 2012). The impact of the acts on the wage gap between regular and nonregular workers varies by firm size. For small and medium-size firms, the wage gap narrowed with the acts as the relative wages of nonregular workers moderately increased. For large firms, the relative wage of nonregular workers showed a moderate downward trend after the acts, causing the wage gap to widen somewhat over the years (figure 6.20).

YOUTH LABOR FORCE PARTICIPATION

Korea's youth unemployment rate (ages 15–24 years) has been hovering around 11 percent in recent years, similar to the OECD average of around 12 percent.[21] The COVID-19 pandemic had little impact on youth unemployment in Korea, unlike other OECD countries, such as Canada and the United States, which saw youth unemployment rates increase by 17 percentage points to 27 percent in April 2020 (OECD 2021). The government's emergency employment responses to the pandemic, including providing firms employment retention subsidies and the creation of temporary, short-term employment for public works projects targeting youths, helped contain the impact of the pandemic on youth unemployment. However, the job market for the youth in Korea has deteriorated in recent decades. The youth (ages 25–29) unemployment rate was stable at around 6 percent in the 2000s, but it has increased since the global financial crisis, peaking at 9.5 percent in 2017, before dropping to 8 percent in 2020 (figure 6.21). Among the unemployed, those ages 25–29 accounted for 22 percent in 2020, the highest rate among OECD countries.

The employment rate of youths ages 15–29 was 42 percent in 2020, below the OECD average (53 percent in 2017), as few young people combine study and employment (OECD 2019b). Only one in eight students works, as opposed to one in four across the OECD countries (OECD 2019b). Students include those who are not in formal education but preparing to apply for the highly competitive jobs in large enterprises and the public sector or to obtain professional qualifications, such as to become a lawyer or an accountant. On average, it takes about a year for graduates to find a job in Korea (Youth Panel surveys, Korea Employment Information Service [KEIS]), which is longer than in other OECD countries, reflecting the lack of access to job-specific information; mismatches in education, skills, and relevant experience; and high expectations about wages and employment conditions (figure 6.22).

FIGURE 6.20 Relative Wage of Nonregular Workers, by Firm Size, Republic of Korea

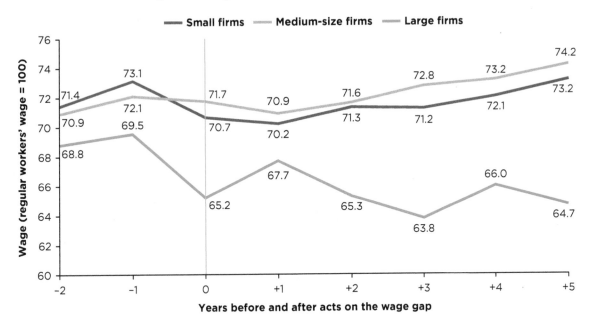

Source: Calculations based on Keum 2015, table 1.
Note: By firm size, the ordinary least squares estimation accounts for workers' attributes, firm characteristics, and year effects. The vertical orange line refers to the benchmark year when the acts on the protection of fixed term/part-time workers and temporary agency workers were implemented. It refers to 2007 for large firms, 2008 for medium-size firms, and 2009 for small firms. The plus and minus values on the x-axis refer to the number of years before (-) and after (+) the respective benchmark year.

FIGURE 6.21 Unemployment Rate among Youth and Young Adults, Republic of Korea, 2000–20

FIGURE 6.22 Job Search Difficulties among Youth and Young Adults, Republic of Korea, 2007 and 2018

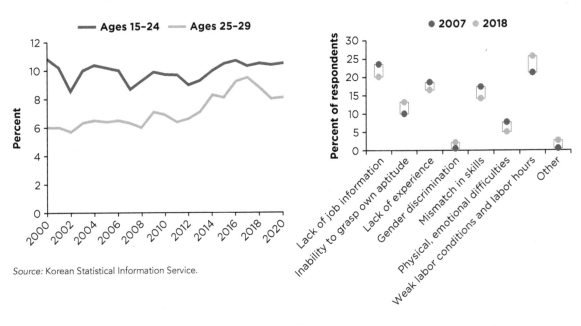

Source: Korean Statistical Information Service.

Source: Youth Panel Survey, Korea Employment Information Service.

Despite the year-long job search, the average employment duration for young employees is only 1.5 years. Half of young workers leave their first job within a year, in particular among university graduates, according to the Korea Labor Institute. The employment period is shorter in smaller firms. The average tenure of young, nonregular workers is only 10 months, as opposed to 23 months for their regular worker counterparts (OECD 2019b). Youth employment has also become more vulnerable. The share of nonregular workers among the youth cohort has been rising steadily—from 33 percent in 2010 to 40.4 percent in 2019.

Youth employment policies have evolved since their introduction during the Asian Financial Crisis in 1997. In 2003, the government aimed to create "decent jobs" to address rising unemployment among university graduates, through new job creation, facilitation of the work-to-study transition through partnerships between schools and industries, and provision of tailored job match services. In 2005, career counseling services and vocational training for youth were expanded. In 2008, the government introduced youth internship systems to support job seekers. In 2010, it introduced programs to incentivize firms to hire graduates from technical high schools, introduced a job academy program to give youths opportunities to learn vocational skills, and allocated financing to universities to provide employment services to students prior to their graduation. In 2013, a European-style study-work dual training system was introduced to ensure that skills development is aligned with industry demand. Subsequent years saw greater government emphasis on enhancing job search assistance and incentivizing firms to hire youths.

The current youth employment policies consist of four blocks—employment/job search services, job training/skills development, employment incentives, and employment continuity—all supported by a youth information center (figure 6.23). Young job seekers from low-income households receive a subsidy of ₩500,000 per month for up to six months to finance training and conduct a job search. Tailored career counseling informs areas for skills development. Job-specific training programs develop skills in areas of high demand. The Additional Youth Employment Subsidy program subsidizes the wages of youths hired as regular employees by SMEs for a three-year period, to encourage young workers to investigate their employment prospects in SMEs. Under the innovative Tomorrow Mutual Aid Program, the young employee, the SME employer, and the government jointly deposit an equal amount into a savings account every month, provided that the young employee remains in the same SME for two or three years. Seventy-eight percent of participants in the savings scheme stay in the same SME for longer than one year, compared with 49 percent among all young workers (T. Kim 2018). In general, research suggests that spending on employment services and vocational training has contributed to reducing youth unemployment (N. Kim 2018).

FIGURE 6.23 **Active Labor Market Programs to Support Youth Employment, Republic of Korea**

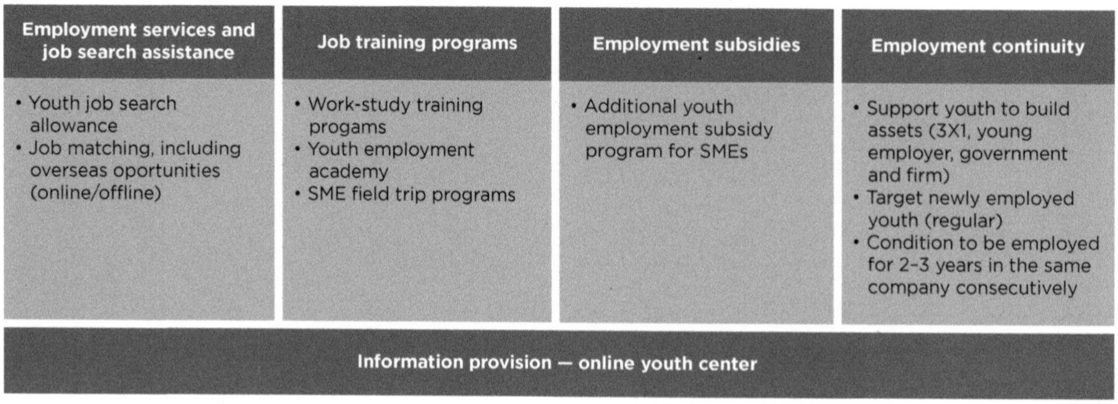

Employment services and job search assistance	Job training programs	Employment subsidies	Employment continuity
• Youth job search allowance • Job matching, including overseas oportunities (online/offline)	• Work-study training progams • Youth employment academy • SME field trip programs	• Additional youth employment subsidy program for SMEs	• Support youth to build assets (3X1, young employer, government and firm) • Target newly employed youth (regular) • Condition to be employed for 2–3 years in the same company consecutively

Information provision — online youth center

Source: Based on MOEL 2020c.
Note: 3X1 = each party contributes the same amount; SMEs = small and medium-size enterprises.

FEMALE LABOR FORCE PARTICIPATION

Rising female labor force participation boosts household income and economic growth. Higher female labor force participation rates can increase the labor supply, offsetting the labor supply effects from population aging, and thus contribute to economic growth over the medium term. Research has found that female participation is related to smaller wage gaps between men and women. At the firm level, female participation in top management is associated with a firm's pursuit of innovation, possibly a result of women's tendency to foster collaborative behaviors that promote innovation (Dezso and Ross 2012).

Female labor force participation in Korea has expanded slowly, from 48.8 percent of the female working-age population in 2000 to 52.8 percent in 2020 (figure 6.24) and remains significantly lower than the average of more than 70 percent in advanced OECD countries. The labor force participation of young women ages 25–29 has increased markedly, from 56 percent in 2000 to 76.3 percent in 2019, benefiting from investments in women's education (Han and Lee 2020). This rate is nearly on par with the male labor force participation rate of 76.7 percent. Yet, half of women with young children do not work. Female employment rises as their children age. For example, in the first half of 2019, 49 percent of women with children ages 6 years or younger were employed, but this increased to 66 percent among women with children ages 13–17 years. Employed women with younger children also work fewer hours compared to the cohort with teenaged children.

There are several obstacles to higher female labor force participation in Korea. Women find it challenging to combine work and family responsibilities. The top five reasons for career breaks for women in Korea are child rearing, marriage, pregnancy/childbirth, children's education, and family caregiving, according to labor force surveys. This results in an M-shaped curve of female labor force participation, as women exit the labor market due to marriage and childbirth and reenter as their children grow older. Women in Korea spend 215 minutes per day on unpaid family work, compared to 136 minutes among their OECD counterparts. The culture of long working hours in Korea makes the significant time devoted to family work challenging. Once interrupted by childbirth and family responsibilities, women find it difficult to return to their careers.

The gender pay gap discourages women's labor force participation. Men earned 1.6 times as much as their female counterparts in 2020 (figure 6.25). The resulting gender pay gap[22] is 36 percent, which is significantly higher than the 12.8 percent average in OECD countries. This gap appears to be linked to the disparity in years of employment—12.2 years for men versus 8.2 years for women in 2020. Significant wage inequality also exists in the young cohort, although young women have a higher share of tertiary education than men. The gender pay gap can incentivize women to choose family care over career and

FIGURE 6.24 Labor Force Participation Rate, by Gender, Republic of Korea, 2000–20

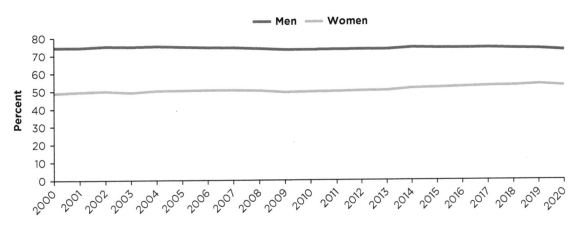

Source: Korean Statistical Information Service.

FIGURE 6.25 **Gender Pay Gap in Average Annual Earnings, Republic of Korea, 2019 and 2020**

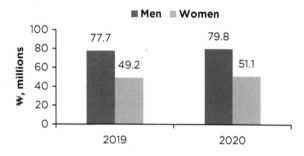

Source: Ministry of Gender Equality and Family, Republic of Korea.

thus push down women's labor force participation (Kinoshita and Guo 2015). Similar to youths, many women are vulnerable workers. Nearly half of female workers have nonregular employee contracts, compared to about 30 percent among their male counterparts (figure 6.26). Women with hourly contracts account for 21 percent of total female employment, compared to only 5 percent for men.

Policies to expand female labor force participation are a combination of ALMPs and gender-neutral workplace policies (figure 6.27). There are efforts to integrate female employment services across various ministries and to focus on females in their forties and fifties who are ready to reenter the labor force after child rearing. Vocational training emphasizes support for women to acquire new technology-related skills (for example, K-Digital training). A special employment promotion allowance is provided for female employees who take leave to provide care to their families. The government has focused on reducing gender discrimination in workplaces by implementing smart labor inspection, providing sexual harassment prevention education to employers and workers, and strengthening consultation and counseling services to improve the overall work environment.

FIGURE 6.26 **Career Challenges for Well-Educated Women, Republic of Korea**

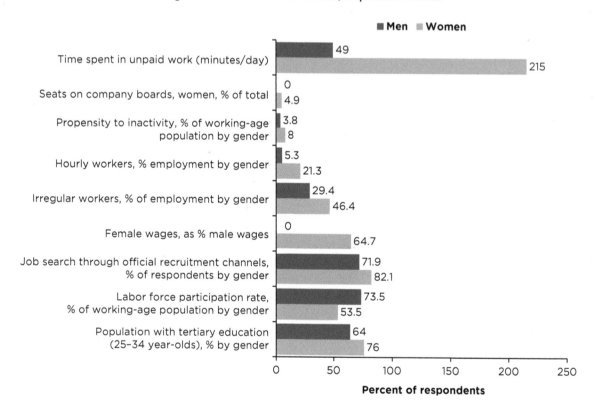

Sources: Organisation for Economic Co-operation and Development; Statistics Korea.

FIGURE 6.27 **Policies to Promote Female Labor Force Participation during the COVID-19 Crisis, Republic of Korea**

Expand employment opportunities for women	Strengthen employment/ entreprenureship support for labor force participation	Care and employment retention programs	Address gender discrimination in the labor market
• Create jobs for women in care, digital, sanitization services • Special employment promotion allowance for women with career breaks • Expand internship opportunities for women	• Employment support systems focusing on women in their 40s and 50s • Targeted job creation through local government-industry coordination • Employment service integrated across ministries • Vocational training in new technology areas, such as through the expansion of K-Digital Credit	• Support for family care expenses • Expansion of public childcare services • Support firms to provide flexible work hours • Reemployment services	• Review to adopt a national license system for care givers • Amend laws related to domestic workers and develop a standard employment contract for domestic workers • Affirmative action at universities with digital innovation specializations • Reduction in gender disaprity in employment across industries through proactive measures to improve employment conditions

Source: Ministry of Employment and Labor, Republic of Korea.

Childcare-related support is particularly critical for female labor force participation, including flexible working time arrangements, parental leave, public childcare services, and childcare subsidies. Simulations show that in Korea, support for childcare would have the largest impact on female labor force participation. Increasing childcare support to Denmark's level would increase the labor force participation of prime-age women by about 12 percentage points (OECD 2005). Paternity leave allows men to spend more time on childrearing activities and women to allocate more time to market activities. Studies have shown that women's employment among firms is significantly higher in countries that mandate paternity leave (Amin et al. 2016).

The government has mandated all companies to provide 90 days of maternity leave. The first 60 days are paid by employers, and the remaining 30 days are financed by the government budget and social insurance. The number of beneficiaries has amounted to around 85,000 per year in recent years. In 2022, the government planned to implement the "3+3 parental leave system": parents with babies (12 months old or younger) can receive government subsidies (up to ₩15 million) if both parents take parental leave for three months, respectively. In this context, policies would support parents with young children to arrange paid leave and shorter work hours with their employers. The government subsidizes companies that provide paid leave for childcare and hire workers to substitute for the workers on paid leave for childcare.

Recent years have seen a marked rise in male workers taking paid leave for childcare. Public spending on early childhood care and education per child aged 0–5 years was US$6,900 in 2017 (adjusted by purchasing power parity), which was higher than the OECD average (US$5,200) (KICCE 2021).

LABOR MARKET POLICY AND SUPPORTING TOOLS

Korea's labor market policies and rules can be categorized into three broad goals: boosting employment, protecting workers while enhancing labor market flexibility, and strengthening social protection of workers. These policies aim to correct market failures: imperfect information, uneven market power between workers and employers, discrimination (especially gender-based), and the inadequate market for insurance of employment-related risks (Betcherman 2012). To boost employment, the government has increasingly utilized ALMPs. To protect workers, the government has introduced employment protection rules such as minimum wages and mandated benefits. The national employment insurance has been a key instrument for strengthening social protection. The Public Employment Service, the Labor Market Information System (LMIS), and financing (subsidies) are key tools to support the implementation of labor market policies and rules.

Korea has emphasized a coordinated approach to the design and implementation of labor market policies. Coordination structures are inter-ministerial and tripartite, and include participation by government agencies, political parties, labor representatives, industry representatives, research institutes, experts, and social partners.

Active Labor Market Policies

Korea has increasingly used ALMPs to improve the employment prospects of labor market participants, including: (a) public employment services (playing a mediating role between job seekers and firms with vacancies), (b) subsidized employment (employment in public works projects and wage subsidies to firms that employ workers from a targeted job seeker cohort, such as youth), (c) skills training, and (d) entrepreneurship promotion.

Korea's public spending on labor markets stood at 0.6 percent of GDP in 2017, far lower than the 1.4 percent in Germany, 2.2 percent in Austria, and 2.8 percent in France (OECD 2020). Half of the spending was on direct job creation to create public sector jobs. Evidence from OECD countries shows direct job creation programs are effective at encouraging employment and reducing poverty among targeted groups, such as youths, women, the low-skilled, or the elderly. However, direct job creation programs tend to be less effective than skills development and training programs and rarely show positive effects on participants' employment probability (OECD 2020). The effects are frequently found to be negative (Kluve 2010). Nonetheless, during the COVID-19 pandemic, direct job creation curbed the dent in total employment (OECD 2020).

Korea's Employment Success Package Program (ESPP) for vulnerable groups (young and elderly job seekers from low-income families) is unique in that it combines ALMPs (assistance with job search, training, and business opportunities) with income support ("participation allowance" and "job seeking allowance"). The program is implemented by commissioning private institutions. The number of ESPP participants increased from 230,000 in 2013 to 361,000 in 2017, and the employment rate of the participants jumped from 55.2 percent to 68.9 percent over the same period. Program evaluations show that overall ESPP has been effective in helping program participants transition to employment, especially middle-aged, older, and low-income job seekers. However, participants reported less satisfaction with their wages and jobs compared to nonparticipants, which suggests that the program requires better coordination with job counseling, vocational training, and job matching services (Kim 2020; Lee et al. 2016).

Minimum Wage

In Korea, the government implemented the minimum wage in 1988. The government sets minimum wages based on recommendations from the Minimum Wage Council, which consists of worker, employer, and social partner representatives. The minimum wage applies to all workers, including foreign workers, other than family and domestic workers. The minimum wage has been raised continuously and in 2020 it was 62 percent of the median wage and 50 percent of the mean wage, ranking seventh and third among

OECD countries, respectively, according to OECD Stat. Korea's monthly minimum wage is $2,096 in purchasing power parity, similar to the minimum wages in Northern European countries, such as $2,076 in the Netherlands and $2,110 in Germany (in purchasing power parity in 2019) (ILO 2020).

In Korea, an increase in the minimum wage has been associated with a decline in work hours, accounting for the labor productivity index (Song, Im, and Shin 2018). However, the impact of the minimum wage must be considered together with other labor market institutions, such as the job stabilization fund, employment protection legislation, and ALMPs. When employment protection legislation is stronger, the effects of minimum wages on youth employment are weaker. An appropriate collective bargaining arrangement reduces the negative impact of minimum wages on employment in high-income countries (O'Higgins and Pica 2019).

Employment Protection and Labor Market Rigidity

Korea's labor market is considered relatively rigid, primarily due to the high level of employment protection based on legislated dismissal protection. The extent of the strictness of employment protection eased after the AFC, but it remained higher than the OECD average as of 2019 (table 6.5). In Korea, employers must notify a dismissal to workers 30 days in advance and must pay 30 days of wages to the dismissed worker as a dismissal notice allowance. Korea also has mandatory retirement allowances, which increase with employment duration, and thus firms find it costly to keep regular workers on long tenures.

Complex dismissal procedures, restrictions on the dismissal of regular workers, and the requirement for retirement allowances increase the cost of dismissing workers and thus incentivize firms to favor nonregular employees, which leads to labor market duality (OECD 2013; Schauer 2018). The high level of employment protection has meant that entry points to the labor market in Korea tend to be nonregular jobs. In response, the government has tried to reduce the regulatory gap between regular employment and nonregular employment, by extending the requirement for the dismissal notice allowance to all workers.

TABLE 6.5 Strictness of Employment Protection: Individual and Collective Dismissals (Regular Contracts), Selected Countries, 1990–2019

Country	1990	1998	2019
Australia	1.17	1.42	1.67
Austria	2.67	2.67	2.29
Belgium	1.64	1.64	2.07
Canada	0.59	0.59	0.59
France	2.52	2.52	2.56
Germany	2.50	2.60	2.60
Japan	1.70	1.70	1.37
Korea, Rep.	3.08	2.42	2.42
Netherlands	3.46	3.25	3.61
New Zealand	1.49	1.49	1.64
United Kingdom	1.35	1.35	1.35
United States	0.09	0.09	0.09
OECD countries	..	..	2.06

Source: OECD (https://stats.oecd.org/Index.aspx?DataSetCode=EPL_OV).
Note: OECD = Organisation for Economic Co-operation and Development.

Social Protection for Workers

Korea started to introduce various elements of its social safety net system in the 1970s and 1980s. The expansion of the social safety net reflected increasing public demands for social equity and efforts to address diverging economic growth across sectors and geographical regions.

The National Health Insurance was introduced in 1977 for workers in large firms and expanded to cover the entire population by 1989. Hence, universal health care coverage was obtained within only a dozen years. Health expenditure in Korea is not high for the country's income level, compared to other OECD countries (figure 6.28), but the public enjoys a relatively accessible health care system, as indicated by the high number of doctor consultations (figure 6.29).

The National Pension Scheme was introduced in 1988 for large firms and expanded in the subsequent years. The EIS, comprising the unemployment insurance program and various ALMPs, was introduced in 1995. In the 1980s, the Constitution was amended to reflect the greater emphasis on social equity.

The AFC resulted in massive unemployment and widespread poverty, quickly exposing the inadequacy of the country's social safety net and leading to a dramatic expansion of existing social protection programs, in particular targeting low-income, working-age individuals. The government introduced short-term measures, such as expanded wage subsidies to employers and public works programs for the unemployed, to protect employees. The EIS was expanded rapidly in 1998 to cover all businesses. In 1999 alone, some 2 million individuals received some form of social assistance benefits, but the coverage remained inadequate, leaving half the poor uncovered.

This prompted the government to introduce the National Basic Livelihood Security program, to provide income support to low-income households while also encouraging beneficiaries to participate in the labor market. It is a monthly cash transfer to eligible individuals, covering livelihoods, housing, medical, educational, childbirth, and funeral assistances. To encourage employment, the program was later

FIGURE 6.28 Health Expenditures in OECD Countries, 2019

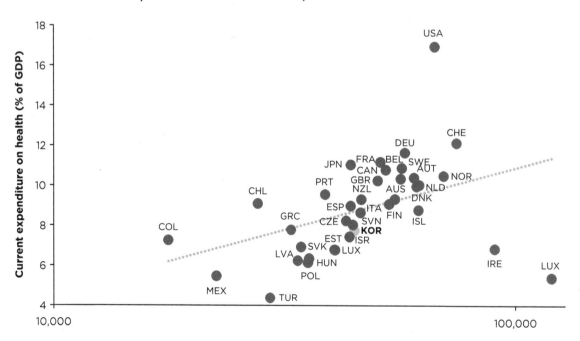

GDP per capita (PPP, log scale)

Source: OECD (https://stats.oecd.org).
Note: The dashed line indicates the trend. GDP = gross domestic product; OECD = Organisation for Economic Co-operation and Development; PPP = purchasing power parity. For a list of country codes, go to https://www.iso.org/obp/ui/#search.

FIGURE 6.29 **Consultations with Doctors per Year, Selected Countries**

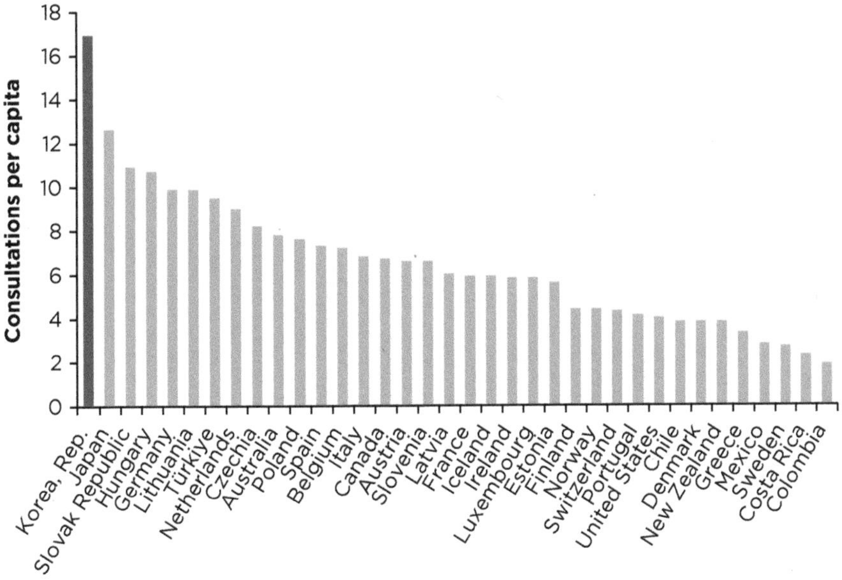

Source: OECD 2022.
Note: Values are for 2020 or the most recent year available.

adjusted so that beneficiaries could continue to be eligible for assistance, depending on their needs, even if they found employment and started to earn income.

Additional social protection programs were added in the 2000s, including Emergency Welfare Support (2006), Earned Income Tax Credit (2007), Basic Old-age Pension (2007), and Long-term Care Insurance (2008). Student loan programs (2010) and scholarship programs (2012) were introduced for college students, with a focus on low-income households. Childcare allowances (2012) were introduced for children younger than age 6 years. ALMPs—wage subsidies, training, and employment services—for workers with low employability were expanded, and local offices of the Ministry of Employment and Labor were established across the country to administer these programs. There were about 170 such local offices, as of 2021.

The expansion of social programs was supported by increased allocation of the government budget. Public expenditures on social protection began to rise in the 1980s, and the increase accelerated post-AFC. Social protection accounted for less than 5 percent of total spending in the 1970s but increased to 22 percent in 2018 (figure 6.30). As a percentage of GDP, it increased from less than 1 to 7 percent. Unemployment-related benefit payouts exceeded ₩8,382 billion in 2019, compared to ₩2,434 billion in 2007. To finance the spending, the tax burden has increased in tandem (figure 6.31). Most notable is the increase in social security contributions since the late 1980s, which now account for a quarter of the total tax burden.

Employment insurance, which is a form of social insurance, is an integral part of Korea's social safety net for workers. Employment insurance finances unemployment benefits, employment services, and vocational skills development training. Employee participation in the insurance scheme is mandatory. The government subsidizes up to 90 percent of the insurance premiums of SMEs with fewer than 10 employees, to protect SME employees who are found to be more likely to have financial difficulties. It has also expanded insurance eligibility to the self-employed and freelancers, including gig workers, recognizing their low job security.

FIGURE 6.30 **General Government Spending on Social Protection, Republic of Korea, 1970–2018**

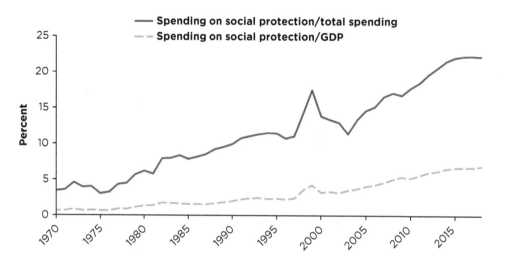

Source: Bank of Korea (http://ecos.bok.or.kr).
Note: GDP = gross domestic product.

FIGURE 6.31 **Total Tax Revenue, Republic of Korea, 1972–2019**

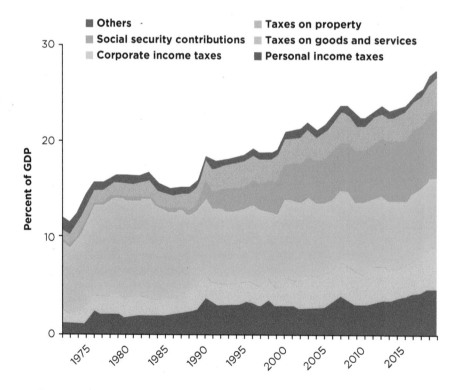

Source: Organisation for Economic Co-operation and Development (http://stats.oecd.or.kr).
Note: GDP = gross domestic product.

Employment insurance is a co-contribution system, with workers contributing 0.80 percent of their remuneration and employers contributing 1.05 to 1.65 percent of the firm's total remuneration. To increase compliance, the government simplified the process for firms to register workers in employment insurance and to pay fines for noncompliance and allowed employees to register themselves for insurance subscriptions. The government expanded its cooperation with the tax authority to identify instances of noncompliance.

Social safety net support for vulnerable groups was extensive during the COVID-19 pandemic. The authorities subsidized employment by providing wage subsidies to firms to retain employees. Emergency security grants supported the livelihoods of the self-employed at risk. Support for vocational training has been expanded to support reemployment of the unemployed and to prepare for the economic recovery from the pandemic. The authorities stepped up support for direct job creation for the vulnerable and increased the childcare support allowance to help parents retain their jobs.

Public Employment Services and the Labor Market Information System

In Korea, the government provides a variety of employment services for job seekers and employees, including employment information services, personalized career counseling and job matching services, and vocational skills development assistance in support of individuals' lifelong careers.

The Employment Welfare+ Center offers integrated support for employment and welfare services. It provides services to help workers to register for unemployment, claim employment insurance, develop a personalized employment plan, and improve their employability. It is a source of real-time information on job offers, job matching services, and employment support programs. The Employment Welfare+ Center's activities include job fairs to connect employers and employees, interview support, and employment intermediation. Currently there are more than 100 job centers across the country.

The LMIS provides labor-related data drawn from surveys on employment and skills and databases from various interconnected KEIS networks, including HRD-net, a job-training platform, and Work-net. KEIS, which is a public agency, uses information in the LMIS to monitor and evaluate policies and create labor market intelligence. It conducts analysis and forecasting for various users, including job seekers, policy makers, employers, and researchers. The law requires all government agencies, such as the national statistics agency, to share requested data with KEIS. KEIS also collects its own survey data to inform employment and skills.

Work-net, a job portal, provides personalized job information, especially for low- and semiskilled workers, using big data. It offers information on vacancies, occupation-specific qualifications and experience requirements, wages, vocational skills development programs, and employment policies, such as eligibility for and benefits of employment insurance. Utilizing artificial intelligence–enabled technology, Work-net offers individually tailored vacancy and training information.

Conclusions and Lessons for Developing Countries

EDUCATION AND TRAINING RECOMMENDATIONS

Governments need to provide strong leadership and sustained commitment to investing in human capital development over the long run. The results of investment in education become evident only after a long gestation period. Korea achieved among the highest levels of human capital development through sustained investments over decades, starting in the 1950s when it was among the poorest countries in the world.

Korea has systematically linked human capital development planning to national economic development planning. Governments must project the labor demanded from economic growth and the capacity of the national HRD system to supply the labor demanded. This requires accurate and timely data on labor market and economic developments and the capacity to analyze the data for policy making. Korea's experience also highlights the importance of a robust coordination mechanism that has the legal mandate and relevant decision-making authority, particularly on budget allocation and personnel appointments.

The coordination of education and economic policies reflected Korea's emphasis on ensuring an adequate supply of skilled and educated labor that was necessary for the country's transition to an innovation- and technology-driven high-income economy. The focus of the country's education and training policies shifted from a government-controlled and supply oriented approach to a more market-based and demand oriented approach, to meet the rapidly changing demand for labor more effectively. It also required the government to work closely with the private sector, including on the curricula, internship programs, R&D, and commercialization of R&D that requires highly specialized research skills.

To transition to an innovation- and technology-driven economy, Korea began prioritizing STEM education and R&D systems when it was still a low-income economy. Even low-income economies must plan ahead to build S&T knowledge and capabilities and research capacity. This requires early and sustained investment in STEM education and R&D infrastructure to educate and train future scientists and researchers. Korea's special purpose science universities, such as KAIST; special purpose science high schools; and dedicated STEAM programs can be examples to benchmark. Korea's promotion of STEAM focused on teamwork, interactive teaching, creative and practical problem solving, and convergence of S&T and the arts.

Korea's experience highlights the importance of integrating the academic and vocational education tracks by ensuring open and integrated horizontal and vertical pathways for vocational school graduates. This makes vocational education an attractive option and promotes a lifelong learning system that enables workers to maintain and enhance their productivity and employability through reskilling and upskilling. Korea developed a national qualification framework and a credit transfer system to ensure open and integrated education and training pathways.

Korea also complemented formal education and vocational training with nonformal vocational training, to respond rapidly to the economy's changing demand for skills. Formal education systems in general have limitations in quickly responding to sharply increasing demand for skilled workers. Through the compulsory vocational training system (1976–98) and the EIS (1995 to the present), Korea's experience demonstrates that nonformal training could play a significant role in supplying skilled workers and retraining incumbent workers and the unemployed.

Industry-academia collaboration is critical for improving the quality and relevance of education, training, and research. Korea's Meister high schools are considered a successful case of industry-academia cooperation that helped to raise the attractiveness of vocational education and produced graduates with high employability. The government, schools, and vocational training institutions in developing countries need to collaborate actively with industries in designing and implementing education and training programs and research projects. This will enhance the efficiency and effectiveness of HRD and R&D systems.

Governments need to diversify funding sources and promote private sector participation in the country's education and training systems. The government budget alone cannot meet HRD demands for national economic development. Furthermore, it may not be justified to provide education and training only through the government budget, considering that private benefits can outweigh the social benefit. It is critical for the government to leverage the private sector's capacity and readiness to provide education and vocational training. For example, if private firms have substantial demand for highly educated workers and households have significant capacity and willingness to pay for higher education, the government could complement household spending by collecting funds from firms to expand and raise the quality of higher education.

LABOR MARKET RECOMMENDATIONS

Labor market policy is critical for achieving inclusive economic growth. Korea's rapid economic growth helped to overcome many labor market challenges by generating employment opportunities and prospects. As the economy grew and demand for high-skilled labor expanded, the tighter labor market conditions gave rise to imbalances in labor supply and demand across sectors. To support more efficient labor allocation, the government invested in building labor market infrastructure, such as public employment services.

As the economy further developed, workers raised their voices for better working conditions and job security, and employers demanded greater labor market flexibility. In response, the government introduced the minimum wage and passed laws to protect disadvantaged groups of workers. Responding to the massive layoffs during the AFC, the government significantly expanded the social safety net and ALMPs, and enhanced labor market flexibility through a tripartite agreement among the government, businesses, and labor. Korea's experience highlights the importance of building consensus among the major stakeholders in society to build support for challenging labor market reforms.

Korea has expanded ALMPs—employment services, direct job creation, skills development, and entrepreneurship promotion—to promote labor market participation and maintain a relatively low rate of unemployment. It combined multiple measures to customize interventions to the needs of job seekers, in particular targeting vulnerable groups. For example, Korea's ESPP promotes the employment of vulnerable young and older workers by integrating social protection with labor market activation measures, including counseling and individual employment plans, training and internship opportunities, and job-matching services tailored to the needs of the program participants.

Social protection programs have been an integral part of Korea's ALMPs. Employment insurance in Korea combines ALMPs, such as skills development and employment services, with income assistance for unemployed workers. Employment insurance addresses uncertainties around job loss risk by imposing entitlement conditions, supports the upgrading of skills by providing vocational training benefits, and encourages job search by making the income benefits conditional on active job search efforts. Unemployment insurance helps to protect the most vulnerable workers, for example, those in the informal sector. The types of income assistance are tailored to the beneficiaries' ability to work, by providing cash transfers to those who have no capacity to work and in-kind transfers or subsidized loans to those who can work. Income support to the vulnerable is maintained for a period after the beneficiaries find new employment, to incentivize job search efforts and prevent beneficiaries from falling back into poverty.

Several lessons can be drawn from Korea's attempts to address labor market duality and promote the labor market participation of women and older workers. Understanding the causes of labor market duality is essential for policy design. In Korea, nonregular employment is preferred by SMEs to save labor costs and by large firms to maintain labor flexibility. Restricting the use of nonregular workers raised labor costs for SMEs and incentivized large firms to switch to dispatched workers and subcontractors, which are less secure forms of employment. To promote the employment of older workers, Korea introduced a wage-peak system to help align the wages of older workers with their level of productivity, and expanded training opportunities for older workers to update their employment skills. To promote female labor participation, Korea increased public spending on childcare and mandated parental leave. In general, Korea has had the most success in addressing drivers of labor market discrimination that are clearly identifiable and actionable, such as discrimination in the coverage of mandatory social insurance. By contrast, gender wage gaps have been more difficult to identify and address.

Finally, Korea's experience highlights the importance of supportive labor market infrastructure and policy instruments. A robust LMIS is critical for monitoring the implementation of labor market policies and programs and supporting evidence-based labor market policies. Korea's LMIS is an integral part of the government's efforts to reduce unemployment, boost the productivity of firms, manage labor market risks, and enhance the impact of labor market programs. Korea addresses the potentially weak cooperation of the ministries in data collection through legislation that mandates that all government agencies, such as the national statistics agency, must share requested data with KEIS. The database enables KEIS to develop and operate several support networks—Work-net, HRD-net, and the Employment Insurance Network. Korea's experience also highlights the benefits to both job seekers and employers of enhancing accessibility to labor market data and services. The Employment Welfare+ Center, for example, provides integrated support for employment and welfare.

Notes

1. World Bank EdStats, datatopics.worldbank.org/education/.

2. KAIST was established as a graduate school, called the Korea Advanced Institute of Science (KAIS), in 1971. KAIS and KIST were integrated into KAIST in 1981, and KAIST was separated from KIST in 1989 and integrated with the Korea Science and Technology University in the same year. In 2009, the Korea Science Academy, a special purpose high school for gifted students, was annexed to KAIST, and Information and Communication University was integrated into KAIST.

3. https://kaist.ac.kr/kr/html/kaist/010101.html (accessed January 17, 2021).

4. The Second National Basic Plan for HR in Science and Technology (2011–15).

5. The Second National Basic Plan for HR in Science and Technology (2011–15).

6. The Second National Basic Plan for HR in Science and Technology (2011–15).

7. The competencies include interest in science, multidisciplinary thinking, communication, creativity, problem solving, real-life applications, self-directed learning, inquiry design skills, persistence, and caring team members.

8. Statistical analysis (difference in differences) showed no difference in the increase in employment between universities that participated in HUNIC and those that did not.

9. VHS included schools in different sectors, such as agriculture, commercial, and engineering. The technical high schools refer to the VHS in engineering.

10. Comprehensive high schools provided both vocational and academic education programs.

11. KRIVET (2020, 26-27 and 29); https://kess.kedi.re.kr/index (accessed January 13, 2021).

12. In Korea, military service is mandatory for young men. This discourages firms from hiring recent VHS graduates who are obligated to join the military in the near future.

13. http://school.cbe.go.kr/jptec-h/M01060104/view/3460475 (accessed January 14, 2021).

14. The program provides support to employers through various forms of assistance, including: (a) Employment Creation Assistance, (b) Employment Adjustment Assistance, (c) Regional Employment Stimulation Grants, (d) Employment Promotion Assistance, and (e) Labor Market Information and Job Placement Service.

15. The fee ranges from 0.25 to 0.85 percent of a company's total payroll, depending on the company's size.

16. Households spent, on average, US$1,200 per month on childrearing in 2015 and 14.6 percent of total household expenditure on children's education (Bak 2019).

17. Households in the top 20 percent of the income distribution spent 20 times more on children's education than those in the bottom 20 percent in 2019, according to Statistics Korea.

18. Jang and Shin (2008) point out that difficulties in finding a job and the immature social welfare system caused the increase in self-employment among the elderly.

19. The relative poverty line is defined as 60 percent of the median income.

20. Nonregular employment includes both temporary and part-time workers. Statistics on nonregular workers have been collected since 2003.

21. Youth are defined as ages 15–24, per the International Labour Organization/OECD definition. Statistics Korea defines youth as ages 15–29.

22. Defined as the rate of men's average pay to that of women.

References

Amin, M., A. Islam, and A. Sakhonchik. 2016. "Does Paternity Leave Matter for Female Employment in Developing Economies? Evidence from Firm-Level Data." *Applied Economic Letters* 23 (16): 1–4.

Bak, H. 2019. "Low Fertility in South Korea: Causes, Consequences, and Policy Implications." In *Global Encyclopedia of Public Administration, Public Policy, and Governance*, edited by A. Farazmand. Springer.

Betcherman, G. 2012. "Labor Market Institutions: A Review of the Literature." Policy Research Working Paper 6276, World Bank, Washington, DC. SSRN: https://ssrn.com/abstract=2181285.

Choo, M. H., Y. S. Kim, C. Y. Ihm, K. G. Kim, and S. C. Song. 2011. *An Evaluation Study on Employment Effect of the Hub University for Industrial Collaboration Project.* Seoul, Republic of Korea: Korea Employment Information Service.

Chung, J. H., J. H. Kim, D. B. Kim, and I. J. Lee 2011. "Aging Workforce and Innovation on Wage System." Research Report 2011-10, Korea Labor Institute, Sejong City, Republic of Korea.

Dezso, C. L., and D. G. Ross. 2012. "Does Female Representation in Top Management Improve Firm Performance? A Panel Data Investigation." *Strategic Management Journal* 33 (9): 1072–89.

Gill, I., and C. S. Ihm. 2000. "Republic of Korea." In *Vocational Education and Training Reform: Matching Skills to Markets and Budgets*, edited by I. S. Gill, F. Fluitman. and A. Dar. Washington, DC: World Bank/International Labour Organization.

Han, J. 2020. "The Effects of Delayed Mandatory Retirement on Elderly and Youth Employment." KDI Policy Forum No. 277, 2020-02, Korea Development Institute, Sejong City, Republic of Korea.

Han, J.-S., and J.-W. Lee. 2020. "Demographic Change, Human Capital, and Economic Growth in Korea." *Japan and the World Economy* 53: article 100984.

ILO (International Labour Organization). 2020. *Global Wage Report 2020–2021.* ILO: Geneva.

IMD (International Institute for Management Development). 2020. *World Competitiveness Yearbook.* Lausanne, Switzerland: IMD.

Jang, J. Y., and H. K. Shin. 2008. "Study on the Determinants of Employment of the Aged: Cross-Country Analysis." Korea Labor Institute, Sejong City, Republic of Korea.

Jones, R., and S. Urasawa. 2012. "Promoting Social Cohesion in Korea." OECD Economics Department Working Papers No. 963, Organisation for Economic Co-operation and Development, Paris.

Kang, N. H. 2019. "A Review of the Effect of Integrated STEM or STEAM Education in South Korea." *Asia-Pacific Science Education* 5: article 6.

Kang, N., M. Lee, M. Rho, and J. E. Yoo. 2018. "Meta-Analysis of STEAM Program Effect on Student Learning." *Journal of the Korean Association for Science Education* 38 (6): 875–83.

Kang, S. H. 2016. "A Study on Reemployment Determinants, Job Satisfaction and Employment Stability of the Aged." *Journal of Employment and Career* 9 (3): 117–40.

KERIS (Korea Education and Research Information Service). 2016. *A Korean Model for Using ICT in Education: Overview.* Daegu, Republic of Korea: KERIS. https://www.keris.or.kr/main/cf/fileDownload.do?fileKey=a352f4d9c4d0f45d0213a9176b5d0728.

KERIS (Korea Education and Research Information Service). 2021. "White Paper on ICT in Education in Korea." KERIS, Daegu, Republic of Korea. https://www.keris.or.kr/main/na/ntt/selectNttInfo.do?mi=1244&nttSn=38410&bbsId=1104.

Keum, J. H. 2015. "Wage of Non-Regular Workers and Transition to Regular Ones." Symposium for Korean Labor Income Panel Studies, Korea Labor Institute, Sejong City, Republic of Korea.

Keum, H.-S., S.-J. Kim, W.-B. Kim, H.-S. Kim, J. T. Song, G.-S. Yoo, K.-Y. Lee, J.-H. Lee, C.-S. Lee, S.-H. Jang, B.-S. Chung, and D.-S. Hwang. 2017. *Labor Market Policy in Korea*. Seoul, Republic of Korea: Seoul National University Press.

KICCE (Korea Institute of Child Care and Education). 2021. "ECEC Statistics of Korea: Services, Enrollment, Workforce, and Financial Resources." KICCE Policy Brief Issue 22, KICCE, Seoul, Republic of Korea.

Kim, B. J., G. R. Cho, S. W. Choi, J. Y. Seo, and S. Y. Kim. 2005. *Evaluation Study on BK21 Program Effectiveness*. Daejeon, Republic of Korea: Korea Research Foundation.

Kim, C. W., and S. N. Kim. 2017. "Employers' Satisfaction with Meister High School Graduates." KRIVET Issue Brief No. 115, Korea Research Institute of Vocational Education and Training, Sejong City, Republic of Korea.

Kim, D. H. 2020. "Effects of Youth Employment Success Package Program on Labor Market Outcomes." *Labor Policy Review* 20 (1): 29–63. Korea Labor Institute: Seoul, Republic of Korea.

Kim, D. J. 2018. "Empirical Analysis on Policy Effect of the LINC Project on Region." *Korean Association for Policy Analysis and Evaluation* 28 (3): 27–47.

Kim, H. K. 2012. "History on Science and Technology Personnel Development Policies and Implications." *Management History Studies* 27 (2).

Kim, N. 2018. "The Analysis of Hysteresis in Youth Unemployment." Bank of Korea WP 2018-37, Bank of Korea, Seoul, Republic of Korea.

Kim, S. N., and C. W. Kim. 2017. "Participation of Meister High School Graduates in Higher Education." KRIVET Issue Brief No. 133, Korea Research Institute of Vocational Education and Training, Sejong City, Republic of Korea.

Kim, T. 2018. "Issues in Policy Design for Employee Oriented Wage Subsidies for Youth: Focusing on Asset Building Program for Youth Employees." *Labor Policy Review* 18 (3): 1–36, Korea Labor Institute, Seoul, Republic of Korea.

Kim, Y. S. 2009. "Research on Labor Mobility of Non-Regular Workers." In *Comprehensive Reviews on Non-Regular Employment*, edited by G. Yoo, chapter 5. KDI Research Report 2009-03. Sejong City, Republic of Korea: Korea Development Institute.

Kim, Y. W., W. Y. Gu, and Y. G. Kim. 2001. "A Study on an Effective Support Plan for ICT and Assistive Technology Application at Special School." *Journal of Special Education: Theory and Practice* 2 (3): 183–201.

Kinoshita, Y., and F. Guo. 2015. "What Can Boost Female Labor Force Participation in Asia?" IMF WP 15/56, International Monetary Fund, Washington, DC.

Kinsella, K., and W. He. 2009. "An Aging World." *International Population Reports*, P95/09-1. Washington, DC: U.S. Census Bureau, U.S. Government Printing Office.

KLI (Korea Labor Institute). 2020. "Labor Statistics on Non-regular Workers." KLI, Sejong City, Republic of Korea.

Kluve, J. 2010. "The Effectiveness of European Active Labor Market Programs." *Labour Economics* 17: 904–18

Koh, Y. 2018. "The Evolution of Wage Inequality in Korea." KDI Policy Study 2018-01, Korea Development Institute, Sejong City, Republic of Korea. https://ssrn.com/abstract=3430270.

Koh, Y. 2019. "Wage Inequality: How and Why It Has Changed over the Decades." KDI Policy Forum No. 274 (2019-03), Korea Development Institute, Sejong City, Republic of Korea. https://ssrn.com/abstract=3465440.

Korea Office of Government Policy Coordination. 2022. "2021 Youth Policy White Paper." Government of Korea, Sejong City, Republic of Korea.

KRIVET (Korea Research Institute of Vocational Education and Training). 2020. *2020 Human Resources Development Indicators in Korea*. Sejong City, Republic of Korea: KRIVET.

Lazear, E. P. 1979. "Why Is There Mandatory Retirement?" *Journal of Political Economy* 87 (6): 1261–84.

Lazear, E. P. 1981. "Agency, Earning Profiles, Productivity, and Hours Restrictions." *American Economic Review* 71 (3): 606–20.

Lee, B. H., H. J. Gil, H. W. Kim, Y. S. Lee, and M. H. Oh. 2016. "Assessment of Implementation of the Employment Success Package and Reform Agenda." Korea Labor Institute, Seoul, Republic of Korea. [Korean]

Lee, J. J. 2019. "Economic Growth and Policies in Aging Society." KDI Policy Forum No. 273, 2019-02, Korea Development Institute, Sejong City, Republic of Korea.

Lee, J., H. Jeong, and S. C. Hong. 2018. *Human Capital and Development: Lessons and Insights from Korea's Transformation.* Edward Elgar Publishing.

Lee, S. I., and Y. S. Park. 2016. "Note on Transition of Non-Regular to Regular Workers." Korea Development Institute, Sejong City, Republic of Korea.

Ministry of Education, Science, and Technology. 2011. "Evaluation Results on the 2nd Stage Hub University/College for Industrial Collaboration." News Conference Material, March 25. Ministry of Education, Science, and Technology, Sejong City, Republic of Korea.

Ministry of Education, Science and Technology. 2012. "Basic Plan for the Leaders in Industry-University Cooperation." Ministry of Education, Science, and Technology, Sejong City, Republic of Korea.

MOEL (Ministry of Employment and Labor, Republic of Korea). 2000. "Current Status of Vocational Competency Development Program." MOEL, Seoul, Republic of Korea.

MOEL (Ministry of Employment and Labor, Republic of Korea). 2004. "Current Status of Vocational Competency Development Program." MOEL, Seoul, Republic of Korea.

MOEL (Ministry of Employment and Labor, Republic of Korea). 2014. "Current Status of Vocational Competency Development Program." MOEL, Seoul, Republic of Korea.

MOEL (Ministry of Employment and Labor, Republic of Korea). 2016. "Measures to Improve Employment Service for Old Workers." MOEL, Seoul, Republic of Korea.

MOEL (Ministry of Employment and Labor, Republic of Korea). 2019. *Vocational Competence Development Innovation Plan.* Seoul, Republic of Korea: MOEL (accessed February 16, 2021), http://www.moel.go.kr.

MOEL (Ministry of Employment and Labor, Republic of Korea). 2020a. "Current Status of Vocational Competency Development Program." MOEL, Seoul, Republic of Korea.

MOEL (Ministry of Employment and Labor, Republic of Korea). 2020b. "Employment Insurance White Paper." MOEL, Seoul, Republic of Korea.

MOEL (Ministry of Employment and Labor, Republic of Korea). 2020c. "Employment and Labor White Paper." MOEL, Seoul, Republic of Korea.

Moon, H. J., and H. Lee. 2015. "Effect of Government Financial Support on the Performance of the Industry-University Collaboration with Focus on the LINC Project." Presented at the Korea Association of Industrial Engineering. Seoul, Republic of Korea.

Nam, J. R. 2017. "A Study on Employment Outcome for Firms with Wage-Peak System." Presented at the Ninth Seminar on the Workplace Panel Survey. Korea Labor Institute: Seoul, Republic of Korea.

Nam, J. R., J. S. Kim, and W. S. Park. 2019. "Searching for Employment System for an Aging Society" Research Report 2019-09, Korea Labor Institute, Sejong City, Republic of Korea.

Nam, J. R., and K. S. Park. 2010. "The Effects of Acts on Protecting Nonstandard Workers on Employment in Korea." *Research on Labor Policy* 10 (42): 65–99.

O'Higgins, N., and G. Pica. 2019. "Complementarities between Labour Market Institutions and Their Causal Impact on Youth Labour Market Outcomes." IZA DP No. 12424, IZA Institute of Labor Economics, Bonn, Germany.

OECD (Organisation for Economic Co-operation and Development). 2005. "Policies to Increase Labour-Force Participation of Women and Older Workers: Highlights of Two Just Released OECD Studies." OECD, Paris.

OECD (Organisation for Economic Co-operation and Development). 2013. *Strengthening Social Cohesion in Korea*. Paris: OECD Publishing.

OECD (Organisation for Economic Co-operation and Development). 2015. *In It Together: Why Less Inequality Benefits All*. Paris: OECD Publishing.

OECD (Organisation for Economic Co-operation and Development). 2017. *Education at a Glance 2017*. Paris: OECD Publishing. https://doi.org/10.1787/eag-2017-en.

OECD (Organisation for Economic Co-operation and Development). 2019a. "Educational Attainment of 25-34 year-olds (2019)." In *Education at a Glance 2019: OECD Indicators*. Paris: OECD. https://www.oecd-ilibrary.org /education/education-at-a-glance-2019_f8d7880d-en.

OECD (Organisation for Economic Co-operation and Development). 2019b. *Investing in Youth: Korea*. Paris: OECD Publishing.

OECD (Organisation for Economic Co-operation and Development). 2019c. *PISA 2018 Results*, volume 1. Paris: OECD.

OECD (Organisation for Economic Co-operation and Development). 2020. *Education at a Glance 2020: OECD Indicators*. Paris: OECD (accessed May 6, 2021), https://www.oecd-ilibrary.org/docserver/045cc436-en.pdf?expir es=1620268341&id=id&accname=guest&checksum=F08F3A8D35127493CD0E3FB0A04D5295.

OECD (Organisation for Economic Co-operation and Development). 2021. *Inclusive Growth Review of Korea: Creating Opportunities for All*. Paris: OECD Publishing. https://doi.org/10.1787/4f713390-en.

OECD (Organisation for Economic Co-operation and Development). 2022. "Doctors' consultations" (indicator). Accessed April 25, 2022. https://doi.org/10.1787/173dcf26-en.

Paik, S. J. 2013. "Pre-Employment VET Investment Strategy in Developing Countries—Based on the Experiences of Korea." KDI School Working Paper, Korea Development Institute, Sejong City, Republic of Korea.

Paik, S. J. 2015. "Education and Inclusive Growth—Korean Experience." KDI School Working Paper, Korea Development Institute, Sejong City, Republic of Korea.

Paik, S. J. 2017. *Strengthening National HRD System for Senegal's Economic and Social Transformation*. National HRD Strategy to Support the Economic and Social Transformation of PASET Member Countries with Focus on Senegal. Sejong City, Republic of Korea: Ministry of Economy and Finance and KDI.

Paik, S. J. 2018. *Make Rwanda's HRD System Perform Better*. National HRD Strategy to Support the Economic and Social Transformation of PASET Member Countries with Focus on Rwanda and Senegal. Sejong City, Republic of Korea: Ministry of Economy and Finance and KDI.

Paik, S. J. 2020. *Redesign the Ethiopian TVET Strategy and Policy*. National HRD Strategy to Support the Economic and Social Transformation of PASET Member Countries with Focus on Ethiopia and Rwanda. Sejong City, Republic of Korea: Ministry of Economy and Finance and KDI.

Park, D. Y. 2011. "Korean Policies on Secondary Vocational Education." Federal Institute for Vocational Education and Training, Bonn, Germany.

Park, H. J., S. Y. Byun, J. H. Shim, Y. S. Baek, and J. S. Chung. 2016. "A Study on the Current Status of STEAM Education." *Journal of the Korean Association for Science Education* 36 (4): 676–77.

Park, W. R., and Y. S, Park. 2018. "Impact the Non-Regular Acts Had on Firms' Employment Decision." KDI Forum No. 271, 2018-4, Korea Development Institute, Sejong City, Republic of Korea.

Schauer, J. 2018. "Labor Market Duality in Korea." IMF Working Paper WP/18/126, International Monetary Fund, Washington, DC.

Science and Technology Policy Institute. 2014. "Programs for Supporting Science and Technology-Centric Universities." Science and Technology Policy Institute, Sejong City, Republic of Korea.

Shin, M. 2018. "Meta-Analysis on the Effects of STEAM Programs for Elementary School Students." *Journal of Curriculum Integration.*

Song, H. J., H. Im, and W. Shin. 2018. "Employment Structure: Evidence from Korean Industry-Level Data." Bank of Korea WP 2018-4. Bank of Korea, Seoul, Republic of Korea.

Song, S. S. 2005. "A Content Analysis on the Science & Technology Comprehensive Plans in Korea: Focusing on Five-Year Plans." Science and Technology Policy Institute, Sejong City, Republic of Korea.

Statistics Korea. 2020. *Survey on Economically Active Population,* August Supplement. Daejeon, Republic of Korea: Statistics Korea.

The Korean Government and the Presidential Committee on the 4th Industrial Revolution. 2017. I-Korea 4.0 to Respond to the 4th Industrial Revolution. Ministry of Science and ICT, Sejong City, Republic of Korea.

World Bank. 2018. *Growing Smarter: Learning and Equitable Development in East Asia and Pacific.* World Bank East Asia and Pacific Regional Report. Washington, DC: World Bank. doi:10.1596/978-1-4648-1261-3.

World Bank. 2020. *The Human Capital Index 2020 Update: Human Capital in the Time of COVID-19.* Washington, DC: World Bank. https://openknowledge.worldbank.org/handle/10986/34432.

Yakman, G., and H. Lee. 2012. "Exploring the Exemplary STEAM Education in the U.S. as a Practical Educational Framework for Korea." *Journal of the Korean Association for Research in Science Education* 32: 10.14697 /jkase.2012.32.6.1072.

Yarrow, N., J. Yoo, and H. Kim. Forthcoming. *EdTech in COVID Korea: Learning with Inequality.*

Yim, C. B., and C. Y. Jyung. 2009. "Performance Evaluation for the University-Industry Cooperation Policy." *Journal of Agricultural Education and Human Resource Development* 41 (4): 241–75.

Yoo, G. J., and C. H. Kang. 2012. "The Effect of Protection of Temporary Workers on Employment Level: Evidence from the 2007 Reform of South Korea." *Industrial & Labor Relations Review* 65 (3): 578–606.